The Final PROPHECIES OF NOSTRADAMUS

ERIKA CHEETHAM

A PERIGEE BOOK

To Alexander

I wish to thank the readers of my previous
books for their many interpretations of the
Prophecies, some of which I have used in this
book. There are far too many to thank
individually.

Perigee Books
are published by
The Putnam Publishing Group
200 Madison Avenue
New York, NY 10016

Library of Congress Cataloging-in-Publication Data

Cheetham, Erika.
The final prophecies of Nostradamus / Erika Cheetham.
p. cm.
Includes selections from the Prophéties of Nostradamus, in Old
Provençal with English translations by E. Cheetham.
Includes index.
ISBN 0-399-51516-X
1. Nostradamus, 1503–1565. 2. Twentieth century—Forecasts.
I. Nostradamus, 1503–1565. Prophéties. English & Old Provençal.
Selections. 1989. II. Title.
BF1815.N8C46 1989
133.3′092′4—dc19   88-34630 CIP

Printed in the United States of America

18   19   20

CONTENTS

ABBREVIATIONS USED IN FOOTNOTES

A.Pr.—Ancien Provençal
L.—Latin
O.F.—Old French
Mod F.—Modern French
Gk.—Greek

INTRODUCTION

Before writing about the life, times and predictions of Nostradamus, I feel I must write about the extraordinary effect he and his works have had upon my personal life. Some are almost beyond belief.

Certainly it was Nostradamus who turned my ideas toward making writing my career. I first came across a book of the Prophecies at Oxford, when I was about nineteen. At that time I was reading medieval Romance Languages, of which Ancien Provençal was one of the most important. I had ordered some set book in the Taylorian—the linguist's equivalent of the Bodleian Library—and in its stead I received the 1568 edition of *Les Prophéties de M. Michel Nostradamus.* While waiting for the correct book to arrive, I idled through the *Prophéties.* It was fascinating. Names such as Hitler, Napoleon, Franco, Pasteur sprang to the eye. There were many dates too, but the only one that stuck in my mind was 1666, "when the city of London would be destroyed by fire." Not easy to forget, even for someone who is not an historian.

One night a great friend, who was then an editor on *Nova* magazine, sadly now long defunct, came to dinner with some friends. At some point I mentioned Nostradamus, this extraordinary prophet, to her. She was interested and I wrote a long article for the magazine, to which they added an amazing collage of pictures of the people I had mentioned.

The article was an enormous success, voted by *Nova* readers as tying with one other as the best in the magazine that year. From that, and thanks to a clever publisher brother-in-law, Putnam's of New York commissioned a book upon Nostradamus. I do not know to this day how I managed to complete it. I was working in the day, lecturing two evenings a week for extramural students at London University, running a house and family. Then one of my brothers had the sense to marry a marvelous girl who took away pages of my rather illegible writing, in which I had attempted to produce an original text, a translation and an explanation of the quatrain when I could. These were returned looking so professional I would gaze at them with amazement. Did I really write this?

The first idea I had that it was not just going to be "a book" occurred on the first day of publication. Foyles, the very reputable bookseller, had taken a journalist on for a week to write about the experience. Whether they knew he was a journalist I don't know, but his article stated that he had sold out all the copies of Nostradamus at Foyles in less than a day. I should have been warned.

During the early 1970s I went down to Nostradamus' home towns of Salon and St. Rémy-de-Provence, and did a lot of work in the local archives. I traced Nostradamus' house off the Place de la Poissonerie. At that time the house was partly unsafe and inhabited by various Arab families and in a state of great decay. This has since been rectified. It has been almost totally restored with a *gardien* to show tourists around. But Nostradamus' study at the top of the house is still out of bounds. Why?

Two years ago an Australian TV company came to France and wanted me to go down to Salon and Saint Rémy to do a piece on Nostradamus. It was then I experienced one of the strangest events in my life.

Nostradamus was buried (for the second time, his body having been disinterred during the French Revolution by drunken soldiers) in a side chapel of Notre Dame Church in the Church of Saint Laurent at Salon. Sadly when we arrived it appeared that the portrait of him, one of only three known likenesses, had been stolen, but the engraving in the wall by his second wife, Anne Ponsart Gemelle, was still there.

We, or rather I, because Australians do not seem to speak French, went to the church on a Friday evening, so that the crew could work out technicalities of lighting and sound. There was to be a burial early the next morning, so we could not start before ten o'clock. The cart used for carrying the coffin doubled up very well for carrying the heavy lighting equipment. I stood under the engraving on the wall commissioned by his wife, dressed all in black, it appeared that I was too tall in shoes, so there I was with frozen feet on the stone flags.

At last we were ready—lighting, sound boom, everything. I launched into my small introductory speech. I spoke these words: *"Ici, dans cette église restent les os de Michel Nostradamus . . ."* At that very moment there was an enormous crack of thunder which reverberated down the church, followed by a huge fireball which traveled from the altar to the great doors. That was the end of the TV program. Every machine was blown. To compound the injury, such heavy rain fell that everyone in Salon with a basement was calling the *pompiers,* the fire brigade. It was like a mini-flood, but everything happened at enormous speed. I have never experienced anything like it—and the superstitious took note that it happened the moment I mentioned the word Nostradamus. The storm flickered around the Alpilles for the rest of the day. It was very spectacular. Having despaired of getting further material from me for the schedule—although we did get some footage in Nostradamus' house the next day—the Australian crew flew off to Rome to interview the Pope.

As to what this book will bring I do not know, except that it is the last book I shall ever write about Nostradamus. This is the reason for giving the reader the original text as published in 1568, instead of bowdlerizing it to make it easier to read. It will be seen that I have changed some of my interpretations. Some are obvious from historical facts that have occurred since my last book, such as Gorbachev—"the man with the mark of blood." Until he appeared I had no idea what man from the East Nostradamus had in mind, but the port-wine stain on his head and forehead gives a convincing touch to quatrains I could not definitely ascribe before he came to office.

Another interpretation is that of "glasnost" which has suddenly arrived upon Gorbachev's heels in Russia. But Nostradamus warns us that the treaty between the US and the USSR will last for only three years and some months. The instigator of the Third World War, as we might designate it, will come from the East. Here we have the option of the Middle East or the Far East. At the moment the former is the volatile keg, but world politics now change so quickly that neither interpretation can be ruled out. I am writing this piece some time after the Americans had shot down the Iran airbus with nearly 300 passengers on board, all dead, and the Iranians have gone to the United Nations to demand peace. Over two hundred and fifty people have been shot down over Scotland by a terrorist bomb. There are so many external influences to bear and understand with all the aids of the modern media to hand, newspapers, radio, television, that we get confused. No wonder Nostradamus may have made mistakes from time to time, although at others, his sense of timing and occasion seem perfect. Maybe the fault lies in the interpreter, as with the Delphic Oracle, whose predictions could always be taken two ways. The resulting success or failure was blamed on the recipient, who was the final judge of his own fate. We can but watch world events and decide for ourselves whether Nostradamus has anything to offer to the present-day world.

We must also remember that the function of the prophet is to warn, and that any event predicted may be averted if we listen with open minds. I think that this may well have happened with the *Prophéties*.

There are some very specific ones that have, quite simply, not happened. This leads to the dual aspect of prediction—if the prophet is heeded his writings are a failure; he is, in an ironic sense, successful only when people fail to recognize the predicted events. He is verified, and the world suffers as a consequence. Job satisfaction is obviously not a concomitant feature of prediction.

Recently, there was a lot of fuss about the White House, in particular, Mrs. Reagan's using astrologers to help the President's timetable. It is the public, not they who are the fools. Throughout history great rulers have let themselves be guided by them. Elizabeth I relied on John Dee, Catherine de' Medicis on Nostradamus and Luc Gauric. But how many people realize that Stalin had a personal astrologer, Yury Yammakin? One would not have thought him capable of that sort of influence during his bloody years of rule of Russia. But he did. Eventually, Yammakin fell into disgrace and was sent to a concentration camp. From this he was rescued and reinstated by Khrushchev. I think the next question to be asked is whether Mickaël Gorbachev has one?

THE LIFE AND TIMES OF NOSTRADAMUS

Most people have heard of Nostradamus, usually in his capacity as a prophet. But he was far more interesting than that. A qualified doctor from the Universities of Avignon and Montpellier, renowned through France as a "plague" doctor, adviser to the queen of France, writer of philosophical treaties and a fascinating book on food and cosmetics, he was indeed a great man of his time. He influenced world events before and after his death and his book of *Prophéties* is probably the only book, apart from the Bible, that has been continuously in print since its first complete publication in 1568, two years after his death. Earlier handwritten versions of books were commonly circulated before publication and this seems to be the case where the *Prophéties* were concerned.

There are two stories about Nostradamus' lineage and background; the second is the true one, but such an overwhelming figure was inevitably bound to be given glamorous antecedents. The legend is as follows, and it is important to know of it because many of his contemporaries believed it, and this must, of necessity, have altered their attitude towards him.

Michel de Nostradame, usually known as Nostradamus after the quarter in St. Rémy-de-Provence where his family were living, was born on December 14, 1503. (This date becomes December 23 by the present Gregorian calendar.) His family were of Jewish ancestry and some of his commentators say from the tribe of Issachar, the tribe that could read the moon and the stars and interpret the heavens. His father, Pierre de Nostradame, had settled in Provence because by the mid-fifteenth century, under the rule of King René of Anjou (1434–80), a comparatively lenient king, many Jews had come to settle in his kingdom, which apart from Anjou included Lorraine and Provence.

It is stated that René's physician was a Jewish doctor and astrologer, Jean de Saint-Rémy, and René's son, the duke of Calabria and Lorraine, had a physician called Pierre de Nostradame. He is reputed to have worked in Arles until his fellow doctors hounded him out of town, possibly on the charge of "falsifying his drugs." Therefore the two physicians followed their masters through Europe and presumably learned much on their travels.

Jean, duke of Calabria, was poisoned and died in Barcelona in 1478. It is said he recommended his physician, Pierre de Nostradame, to his father. René, after the death of his son, left his glittering court at Anjou and settled in Tarascon en Provence. The two physicians became friends and on René's death in 1480 Jean and Pierre teamed up and settled in Saint Rémy. Pierre had a son, a notary called Jacques, and it was arranged that he should marry Jean's daughter, Renée. Nostradamus gave credence to this story during his lifetime as does Chavigny, the biographer who probably coped with Nostradamus' papers after the prophet's death in 1566.

Six years after René of Anjou's death his heir, Charles de Maine, also died, and so not only Anjou, but now Provence and Maine reverted to the king of France. French royalty were not overanxious to create a Jewish ghetto in these *comtés* and in 1488 Charles VIII of France issued a decree à la Pontius Pilate. All Jews had to be baptized. Not much was done to enforce the order but when the throne reverted to Louis XII he decreed, on September 26, 1501, that all Jews were to renounce their religion within three months, or leave Provence. It is clear that Jean de Saint-Rémy and Pierre de Nostradame decided to submit and on the tax list for Aix, December 12, 1512, both their names appear as being taxpayers in the new Christian Community.

The truth was somewhat different. Many great researchers, including Reynard-Plense in 1940 and Buget 1862, found that there was no one of the name of Pierre de Nostradamus in the court of King René. But there was a Jewish doctor called Abraham Salomon, who was baptized and then ennobled by King René. It remained to Dr. Edgar Le Roy, a fanatic anti-Nostradamus researcher, to find out the whole truth, in his *Mémoires de l'Institut Historique de Provence.*

The father of Nostradamus was Jaume (Jacques), the son of a certain Peyrot (Pierre) de Nostradame, who came of a long family of Avignon grain dealers. The grandfather, Pierre, was converted when he married a Christian woman, Blanche. His son, Jaume, also dealing in grain, gave it up on his marriage to Reynière de Saint-Rémy. She was the granddaughter of a failed doctor, Jean de Saint-Rémy, who had become a tax collector. All of his family were also converted Jews.

We don't know the date of Jaume de Nostradamus' marriage to Reynière de Saint-Rémy, but Michel de Nostradamus was born in 1503 and he was the eldest son. This helps support the idea that the couple were married before September 26, 1501, when all Jews had to become Christians within three months or leave Provence. Nostradamus had one definite brother, César, who became Procureur du Parliament de Provence. Later it was his son César who wrote the famous *Histoire de Provence,* which sustains the myth of the Nostradamus royal line. He is also credited with three other brothers, Bertrand, Hector and Antoine, but almost nothing is known of them apart from their names.

Nostradamus showed his extraordinarily free thinking and intelligent mind early on. He was educated by his two grandfathers. First Peyrot, who had been a great traveler, brought him up in his home. We are told that he taught his grandson the basics of mathematics, Greek, Latin, and interestingly, Hebrew, and also the rudiments of "Celestial Science," now known as astrology.

After Peyrot de Nostradamus' death—again the exact date is missing in the archives—Michel de Nostradamus returned to his parents' house in the rue de Barri. It appears that his other grandfather then took over his education for a while, but the family decided to send the boy to Avignon, which was at that period the center of Renaissance learning. A century earlier Avignon had been the capital of French Christendom. Imagine the effect it must have had on the brilliant and youthful mind of Nostradamus. It is related that although good in grammar, philosophy and rhetoric, his greatest passion was the study of the stars. Because of this interest and the dialogues Nostradamus had with fellow pupils he became known as *"le petit astrologue."*

It was here, at Avignon, that Nostradamus is reported to have spent many hours in the University libraries, and it is likely that this was the source of his interest in magic and the occult which was to remain with him until his death. Probably on these ancient shelves he first read Ficino's translation of *De Mysterius Aegyptorium.* This book was used as the source of his method of prediction. He quotes from it in Century I, quatrains I and II.

This interest in astrology, the Celestial Sciences, began to worry his parents and on the advice of his old grandfather he was sent off to study medicine at the University of Montpellier, a university regarded as second only to that of Paris in the whole of France. Indeed, in 1376, Louis I of Anjou bequeathed upon it the dubious right in perpetuity of the body a year for dissection, that of an executed criminal.

Nostradamus arrived there in 1522, aged nineteen, and settled down well. For the first three years he read all those subjects needed for his baccalauréat, tutored by some of the most celebrated doctors in Europe. The process of getting a degree was far more arduous than in the present day, and lasted much longer. The examinations consisted of the following routine. From 8:00 A.M. until noon the pupil was given an oral examination, in Latin, during which he was asked questions demanding complicated answers, having to avoid traps and prove his own learning in return. Once successful, the newly fledged doctor changed his black robes for the red ones of the learned doctor.

But, in the sixteenth century, to get one's degree did not qualify a candidate to practice. Far from it, Nostradamus now had to give five lectures chosen by the Dean of the University over three months. Again in Latin. One must always remember that none of the teaching or work was done in the pupils' mother tongue. Medieval Latin was the *lingua franca* of doctors and other professions. The lectures approved, Nostradamus had to pass the *"per intentionem"* examinations, which consisted of four different questions, each presented one day in advance and each of which had to be discussed for an hour and the format varied. If you were unlucky all four subjects had to be discussed on the same day, or otherwise two on two consecutive days.

That ordeal passed, the candidate was given a further subject eight days later and this was discussed extemporaneously in front of the Chancellor of the University himself. The subject was usually one that had not been discussed earlier. To crown all this, Nostradamus would then be given an aphorism of Hippocrates on which he had to produce a thesis the next day. These last two tests were rightly known as *les points rigoreux,* which they really were. A successful candidate was then given his license to practice by the Bishop of Montpellier. Nostradamus achieved this in 1525.

During this period there was yet another outbreak of the plague then endemic in southern France, and Nostradamus left the University in order to help the victims. He would return later to get his doctorate, our equivalent of a D.Phil., Doctor of Philosophy. It appears that his remarkable reputation as a healer—often the other aspect of prophecy—started there. He was already known to use his own formulas and prescriptions, and to refuse to wear the magic coat of seven colors known as such by contemporaries, worn by all medieval doctors for protection. He is recorded as being very successful. From Montpellier he went to Narbonne where it is rumored he attended courses held by Jewish alchemists. He then moved on to Carcassonne in the service of the Archbishop of Fays. In his book *Moulte Opuscule* of 1555 he prescribes an elixir of life, a love potion for the bishop of interesting content for any jaded man. There is some confusion here. The Bishop of Carcassonne during this period was a certain Martin de Saint-André. Either Nostradamus got the name wrong when he wrote about it or he was thinking of Amaníen de Foix, who was Bishop of Mâcon from 1557. Nostradamus was a shrewd psychologist. The richer the patient, the more expensive the ingredients, so this recipe contains such delicacies as ground pearls. Perhaps the expense justified the means to both patient and doctor. Bishops were not notorious for their celibacy in the sixteenth century.

The next reference we have of him is living in Toulouse in the rue de la Triperie; then on to Bordeaux where the plague was raging particularly virulently. He seems to have been successful in his cures, which included running instead of well water, fresh air, and he refused to bleed the patient. This inevitably earned him the enmity of the local doctors, a reputation which preceded him on his return to the University of Montpellier.

It was four years since he had left and he decided now to return to take his doctorate. He must have felt that he had gained much by his experience in the field, so to speak. His name is recorded as rejoining on October 23, 1529. He now had to submit to a further series of examinations, known as *"les triduanes."* For this the candidate had to present a list of twelve subjects for questioning; six were chosen. He would be questioned on three chosen by lottery, and on the other three by the dean. He had to argue and discuss his views with the University professors. It is reported that Nostradamus was mainly questioned about his unorthodox remedies. He must have convinced them, at least partially, for he was awarded his doctorate in 1530 together with the distinctive doctor's cap (seen in the two portraits still remaining of him), a gold ring and a book of Hippocrates' works.

Surprisingly, Nostradamus was offered a job in the faculty at Montpellier and he accepted. Perhaps he wished to solidify his position as doctor and physician with the more conservative element? But he was unable to prescribe or teach his own more unorthodox remedies and had to be led by the prescribed texts. So, inevitably, he decided to travel again. It was in his blood; he was the epitome of the Wandering Jew except during the brief period of his first marriage. It was not much later that he settled and married his second wife Anne Ponsarde Gemelle at Salon, whose name is also recorded elsewhere as Anne Pons Gemelle and Anne Ponsart Gemelle.

He left the University in 1532 and according to his biographer Bareste he was received in great triumph by all those towns he had earlier visited. We know he went to Bordeaux again, to La Rochelle and Toulouse. It was during his stay here that one of the turning points in his life occurred. Jules César Scaliger, who was considered the second most learned man in Europe to Erasmus, wrote to him saying that he had heard so much of Nostradamus, he wished to see if the man lived up to his reputation. According to Chavigny, writing in 1594, Nostradamus replied with a letter that was "ingenious, learned and spirited." As a result, he was invited by Scaliger to come and stay with him at Agen.

Scaliger and Nostradamus were well pleased with each other's companionship and friendship. The former was considered a master of mathematics, biology, medicine, poetry and philosophy. This must have added to Nostradamus' breadth of thought, and he decided to take a house nearby at Agen. Finally he decided to marry a young girl "of high estate, both beautiful and amiable." Her name has been given by some as Adrièta de Loubéjac, but this is almost certainly a mixup with Scaliger's wife, Andiethe de Roques-Lobejac. Soon his family was complete with the births of a son and a daughter. We still do not know her name. Nostradamus' only surviving children came of his second marriage, to Anne Ponsart Gemelle.

The next three years were those of great happiness. His practice was lucrative, he had a beautiful family and the friendship of Scaliger, together with the many important people who visited him. But, the fates then struck, as they do all who have so much. His wife and both children were killed by the outbreak of some type of infectious disease, probably the plague.

It was both tragic and ironic that he could not save his own family, having saved the lives of so many others. Naturally, after this, his patrons deserted him. Who wants a doctor who cannot save his own family? Upon this followed a severe and final quarrel with Scaliger. We don't know the cause, but Scaliger's quarrelsome character is well documented. Sadly, they ceased their friendship and Scaliger was very abusive of him in later years. Interestingly enough, Nostradamus did not retaliate. In 1552 he writes of Scaliger in his *Traité des Fardemens* as one "who seems to have inherited Cicero's soul in the subject of eloquence, Virgil's in poetry, and Galen's twice over in medicine. I owe him more than to anyone else in the world." To crown all those troubles, Nostradamus' dead wife's family sued him to recover his dowry. It is not known whether it was returned.

But the final blow fell when Nostradamus was officially summoned in 1538 to attend the Inquisition at Toulouse—just as much to be feared as its Spanish equivalent. It was reported that when, in 1534, Nostradamus, seeing some workman making a bronze cast of a statue of the Virgin, remarked to the man that he was only "making devils." Whatever he did in fact say, it was extremely unwise of him to say anything derogatory at that period. His defense, which appears somewhat weak, was that he was only referring to the lack of artistic form of the statue. It was time, in every sense, for Nostradamus to move on.

The next period of his life, 1538–1544, is little documented. We glean odd bits of information from his later books *Moultes Opuscules* and *Le Traité des Fardemens.* We learn that he visited Lorraine, Venice and traveled even as far as Sicily.

Certainly, he was well known and much thought of despite his personal tragedy. He seems to have been intent on building up his medical knowledge and presumably visited many important astrologers, cabalists, alchemists and physicians. Many oral legends come down to us about this period of his life. While in Ancona in Italy we learn that he met a young swineherd called Felix Peretti. Nostradamus knelt in the road as the boy passed. Replying to questions as to why he had done this, Nostradamus replied that he must kneel before His Holiness. Felix Peretti became Pope Sixtus V in 1585, twenty-odd years after Nostradamus' death.

Another widely circulated story was related in print in 1656 by Etienne Jaubert. He says, "In this same place when visiting Monsieur and Madame de Florinville, I learned that Nostradamus had stayed there and treated Madame de Florinville, the grandmother of the present Seigneur de Florinville, who is still alive . . . Monsieur de Florinville, walking in the courtyard of his château in the company of Nostradamus, noticed two suckling pigs, one black and one white. Determined to have some sport, he asked Nostradamus what would happen to the two animals, to which the reply was that 'the wolf will eat the white one and we will eat the black one.'

"So, Monsieur de Florinville, wishing to disprove Nostradamus' powers, secretly commanded his cook to kill the white one for that night's supper. This was done, and the pig was dressed and placed on the spit in the kitchen. But while the cook was out on an errand, a tame wolf cub belonging to the household, gnawed at the prepared pig. When the cook returned and saw what had happened, he took the black pig and prepared it, serving it up at dinner.

"Monsieur de Florinville, knowing nothing of this because the cook was afraid to tell him, said to Nostradamus that they were eating the white pig. The prophet disagreed and insisted that the black pig had been served up at table. The cook was then asked to come in and eventually confessed what had happened. This gave the company another more agreeable dish to discuss." He goes on to say that "All France recounts diverse events predicted by the author, but I omit them, because I have not been personally assured about them. . . ."

We next come across Nostradamus in Marseilles in 1554, where he

apparently thought of settling down. But there was a fresh outburst
of the plague in the city during that year, and together with the doctor
Louis Serres, Nostradamus worked unceasingly. Then, in November,
1554, Provence suffered one of the worst floods in its history. The
plague became even worse, the rivers and springs being polluted with
bodies of men and animals. By 1546, the plague was at its height.
Aix-en-Provence, the capital town, was in a desperate plight. César
de Nostradame, in his *Histoire de Provence,* 1614, says that his father
described the situation which faced him when the town sent for him
just after May 1, 1546, soon after the plague had broken out.

"People struck by the fever of this illness completely abandon all
hopes of recovery, wrap themselves into two white winding sheets
and, even while they are still alive say the prayers for the dead—an
unheard of thing. The houses are abandoned and empty, men disfigured, women in tears, bewildered children . . . the brave gone and
the animals fled. The palace is locked and silent, justice silent and
deserted . . . shelter bearers and street porters work on credit as there
is no money to be had. The shops are shut, there are no arts, the
churches are empty and the priests confused. In short, the streets are
foul, wild and full of weeds because of the absence of man and beast
during all the 270 days that the plague lasted. . . ."

Nostradamus remained among the sick and dying all that time and
ascribed the immunization acquired by his patients to the plague to
his rose pills, the recipe for which is given below and appears in his
Moultes Opuscules, 1555. But one should also remember his insistence
on fresh air, running water and his refusal to bleed patients. He also
refused to wear the typical cloak of many colors, said to be magical
and protect its wearer from sickness. Unfortunately he does not say
anything about hygiene except that the rose pills killed bad breath,
bad odors and cleansed teeth, preventing decay, and had to be
sucked continuously.

The recipe is not at all unusual for medicine of the time. The
ingredients were as follows.

300–400 red roses, picked before dawn.[1]
1 oz. sawdust from green fresh cyprus.
6 oz. Iris of Florence.
3 oz. cloves.
3 drams. sweet smelling calamus, tiger lily.
6 drams. lignaloes.

[1]As with all recipes using flower petals for medicines or scent it was necessary to
pluck them before dawn while the dew was still on them. This is still done with many
flower-based perfumes today.

Pulverize the rose petals, in a mortar, mixed with a powder made from the above. Make the mixture into lozenges, dry and keep enclosed, away from the air. Keep one in the mouth at all times.

Bareste says that the Parliament at Aix voted Nostradamus a pension for life. He is also said to have given many of the rich presents from his wealthy patients to the poor, the widows and orphans of the plague. It is difficult to know how much of this is generosity or hearsay, but there must be a foundation for it as this reputation for generosity follows Nostradamus throughout his life.

The plague then afflicted the small, charming town of Salon-de-Provence. Again Nostradamus decided to settle down when it was over, and it became his home until his death.

From a medical point of view, the town was ideally situated for him, between Marseilles, Aix and Avignon. Nostradamus was proved right in his choice because he was settled between the most important cities of Provence and the Midi. He moved there in 1548. In 1547 the town of Lyons sent for him, afflicted by something which may not have been the plague, but possibly whooping cough, still a deadly disease at that period. Nostradamus mentions in his *Traité des Fardemens* a certain chemist, René Hepilievard of Lyons, who produced his prescriptions to a very high quality.

Bareste again recounts Nostradamus' activities at this time, but they are of dubious source. He states that at Lyons Nostradamus quarreled with Antoine Sarrazin, a colleague, who did not agree with his medical advice. The town is said to have sent a delegation to Nostradamus, begging him not to desert them. He answered that the townspeople must choose between them. They are said to have replied, "We choose Nostradamus, the liberator of Aix." In fact, whoever the doctor was, it was not Sarrazin. He did not get his license, yet alone doctorate, until much later, so the story is somewhat suspect. Researches in the various archives have not been able to support this story. Its only source is Bareste plus the indubitable fact that Nostradamus was in Lyons in 1547.

Now comes the final, and it appears the most contented, period of Nostradamus' life, when he obtained international recognition and became adviser to Catherine de' Medicis, queen of France. He was a solid citizen, laden again with honors and gifts, and now he married for a second time. Anne Ponsarde Gemelle, a rich and definitely young widow, in view of their numerous future offspring, gave Nostradamus the solid base that had been lacking until then in his life. They were married at Salon on November 11, 1547, before the notary of Salon, Etienne Hozier.

The marriage contract is still in the archives at Salon. They bought a house off the rue de la Poissonnerie, and settled there for the rest of Nostradamus' life.

Salon did not offer much medical competition. Nostradamus appears to have spent most of his time making medicinal and cosmetic preparations for the town notables, by whom he was accepted. But there was an element of distrust and dislike among the ordinary townspeople; presumably his reputation had gone before him. The townspeople abused him as a Jew, his conversion in childhood did not impress them, and he was suspected of being a Huguenot (Protestant) sympathizer. This last was patently untrue as is seen throughout his writings, but it was the age of Calvin and Luther, and the wars of religion which would ravish France for nearly a century were about to begin. The fact that many of the Provençal nobility turned Huguenot did not help. The Catholic peasants banded into groups called Cabans, and became notorious for pillaging the rich Huguenot houses. To the cynical it may well appear that their motive was greed rather than religion. Nostradamus had a low opinion of the Cabans. In the *Traité des Fardemens* he wrote in 1552, "Here where I reside I carry on my work among animals, barbarians, mortal enemies of learning and letters."

It was around this time that he converted the top floor of his house into his study and spent his time reading occult books which were eventually to make him one of the best-known persons in France. He started upon his literary predictive career with a series of *Almanachs.* The first one was published in 1550, which presumably means he wrote it at some period in 1549. It was very successful although it contained only limited information about the weather, crops and the odd supernatural occurrence. Many of these predictions were wrong, but the *Almanachs* were a great success. La Croix du Maine in 1594 wrote that Nostradamus wrote an "infinite number of *Almanachs* and *Prognostications* which were very well received and sold so well that several imitations of them were made in his name."

The so-called *Prophecies of Orval,* by Philip Olivarious, supposedly printed in 1542 and which predicted the coming of Napoleon, were fakes printed around 1820. There is no record of Nostradamus going to Orval although he may have passed through it. However, according to Mlle Le Normand, Napoleon always carried a copy of the Orval prophecies around with him. Le Normand was a great friend of the Empress Josephine: she was a mystic and soothsayer who was very successful and made a great deal of money during and after the Revolution.

It is certain that Nostradamus continued to produce these even while writing the *Prophéties* because in the Salon archives there is a receipt from two Lyons printers for twenty crowns for the *Almanachs* of 1562. One wonders if their success led him to conceive the idea of the *Prophéties*? At the same time however he produced his *Traité des Fardemens* in 1552; in modern terms one might have called him a workaholic.

He also became involved around this period with something quite different. A young man called Adam de Craponne dreamed of building a canal which would connect the Rhône with the Durance, and bring water to the arid land around Salon. Nostradamus became his patron, giving money and doubtless offering advice as well. The canal was started in 1557 and finished in 1559 and is still functioning, bringing water to Salon and the surrounding communities. He was a sound businessman as well as a prophet. We don't have records of his percentage revenue on this venture but I don't doubt it was substantial. There is an impressive statue to Adam de Craponne at Salon, just as grand as that to Nostradamus.

It was approximately in 1554 that a certain Jean Aymes de Chavigny, ex-mayor of Beaune, arrived in Nostradamus' life. Jean Aymes de Chavigny, from now on referred to as Chavigny, was thirty years old in 1554 and held a doctorate in law and theology. He had been elected mayor of the town of Beaune in 1548 and had a brilliant future awaiting him. But he suddenly decided to give all this up, and was advised by Jean Dorat, a court poet and professor of Greek at the Collège de France, to go to Nostradamus as a pupil. He was obviously close to the prophet during his life, but not enough to be mentioned in Nostradamus' will. He is important in that it was he and Anne Ponsarde Gemelle who published together the first final and definitive copy of *Les Prophéties* in 1568, two years after Nostradamus' death. His influence on Nostradamus' widow has long been a matter of question, but one that I think shall never be resolved.

How much Chavigny influenced Nostradamus' widow over the publication of the second part of the quatrains is impossible to estimate. Not only did Chavigny claim to be the adopted son of Nostradamus, but of this there is no proof, he was also his scribe and amanuensis. It is unlikely that Anne Ponsart Gemelle Nostradamus was a very literate woman, and nowhere during Nostradamus' lifetime is she referred to in connection with the *Prophéties*. But it is Chavigny who gives some of the best definite biographical information on Nostradamus. He wrote a book, now lost, the *Receuil des présages prosaïques de M. Nostradamus*. This was followed in 1594 by his major work, *La Première face de Janus François*. Chavigny studied his master's work for a good thirty years. Chavigny used Nostradamus' writings to ally himself with Henri de Navarre, which proved an extremely wise political move. To research Chavigny in depth is a purely academic effort, and I think it is sufficient here to leave him with his second book, *Janus François,* a discussion of various predictions chosen by Chavigny.

The other main source of reference to the prophet was Nostradamus' eldest son, César, who states in his *Histoire de Provence* that Nostradamus was convinced great historical change would occur in France during the 1550s. He writes of one episode which affected Nostradamus deeply.

"In the year 1554, what tragic and unhappy events occurred . . . fellow creatures born deformed and hideous . . . At the end of January a child was born at Senas, monstrous, with two heads. . . . He was brought to my father and seen by several people." After the birth of a two-headed horse which Nostradamus seems to have been persuaded to see, he diagnosed it as being the forerunner of a great split due in French history. With all the trouble brewing between the Catholics and the Huguenots it would not be a difficult interpretation. A child born in England in 1988 with two heads has been declared by its doctors to be "viable." A dreadful thought. However, in the twentieth century, we do not allot meanings to these tragic freaks. Nostradamus was a shrewd psychologist. He understood the value of symbols in his society and used them accordingly.

During the first part of the 1550s Nostradamus was working at full stretch. He was writing his monthly *Almanachs* and *Prognostications.* He was treating his patients and above all he was writing the first part of the book for which he is most remembered, *Les Prophéties de M. Nostradamus,* which first appeared in 1555. However, as far as this book is concerned I shall take the total edition of the *Prophéties* to which were added the further Centuries VIII–X to give us the first definitive complete version, which was published by Benoît Rigaud in 1568. Since Nostradamus had been dead for two years, it seems fair to contemplate the possibility that Chavigny, the faithful pupil, may have tampered with some of the *Prophéties* with the consent of Nostradamus' wife. But this is still Nostradamus' essential work.

The Prophéties of Nostradamus were intended to contain predictions until the end of the world. The *Almanachs* were a yearly publication. How Nostradamus worked out his date for the end of the world is difficult to decide. In many ways he is a Millennium man, believing that the world will come to an end at A.D. 2000 or maybe, but with far less reason, A.D. 3000. Although civilized and cultured, Nostradamus belonged more to the fifteenth century than to the Renaissance. His thoughts went backwards to the First Millennium, A.D. 1000, rather than forward to A.D. 2000. The influence of the Church during the first Millennium had been enormous, preaching that the world was coming to an end and its influence was widespread. Therefore people let their fields lie fallow, neglected their beasts, made no plans for the future. When the year A.D. 1000 was reached and passed without singular incident, it took at least two years for a semblance of normality to return to people's lives. And the Church? It preached that an error had been made and that all would be fulfilled in the next millennium, A.D. 2000. From most of Nostradamus' prophecies it seems that he inclined to A.D. 2000, but was not wholly certain due to the influence of such writings as *The Book of Enoch,* which stated the Millennium would come in 7000 years. Unfortunately this book does not say from when this date should be calculated. Perhaps the worldly side of Nostradamus was hedging his bets.

It is now necessary to say how the *Prophéties* were composed. They were intended to be a series of one thousand predictions, divided into books of a hundred centaines. The word *"centaine"* has nothing to do with time, a hundred years, but refers to the fact that it is a set of 100 four-line predictions. These were joined together in a book, for the first time, in 1568: *Les Prophéties de M. Michel Nostradamus. Dont il y en a trois cens qui n'encores iamais este imprimées. A. Lyon. Par Benoît Rigaud. Auec permission.* But since this book was published after his death, there is room for some speculation. The seventh Century contains only 42 quatrains and there seems no evidence to prove that the remaining quatrains were used elsewhere. My personal opinion is that possibly Nostradamus had simply not completed the 1000 before his death. The Benoît Rigaud edition also contains the Préface, the first seven Centuries (as seen in an edition by Antoine du Rosne of Lyons), and also the Epistle to Henri II and Centuries VIII–X inclusive. This definitive publication resulted in an immediate spate of copies and fakes throughout Europe, and gives one some idea of the influence the name of Nostradamus carried in its wake. They all contain material, much of it very crudely faked, of forged quatrains not in the editio princeps of 1568.

The *"Sixaines,"* a series of predictions in six lines, first turned up in 1605, at Chantilly. They were presented to Henri IV. They purported to have been in the possession of a certain Henry Nostradamus, a nephew of Nostradamus. This cannot be verified either way. Nostradamus had two other brothers, and we have no record as to whether he had any sisters. But the *Sixaines,* in my opinion, are forgeries, which is why I do not include them in this book. The style is not similar to that of Nostradamus, neither were they mentioned by his great follower and pupil Chavigny.

Another fact that makes them suspect is that many appear to be retrospective, applying to the conspiracy of the duc du Biron which rocked the French court in 1602. Anyway, there seems no reason for Nostradamus to change from his successful convoluted style of the quatrains, which had made him famous; they were his trademark, after all.

To return to the *Prophéties:* Chavigny, in a short biography of Nostradamus in 1594, wrote as follows: "Nostradamus . . . foreseeing the important changes and revolutions which were to occur throughout all Europe, the bloody civil war and the dangerous troubles fatally approaching the French realm . . . set out to write his Centuries, which he kept a long time without wishing to publish them feeling that the novelty of the content could not fail to cause infinite attacks, calumnies . . . as indeed happened. Finally, overcome by a wish to be of service to the public, he produced them, with the result that their fame rang throughout the mouths of both Frenchmen and foreigners, with great wonderment."

The reaction of the ruling class was enthusiastic. They had time to read this tiny book, 6" × 4" approximately, a size convenient to carry around in their pockets. Its influence spread downward from the court to other areas often through oral tradition as well as book form.

The *Prophéties* became the rage and greatly influenced the queen, Catherine de' Medicis. But equally Nostradamus was vilified on all sides; doctors, philosophers even astrologers objected to the quatrains. A clever Latin verse was soon repeated all over France.

Nostra damus cum falsa damus nam fallere nostrum est;
Et cum falsa damus, nil nisi notra damus.

Roughly translated this means, "When we give our own we give false things. And when we give false things, we give but our own."

We don't know exactly when the name of Nostradamus came to the ears of Catherine de' Medicis. She had for some time been interested in astrology and possibly necromancy, particularly during those first ten years of her marriage, when she was barren. We know that the king sent a royal command for Nostradamus to come to Paris.

He set out on July 14, 1556. Because of his mission he was able to make use of the royal post, and the journey took about half the time it would have taken an ordinary traveler. He reached Paris on August 15 and lodged in the Inn of Saint Michel at Nostradame. The following day the Constable of France himself, Anne de Montmorency, ordered Nostradamus to the court, which was based that month at Saint-Germain-en-Laye.

We know little of this visit other than that Nostradamus spent several hours with Catherine. What they discussed is impossible to guess but it is generally agreed that the quatrain I.XXXV particularly occupied the queen, as she had also been warned by her Italian astrologer, Luc Gauric, that her husband would die in a duel. The letter Gauric sent to Henri is dated February, 1556, and warns the king "to avoid all single combat in an enclosed place, especially near his 41st year." Henri is said to have told Montgomery, the captain of his Scottish guard, who, ironically, was the person to be involved in his death, "I care not if my death be in that manner more than in any other. I would even prefer it, to die by the hand of whoever he might be, so long as he was brave and valiant and that I kept my honor."

Returning to Paris, rather dissatisfied with the payments he had received, which totaled one hundred and thirty crowns, Nostradamus was lodged at the palace of the Archbishop de Sens. Since his journey had cost him a hundred crowns he was soon short of money and borrowed money from a stranger, Jean Morel. Nostradamus later acknowledges a loan of two rose nobles and twelve crowns in the only authenticated letter that has remained signed by himself, underneath the name of a secretary. All other communications relating to Nostradamus that have survived have been written by scribes.

However, once comfortably settled in Paris, Nostradamus resolved to make good use of his reputation and gain something from it. We learn that he had an attack of gout and was confined to his rooms for ten days. But that did not stop the rich and the credulous from seeking him out. There is a pleasant legend about this period. Nostradamus was in bed when he was woken by a loud knocking at his door. The intruder was a page of the Beauveau family, who had lost one of their dogs. Before he could state the reason for his interruption, Nostradamus is said to have cried out, "You are making a lot of noise over a lost dog. Go and look on the road to Orléans. You will find it there on a leash." According to the page's story he found a servant on the road leading the dog back. This story spread mightily around the court and increased the Nostradamus legend.

Eventually the other reason for his journey was made clear. Catherine wanted to know the fates of her children. Nostradamus was summoned to Blois to draw up their horoscopes. It must have been a difficult task as all the Valois children would die, leaving France no direct heir. Her first son, François II, would be king for a year and leave his child bride, Mary Queen of Scots, to her tragic destiny.

Eleven-year-old Elisabeth would be married off to old Philip II of Spain, as his third wife, and die in childbirth. The next daughter, Claude, who became the duchesse de Lorraine, was also to die in her twenties. Then came Charles IX, who would celebrate his coronation dinner wearing a woman's dress and in whom lurked the tragedy of St. Bartholomew, the massacre of the Huguenots, noble and otherwise, which took place in Paris on St. Bartholomew's Day, August 24, 1572. The Huguenots had flocked to the city to celebrate the marriage of the Huguenot king Henri of Navarre to Marguerite de Valois. It was an attempt to quash the influence of the Huguenot Admiral Coligny, who was attempting to draw Charles IX into a war with Spain, which Catherine, his mother, greatly opposed. She persuaded the king that the massacre was a measure of public safety. The king himself arranged the manner of the execution of the massacre. It began on Sunday, August 24, at daybreak and lasted until September 17. It is reported that Charles himself fired upon Huguenots from a window of the Louvre. The Catholic powers rejoiced greatly at this slaughter and Pope Gregory XIII commanded bonfires to be lit and a medal struck to commemorate the event.

Charles IX was followed by Henri III, king of Poland and France, twice times king, killed by the assassin Clément. Then there was the duc d'Alençon, Elizabeth I of England's perpetual suitor, her "little frog," titular ruler of the Netherlands. Finally, la belle Marguerite, who married the Huguenot king of Navarre, and because she became bored with his provincial court and sought solace in various love affairs, was imprisoned by her husband in a grim convent for the rest of her life. A tragic life for two reasons. She would outlive all her siblings and also see her former husband take over France as Henri IV.

It is difficult to imagine what Nostradamus did tell Catherine, but obviously it sufficed, because she retained her faith in him until her death. As we know, she visited Salon with Charles IX in 1554 and conferred upon Nostradamus the title of Physician in Ordinary and a present of 200 crowns. How he explained away the predictions he had already written one cannot guess.

It was soon after this that Nostradamus began to see the danger signs in Paris. He was burned in effigy in one of the city squares. The Justice of Paris wished to question him. So he returned, triumphantly, to Salon. Here, it appears, he received many important visitors. The canal was at the point of completion, and his second son, André, was born. Presumably, he was also finishing off the *Prophéties*. There is another typical Nostradamus story at this period.

The prophet was seated in front of his house one evening, and a young girl passed him on her way to the woods. She greeted him: *"Bonjour, Monsieur de Nostradame."* He replied, *"Bonjour fillette."* On her return she again greeted him, to which his reply was, *"Bonjour petite femme."* He knew what she was doing in the woods. A charming tale.

In the summer of 1559 the court celebrated the double marriage of Elisabeth, Henri's eldest daughter, aged fourteen, to Philip II of Spain, and of his sister, Marguerite, to the duc de Savoie. To celebrate these events a grand tourney was planned. It started on June 28 and was to be held for three days in the rue Saint-Antoine. The king joined in the jousting and was very successful for the first two days. But on the third, the mood changed. Catherine sent him a note begging him not to proceed as she felt a great unease.

An unknown boy among the spectators is said to have cried out, "The king will die." But Henri disregarded these warnings and towards evening rode against the Captain of his Scottish guard, Montgomery. They jousted twice, neither succeeding in unseating the other. Then Montgomery, too, became afraid and begged the king to ride no more. But Henri insisted. They clashed lances, but unfortunately Montgomery did not raise his in time, and he struck the king in the head, through his gilded helmet. Some record a second wound in the head, thus fulfilling Nostradamus' prediction: I.XXXV, *deux claffes un.* He died ten days later in great agony, pleading with Catherine and the court not to take action against the wretched Montgomery. The latter, however, had the sense to flee the court immediately, but ultimately Catherine caught up with him and wreaked her revenge. Montgomery is said to have exclaimed of Nostradamus, "Cursed be the magician who predicted so evilly and so well."

The immature François II, already married to Mary Stuart, Mary Queen of Scots, from childhood, succeeded his father. Like all his family he had a passion for hunting and probably initially caught a chill in his ear in November, 1560. It is interesting to note that the various court ambassadors were extremely worried about the young king, each remembering quatrains X.XXXIX and X.LV. The remaining centuries had been circulated in handwritten form, a common practice. The Venetian ambassador, Michele Suriano, wrote on November 20, 1560, to the doge at Venice, "Each courtier now remembers the XXXIX quatrain of Century X of Nostradamus and comments upon it under his breath." The Tuscan ambassador, Niccolò Tornabuoni, wrote to Duke Cosimo of Florence on December 3, "The health of the king is very unsure and Nostradamus in his predictions for this month says that the royal house will lose two young members from unexpected illness." I cannot find the quatrain which predicts the death of two young men of the royal house, but François II died two days later on December 5 and a young cousin, the son of the duc de Roche-sur-Yon, died in the same month.

It is probable that sitting quietly down in Salon, Nostradamus was not aware of the political impact of his predictions throughout Europe.

In January of the following year, 1561, the Spanish ambassador, Chantonnay, wrote to his master, Philip II: "It has been noticed that in the period of one month both the first and least members of the royal house have died. These troubles have stupefied the court, together with the prediction of Nostradamus: it would be better to chastise him than allow him to sell such prophecies which lead to ignorant and superstitious beliefs."

In 1561, Nostradamus was asked by Marguerite of Savoie and her husband to predict the future of the child she was bearing. He went to Nice to draw up the horoscope of the future Charles-Emmanuel. Nostradamus claimed he would be the greatest captain of his age. He was known as Charles-Emmanuel the Great; but apart from disagreeing totally about the rights of Henri IV to the French throne, his main claim to fame was as the ruler of Savoie. In May, 1561, Suriano again voiced his suspicions to the doge: "There is another prediction very widely spoken in France, coming from the famous astrologer Nostradamus, which threatens the three sons, in claiming that the Queen Mother will see them all as kings." Which indeed she did.

Nostradamus' reputation was again increased by the prediction X.XXXIX, which was now openly quoted at the court: "The eldest son; a widow, an unfortunate marriage without any children; two islands in discord, before eighteen still a minor. For the other one, the betrothal will be even younger."

This was widely believed to apply to François II, eldest son of Henri II. He died six weeks before reaching the age of eighteen, leaving a widow, Mary Queen of Scots, whose return to her own country as a rightful queen was to put two realms in discord. To compound the interest, François' younger brother Charles, later to become Charles IX, had been betrothed at the earlier age of eleven to Elizabeth of Austria.

It was in 1564 that Catherine de' Medicis decided to make a grand progress throughout France, partly to try to help to quell the religious troubles and also to meet her daughter Elisabeth, whom she had not seen for five years. Perhaps she had memories of her own unhappy arrival in France aged fourteen, exactly the same age as Elisabeth had been when she set off to marry the dour king of Spain. All her family came with her, but because of the length of the trip—it was to last nearly two years—she took with her a reduced court of eight hundred.

During this progress, which included Provence, Catherine decided that she would visit Nostradamus and Salon. César Nostradamus, his son, gives us a vivid but lengthy description of the visit. The royal family arrived at Salon on October 17 at 3.00 P.M. But a few days before, the plague had reappeared and five people died, so the town was almost empty. King Charles IX ordered that people return to welcome the royal party under threat of penalty.

It is worth noting Charles's attire. "He was seated on an African horse, with a harness of black velvet with large trimmings and fringes of gold. His person was robed in a cloak of Tyrian purple, adorned with silver ribbons. He wore an amethyst in one ear and a sapphire in the other. . . ."

The two consuls of Salon received their king and "at once begged Michel de Nostradame . . . to speak to Her Majesty at the reception, guessing quite correctly that she would especially desire to see him." Nostradamus, with unusual modesty told his friends "he wanted to move about independently and greet Her Majesty away from the vulgar people and this crowd of men, being aware that he would be asked for and sent for when she arrived." Apparently Nostradamus was pointed out to the king by the consuls and greeted him suitably in Latin. According to César, he never left his father's side during this occasion. Nostradamus, with his velvet hat in one hand and a Malacca cane with a silver handle in the other, which he used because he suffered from gout, went up to the château where the royal family were staying and spent a long time talking with the king and queen regent.

Here is an interesting anecdote omitted by César but quoted by many other commentators. The queen, Catherine, asked Nostradamus to cast the horoscope of her youngest son, the duc d'Anjou, which Nostradamus did, saying he would become king.

This, as at their first meeting at Blois four years earlier, seemed to satisfy Catherine. But Nostradamus was far more interested in a ten-year-old page in the king's suite. He tried to see the boy, who was frightened and ran away. He therefore arranged to see him at his levée the following morning. Henri IV often told this story in later years, saying that his servants delayed in giving him his shirt so that Nostradamus could see him at his leisure, while he feared that a whipping was awaiting him. As the boy stood naked, waiting to be ceremonially dressed as usual, Nostradamus remarked the moles upon his body. This was a common method of prediction akin to chiromancy or reading the hand. Nostradamus was convinced this was the boy who would be the future king of France. He said to the servants at the levée, "You will have as a master the king of France and Navarre." The boy was a cousin of the king, of the family of Navarre, and thus united France and Navarre on his accession to the French throne after his defeat of Henri III in 1589 as Henri IV of France.

There is a painting of this episode by Valverane which is in the Old Museum at Salon. It happened on October 18, 1564, shortly before Nostradamus' death in 1566.

After the court's leaving Provence Nostradamus sank back into obscurity—but that was only technically, as it were. The corridors of the royal court were still humming. The new ambassador to Spain was Don Francisco de Alava. He reports upon one of the quatrains concerning the duc d'Anjou, the permanent courtier, and Elizabeth I of England. "Tomorrow, there leaves secretly a gentleman sent to visit the queen of England. The first day that the King and Queen saw Nostradamus [at Salon] he declared to them that the king would marry the aforesaid Queen." Another dispatch, sent some months later, shows de Alava's low opinion of the prophet, and his certainty that Nostradamus was acting for personal motives of greed, which I believe to be probably untrue. "To the king of Spain: In order that Your Majesty may see how duped people are here in France, I report that the Queen, when she passed through the place where Nostradamus lives, summoned him and presented him with two hundred crowns. She ordered him to draw up the horoscope of the King and the Queen." (It is uncertain whether the Queen here is Charles IX's fiancée, Elizabeth of Austria, or Catherine herself.) "Since he is the most diplomatic and never wishes to displease anyone, he drew up two horoscopes which flattered them, and they ordered him to follow their court as far as Arles . . . The Queen spoke with me today. 'Do you know,' she said, 'Nostradamus has assured me that in 1566 a general peace should reign all over the world' . . . and when saying this she had as confident an air as if she were quoting the gospels of St. John or St. Luke."

But by the end of 1565, Nostradamus was seriously ill. Suffering from arthritis and gout, he was confined to his house at Salon. Joseph Roche, his notary, was summoned on June 17, 1566, to draw up his will. His detailed estate included coins to the value of 3,444 crowns. (For contemporary evaluation, Leoni states that a room in a good house in Paris could be rented for four crowns a year.) His daughter Madeleine received the largest legacy of 600 crowns, while her two sisters Diana and Anne received 500 each. Anne Ponsart Gemelle Nostradamus received 400 crowns and most of the contents of the house. His sons, unnamed, received 100 crowns each, but not until they were twenty-five. There were several minor bequests to charities and beggars of the parish—six sous each! He also gave instructions for his burial. His body was to be placed between the great door and the altar of Saint Martha in the local Franciscan monastery.

This was changed on June 30, when a codicil was drawn up, giving his eldest son, César, his astrolobe and his large gold ring, and Madeleine, obviously his favorite daughter, two walnut chests with their contents, without having to wait for her marriage.

Chavigny states that dropsy set in around June 25. On July 1, the superior of the Franciscan monastery, Father Vidal, was sent for to give the last rites. Nostradamus knew he was dying. Despite being a doctor he had predicted it, stating that Chavigny would find him the next morning, *trouvé tout mort entre le lit et le banc.* The *banc* had been set by Nostradamus' bed to enable him to climb into it in his weakened state. He also told Chavigny he would not find him alive at sunrise. He died sometime during the early morning, after eight days of severe pain.

Nostradamus was buried as he asked, upright in the monastery "so that the feet of the vulgar should not walk over him." His headstone, written in Latin, composed by his wife, reads as follows: "Here lie the bones of the illustrious Michel Nostradamus, alone of all mortals judged worthy to record events of the entire world with his almost divine pen, under the influence of the stars. He lived 62 years, 6 months and 7 days. He died at Salon in the year 1566. Let not prosperity disturb his rest. Anne Pons Gemelle wishes her husband true happiness."

Of Nostradamus' wife, Anne Ponsart or Pons Gemelle, we have no further information. César, his eldest son and author of the *Histoires de Provence,* died in 1631. He was described by Pitton as "a good poet, painter and good historian." He was twice consul of Salon.

He married, but had no children. It seems that any descendants of Nostradamus came from the female line. The second son, André, who went to Paris soon after his father's death, killed an adversary in a duel and was arrested. He vowed to take Orders if freed, and it is said that he became a Capuchin monk and was buried at a monastery near Toulon. The third son, Charles, tried, unsuccessfully, to make his name as a Provençal poet.

An interesting story of a charlatan can be introduced here. He normally called himself Michel le Jeune. He made a glorious exit at the siege of Poussin, 1574, as related by Théodora-Agrippa d'Aubigné, the mother of the wife of Louis XIV, Madame Maintenon. It appears that Poussin was under siege and the "young Michel" was asked by the commander, Saint-Luc, what would happen to the town. Michel le Jeune gave the deliberated reply that the town would be burned down by fire. Sadly, he was caught setting fire to sites all over the town. He was killed by the troops. Already Nostradamus' name was one to conjure with.

All that remains to add is that Nostradamus' tomb soon became a place of pilgrimage. During the Revolution it was sacked, despite the solemn warning on the headstone. The soldiers scattered his bones, and there is a rumor that they drank wine out of his skull. However, his bones were collected under the order of the then mayor, a M. David, and reinterred in the Church of Saint-Laurent at Salon. The town put up a new epitaph in 1792: "In this year 3 of Liberty, the tomb of Nostradamus, who honored Salon, his native land, and whose memory will always be cherished by French patriots, was opened because of his predictions of the rule of Liberty. The citizens divided his bones amongst one another. The municipality has recovered part of them, which are contained in this tomb."

But, once the fervor of the Revolution had passed, the old epitaph of his wife, Anne Ponsart Gemelle, was replaced in marble over Nostradamus' new resting place. One other small touch. The locals of Salon were so convinced that Nostradamus did not die in 1566 that a legend ran that he was shut up in his tomb with pen and ink and would continue to write the *Prophéties*.

Perhaps this is time to give a physical description of Nostradamus. Chavigny describes him thus: "He was a little under medium height, robust, nimble and vigorous. He had a large and open forehead, a straight nose and gray eyes which were usually pleasant but which blazed when he was angry. His face was both severe and smiling, but along with this severity there was a great kindness. His cheeks were red, even in his old age, and his beard long and thick. Except in his old age his health was good and his senses acute. He had a lively and inquiring mind and a remarkable memory. He spoke little, but thought a great deal. He slept only four or five hours a night. He praised freedom of speech and approved of the Catholic Church, outside of which he believed there was no salvation. He hated vice. I can remember his charity to the poor towards whom he was very generous."

JEWISH SOURCES WHICH INDICATE THE COMING OF THE MILLENNIUM

As I have mentioned, Nostradamus' family had declared themselves converts to the Christian religion by 1502, two years before he was born. But they never entirely left their Judaism behind. We learn that among the first things Nostradamus was taught by his grandfather was Hebrew, so the ancient creed must have been a strong tradition among the family.

The Old Testament predicts that seven great events will happen at roughly the same time, all of which shall be indicators that mankind is approaching Armageddon, Nostradamus' Millennium. Horrifyingly enough, these events appear to have already started and mankind will have to act quickly if the predictions are not to be fulfilled.

The first is religious deception, false religions. The movement away from major Christian, Islamic and Hindu beliefs is increasing daily. Particularly we see the basic tenets of the Church being changed or ignored. Women deacons, and already some women priests, married priests, and the schism in early 1988 by Archbishop Lefèbvre and his followers plus the intransigence of Muslim fundamentalists.

We have a spate of newly founded mystic religions, quite apart from television evangelists and Bible Thumpers. One of the most dangerous and prolific of these religions is that of Sun Myung Moon, a Korean, who has houses all over the world. Induction into this cult is so severe that parents have been known to kidnap their children to get them away from this pernicious sect and actually have them deprogrammed. He claims among other things to be the second coming of the Messiah.

Maharaj Ji of India also claims to be the Messiah and has a large following. He sometimes calls himself "The Lord from Heaven in a 747." All these sects accrue immense sums of money from their followers and most are impenetrable due to their claiming charity status where taxes are concerned and are therefore difficult to prosecute under the law.

David Moses is another. His cult are known as The Children of God. He has a strong following among young people and sends messages to his followers, apparently known as the "Mo Letters" to his "families" of adoring disciples. He too claims to be the Messiah.

The most dreadful of these cult leaders was the Reverend Jim Jones. He led some nine hundred people into the jungles of Guyana in the 1970s, only to serve them a cocktail of death; men, women and children together.

Another aspect of these "false gods" is the current revival of the occult. It was not taken too seriously in the early sixties but now one can read about it regularly in even the more serious newspapers. Whether these so-called covens actually do much harm is improbable, but they worship Satan as their God.

Under this heading may also come the amazing advance of astrology. Not only is it found in its most basic form in every daily newspaper and magazine that is published, but there is a wide network of people who today use personal astrologers to conduct their daily lives. Some astrologers are serious in their work, but many are charlatans. The average person accepts occult and psychic phenomena as normal. This is not to be confused with the few scientific experiments in laboratories working upon ESP and telepathy. They are attempting to sound out the extent of man's unconscious brain power.

It must be realized that not all supernatural or psychic phenomena are essentially good. There is a malevolent side to all these happenings, very often desired by those who dabble in it. Timothy 4.1 says, "The spirit clearly says that in later times some will abandon the faith and follow deceiving things." This is the demonic aspect of psychic phenomena, which although fortunately very rare, is desperately dangerous. Exorcisms are hard and sobering events to go through. The spate of films such as *The Exorcist* have made people more aware of the possibility of this happening, but not of the savage truths behind it.

The second Biblical warning Nostradamus would have us heed is one of internal revolution. The end of the eighth decade of this century makes it appear worldwide. In Russia we have the revolt of the Armenians trying to regain control over the Azerbaijan. Burma, Korea, Kampuchea, Ethiopia, Sudan, Latin America, South Africa, let alone the Gulf War, the tragic position of the Kurds, and the position of the Christian Lebanese against their terrorist-backed countrymen. The list can go on forever. I don't believe the world has ever been in such a state of insurrection. Most of these wars and uprisings are upheld in the name of liberation, and are financed mainly by the USSR or the USA. Not even embassies are safe places anymore. They are shelled or burned. It appears that not a year goes by without at least one national government being overthrown.

The third event that should warn us is war: "You will hear of wars and rumours of war," Matthew 24.6. No century has witnessed such an escalation of war as we have since the Second World War. Some are front-page news. Others, such as that in Burundi, are hardly heard of, but there is practically no country in the world today that is not fighting some kind of war. Even Britain has the problem of the indiscriminate terrorism of the IRA, although at the time of writing this, Europe does seem to be the most stable area.

When General MacArthur signed the peace treaty after the Second World War in 1945 he gave his warning, unfortunately unheeded: "We have had our last chance. If we do not devise some greater and more equitable system, Armageddon will be at our door."

Since then we have had wars in the Middle East, the Israel/Palestine problem, the Cold War (now hopefully coming to an end with "Glasnost"), the Korean War, the Vietnam War, the war in Afghanistan and the Gulf War. These have all been full-fledged wars, killing as many civilians as soldiers. Many countries now appear to have the capacity both to make atomic bombs and to utilize chemical weapons. There is always a chance that there may be a nuclear war by the end of the 1990s. That is the Holocaust, the Armaggedon, the Millennium.

As Nostradamus says, our chances of survival are slim. They depend upon the intelligence of our world leaders. At least, in this, Reagan and Gorbachev have started down this path of defusing world pressures. A small start, but a definite one.

The fourth warning is famine. Of course, famine is partly caused by the enormous population explosion, particularly in the Third World. However, despite many dying in disasters such as local wars, floods and famine, the world population is growing at an alarming rate. This is even despite the many sophisticated forms of contraception we now have. This decade has never been more conscious of the widespread famine throughout the Third World. First there was Ethiopia, and it still remains. Now we have the Sudan, Bangladesh, the great exodus of the boat people from Vietnam and Cambodia, the Iraqi Kurds in inadequate camps in Turkey and even the dreadful drought that has ruined so many farmers in the United States. Famine now appears to be ever present. Dr. William Paddock, a noted environmentalist, wrote a book in 1975 called *Famines,* and in it he predicted an age of famine which would begin in the 1970s and escalate beyond all our control. He appears to have been right. Dr. Borlaug, one of the world's greatest nutritionists, states, "The hunger and misery of millions would provoke a great global holocaust." We seem to be at this point now. Creations such as the European food and wine "mountains" now in storage should immediately be given as famine relief.

The fifth problem we are warned to face is the poisoning of the earth, pollution. The overwhelming impact of industrial pollution now affects every area of our lives. The earth is troubled by the "greenhouse effect" due to our constant use of fluorocarbons. The seas are so contaminated with over a thousand different chemicals being pumped into them in enormous quantities that we are now losing our sea mammal population. Seals, dolphins, porpoises, all at the top of the food chain, die of dreadful disfigurements, and the present epidemic of seal distemper is certainly partly due to the fact that the seals' immune systems have been lessened by the effluent. What should worry us more is that the fish we eat often contain dangerous levels of these same pollutants. Add to this the problems of acid rain and the deforestation of the globe, it makes one wonder where mankind will be in fifty years' time. Many of us now will drink only bottled water and with reason. Nitrites and nitrates used by farmers to increase their crops are leached into the rivers and reservoirs, the source of all our tap water.

The changing weather pattern, extreme heat (such as in the USA in 1988) and the appalling summers we have been having in Europe are another variable which affects food production. Dr. John Gribbin, scientist and co-author of *The Jupiter Effect,* says that these problems are aggravated by shifting planet orbits: "The unusual planetary alignment due to occur in the early 1980's will affect the sun. This in turn shakes up the planet earth. But we realized while studying the repercussions in the area of earthquakes that the link works through the atmosphere. What we are really talking about is an effect of the sun on the circulation of the atmosphere. This determines weather pattern shifts."

The sixth warning given is the Earthquake. "In various places there will be great earthquakes." These are something Nostradamus worries about, an interesting fact in that his France was not an "earthquake zone." Earthquakes are dreadful, sudden and devastating. The one that occurred recently on the Nepal/India border at about 6.7 degrees on the Richter scale has still left that part of the world greatly isolated. No communications, no railways, no roads, and—worst of all—no shelter for those fortunate enough to survive. Since then there has been the dreadful earthquake in Armenia with a total of over 70,000 dead and 100,000 injured.

It is a fact that there has been an unprecedented increase in earthquake activity in the twentieth century. The number of earthquakes has roughly doubled in each of the ten-year periods since 1950. Nostradamus may well therefore not be so far off when he predicts an enormous earthquake on the west coast of America in the near future, which will occur in May. One of the unpleasant side effects of earthquakes is great floods, should dams built over faults be destroyed. This would also apply to nuclear plants built near them. It has been stated by contemporary astrologers that May, 1989, is an extremely dangerous period because on the 8th of that month the three planets Mars, Uranus and Saturn will turn into retrograde action, which is malevolent and associated with earthquakes.

The final seventh sign of the Millennium will be plagues and disease. Plagues such as the Black Death, polio and smallpox seem to have been eliminated through medical development in most parts of the world. But a new and far more dreadful one has appeared, AIDS, for which as yet we have no cure, only means to retard its inevitable progress. Nostradamus certainly was aware of this new mutation in disease. He says unfortunately that "although relief will be found, the remedy will be far off." Let us hope that, in this prediction at least, he is partially wrong. The number of AIDS victims is multiplying at an appalling rate, and hospitals say that within a few years the majority of their beds will be occupied by people suffering from this disease.

It is a dreadful decade we have to look forward to.

THE MODERN MILLENNIUM

Apart from the Jewish influence on Nostradamus' opinions concerning the Millennium, as well as the Christian aspect, it appears to me that we could do much by simply sitting down, as it were, and analyzing the state in which the world finds itself at the end of the ninth decade of the twentieth century.

Never have there been so many continual disasters, both natural and manmade. Never have there been so many wars, so many available instruments of global destruction, so much wealth in the Western World and so much unimaginable poverty in the Third World, let alone those natural phenomena such as earthquakes and enigmatic plagues such as AIDS which threaten to decimate the human race.

There are many disaster areas worldwide. Bangladesh admits to hundreds of thousands drowned, millions homeless and 80 percent of the whole country underwater during the floods in 1988. That tragedy came a month after the catastrophic flooding in Sudan. The problem was caused just as it was in the Sudan according to scientists by "the thin end of the deforestation wedge." That is, the effect upon the climate by our relentless policy of destroying the great forests of the world, which causes changes in the weather. It is now much more generally understood that deforestation could cause the destruction of the world's entire ecological balance, changing everything from the air we breathe to the food we eat.

The human race is destroying areas of rain forest about the size of two hundred football pitches every minute. In this century alone we have removed about 50 percent of the forests. If we continue at this rate, another 20 percent will be destroyed by the year 2000.

Deforestation has four definite and tragic side effects. The first is flooding. When the soil is eroded by wind and rain, water from the melting snow caps of Tibet (in the case of Bangladesh) is not absorbed into the earth. Were there trees, the roots would absorb the water and bond the topsoil. Later, the water would be drawn up through the branches and released into the atmosphere, forming rain clouds. Where the land is subject to deforestation, the rain simply washes away the topsoil.

Secondly, there is what is now known as the greenhouse effect. This happens when gases created by the burning of timber form a layer of carbon dioxide around the planet, trapping heat and raising the atmospheric temperature. The earth's average temperature has already been raised by 0.5°C in the past ninety years. If the current destruction rate continues, the earth's temperature will rise by a further .5°C, thus raising the world sea level by anything up to sixty meters due to the melting of the polar ice cap. This would obliterate many cities, including London and New York.

Environmentalists have claimed that another side effect of deforestation is the extinction of many plant and animal species, and that at least one plant or animal species becomes extinct every half hour, an enormous environmental disaster. Another school of thought says that of the five to ten million species of organisms now inhabiting the earth, one million could die within the next ten years. Tropical forests have also been the main dispensary of raw materials for medicines, in particular those containing anticancer properties.

Plant and animal destruction in turn leads to the destruction of our few remaining primitive tribes. In the Carajas region of the Amazon, an area of rain forest the size of England and France combined was cleared in 1982 for a $600-million iron-ore project. The removal of essential sources of food and shelter forced the last nomadic tribe in South America, the Guajas, to near extinction, and two neighboring tribes, the Parakana and the Xikrin, now exist only in photographs or the slums of Rio de Janeiro.

What has happened to man's sense of proportion, his value of nature, his ultimate source of survival, his sense of decency? We have become, however unwittingly, the victims of those people selfish and greedy enough to attain their aims at whatever cost to others. The age of individual protest is past. It is pointless. Very often it is circumvented by those same exploiters who change the names of sources of food and other requirements on a ship's manifest, and usually succeed, as has happened recently in Britain. An individual is hard put to boycott the products of an individual country. Man must unite. Ten more years is a very short time indeed. Whether one gives credence to what Nostradamus writes or not, it must appear obvious to any right-minded, thinking person that the cooperation between nations is rapidly becoming impossible and that only global intervention will be of any use. The Millennium will arrive for the disbelievers as well. The Apocalypse (whatever one wishes to call it) which is already wiping out human, plant and animal life, has its roots in the acts of mankind as well as the will of God.

Michael Robinson of Washington's Smithsonian Institution said recently, "We are facing the first human-created extinction style cycle that is on the same scale as major geological events of the past, but condensed into an incomparably smaller span of time. This is not hyperbole, not even hypothesis, BUT IMMINENT ACTUALITY."

An example of this is Sir Edmund Hillary's first ascent of Everest. The steep sides of the Khumbu Valley in 1953 were covered with juniper brushes. Now 75 percent of these are destroyed, by climbers and environmental changes.

In the Third World Pakistan, India, Nepal, and Tibet—in addition to Bangladesh—have all suffered deforestation. This has eroded the fertile topsoil from the hills, caused landslides, and clogged rivers and reservoirs with so much silt that they cannot cope with the waters from the mountains so that they overflow, well before they reach their natural outlet, the Ganges.

It is estimated that at the present rate of cutting, the Himalayas will be treeless in twenty-five years and the climatic effects will probably turn the now fertile plain into a new Sahel, a severely drought-stricken region of Central Africa.

In Nepal, where the population is expected to double to 38 million by A.D. 2000, they clear an average of 120,000 acres of forest annually. Most of the wood is used for firewood. The rest is cleared to make room for crops and livestock.

Three decades ago, floods afflicted 62 million acres of India each year. Now it is well over 100 million acres. Appallingly, the high-water mark on the river Brahmaputra at Dibrugarh in East Assam has *never once* been below danger level since 1960.

Still in the Third World, but on the other side of the globe, the Brazilians will celebrate the onset of the next dry season by torching the rain forests. Before the next rainy season it is estimated that they will have burned down approximately 100 million acres of forest. This will compound the world's problems and is an area over which governments seem to have little control.

One may continue in this vein indefinitely. Blame cannot be placed on the Third World alone. The West German Danzer Group are ripping out vast areas of jungle to give us teak coffins and mahogany kitchen units. But there are a few tiny grounds for optimism.

Perhaps the last word, however, lies with an environmentalist quoted in the London *Sunday Times* September 11, 1988. "Peasants don't listen to biology lectures." They don't. They live off the land and fulfill their immediate needs. What they cannot understand is that this fulfillment may well not only drown or starve their families but also affect the rest of humankind.

I could continue quoting problems such as the Kurds in the Middle East, the tragedies in Ethiopia and Sudan, Somalia, etc., but the principle in each case is the same. Deforestation leads to famine, drought and flooding. Add to this disease, chemical pollution, warfare; you have the perfect ingredients for Nostradamus' Millennium.

CENTURY I

I.I

Estant afsis de nuict fecret eftude
Seul reposé sur la fcelle d'aerain:
Flambe exiguë fortant de folitude
Fait fperer q n'est à croire vain.

Sitting alone at night in secret study, it rests solitary on the brass tripod. A slight flame comes out of the emptiness, making successful that which would have been in vain.

This and the following quatrain I.II are an attempt to describe Nostradamus' methods of divination, a prelude to his predictions. The method he uses is that of the fourth century neo-Platonist, Iamblichus, a reprint of whose book was published at Lyons in 1547. It was almost certainly read by Nostradamus, and may even have been the source of his experiments once he realized he had a gift for prediction or second sight. It was soon after its publication in France that Nostradamus' first attempt at written prediction appeared—the *Almanachs*. Admittedly they were not up to much—a bucolic *Moore's Almanach*—but they were read seriously in the region. As to when he first decided to write the Centuries is not known, but my impression is sometime during the early 1550s.

All the ingredients necessary for magic practices are in this quatrain. It is night—solitude. Nostradamus is alone in his study. The brass tripod which held a bowl of water is identical to the method used by Iamblichus. The seer gazed into the water until it became cloudy and pictures of the future were revealed. Interestingly enough, Nostradamus was not only a clairvoyant but an audiovoyant as well, which will become clear in the second quatrain. He heard as well as saw his visions. The *flambe exiguë* is the tenuous light of inspiration which takes over Nostradamus as he begins to prophesy.

Century I

I.II

La verge en main mife au milieu de
  BRANCHES, [1]
De l'onde il moulle[2] & le limbe[3] & le
  pied:
Vn peur & voix fremiffent par les
  manches:
Splendeur diuine. Le diuin pres s'afsied.

The wand in the hand is placed in the
middle of the legs of the tripod. He sprin-
kles with water both the hem of the garment and its (his) foot. Fear, a voice runs
trembling through the sleeves (of his robe).
Divine splendor; the God sits nearby.

Nostradamus here reveals more of his method. He touches the
water on the tripod with his wand and then moistens his robe and his
feet with it. The Apollonian prophetesses used the same method at
the oracles of Branchus in Classical times. Nostradamus appears to
be afraid of the power thus evoked. He both hears and sees the
visions as they appear to him, and writes them down while still possessed. But once the God—the gift—sits down beside him, he feels
unafraid. This dual aspect of prophecy is rare enough to be worth
noting when trying to interpret the Prophéties.

Century I

I.III

Quand la licture du tourbillon verfee
Et feront faces de leurs manteaux
  couuers:
La republique par gens nouueau vexée,
Lors blancs & rouges ijouent à l'enuers.

When the litter is overturned by the whirlwind and faces are covered by their cloaks,
the republic will be troubled by its new
people. At the time, both reds and whites
will rule badly.

The key word to this quatrain is "republic." Nostradamus always
calls France a kingdom until the time of the Revolution of 1789. The
aristocracy were always carried in litters and this, their symbol, is
overturned by the violent whirlwind of the Revolution. The line
about faces covered with cloaks is interesting. It could possibly refer
to the many exiles who fled from France at that time, or possibly to
the many heads which fell from the guillotine and were thence hidden
from sight in quicklime. Nostradamus feels that the republic will be
greatly troubled by its new rulers.

[1]*BRANCHES.* Capitals in the original text. Refers to the three limbs or branches of
the brass tripod. It could also be an indirect reference to the prophetess at Branchus.
[2]*moulle.* Mod. F. *mouille,* to moisten.
[3]*limbe.* L. *limbus,* the hem of a garment.

White was the color of the Bourbon kings and red that of the revolutionaries. Both committed excesses during their terms of power, *à l'enuers.*

Century I

I.IIII

Par l'vniuers fera faict un monarque,
Qu'en paix & vie ne sera longuement,
Lors fe perdra la pifcature[1] barque,
Sera regie en plus grand detriment.

An universal monarch shall be created, who both in life and peace will last for a short time. At this point the ship of the Papacy will founder, governed to its greatest detriment.

Napoleon crowned himself *(fera faict)* King and Emperor of France on May 18, 1804, and reigned for ten years, abdicating in April, 1814—not a long reign. Peace was certainly not a characteristic of his era—the Napoleonic Wars are still remembered. Under General Miollis, the French army captured Rome, the *pifcature barque,* in 1809.

Pius VII (1800–1823) first came to France to crown Napoleon, but on his second visit he was held prisoner and only released by Napoleon's abdication at Fontainebleau on January 23, 1814. The last line probably refers to the religious anarchy that held sway in France after the dissolution of the clergy in 1792.

Century I

I.V

Chafsés feront pour faire long combat,
Par le pays feront plus fort greués:
Bourg & Cité auront plus grand debat,
Carca[2] Narbonne auront coeur
efprouvez.

They will be driven away for a long drawn out fight, those in the countryside will be the most troubled. Town and city will have the greater struggle; Carcassonne and Narbonne will have their hearts tried.

This almost certainly refers to the Huguenot troubles in Provence, officially dated as starting in 1502. However, sporadic trouble had been breaking out long before that and Nostradamus would have been aware of it. Technically the wars broke out between Huguenots and Catholics before the succession to the French throne of Henri de

---

[1]*pifcature barque.* L. *pifcature,* to fish, and the barque of Saint Peter. The fish has been a common symbol of Christianity since the early centuries, and its significance has remained.

[2]*Carca.* simply an apocope of Carcassonne to fit the scansion.

Navarre. But since Nostradamus had seen the young boy, when aged ten, and declared him to be the future king of France, he would have been in little doubt. Carcassonne declared itself for the Catholic League, but the Huguenots seized part of the town, and Narbonne also suffered a great deal from the fighting. Henri IV was a Huguenot but on taking Paris became a Catholic with the cynical statement, "Paris is worth a Mass."

Century I

I.VI

L'oeil de Rauuene sera deftitué,
Quand à fes pieds les aelles failliront:
Les deux de Breffe auront conftitué
Turin, Derfeil que Gaulois fouleront.

The eye of Ravenna will be destitute, when his wings will fall at his feet. The two of Bresse will have made a constitution for Turin and Vercelli, which the French will trample (underfoot).

The clues to this quatrain are in the place names: Ravenna has been part of the Papal States since 1509 and Bresse, 1601, Turin, 1640 and Vecelli, 1904, were all occupied by the French. All that is certain is that all these States, except for Varenne, were occupied after the death of Nostradamus.

Century I

I.VII

Tard arriué l'execution faicte,
Le vent contraire lettres au chemin
*   prinfes;*
Les coniurez xiiii d'une fecte:
Par le Rousseau femez les entreprinfes.

Arrived too late, the act has been done. The wind was against them, letters intercepted on the way. The party of conspirators numbered fourteen. By Rousseau will these enterprises be undertaken.

The minister who was called upon to review the case of Alfred Dreyfus in 1899 was a Monsieur Waldeck-Rousseau. It is on this name that I base my interpretation. Dreyfus, a Jewish man and French soldier, was condemned for the treasonable act of selling military secrets *(lettres)* to the Germans in 1894. He was publicly degraded and transported to a penal colony, l'Ile du Diable, in 1895. But in 1899 he was brought back for a retrial. Due to the strong anti-Semitic bias of the period he was again found guilty, but with extenuating circumstances. Ten days later he was publicly pardoned by President Loubet and a further investigation of the case was ordered. The letters were declared to be forgeries and Dreyfus to be innocent. The case troubled the French social conscience for some years.

There was much debate as to where to put up a statue in his honor. It has been decided to place it in the Tuileries. The original plan was to place it on the playground of the Ecole Militaire, where Dreyfus was degraded before being sent to l'Ile du Diable. This was refused by the Socialist former French minister Charles Hernu, who did not think it was "suitable that the military college should be constantly reminded of the injustice."

Nostradamus describes the proof of Dreyfus' innocence as arriving too late, because his sentence had been passed and he had been sent to l'Isle du Diable. The *vent contraire* is the anti-Dreyfus element of public opinion. Monsieur Waldeck-Rousseau, who sentenced Dreyfus the second time, was a known anti-Semite. This sentence was overturned by a public pardon. The number of conspirators may well have been fourteen—this subject has never been cleared up.

Century I

I.VIII

Combien de fois prinfe cité solaire
Seras changeant les loys barbares &
vaines:
Ton mal s'approche. Plus sera
tributaire,
Le grand Hadrie recouira tes veines.

How often will you be captured, O city
of the sun?
You will change laws that are barbaric
and strange:
Bad times approach you. No longer will
you be enslaved.
The great Hadrie will revive your
veins.

Paris has often been known as the City of the Sun, after Louis XIV, the Sun King. This quatrain possibly refers to the siege in 1590 by Henri IV of Navarre (Hadrie) who stormed Paris for six months (from April to September) before the city capitulated. The barbarous and strange laws then refer to the innovations of the *Seize,* the first truly revolutionary parliamentary faction to govern Paris. The siege occurred less than twenty years after Nostradamus' death, *ton mal s'approche.* The last line could mean that there is a new bloodline (Navarre) on the French Valois throne, and it could also refer to the fact that during the siege Henri allowed food to be passed through the lines to the starving people of Paris.

Century I

I.IX

De L'Orient viendra le coeur Punique
Fafcher Hadrie & les hoirs[1] Romulides
Accompagné de la claffe[2] Libique
Temples Mellites & proches ifles vuides.

From the Orient will come the African heart to trouble Hadrie and the heirs of Romulus. Accompanied by the Libyan fleet the temples of Malta and nearby islands shall be deserted.

I think this is a dual quatrain, the first two lines referring to Henri IV and the Duke of Palma, the second two to the siege of Malta in 1565. If that is the case, Henri IV was troubled from the East by the duke of Palma, who in 1590 compelled Henri to raise his siege of Paris to confront the Spanish army marching from Flanders. This annoyed the Pope, *les hoirs Romulides,* who favored the Navarre claim and was hostile to Spanish policy at this point. The siege of Malta took place in 1565, just before Nostradamus' death. The Libyan fleet would represent the Turkish navy, then roaming the Mediterranean.

Century I

I.X

Serpens[3] tranfmis dans la caige de fer,
Où les enfans feptaines[4] du Roy font
  pris:
Les vieux & peres fortiront bas de
  l'enfer,
Ains mourir voir de fruict mort & crys.

A shroud is put into the iron vault, where the seven children of the king are held. The ancestors and forefathers will come forth from the depths of hell, lamenting to see thus dead the fruit of their line.

This quatrain must refer to the fall of the House of Valois, and in particular to the removal in 1610 of the remains of the last Valois king, Henri III, to the family sepulcher at Saint Denis.

The seven children, referred to several times during the quatrains, are those of Henri II and Catherine de' Medicis, who, as is related earlier, was a great follower of Nostradamus. The prophet seems quite certain the Valois line will die out; he predicted it earlier when he saw the then ten-year-old Henri of Navarre as a page in the royal

[1]*hoirs.* O.F. heirs. The heirs of Romulus are the Italians and by extension, the Vatican.

[2]*claffe.* L. *classus,* a fleet. A word commonly used in Nostradamus' Centuries.

[3]*Serpens.* Gk. *serpos,* shroud.

[4]*enfans feptaines.* 1) François II, 1549–60; 2) Elisabeth, 1545–1568; 3) Claude, 1547–1575; 4) Charles IX, 1550–1574; 5) Henri II, 1551–1589; 6) Marguerite (de Navarre), 1552–1615; 7) François, duc d'Alençon, 1554–1584.

suite, but it must be said that Henri III was not the last to die. Marguerite de Navarre, the sixth Valois child, lived until 1615, but she had been discarded by the king for adultery and spent a good thirty years shut up in a convent. So perhaps Nostradamus felt that Henri III was the last Valois of any political importance.

Century I

I.XI

Le mouument de fens, coeur, pieds, &
mains,
Seront d'accord Naples, Lyon, Sicile;
Glaiues, feux, eaux puis aux nobles
Romains,
Plongez tuez mors par cerueau debile.

The movement of senses, heart, feet and hands will be in agreement between Naples, Lyon and Sicily. Swords, fire, floods; the noble Romans drowned, killed or dead, because of a degenerate brain.

The only comment I can make on this is that if one reads *Leon* for *Lyon,* these cities were part of the Spanish Hapsburg empire. This may be a prediction that was avoided. It seems to have no relevance to the present day.

Century I

I.XII

Dans peu dira faulce brute fragile,
De bas en hault efleue promptement:
Puis en instant defloyale & labile,
Qui de Veronne aura gouuernement.

Soon they will talk of a treacherous man, quickly raised from low to high estate. Suddenly he will become disloyal and volatile, and will become the governing power in Verona.

Verona was governed by a podestà between 1405 and 1562, who was meant to be replaced yearly. It was the equivalent in rank to the office of captain. The last podestà was Jacabo Sansabastiani, 1539–62, but there is no proof he was ever a traitor.

Century I

I.XIII

Les exilez par ire, haine inteftine,
Feront au Roy grand conjuration:
Secret mettront ennemis par la mine,
Et fes vieux fiens contre eux fedition.

Through anger and internal hatreds, the exiles will hatch a great conspiracy against the king. Secretly they will place enemies to threaten him, and his own old party against them: there will be sedition.

This quatrain describes the Conspiracy of Amboise, which occurred in 1560, during Nostradamus' lifetime. The power of the Guise family in France—Mary Stuart was the bride of François II for a year until his death, and her mother was a Guise—caused other parties, in particular the Montmorencys and the Bourbons, to conspire to kill the duc de Guise and to kidnap the king, François II. But the plot was leaked out in advance and suppressed.

Century I

I.XIIII

*De gent efclave chanfons, chants &
    requeftes,
Captifs par Princes & Seigneur[1] aux
    prifons:
L'aduenir par idiotz fans teftes,
Seront reçeus par diuaines oraifons.*

From the enslaved populace come songs, chants and demands, while Princes and the Ruler are captive in prison. In the future they will be seen as headless, through idiots by holy prayers to heaven.

Most commentators believe this quatrain refers to the songs and demands of the French populace while Louis XVI was imprisoned with his family in the Temple. The headless idiots therefore become the early ringleaders of the terror. At first these people are regarded as inspired leaders; then all changes and they follow the aristocracy to the guillotine.

Century I

I.XV

*Mars nous menaffe par la force
    bellique,
Septante fois fera le fang efpandre:
Auge[2] et ruyne de l'Ecclefiaftique,
Et plus ceux qui d'eux rien voudront
    entendre.*

Mars threatens us with warlike strength and will cause blood to be shed seventy times. Moreover, the clergy will be both exalted and reviled, even more by those who wish to know nothing of them.

Serious commentators of the nineteenth century, such as Nicollaud, take the first two lines as referring to Napoleon (Mars) and the many wars of his Empire. The clergy suffered much during this period. It was disbanded in 1792 and religion had almost disappeared from France during the early days of the Directoire (the government of the Revolutionaries). But by 1804, Napoleon had to recognize the

[1]*Seigneur.* Used in the singular may indicate King Louis XVI himself.
[2]*Auge.* L. *augere*, to increase.

Pope, and therefore the clergy, to legitimize his coronation. General talk of trouble facing the Catholic Church is a common theme throughout the Centuries, and religious practice is certainly on the decline almost everywhere. However, there is no use of the key word "empire" which normally, but not always, indicates Napoleon.

Could a possibility be modern Iran, where the clergy, led by the Ayatollah Khomeini, are both at their height and decline, and certainly not welcome in the West? They have now ended their eight-year-long war with Iraq, and due to the intervention of the United Nations, initiated by the failing Iran, the fighting has ceased.

Century I

I.XVI

Faulx[1] à l'eftang[2] ionct vers le
    Sagitaire,
En fon hault AUGE[3] de l'exaltation,
Pefte, famine, mort de main militaire,
Le siecle approche de renouation.

A scythe joined with a pond in Sagittarius at its highest ascendant. Plague, famine, death from the military hand, the century approaches its renewal.

According to this quatrain when Saturn (scythe) and Aquarius (pond) are in the ascendant towards the end of a century, a great war should be expected, with the usual concomitants of disease and famine. This description is so general it could fit the twentieth century as well as any other. Nostradamus refers later in the Centuries to a possible war toward the end of our present century.

Century I

I.XVII

Par quarente ans l'Iris n'apparoiftra,
Par quarante ans tous les lours fera
    veu:
La terre aride en ficceté croistra,
Et grans deluges quand fera aperceu.

For forty years the rainbow will not be seen. Then for forty years it will be seen every day. The dry earth will grow even more parched, and there will be great floods when it is seen.

A general quatrain of doom and gloom. Even in Africa there is no record of a forty-year drought followed by forty years of rain and flooding, nor has there been so anywhere else, to my knowledge.

[1]*Faulx.* O.F. scythe, the zodiac sign of Saturn.
[2]*l'eftang.* O.F. pond, a water sign designating Aquarius.
[3]*AUGE.* L. *augere,* to increase. No reason to be seen for capitals.

Century I

I.XVIII

Par la difcorde negligence Gauloife,
Sera paffaïge à Mahommet ouuert:
De fang trempé la terre & mer Senoife,
Le port Phocen[1] de voilles & nefz
couuert.

Because of French discord and negligence,
a passage will be opened to the Mohammedans. Both the land and sea of Sienna will
be soaked in blood and the port of Marseilles covered with ships and sails.

One tentative opinion is that this quatrain relates to the chaos in France and its colonies in 1940, which allowed the Italian armies into North Africa. The blood spilled would refer to the various battles. The harbor of Marseilles was constantly operative during the war, although it was in German hands.

Century I

I.XIX

Lors que ferpens viendront circuir
l'arc,[2]
Le fang Troyen vexé par les Efpaignes:
Par eulx grand nombre en fera faicte
tare.
Chef fruict,[3] caché aux mares[4] dans les
faignes.[5]

When the serpents will surround the altar,
the Trojan blood is troubled by the Spanish. A great number will be decimated by
them. The leader flees, hidden in the
marshy swamps.

After the death of her husband Henri II, Catherine de' Medicis, Regent of France, changed her personal emblem to a serpent curled around a star, biting its tail. Nostradamus usually calls French royal blood Trojan, a derivation from the medieval legend that the French royal family were descended from Francus, a mythical son of Priam. French troubles with Spain did not really come to a head until the interregnum of 1589–94 and the later wars of the Spanish succession. The last line is unclear.

---

[1]*Phocen.* Marseilles; founded by the people of Phocaea, its mother city is in west Asia Minor.
[2]*arc.* L. *are,* altar.
[3]*fruict.* here equals L. *fuit,* fled.
[4]*mares.* O.F. swamp, marsh.
[5]*faignes.* O.F. swamp, marsh.

Century I

I.XX

Tours, Orleans, Blois, Angiers, Riems,
  Niãtes,
Cites vexées par fubit changement:
Par langues eftranges feront tendues
  tentes,[1]
Fleuues, dards Renes, terre & mer
  tremblement.

The cities of Tours, Orléans, Blois, An-
gers, Reims and Nantes are troubled by a
sudden change. People of foreign tongues
will pitch their tents. Rivers, darts at
Rennes, the earth will quake by land and
sea.

Another fruitless quatrain. All the cities mentioned, except for Reims, are situated on the Loire and have suffered various foreign invasions, mainly the Prussian and Russian armies in 1815, the Prussians again in 1870 and 1940, and the Americans in 1917–1919 and 1944–1945. There has been no notable earthquake at Reims since publication in 1566.

Century I

I.XXI

Profond argille blanche nourrit rochier,
Qui d'vn abifme iftra[2] lactineufe[3]
En vain troublez ne l'oferont toucher,
Ignorans eftre au fond terre argilleufe.

The depths of the rock contain white clay
which will come out milk white from a
cleft. People, needlessly troubled, will not
dare to touch it, not realizing that the
foundation of the earth is of clay.

I have no explanation for this quatrain. Perhaps the language has alchemistic undertones?

Century I

I.XXII

Ce que viura & n'ayant aucun fens,
Viendra lefer à mort fon artifice:
Auftun, Chalon, Langres & les deux
  fens,
La grefle & glace fera grand malefice.

A thing living without any senses will
cause its own death through artifice. At
Autun, Chalon, Langres and the two Sens
there will be great damage through hail
and ice.

Garencières gives a highly improbable solution to this quatrain. He states that in 1613 a petrified embryo was removed by an operation

---

[1]*tentes.* L. *tentere,* to attack, i.e., a position taken by attackers.
[2]*iftra.* O.F. *aller,* to go (*ira*).
[3]*lactineufe.* L. *lac,* milk or *lacticineum,* milky food.

(artifice) from a woman named Colomba Chantry who lived in Sens. A woman in her sixties had been discovered seven years earlier in Italy carrying a petrified embryo. But these medical facts—which would be of interest to Nostradamus, who was a well-qualified doctor—do not seem to me to merit a quatrain. Also, a petrified embryo could not be called live *(viura)*. So I can offer no explanation.

On the factual side, all the towns mentioned belonged to the Duchy of Burgundy. There is a second town of Sens near Louhans. The comments about the weather are equally imprecise.

Century I

I.XXIII

Au moys troifiefme fe leuant le Soleil
Sanglier, Liepard au champs Mars
    pour cobâtre:
Liepard laiffé, au ciel extend son oeil,
Vn Aigle autour du Soleil voit
s'esbattre.

In the third month, at sunrise, the Boar and the Leopard meet on the battlefield. The fatigued Leopard looks heavenwards and sees an Eagle battling around the sun.

This is one of Nostradamus' more impressive quatrains, with some of the visual qualities we seldom get from his predictions. The background is the battle of Waterloo, June 18, 1815. Blücher, the Prussian boar *(Sanglier)*, had been beaten back at Ligny. The British forces, with Wellington at their head, had not been able to make a coordinated stand with the Prussians at Waterloo.

The French troops battered the English *(Liepard)* from sunrise to evening. Wellington waited for the arrival of his ally Blücher to arrive and turn the French flank. Wellington's position faced south, so he would have seen the Imperial standards, the French eagle, flying against the sun. As the day drew to a close, the British were exhausted. Then a cloud of dust was seen. Napoleon thought it was Grouchy, but it was Blücher. The end had come.

The Imperial Eagle, symbol of Revolutionary France, is often used in the Centuries to describe Napoleon himself. On this occasion it applies both to the standards and the man. Napoleon used to call the English heraldic lion "the Leopard of England."

The battle took place in June, just over three months after Napoleon's return from Elba *(au moys troifiesme)*. This cryptic comment may also contain references to Napoleon's reign of one hundred days, which ended with this battle. Equally, dating the year from the March solstice, as Nostradamus would have done by the then-current Julian calendar, June would be the third month. This is Nostradamus at his most convoluted and is typical of his style.

Century I

I.XXIIII

A cité neufue penſif pour condemner,	*At the New City he thinks to condemn.*
L'oifel de proye du ciel ſe vient offrir:	*The bird of prey offers itself to the heavens.*
Apres victoire à captifs pardonner,	*After victory he pardons his captives. At*
Cremone & Mâtoue grâs maulx aura	*Cremona and Mantua great hardships*
fouffert.	*will be suffered.*

This appears to continue the Napoleonic theme. During his campaigns in Italy, 1795–97, when Napoleon arrived at Villa Nova (*cité neufue*) he was uncertain what to do, having received no instructions from the Directoire. By June 1796, Napoleon had laid siege to Mantua, a city which, despite horrendous bombardments, held out until February, 1797. Napoleon is reputed to have treated his prisoners generously in their defeat, *à captifs pardonner*. Since Cremona is situated near Mantua, it must have suffered from the French siege.

Peace with Mantua, however, was of short duration. In 1799 it was retaken by the Austrians, and although restored to the French in 1801 (as Lunéville), it once again reverted to the Austrians from 1814 to 1836. The whole of Lombardy suffered severe political persecution between 1849 and 1859, after the peace of Villafranca. Note again the bird of prey as a symbol of Napoleon.

Century I

I.XXV

Perdu trouué, caché de ſi long ſiecle,	*The lost thing is discovered, hidden for*
Sera Pasteur demy Dieu honoré,	*long centuries. Pasteur will be celebrated*
Ains que la Lune acheue ſon grand	*almost as a god. This is when the moon*
ſiecle,	*completes her great cycle, but he will be*
Par autres vents sera deshonoré.	*dishonored by other rumors.*

This quatrain contains not only a proper name, Pasteur, but also a specific dating, towards the end of the cycle of the moon, *acheue son grand ſiecle*. This cycle ran, in astrological terms, from 1535 to 1889.

Pasteur founded the Institut Pasteur on November 14, 1889. His discovery that germs polluted the atmosphere was vital to medical history and led to Lister's theory and practice of sterilization. The *Encyclopaedia Britannica* says that Pasteur, the *demy Dieu,* was the acknowledged head of the greatest chemical movement of the time. The reference to rumors that dishonored him may well refer to the violent opposition that his methods aroused among powerful members of the French Academy, particularly against the new practices of the Institut with vaccines, such as those against hydrophobia.

Century I

I.XXVI

*Le grand du fouldre tumbe[1] d'heure
     diurne,
Mal & predict par porteur poftulaire:
Suiuant prefage tumbe d'heure
     nocturne,
Conflict Reims, Londres, Etrufque
     peftifere.*

*The great man will be struck down in
daytime by a thunderbolt. An evil deed,
foretold by a bearer of a petition. According to the prediction another is struck at
night. Conflict in Reims, London, pestilence in Tuscany.*

The first three lines of this quatrain could apply to the assassinations of the two Kennedy brothers. John F. Kennedy was struck down
(fouldre) in broad daylight in Dallas, Texas, November 22, 1963, by
the presumed assassin Lee Harvey Oswald. Linked with him is another killed at night, in fact early dawn, Robert F. Kennedy, shot
down on June 5, 1968, during the celebrations for his presidential
primary elections at an hotel by Sirhan Sirhan. Line 2 may refer to
the fact that both men received death threats and warnings during
their terms of office. Then, presumably, line 4 refers to the world
repercussions to the assassinations.

Century I

I.XXVII

*Deffouz de chaine[2] Guien du ciel
     frappé,
Non loing de là eft caché le trefor:
Qui par longs fiecles auoit efte grappé,
Troué mourra, l'oeil creué de reffort:*

*Beneath the oak tree of Guienne, struck by
lightning, not far from there is the treasure hidden. That which for long centuries
had been kept, when found, he will die, his
eye pierced by a spring.*

This is one of several puzzling quatrains linking the finding of a
tomb, a man dead for many centuries, and a treasure (see quatrain
IX.VII for another example). None of these quatrains, unfortunately,
make much sense. Guienne was an ancient province of southwest
France, therefore this quatrain does not refer to the violation of
Nostradamus' tomb, which took place during the Revolution, after
which his remains were transferred to a side chapel of Nôtre Dame
in the Church of Saint Laurent at Salon. Alternatively, *Guien* could
stand for *gui*, meaning mistletoe, but that meaning gets one no further in deciphering the quatrain.

[1]*tumbe.* O.F. *tumber*, to fall.
[2]*chaine.* O.F. *chene*, oak tree, but could possibly mean *chaine*, chain of mountains, etc.

Century I

I.XXVIII

*La tour de Boucq craindra fufte[1]
    barbare
Vn temps, long temps apres barque
    hefperique:
Beftail, ges, meubles tous deux feront
    grand tare[2]
Taurus & Libra quelle mortelle pique?[3]*

Tobruk will fear the barbarian fleet for a long time, then much later the western fleet. Cattle, people, possessions for both will be quite lost. What a great struggle in Taurus and Libra.

If one accepts *tour de Boucq* as Nostradamus' version of Tobruk, then the quatrain is placed definitely in North Africa. The first line would apply to Tobruk's checkered history as a trading port between the Greeks and Libyans, until, for strategic reasons, it fell under the interest of the Italians.

In modern times, Tobruk suffered invasion by the British in 1941 during the Second World War. The word *"hefperique"* in line 2 is ambiguous. It can mean either "western" or "Spanish," but in view of the word "fleet," I take the first meaning. The British Army was fighting the Italians in Tobruk in 1941, but the attack on Pearl Harbor occurred in December, the same month as Tobruk was liberated, so *hesperique* may well refer to the American (Western) fleet. Rommel reached Tobruk on April 8th (the time of Taurus) and besieged it until December, 1941, when it was relieved by British reinforcements. As Libra is October, not December, Nostradamus was two months off in his calculations, but that's not so bad over five centuries.

Century I

I.XXIX

*Quand le poiffon tereftre & aquatique,
Par forte vague au grauier fera mis:
Sa forme eftrange fuaue & horrifique,
Par mer aux murf bien toft les ennemis.*

When the fish that travels over land and sea is cast up on the shore by a great wave; its shape foreign, smooth and frightful. From the sea the enemies soon reach the walls.

This quatrain could possibly describe a missile fired from a submerged submarine, which causes a great upheaval of the water.

---

[1]*fufte.* low draught galley with both sails and oars.
[2]*tare.* O.F. loss
[3]? presumably printer's error for full stop (period).

Equally well it may describe the American equivalent, SUBROC which, although fired under water, flies through the air to its target.

Century I

I.XXX

La nef eftrange par le tourment marin,
Abourdera pres de port incogneu:
Nonobftant fignes de rameau palmerin,[1]
Apres mort pille bon auis tard venu.

Because of the storm at sea the foreign ship will approach an unknown port. Notwithstanding the signs of the palm branches, afterwards, death and pillage. The good advice comes too late.

An unspecific quatrain. The *rameau palmerin,* palm branches, usually indicate peaceful intent, which seems in this case to be trickery on the part of the inhabitants of unknown harbor.

Century I

I.XXXI

Tant d'ans les guerres en Gaule
*   dureront*
Oultre la courfe du Caftulon[2]
*   monarque:*
Victoire incerte trois grands
*   couronneront,*
Aigle, coq, lune, lyon, foleil en marque.

The wars in France will last for so many years beyond the reign of the Castulon kings. An uncertain victory will crown the great ones, the Eagle, Cock, Lion, Sun in its house.

Despite many ingenious interpretations of this quatrain concerning the French Revolution, it seems to be dated by means of a great war in France after the downfall of the Spanish monarchy, and therefore from the founding of the Spanish Republic in 1923. This leads us to the period of the Second World War, 1939–45, from which Spain remained officially detached, neutral, and during which time there were *guerres en Gaule.* The uncertain victory was won by the USA (Eagle), France (Cock), and Britain (Lion). The final capitulation of the Japanese (Sun) was to herald the end of the war. Also the Japanese surrendered on August 12, during the period of a sun sign. The double meaning is typical of Nostradamus.

The sheer immensity of all these ideas by a medieval mind is astonishing. Spain was one of Europe's greatest contemporary monarchies, but Nostradamus envisages a war on a global scale!

[1]*palmerin.* L. *palmarins,* of a palm tree.
[2]Caftulon: an old Iberian city, standing for Spain.

Century I
I.XXXII

Le grand empire fera toft tranflaté
En lieu petit qui bien toft viendra
   croiftre:
Lieu bien infime d'exigue comté,
Ou au milieu viendra pofer fon fceptre.

The great empire will soon be exchanged for a small place, which will soon begin to grow. A very small place of tiny area in the middle of which he will come to lay down his scepter.

The key word in this quatrain is "empire"; Nostradamus practically never calls France a kingdom after the Revolution. The great Empire of the Imperial Napoleon soon dwindles to the island of Elba. It begins to grow again on Napoleon's escape, but only for the Hundred Days. Then he is sent to an even smaller place, St. Helena, where he finally relinquishes all claim to power, putting down his scepter for good.

Century I
I.XXXIII

Pres d'vn grand pont de plaine
   fpatieufe,
Le grand lyon par forces Cefarées:
Fera abbattre hors cité rigoureuse,
Par effroy portes luy feront referées.

Near a great bridge a spacious plain. The great lion with the Imperial forces will cause ruin outside the austere city. For fear the gates will be reinforced against him.

If one takes the "austere city" to be Geneva, home to the rigorous doctrine of Calvinism, then the plain may be Lombardy and the Lion an imperial troop. The bridge is probably a mountain pass.

But if Nostradamus hoped for the fall of Geneva through the pressures of the Holy Roman Empire he was completely wrong. It is necessary to remember Nostradamus' strong anti-Protestant feelings, which sometimes surface almost in spite of himself. He may well have seen and comprehended this quatrain quite wrongly. See, however, I.XLV.

Century I

I.XXXIIII

L'oyfeau de proye volant à la feneftre,[1]
Auant conflict faict aux Francoys
*   pareure:*[2]
L'vn bon prendra l'vn ambigue finiftre,
La partie foyole tiendra par bon
*   augure.*

The bird of prey flying to the left makes preparations before joining with the French. Some will regard him as good, others bad or wrong. The weaker party will regard him as a good omen.

Although Nostradamus often applies the bird of prey to Napoleon, here Hitler seems more appropriate. The "left" would have meant little to Nostradamus other than in a geographical sense, that is the low countries. Hitler invaded France through Holland and Belgium, having made his preparations, *pareure,* well in advance. Corruption and uncertainty among French (and other) politicians follows in the early days of the war, finding its culmination in the Pétainists who colluded with Hitler, and the Vichy cabinet *(partie foyole).*

Century I

I.XXXV

Le lyon jeune le vieux furmontera,
En champ bellique par fingulier duelle:
Dans caige d'or les yeux luy creuera,
Deux claffes[3] *vn, puis mourir, mort*
*   cruelle.*

The young lion will overcome the old, in a field of combat in a single fight. He will pierce his eyes in a golden cage, two wounds in one, he then dies a cruel death.

This is the quatrain that made Nostradamus' reputation in contemporary France. Although the Centuries had not yet been published at the time of its fulfillment, it was known and understood by the queen, Catherine de' Medicis and referred to in letters by several important foreign diplomats. Presumably, therefore, Nostradamus circulated the first part of his still-unpublished book in handwritten or pamphlet form. In 1555 he published the first 353 quatrains of the Centuries.

The queen was greatly perturbed by this quatrain, which she understood to predict the death of her husband in a duel. It so troubled her that in July, 1556, she sent for Nostradamus to come to Paris and explain the prediction to her. Nostradamus was not the only person

---

[1]*feneftre.* L, *sinistre,* left, F. *sinister.*
[2]*pareure.* O.F. preparation.
[3]*claffes.* Gk. *klasis,* a fracture. The Latin *classus,* fleets, makes no sense here, since there was no union of fleets anywhere in the world at this time.

to predict this event. The Italian astrologer Luc Gauric had warned Henri that both the beginning and the end of his reign would be marked by duels.

The first duel took place soon after his accession—an extraordinary event when one realizes that under French court etiquette, the king could not technically be challenged to a duel. But Henri, who had little time for prophets, took no notice of this early warning.

The second duel was fought in 1559, on the occasion of the marriage of his daughter Elisabeth to old King Philip of Spain—the same one who had married Mary Tudor of England so long before—and that of his sister Marguerite to the duc de Savoie. The latter couple would visit Nostradamus several times in his house at Salon. During the festivities, which lasted three days, the king joined in the jousting at St. Antoine. He was victorious for the first two days but on the third he insisted on riding against the Captain of his Scottish guard, Montgomery.

The reference to *lyon* is interesting in that both the king and Montgomery had a lion in their coat of arms. In the first bout, Henri failed to unseat his opponent; it was only on the third bout that they splintered lances successfully. But Montgomery's lance pierced the king's gilt helmet and entered his face and brain just above the eye. Some report he received a second wound in the throat, which turned into a severe ulcer before he died in agony ten days later.

Century I

I.XXXVI

Tard le monarque fe viendra repentir,
De n'auoir mis à mort fon aduerfaire:
Mais viendra bien à plus hault
*   confentir,*
Que tout son sang par mort fera
*   deffaire.*

Too late the king will repent that he has not put his adversary to death. But he will soon come to agree to far greater things which will cause the death of all his line.

This is another of Nostradamus' famous double quatrains. It can equally possibly refer to the death of the Guise brothers in 1588 through the influence of Henri III, or possibly to Louis XVI.

Henri III caused both the duc de Guise and his brother to be murdered at Blois on Christmas Day, 1558, in an effort to quash the increasing influence of the Guise family in French politics. However, he did not kill the real ringleader, the duc de Mayenne, and he was forced to take further action to eliminate their powers, *à plus hault confentir.*

Other commentators interpret this quatrain as describing Louis

XVI and his brother and adversary, the duc d'Orléans. It is certain that Orléans intrigued against the king, was a sworn enemy of the queen, Marie Antoinette, and even debated joining up the revolutionaries at one point. If one accepts this interpretation, then line 3 refers to the constitutional monarchy that Louis was forced to accept, and to the later imprisonment of himself and his family which led to their deaths by the guillotine. But Orléans did not die *(tout son sang)*, he returned to France in 1814 as Louis XVIII, so I regard this as a less satisfactory interpretation.

Century I
I.XXXVII

Vn peu deuant que le foleil s'efcufe,
Conflict donné grand peuple dubiteux:
Profliges, port marin ne faict refponse,
Pont & sepulchre en deux eftranges
lieux.

Shortly before the sun sets battle is engaged, a great nation uncertain. Overcome, the port cannot reply, both bridge and grave in foreign places.

I cannot make any sense of this quatrain except that its subject is probably a sea battle. *Pont* in line 4 often stands for Pope *(Pontifex)* in Nostradamus' writings. There might then be a tenuous link with Pius V, who died at Valence in 1799, captured by the French. His death occurred in August, so the first line might refer to the summer. The French people were certainly *dubiteux* in 1799, as the Directoire had suffered defeats in both Italy and Germany and the success of Napoleon's Egyptian campaign was not yet assured. Line 3 cannot refer to the English fleet, who were scouring the seas for Napoleon, not resting in port.

Century I
I.XXXVIII

Le sol & l'aigle au victeur paroiftront
Refponse vaine au vaincu l'on affeure:
Par cor ne crys harnois n'arrefteront,
Vindicte paix par mors fi acheue à
l'heure.

The sun and the eagle will appear to the victor. An empty answer is given to the defeated. Neither bugle nor shouts will stop the soldiers. Peace will be vindicated by death, if achieved in time.

This quatrain probably followed upon I.XXIII in Nostradamus' original writings, before he deliberately confused the order of the verses. It continues the description of the Battle of Waterloo—the Imperial Eagle, Napoleon, coming out of the mist to attack Wellington. Both generals were aware that it was a fight to the finish, but for Napoleon it was even more desperate, as it was his final stand after the frantic Hundred Days. No reasonable terms awaited if he lost (*refponse vaine*) nothing but permanent exile on St. Helena. Once the men engaged in battle they could not be stopped, *par cor ne crys harnois narrefteront*. Napoleon's Grenadiers fought until the last man dropped, refusing to retreat. Nostradamus saw that liberty and peace would return eventually to Europe, but only through Napoleon's end, whether political or through his death.

Century I

I.XXXIX

De nuict dans lict le sufprefme eftrangle, *Par trop avoir sejourné, blond efleu:* *Par troys l'empire fubroge exancle,*[1] *A mort mettra carte, et pacquet ne leu.*	*At night the final (claimant?) will be strangled in his bed because he became too involved with the blond heir-elect. The Empire is enslaved by three and substituted. Dead, neither letter or packet are read.*

The last of the Condé line, supporter of the Royalist claim, was found dead in his bedroom, but he had been hanged, not strangled. But both of these methods of death involve squeezing by the throat. Perhaps the duc was hanged after his death to cover the signs of strangulation? It has been suggested that he was murdered because he supported the cause of the duc de Bordeaux, the comte de Clambord, whom Nostradamus rightly describes as *efleu*, as he was the grandson of Charles X and the legitimate heir to the French throne.

As to the three who usurped power, there are two possible explanations: the three are either the régimes which followed Charles X—Louis Philippe, who became king in 1830, the Republic, and then the Buonapartes; or more specifically, the three who intrigued against the Condé family—Charles X, the duc d'Angoulême and the duc de Bourgogne. According to the nineteenth century commentator Le Pelletier, Condé was fair-haired and had written a will (*carte et paquet*) in favour of Bordeaux. This was said to have been destroyed and replaced by an earlier will in favor of the duc d'Aumale, son of Louis Philippe.

---

[1]*exancle.* L. *exancilatus*, enslaved.

Century I

I.XL

La trombe fauffe difsimulant folie,
Fera Bifance vn changement de loix:
Hyftra d'Egypte qui veut que l'on
  deflie,
Edict changeant monnoyes & aloys.[1]

The false trumpet pretending madness will cause Byzantium to change its laws. From Egypt will come forth a person who wants the edict withdrawn, changing money and values.

This is another difficult quatrain. It seems to refer to a political situation between the Ottoman Empire *(Bisance)* and Egypt. The debasement of coinage was an old practice of various Christian monarchies, and may have been copied by Byzantium. But Egypt only revolted under Napoleon, so this may therefore refer to the new values established in France under the Directoire.

Century I

I.XLI

Siege en cité de nuict affaillie,
Peu efchapé non loin de mer conflict:
Femme de joye, retour de fils defaillie,
Poifon & lettres cachees dans le plic.

The besieged city is assaulted by night, few escape; a battle not far from the sea. A prostitute faints with joy at the return of her son, poison in the fold of the hidden letters.

Some commentators believe this quatrain refers to the French invasion of Italy, 1556–57, others to Dunkirk, 1940, when the French Revolution came to be regarded as a prostitute, and the poison would be the Nazi doctrines, *lettres dans le plic.* I find neither explanation at all convincing.

Century I

I.XLII

Le dix Kalende d'Auril de faict
  Gotique,
Refufité encor par gens malins:
Le feu eftainct affemblé diabolique,
Cherchant les os du d'Amant & Pfelin.

The tenth day of the April Calends, calculated in Gothic fashion, is revived again by evil people. The fire put out, the diabolic gathering seek the bones of Amant and Pselin.

A fascinating quatrain. Nostradamus seems clearly to understand the change in 1582 from the Julian calendar of his day to the

---

[1]*aloys.* alloy, a standard of metal.

Gregorian calendar, which is still used today. This, of course, leads to another complication. Most of his futuristic dates appear, because of affirming circumstances, to be by the modern calendar, but I feel there are other predictions in which he may be using the Julian, for confusion's sake. He was, after all, a past master where confusion is concerned.

The tenth day of the Kalends of April is the 10th, as the Kalends were the first day of the Roman month. When the Gregorian calendar was introduced, ten days were removed—much to the annoyance of most of the populace of Europe, who demanded their ten days back! Possibly here Nostradamus means the April 1, Gregorian-style, a Good Friday, which is regarded as the best day for magical evocations. Possibly Nostradamus is indicating that this was the first day on which he started writing the Centuries. (He is believed to have started them circa the end of March, 1554.)

It is believed that the last line should read *"Cherchant les os du Demon & Psellus,"* but Nostradamus suppressed it, remembering his earlier troubles with the Catholic authorities. Psellus mentions that he used a bowl of water in order to predict, "which seems to bubble and a faint voice murmurs words which contain the revelation of future events."

Century I

I.XLIII

*Auant qu'aduienne le changement
    d'empire,
Il aduiendra vn cas bien merueilleux:
Un champ mué, le pillier de porphire,
Mis tranflaté fur le rocher noilleux.*

Before the coming of the end of the empire a miraculous event will take place. A field moved, the pillar of porphyry put in place on the gnarled rock.

Line 1 probably places this quatrain before 1789. There are several other references to pillars of porphyry in the Centuries. I cannot decipher them.

Century I

I.XVIIII

En bref feront de retour facrifices,
Contreuenans feront mis à martire
Plus ne feront moines, abbez, ne
  nouices,
Le miel fera beaucoup plus cher que
  cire.

Shortly sacrifices will be resumed, those
opposed will be martyred. There will no
longer be monks, abbots or novices. Honey
will be far more expensive than wax.

The worship of God was forbidden by the French Revolutionary
government in 1793. The sacrifices in line 1 symbolize the restoration of paganism. The Cult of Reason was established in 1794 and
this was followed by a Festival of the Supreme Being on June 8. The
Constitution of 1790 had declared the dissolution of the clergy, *plus
ne feront moines, abbez, ne nouices,* and of all ecclesiastical orders. Many
who refused to embrace the new ideology were persecuted, *mis à
martire,* and priests who refused to accept the Civil Constitution of the
Clergy were expelled as citizens. The last line is interesting. It implies
that under the new order, when fewer church candles will be needed,
the price of wax will drop to less than that of honey. Guesswork
perhaps, but astute all the same.

Century I

I.XLV

Secteur de fectes grand peine au
  delateur,
Befte en theatre, dreffe le ieu fcenique,
Du faict antique ennobly l'inuenteur,
Par fectes monde confus &
  fchifmatique.

A founder of sects, much trouble to the
informer. A beast in the theater prepares
the scene and plot. The author ennobled by
acts of older times: the world is confused
by schismatic sects.

I think this is probably a tirade against the schisms and heresies of
the sixteenth century, rather than a prediction, and probably directed
against Calvinism. (See I.XXXIII.)

Century I
I.XLVI

Tout aupres d'Aux, de Lestore &
*   Mirande,*
Grand feu du ciel en trois nuicts
*   tumbera:*
Cause aduiendra bien stupende &
*   mirande,*
Bien peu apres la terre tremblera.

Very near Auch, Lectoure and Mirande a
great fire will fall from the sky for three
nights. The cause will appear both stupe-
fying and marvelous; shortly afterwards
there will be an earthquake.

One of the many earthquake quatrains, but unfortunately Nostradamus does not say where it will occur. He links it with amazing events which will occur in Auch, Lectoure, and Mirande, all towns in the Département of Gers in southwest France. But the question remains for the reader—is the earthquake linked to the five geographically or by a time factor? We have no way of knowing.

Century I
I.XLVII

Du lac Leman[1] les sermons fascheront,
Les iuors feront reduicts par les
*   sepmaines:*
Puis moys, puis an, puis tous
*   desfailliront,*
Les magistrats damneront leurs lois
*   vaines.*

The speeches at Lac Leman will become
angry, the days will drag out into weeks,
then months, then years; then everything
will fail. The authorities will damn their
useless powers.

Lac Leman, Lake Geneva, was important as the situation of the League of Nations whose first assembly was held there on November 15, 1920. The quatrain describes vividly the years of fruitless argument and failure until its final disbandment after the war, in August 1947. One must admit it really ceased to be effective after early 1940. This is a clear achieved quatrain. There may also be a somewhat oblique reference to the League of Nations in V.LXXXV.

---

[1]Lac Leman, in Switzerland, Lake Geneva.

Century I

I.XLVIII

Vingt ans du regne de la lune paffez,	When twenty years of the Moon's reign
Sept mil ans autre tiendra fa	have passed, another will take up his rule
monarchie:	for seven thousand years. When the Sun
Quand le Soleil prendra fes iours laffez,	takes up his final cycle then will my proph-
Lors accomplit & mine ma prophetie.	ecy and warnings be accomplished.

According to Nostradamus, and quite correctly as early printings show, his predictions, although not the complete version, will be published after twenty cycles of the Moon. According to Roussat this lasted from 1535 to 1889, and 1555, twenty cycles after the moon, was the year of the publication of the first part. Nostradamus seems to envisage here that the world, and his predictions, will last for another seven thousand years. This contradicts many of his other predictions which seem to envisage world destruction at the time of the second millennium, A.D. 2000.

However, it is interesting that this quatrain gives the date of publication, although it can hardly be regarded as precognitive, as Nostradamus was alive when the first part was printed.

There was a commonly held view in the Middle Ages that the world would come to an end at the end of the seventh millennium. This theory originated from the Book of Enoch, which was general reading during the first and second centuries A.D., until it was removed from the Church Canon in A.D. 300.

Nostradamus also refers to seven thousand years in X.LXXIIII, but since it seems that no commentator can agree as to the date from which this calculation should begin, this dating remains somewhat abstruse.

Century I

I.XLIX

Beaucoup auant telles menees,	Long before these events those in the East,
Ceux d'Orient par la vertu lunaire:	influenced by the Moon, in the year 1700
L'an mil sept cens feront grands	will cause many to be carried off, and will
emmenees,	almost subdue the Northern area.
Subiugant prefque le coing Aquilonaire.	

Several astrologers (Roussat as well as Nostradamus) believed the years 1700–1702 would be the start of great upheavals, but it appears they were all wrong.

There were several invasions in the north, *Aquilonaire,* in 1700, but none of the import described in the quatrain. In February, 1700, August II invaded Livonia. Peter the Great of Russia took Azov and Kouban from the Turks. Charles XII occupied Iceland and Peter the Great then declared war upon Sweden. None of these events subdued (*subiugant*) northern Europe, so this quatrain must be regarded as hit and miss.

Century I

I.L

De l'aquatique triplisté naiftra.	From the three water signs will be born a
D'vn qui fera le jeudy pour fa fefte:	man who will celebrate Thursday as his
Son bruit, loz, regne, sa puiffance	feast day. His renown, praise, rule and
croiftra,	power will grow by land and sea, bringing
Par terre & mer aux Oriens tempefte.	trouble to the East.

All one can say of this quatrain is that it describes a person with the signs of Aries, Cancer and Aquarius in his birth chart. He is presumably not Christian or a follower of any of the great religions of today, *jeudy pour sa fefte.* His power will become so great it will bring wars to the East. This may be one of the many quatrains referring obliquely to the third Antichrist.

Century I

I.LI

Chef d'Aries, Iupter & Saturne,	At the height of Aries, Jupiter and Saturn,
Dieu eternel quelles mutations?	eternal God what changes! Then after a
Puis par long fiecle fon maling[1] temps	long century the bad times will return;
retourne	great upheavals in France and Italy.
Gaule, & Italie quelles efmotions?[2]	

The conjunction of Jupiter, Saturn and Aries took place on December 13, 1702, during the War of the Spanish Succession waged by Louis XIV. Presumably therefore, the bad times which return after a century, give or take a few years, refer to the French Revolution. By 1802, France was embroiled in the Italian campaign and it was in January of that year that Napoleon was declared President of the Italian Republic. The next time this inauspicious conjunction will occur is December 2, 1995; possibly an indicator of the Third World War?

[1]*maling.* O.F. *malin,* evil.
[2]I think the question marks in lines 2 and 4 are simply printer's errors.

Century I

I.LII

Les deux malins de Scorpion coniouint,
Le grand feigneur meutry dedans fa
  salle:
Pefte à l'Eglise par le nouveau Roy
  ionct,
L'Europe baffe & Septentrionale.

Two evil influences are in conjunction
with Scorpio. The great lord is murdered
in his hall. A newly anointed king perse-
cutes the Church, in lower Europe and in
the north.

The two evil influences in Scorpio are Mars and Saturn; unfortunately, this conjunction has occurred fourteen times since 1555. A particular example occurred in 1807, when the Sultan of Turkey, whose title was *seigneur,* was deposed, although he was not murdered until the following year. The newly anointed king who persecutes the Church is, of course, Napoleon, who restored the Catholic hierarchy in France but at the same time held Pope Pius VII prisoner. By this time Napoleon had also defeated Austria and Prussia *(l'Europe basse)* and Russia *(Septentrionale).*

Century I

I.LIII

Las qu'on verra grand peuple
  tourmenté,
Et la loy faincte en totale ruine:
Par autres loyx tout la Chreftienité,
Quand d'or, d'argent trouue nouuelle
  mine.

Alas, we shall see a great nation sorely
troubled and the holy law in utter ruin.
All Christianity taken over by other laws,
when a new source of gold and money is
discovered.

I believe this quatrain refers to the discovery of oil, particularly in the Middle East, where the laws of Islam prevail, *autres loyx tout la Chreftienité.* The great nation that is tormented may well refer to Iran, subjected to the barbaric laws of the Ayatollah Khomeini and his followers. Certainly, oil is the twentieth century source, *nouuelle mine,* of immense fortunes.

Century I

I.LIIII

Deux reuolts faicts du maling falcigere,[1]
De regne & fiecles faict permutation:
Le mobil figne à fon endroit fi ingere,[2]
Aux deux egeaux & d'inclination.

Two revolutions caused by the evil scythe-bearer marks a change of reign and centuries. The mobile sign moves into its house, equally favoring both sides.

The evil scythe-bearer is Saturn, who caused a change of reign in two centuries. The first is the French Revolution and the second the Russian. An interesting double meaning here, when one considers communist Russia's insignia of the hammer and sickle.

The mobile sign is Libra, the Balance, which according to astrologers governs Austria as one of its countries. Nostradamus seems to feel that Libra's influence was not strong enough to tip the balance in favor of Austria, *aux deux egeaux,* and so the malign influence of Saturn is able to cause war in Austria too—the assassination of the Archduke Ferdinand at Sarajevo, with the consequent result of the First World War.

Century I

I.LV

Soubs l'oppofite climat Babylonique,
Grand fera de fang effufion:
Que terre & mer, air, ciel fera inique,
Sectes, faim, regnes, peftes, confufion.

In the land opposite to Babylon there will be a great shedding of blood. Both on land and sea and in the air the heavens will seem unjust. Sects, famine, kingdoms, plagues, confusions.

This is a totally obscure quatrain, the only point of interest being the use of the word *air* in line 3. As in further quatrains it will be seen that Nostradamus envisages that man will move in this dimension, both personally and with the use of rocket-type weapons, in the future.

---

[1]*falcigere.* L. a compound word, *falcams geruns,* bearing a scythe.
[2]*ingere.* L. *ingerere (se),* to penetrate, enter. The *"si"* may be a misprint for *se.*

Century I

I.LVI

*Vous verrez toft & tard faire grand
    change,
Horreurs extremes, & vindications:
Que fi la lune conduicte par fon ange,
Le ciel s'approche des inclinations.*

*Sooner or later you will see great changes
made, dreadful horrors and vengeances.
For as the moon is led by its angel, the
heavens draw nearer to the Balance.*

Another astrological quatrain promising disaster in Libra, either the sign itself or one of the countries under its aegis. If it means the domination of Libra in astrological terms, that ended in 1879. (See I.LIIII.)

Century I

I.LVII

*Par grand difcord la trombe tremblera
Accord rompu dreffant la tefte au ciel:
Bouche sanglante dans le fang nagera,
Au fol la face ointe de laict & miel.*

*The trumpet will shake with great discord.
An agreement broken, lifting the face to
heaven. The bloody mouth will swim with
blood; the face anointed with milk and
honey lies on the ground.*

In 1793, amidst the horrors of the French Revolution, Louis XVI accepted the new decrees of the National Assembly which negated his position as absolute monarch, *accord rompu.* As Louis went to his execution on the tumbril he is recorded as reciting the Third Psalm, which he had sung at his coronation, *exultus caput meum, dressant la tefte.* When a victim is guillotined blood rushes out of his month, *bouche sanglante.* One of Nostradamus' grisly details: the head of Louis, anointed with milk and honey at his Coronation, *ointe de laict & miel,* lay on the ground after his execution before being placed in a basket. A tragic yet successful quatrain.

Century I

I.LVIII

Tranché le ventre, naiftra avec deux
* teftes,*
Et quatre bras: quelques ans entiers
* viuera:*
Tour qui Aquiloye[1] celebrera ses feftes,
Foffen, Turin, chef Farrare fuyura.

Through a slit in the belly a creature will
be born with two heads and four arms. It
will survive for some years. The day that
Aquiloye celebrates its holidays, Fossana,
Turin and the ruler of Ferra will follow.

This is an involved political quatrain dealing with both Napoleon and the Bourbon family, but in which Nostradamus has reversed the time sequence.

One could possibly refer to the first line literally, as a Cesarian section. But elsewhere Nostradamus uses the word *tranche* quite specifically to mean the blow of the guillotine. Therefore, if Louis XVI, the guillotined, is the belly, *ventre;* from him came forth two heirs, Louis XVIII and Charles X, *deux teftes.* The four arms may then be understood as the dukes of Angoulême, Normandy, Berry and Bordeaux. The family was deposed by *Aquiloye*—the rule of the Eagle, Napoleon. The ruler of Farrare (Fossana) was the Pope, who "followed" Napoleon back to France as a prisoner. Alternatively, one may interpret Fossana and Turin as standing metaphorically for the rest of Italy, captured by the French.

Century I

I.LIX

Les exilez deportez dans les ifles,
Au changement d'vn plus cruel
* monarque*
Seront meurtris: & mis deux les
* fcintiles,[2]*
Qui de parler ne feront eftez parques.[3]

The exiles deported to the islands, at the
advent of an even crueller king will be
murdered. Two will be burned to death,
who were not sparing in their speech.

Nicollaud ascribes this quatrain to the events of the Coup d'Etat of 1857, when many members of French secret societies were deported to the Cayenne Islands. The even more cruel king was Napoleon III, who imprisoned and deported people who spoke against his régime, *ne feront eftez parques.*

[1]*Aquiloye.* L. *Aquila lex,* the rule of the Eagle.
[2]*fcintiles.* L. *scintilla,* sparks, flames.
[3]*parques.* L. *parcus,* sparing, economic.

The lines fit this reading, but I am not wholly convinced. Some commentators, like Henry C. Roberts, believe this refers to the cremation of the Jews, but if he can believe that a man of Jewish blood, as Nostradamus was, could reduce six million deaths to two, *mis deux les scintilles,* he is completely mistaken to say the least.

Century I

I.LX

Vn Empereur naiftra pres d'Italie,
Qui à l'Empire fera vendu bien cher:
Diront auec quels gens il fe railie,
Qu'on trouuera moins prince que
  boucher.

An Emperor will be born near Italy who will cost the Empire very dear. When they see the people who ally with him they will say he is less a prince than a butcher.

Another Emperor quatrain. Napoleon was born in Corsica, near Italy. He cost his Empire dearly in both manpower and strength. The last two lines may refer either to the Créole blood of his wife, the Empress Josephine, or to the fact that his non-royal brothers were made kings of Naples, Spain, Holland and Westphalia. The butchery of line 4 must refer to the enormous number of troops killed in the Napoleonic campaigns. A good quatrain.

Century I

I.LXI

La republique miferable infelice,[1]
Sera vaftee[2] de nouueau magiftrat:
Leur grand amas de l'exile malefice,
Fera Sueue[3] rauir leur grand contracts.

The wretched, unfortunate republic will again be ruined by a new authority. The great amount of ill will accumulated in exile will make the Swiss break their important agreement.

The republic, created by Napoleon, will be in trouble again with the German Swiss. This may apply to the French Prince-President Napoléon III, 1852–70. If the German Swiss are the Prussians, this may refer to the Franco–Prussian war of 1870. However, I feel this is a poor interpretation.

[1]*infelice.* L. *infelix,* unhappy.
[2]*vaftee.* L. *vastus,* ruined, devastated.
[3]*Sueue.* L. *Suevi,* German Swiss tribe.

Century I

I.LXII

La grand perte las que feront les lettres,
Auant le cycle de Latona parfaict:
Feu, grand deluge plus par ignares
*   fceptres,*
Que de long fiecle ne fe verra refaict.

Alas! what a great loss there will be to learning before the cycle of the moon is completed. By fire, great floods, ignorant rulers; how long the century until it is seen to be restored.

Scholarship is seen to be suffering a great loss before the end of the Moon's cycle (in 1889). This quatrain appears to be open to two possible interpretations. One, that a piece of scholarship is lost through a series of disasters, *Feu, grand deluge*. The alternative is that true scholarship becomes vulgarized by lower standards and general availability to the public. Like all scholars of his day—and one must remember, even without taking into account the Centuries, Nostradamus was definitely a scholar—he regarded himself as a member of the intellectual elite.

Century I

I.LXIII

Les fleurs¹ paffés diminue le monde,
Long temps la paix terres inhabitées:
Seur marchera par ciel, terre, mer &
*   onde:*
Puis de nouueau les guerres fufcitées.

Pestilences passed, the world becomes smaller, for a long time lands will be inhabited peacefully. People will cross through the skies, safely, over land and seas; then wars will start up again.

The most remarkable thing about this quatrain is that Nostradamus predicts the world will become a smaller place, *diminue le monde*. This must refer especially to the air travel mentioned in line three, as well as to the then-known methods of travel over land and sea.

As to the placing of the age of pestilence (*fleurs*), there is no indication as to when this, war or pestilence, will pass—but after the two great wars of this century followed by a time of peace, he envisages that wars, note the plural, will start up again. Certainly, from 1945 until the present there has been no global war, but Korea, Algeria, Cambodia, Vietnam, Afghanistan, Pakistan, Iran and Iraq have been or are still at war. But since Nostradamus always considers France above all, the *paix terres inhabitées* should certainly be included in this line, possibly its influence in the Middle East and Africa?

¹*fleurs.* misprint for *fleaux*, scourge, pestilence.

There are several other vague and not so vague references to this state of affairs in the Centuries. The last line may simply apply to a Third World War but the plural *guerres* makes it unlikely.

Century I

I.LXIIII

De nuict foleil penferont auoir veu,
Quand le porceau demy homme on
  verra:
Bruict, chant, bataille, au ciel battre
  aperceu:
Et beftes brutes à parler lon orra.

At night they will think they have seen the sun, when they see the half pig man. Noise, screams, battle fought in the skies. The dumb beasts will be heard to speak.

Despite the apparently nonsensical aspect of this quatrain on first sight, it is, to the modern eye, a vivid picture of an air battle. The sun appearing at night is a searchlight piercing the sky, or possibly the glare of exploding bombs. The piglike man, which no one to date has interpreted, seems a clear picture in silhouette of the pilot in an oxygen mask, helmet and goggles. The breathing apparatus would certainly look like a pig's snout to Nostradamus, gazing into the water on the tripod, trying to decipher what the picture meant.

This interpretation is supported by the noises that Nostradamus also hears: screams, and battles in the skies. He hears these creatures speaking to each other, *Et beftes brutes à parler lon orra.* The *beftes brutes* could of course be the sounds of the battling planes, or the whine of the bombs as they fall to earth and explode, or possibly even radio instructions. The word *aperceu,* seen, watched, indicates that the battle was also seen from the ground.

This quatrain is an excellent prediction that is both aural and visual. I think it is very successful, when one considers that Nostradamus is trying to describe something completely beyond his ken.

Century I

I.LXV

Enfans fans mains iamais, veu fi grand
  foudre,
L'enfant royal au ieu d'oesteuf blefsé:
Au puys brifes[1] fulgures[2] allant
  mouldré,
Trois fouz les chaines par le milieu
  trouffés.

A child without hands, never so great a thunderbolt seen, the royal child wounded at a game of tennis. At the well lightning strikes, chaining together three by the middle.

An unsuccessful quatrain. There have been several royal children born with various defects, mostly mental, as for example in the Hanover/Windsor line, but none with such a specific deformity, which sounds something like a Thalidomide victim.

Century I

I.LXVI

Celuy qui lors portera les nouuelles,
Apres vn peu il viendra refpirer
Viuiers, Tournon, Montferrant &
  Pradelles,
Grefle & tempestes les fera soupirer.

He who then brings the news after a short while will (stop) for breath. Vivers, Tournon, Montferrant and Pradelles; hail and storms will make them suffer.

I cannot decipher this quatrain. Viviers and Tournon are in the Ardèche and Pradelles is across the border in east central France. Montferrant was in the Puy-de-Dôme until it joined Clermont (Clermont-Ferrand) in 1731. However, this gets me nowhere.

Century I

I.LXVII

La grand famine que ie fens approcher,
Souuent tourner, puis eftre vniuerfelle:
Si grande & longue qu'un viendra
  arracher,
Du bois racine, & l'enfant de mamelle.

The great famine that I sense approaching will often appear in different areas, then become worldwide. It will be on such an enormous scale and last such a long time that roots will be grubbed from trees and children from the breast.

Famine is now global and we are far more aware of it these days than people would have been in Nostradamus' time. However, he

---

[1]*brifes.* O.F. *briser,* to fracture, break.
[2]*fulgures.* L. *fulgur,* flash of lightning.

seems to see it traveling from one country to another, *souuent tourner.* At the moment, many parts of Africa are in a dreadful state, and at the time of writing the corn belt of America has been reduced to about 30 percent of its normal production.

Considering that millions of tons of grain and other help have been pouring into Africa over the past few years, it seems tragic that the present state of that continent is worse than before. This quatrain should be regarded as a warning.

Century I

I.LXVIII

O quel horrible & malheureux
tourment,
Trois innocens qu'on viendra à liurer;
Poifon fufpecte, mal gardé tradiment,[1]
Mis en horreur par bourreaux enyurez.

O to what a dreadful and wretched tor-ment three innocent people will be deliv-ered. Poison suspected, badly guarded, be-trayal. Delivered up to horror by drunken executioners.

A quatrain too vague to be of use. One is tempted to place it in the French Revolution when Louis XVI, Marie Antoinette and their son, technically *innocens,* were delivered up to the guard of the mob. The *poifon fufpecte* has no meaning here, and they were certainly *mis en horreur* by drunken executioners, but their son did not go to the guillotine. He was most probably walled up in his own excrement until his early death.

Century I

I.LXIX

La grande montaigne ronde de fept
ftades,[2]
Apres, paix, guerre, faim, inondation:
Roulera loin abifment grans contrades,
Mefmes antiques, & grand fondation.

The great mountain will measure seven stadia around, after peace, war, famine, flooding. It will spread far drowning great countries, even antiquities and their mighty foundations.

This probably describes an enormous flood after a time of peace, war, and famine. The flood will apparently inundate many areas including antiquities which happened in Lyons at the end of 1988. It could possibly arise as the result of an earthquake, either on land or sea.

---

[1]*tradiment.* O.F. betrayal.
[2]*ftades.* L. *status,* a measure roughly a furlong in length; seven stadia would be just under a mile in circumference.

Century I

I.LXX

Pluie faim, guerre en Perfe non ceffée,
La foy trop grand trahira le monarque:
Par la fini en Gaule commencee,
Secret augure pour à vn eftre parque.

Nonstop rain, famine and war in Persia;
too great a trust will betray the monarch.
The result, started in France, will end
there, a secret treaty for someone to be
lenient.

The linking of the two place names, Persia and France, makes it likely that this quatrain refers to the Ayatollah Khomeini, who toppled the monarch, the Shah of Iran, because the Shah placed too much trust in him, or held him in too little suspicion.

The Ayatollah spent years of exile in Paris plotting the Shah's downfall. Since these events will also end in France, the secret treaty, *secret augure,* may well refer to France's methods in modern years of paying Iran with both large sums of money and arms for the release of their hostages. However, at the time I am writing the Ayatollah is reported to be dying of terminal cancer, and so the last line may contain a reference to things to come.

Century I

I.LXXI

La tour marine trois fois prife &
*   reprife,*
Par Hefpagnols, Barbares, Ligurins:[1]
Marfeille & Aix, Arles par ceux de
*   Pife,*
Vaft,[2] feu, pillé Auignon des Thurins.

The marine tower will be captured and
retaken three times by Spaniards, Barbar-
ians and Ligurians. Marseilles, Aix and
Arles by men of Pisa, devastation, fire,
sword. Pillage at Avignon by the Turi-
nese.

This is an irritating quatrain, which I cannot decipher despite the plethora of proper names. The keystone is probably the meaning of *la tour marine,* which could be related to the conflict between the Spaniards, French and Italians. Could it possibly refer to the Tour de Boucq in I.XXVIII?

---

[1]*Ligurins.* L. people of Ligurin in Italy.
[2]*Vaft.* L. *vastus,* laid waste, devastated.

Century I

I.LXXII

De tout Marseille des habitans changee,
Course & pourfuitte iusqu'au pres de
*   Lyon,*
Narbon, Tholoze par Bordeaux
*   outragee,*
Tuez captifs prefque d'vn million.

The inhabitants of Marseilles are completely changed, fleeing and pursued as far as Lyons. Narbonne and Toulouse are angered by Bordeaux. The killed and captive amount to almost a million.

The enormous number of dead must place this quatrain in modern times (*Tuez captifs prefque d'vn million*). For the last war, the official casualty list for soldiers in France gives a total of 675,000 dead or wounded. Since this sum does not include any Allies who fought beside the French, Nostradamus' total may be nearer the mark.

Century I

I.LXXIII

France à cinq pars par neglect
*   affaillie,* [1]
Tunys, Argel efmeuz par Perfiens:
Leon, Seuille, Barcelonne faillie
N'aura la classe par les Venitiens.

France will be accused of neglect by her five partners. Tunis, Algiers stirred up by the Persians. Leon, Seville and Barcelona having failed, they will not have the fleet because of the Venetians.

Towards the end of de Gaulle's presidency, France was under pressure from her Common Market partners (at that time, five of them) over various policies. This would agree in time with the trouble in North Africa, *Tunys,* in 1969, when Gadaffi's revolution toppled King Idris. The reference to Persia is interesting. In Nostradamus' day, Persia was part of the Ottoman Empire, part of which now belongs to the USSR. Are the Soviets, by implication, involved in the Middle Eastern troubles? This is obviously the case, even though they are now withdrawing from Afghanistan.

---

[1]*affaillie.* F. *assaillir,* to assault. France has only once been attacked on five sides—in 1813–14, and then it was by European allies, so this cannot apply here.

Century I

I.LXXIIII

Apres fejourné vogueront en Epire
Le grand fecours viendra vers Antioche:
Le noir poil crefpe tendra fort à
*   l'Empire,*
Barbe d'aerain fe rouftira en broche.

After a rest they will travel to Epirus,
great help coming from around Antioch.
The dark curly-headed one (king?) will
strive greatly for the Empire. The bronze
(brazen) beard will be roasted on a spit.

Sometimes in the Centuries Nostradamus uses the anagram *noir* for king, *roi*. It seems impossible here to indicate whether he had a single meaning or both in mind. The dark-haired king recurs in other quatrains, as does the red-headed man. I am tempted by the explanation that it refers to the family of Algerian pirates called Barbarossa, but their plunderings were contemporary with Nostradamus, so that this quatrain, in this sense, is not predictive.

Century I

I.LXXV

Le tyran fienne occupera fauone,
Le fort gaigné tiendra claffe marine:
Les deux armees par la marque
*   d'Anconne,*
Par effrayeur le chef s'en examine.

The tyrant of Siena will occupy Savona,
having won the fort he will restrain the
marine fleet. Two armies under the standard of Ancona; the leader will look upon
them with fear.

Until April, 1535, roughly at the time of the publication of the first part of the predictions, of which this quatrain was one, Siena was a free town, and held out with French help against the Florentines. Otherwise, all that is of note is that Savona was a protectorate of the Genoese republic and Ancona part of the Papal States. It is impossible to get much information out of this quatrain.

Century I

I.LXXVI

D'vn nom farouche tel proferé fera,
Que les trois foeurs auront fato[1] le
*   nom:*
Puis grand peuple par langue & faict
*   dira*
Plus que nul autre bruit & renom.

This man will be called by a barbaric
name that the three sisters will receive
from destiny. He will speak then to a great
people in words and deeds, more than any
other he will have fame and renown.

[1]*fato.* L. *fatum,* destiny.

This quatrain almost certainly refers to Napoleon, as Le Pelletier, another commentator, believed. This is due to the Greek derivation of his name *(nom farouche) NEAPOLLUON,* meaning destroyer. That his name was spelled this way, with the extra *e,* is evident from the inscription on the Column in the Place Vendôme: NEAPOLIO. IMP. AUG.

Napoleon was also barbaric in a more general sense, being the younger son of a Corsican family whose language and manners were not those of polite Parisian society. He was also renowned for his great speeches to his troops *(par langue dira)* before battle, a characteristic he shared with Hitler.

Century I

I.LXXVII

Entre deux mers dreffera promontaire,	*Between two seas there stands a promon-*
Que puis mourra pars le mords du	*tory; a man will die from the bite of a*
cheual:	*horse. Neptune unfurls a black sail for his*
Le fien Neptune pliera voille noire,	*man; the fleet is between Gibraltar, near*
Par Calpre & claffe aupres de	*Rocheual.*
Rocheual.	

This is an excellent quatrain describing the Battle of Trafalgar, October 21, 1805. Gibraltar is the promontory separating the two oceans, the Atlantic and the Mediterranean. The French and English fleets fought the battle of Trafalgar between Gibraltar and Cape Roche *(Rocheual),* Trafalgar itself being a point between two bays.

The Admiral of the French fleet, Admiral Villeneuve, was reputedly strangled by one of Napoleon's Mamelukes with the bridle of a horse, when at an inn in Rennes in 1806. He had returned to France after being captured by the English. When the English Admiral, Nelson, was mortally wounded, his ship raised a black sail on its return voyage to England.

Rocheual may just be Nostradamus' word for *"roche,"* rock, which is the name often given to Gibraltar itself, The Rock.

Century I

I.LXXVIII

D'vn chef naiftra fens hebeté	*To a leader will be born an idiot heir,*
Degenerant par fauoir & par armes;	*weak both in knowledge and in warfare.*
La chef de France par fa foeur redouté,	*The head of France is feared by his sister,*
Champs diuifez, concedez aux	*battlefields divided, conceded to the mili-*
gendarmes.	*tary.*

Several commentators believe the weak leader is Marshal Pétain, who took over the government from Reynaud in 1940. If the sister stands for France itself, she had reason to fear the duplicity of her leaders and the horrors of the Second World War. However, I find this too general a quatrain to be satisfactory.

Century I

I.LXXIX

Bazaz, Leftore, Condon, Aufch, Agine,
Efmaus par loix querelle & monopole:
Car[1] Bourd. Toulouze Bay[2] mettra en
  ruine.
Renouueller voulant leur tauropole.[3]

From the sixth bright celestial planet, there will be great storms in Burgundy.

Basas, Lectoure, Condom, Auch and Agen are troubled by laws, disputes and monopolies. Carcassonne, Bordeaux, Toulouse and Bayonne will be ruined when they wish to renew the slaughter.

All of these towns are in southwest France. The quatrain may contain a reference to a trading dispute and the granting of monopolies in the locality. But the massacre is unclear.

Century I

I.LXXX

De la fixieme claire fplendeur celefte,
Viendra tonner fi fort en la Bourgogne:
Puis naistra monftre de treshideufe
  befte,
Mars, Auril, Mai, Iuin grand charpin[4]
  & rongne.

From the sixth bright celestial planet, there will be great storms in Burgundy. Then a monster will be born of a very hideous beast; in March, April, May and June, great wounding and trouble.

This general quatrain is believed by many commentators to refer to spring, 1918. Saturn being the sixth planet, the portents of war will occur during the period governed by him. But why the great storms in Burgundy? There is no record of anything outstanding occurring there during this time. The monster born *de treshideufe befte* must presumably refer to the war, but it is an exceptionally muddled quatrain, even for Nostradamus.

---

[1]*Car.* F. because, or apocope of Carcassonne.
[2]*Bay.* F. apocope of Bayonne.
[3]*Tauropole.* L. *Taurobolium,* the sacrifice of a bull, metaphorically massacre, slaughter.
[4]*charpin.* O.F. wound, or rags to dress wounds.

Century I

I.LXXXI

*D'humain troupeau neuf feront mis à
    part,
Du iugement & confeil feparez:
Leur fort fera diuifé en depart,
Kappa, Thita, Lamda, mors bannis
    efgarez.*

*Nine will be set apart from the human
race, separated from judgment and advice. Their fate is to be divided as they
depart. Kappa, Theta, Lamda dead, banished and scattered.*

This quatrain certainly has no reference to the past that one can
see. Leoni believes that it suggests pioneer astronauts. But the implication is that the expedition will be unsuccessful *(mors bannis efgarez)*
and those hurt will have names beginning with the letters K, T (Th),
and L, here produced as letters of the Greek alphabet.

Century I

I.LXXXII

*Quand les colomnes de bois grand
    tremblee,
D'Aufter conduicte couuerte de rubriche:
Tant vuidera dehors grande affemblee:
Trembler Vienne & le Pays d'Auftriche.*

*When the columns of wood tremble greatly
in the south wind, covered with blood then
such a great multitude pours forth that
Vienna and the land of Austria will tremble.*

It was in the autumn of 1918, when the leaves trembled in the wind,
that Austria was overturned and the new revolutionary rule, *rubriche,*
replaced the autocratic reign of the Hapsburgs. The great assembly
represents the World Powers, whose Triple Entente annoyed
Austria. Austria's problems first arose in the south *(Auster),* in Turkey
and Balkan States. The last line speaks for itself.

Century I

I.LXXXIII

*La gent eftrange diuifera butins,
Saturne en Mars fon regard furieux:
Horrible eftrange aux Tofquans &
    Latins,
Grecs qui feront à frapper curieux.*

*A foreign nation will divide the spoils;
Saturn in a dreadful aspect with Mars.
Terrible and strange to the Tuscans and
Latins; Greeks who will wish to strike.*

The last two lines seem to place this quatrain in the midst of the
struggles with Mussolini's Italian forces who occupied Greece in
1940. The booty *(butins)* taken by the Germans was proverbial. It is

still appearing sometimes in the various *diuifera,* sale rooms, of the world. Mars is the God of War with Saturn, a bad aspect, which indeed did turn out so for the Italians who allied themselves to the losing Nazi side.

Century I

I.LXXXIIII

Lune obfcurcie aux profondes tenebres,	*The moon eclipsed in great gloom, his*
Son frere paffe de couleur ferrugine:[1]	*brother becomes the color of blood. The*
Le grand caché long temps foubs les	*great one, hidden for a long time in the*
tenebres,	*shadows, will hold a blade in the bloody*
Tiedera fer dans la plaie fanguine.	*wound.*

The comte d'Artois is the man in eclipse, for he was in exile when his brother died bloodily *(paffe ferrugine)* on the guillotine. D'Artois remained away for a long time before he returned to France with his family, as Charles X.

The reference to blades and blood applies very neatly to his son, the duc de Bercy, who was attacked and fatally stabbed, *fer dans la plaie fanguine,* at the Opéra on the night of February 13, 1820. As he died clutching the hilt of the knife he said, "I am murdered, I am holding the hilt of the dagger." His attacker was Louvel, keeper of the royal greyhounds, a fanatic Republican, who actually accompanied Napoleon to Elba.

Century I

I.LXXXV

Par la refponse de dame Roy troublé	*The king is troubled by the queen's reply.*
Ambaffadeurs mefpriferont leur vie:	*Ambassadors will fear for their lives. The*
Le grand fes freres contrefera doublé	*greater of his brothers will doubly disguise*
Par deux mourront ire, haine enuie.	*his action. Because of the two, they will*
	die of anger, hatred and envy.

The king who is troubled by the queen's reply is Henri III of France, because Catherine de' Medicis, the queen mother, was furious at Henri's action in killing not only the powerful duc de Guise but also his equally powerful brother, the Cardinal de Guise, on December 23, 1588.

Catherine quite rightly saw the political troubles these murders would bring in their wake. The ambassadors who fear for their lives

---

[1]*ferrugine.* L. *ferruginus,* blood colored.

are almost certainly the Estates General, whom the king assembled to meet him at Blois. They protested the murders as strongly as they could.

The greater brother who survived was the duc de Mayenne, who at that time led the Catholic League, and became an important figure at the French court as lieutenant general of France *(contrefera doublé)*, although these words could also apply to the king himself.

Century I
I.LXXXVI

La grande royne quand fe verra vaincue, *Fera excés de mafculine courage:* *Sus cheual, fleuue passera toute nue,* *Suite par fer: à foi fera outrage.*	*When the great queen sees that she is conquered, she will show an excess of masculine courage. Naked, on horseback she will cross the river pursued by the sword: she will be an outrage to her faith.*

Mary, Queen of Scots, is almost certainly the subject of this quatrain. In May, 1568, having been defeated for the second time by Murray, her half-brother, she escaped from her prison and fled to England to the hoped-for mercy of Elizabeth I, taking with her only the clothes she was wearing, *toute nue.* She fled on horseback, but crossed the border by ferry. Both Catherine and Protestants believed she had outraged her faith, *à foi fera outrage,* because of her affair and subsequent marriage to Bothwell.

Century I
I.LXXXVII

Ennofigee[1] feu du centre de terre, *Fera trembler un tour de cité neufue:* *Deux grands rochiers long têps ferôt la guerre,* *Puis Arethufa rougira nouueau fleuue.*	*Earthshaking fire from the center of the earth will cause tremors around the New City. Two great immovable powers will war for a long time, then Arethusa will redden a new river.*

This quatrain talks of a "great explosion" near a new city, which normally in Nostradamus' writings refers to New York. But this particular verse seems to give a clear indication of a volcanic explosion. Lava forms red rivers, and pours from the earth's center.

I think therefore that we have here a possible description of the eruption at Mount St. Helens on May 12, 1980. Later Nostradamus links this eruption with a city at 45° parallel. The town of Newberg in Oregon is also on this standard. At the time of its explosion, Mount

---

[1]*Ennofigee.* Gk. *ennosigaeus,* earthshaking. A name often given to Neptune.

St. Helens literally became a hollow mountain. The volcano's ash-type debris could be seen as far away as New York. The destruction this explosion wrought upon miles of forests and farmland will take generations to renew. (See X.XLIX.)

Century I
I.LXXXVIII

Le diuin mal furprendra le grand prince,	Divine wrath overtakes the great prince a short time before he will marry. Both his
Vn peu deuant aura femme efpoufee.	supporters and his credit will suddenly diminish. Advised, he will die because of the
Son apuy & credit à vn coup viendra mince,	shaven heads.
Confeil mourra pour la tefte rafee.	

The key phrase here is *la tefte rafee.* This was a common term for the Roundheads in England who wore their hair short, as opposed to the curled wigs of the Royalist following of Charles I of England. It appears several times in the *Prophecies*. Divine retribution overtook Charles I when he was sentenced by Parliament, but the real trouble arose originally around the time of his marriage in 1625 to Henrietta of France. On his wedding day Charles proclaimed an edict that the persecution of Catholics should cease. Parliament refused this and demanded instead subsidies for the war against Spain. This lead to his death, demanded by the Roundheads, in 1649. (See IX.XLIX.)

Century I
I.LXXXIX

Tous ceux de Ilerde[1] feront dans la Mofelle,	Everyone from Lerida will be in the Moselle, killing all those from the Loire and
Mettant à mort tous ceux de Loire & Seine:	the Seine. The sea route will come through a high valley, when the Spanish open up
Le cours marin viendra pres d'haulte velle,	every way.
Quand Efpagnols ouuira toute veine.	

This seems to be a general quatrain about the Peninsular Wars, 1808–1814, when Wellington pushed up through Spain and Portugal across the Pyrenees to Bordeaux. The killing of the people in the Loire and further north towards Paris, *Seine*, does not occur until later. James Laver suggests that *haulte velle* may be Nostradamus' groping towards the unfamiliar name of Wellington.

[1]*Ilerde.* Lerida, a city in Spain.

Century I

I.XC

Bourdeaux, Poitiers au fon de la
   campane,
A grand claffe ira iusques à l'Angon:
Contre Gauloys fera leur tramontane,
Quand monftre hydeux naistra pres de
   Orgon.

At the sound of the bell Bordeaux and
Poitiers will go with a fast fleet as far as
Langon. A great anger will surge up
against the French, when an hideous
monster is born near Orgon.

This quatrain does nothing but describe an invasion by the French which is countered with strong resistance.

As for hideous monsters, Nostradamus was very interested in them. During the Protestant troubles, a calf with two heads was born near Salon. Nostradamus predicted that it would mean the separation of France through the two religions, Catholicism and Calvinism. He was right, of course, but any thinking politician of the day would have said the same thing. For what it is worth, a two-headed child was born in England in May, 1988, so these strange abnormalities still go on. The doctors have declared that the child will live, a truly tragic situation.

Century I

I.XCI

Les dieux feront aux humains
   apparence,
Ce qu'ilz feront auteurs de grand
   conflict:
Auant ciel veu ferein efpee & lance,
Que vers main gauche fera plus grand
   afflict.

The gods will make it seem to mankind
that they are the authors of a great war.
Before the sky was seen to be free of weapons and rockets: the greatest damage will
be afflicted towards the left side.

There have been many great wars, but my inclination is to say that this one has yet to happen. Here Nostradamus states that we will not know which side starts the war, although he contradicts in later quatrains when he places the responsibility on the East, China. He says that after a peaceful interlude (I.LXIII) the air will be full of weapons of combat, rockets pointing like lances to the skies. Visually, the left-hand side of a map or globe is America, and he states that this country will face great losses. However, the redeeming factor is that in IV.XCV he states that the war's victor will be born in America. It is to be hoped that the factors in this quatrain remain allied to the Western cause. With Nostradamus, there is no guarantee.

Century I

I.XCII

Souz vn la paix partout fera clamee
Mais non long temps pillé & rebellion:
Par refus ville, terre, & mer entamee,
Mors & captifs le tiers d'vn million.

Under one man peace will be proclaimed everywhere, but not long afterwards will be looting and rebellion. Because of a refusal, both town, land and sea will be broached. A third of a million will be captured or dead.

If the universal peace, *la paix partout,* refers to the French Empire, one might bear in mind Napoleon's statement, *"L'Empire, c'est la paix."* The Franco-Prussian war, which started when the king of Prussia refused to give in to humiliating French demands, is depicted in the remainder of the quatrain. The *Encyclopaedia Britannica* gives the number of dead and wounded in the war as approximately 300,000, which is close enough to Nostradamus' estimate.

Century I

I.XCIII

Terre Italique pres des monts tremblera,
Lyon & coq non trop confederez:
En lieu de peur l'vn l'autre s'aidera.
Seul Castulon[1] & Celtes moderez.

The Italian land near the mountains will tremble. The Cock and the Lion are not strongly united. Instead of fear they will help each other. Freedom alone moderates the French.

The Italians certainly trembled when Napoleon mounted his Italian campaign in 1795. Having captured Toulon, he set out upon the Italian wars and France *(coq)* saw the start of the enmity which grew up between her and England *(Lyon).* This situation is followed by one of mutual alliance, *l'vn l'autre s'aidera.* After the accession of Louis XVIII, the French, *Celtes,* regain their freedom from tyranny.

Century I

I.XCIIII

Au port Selin le tyran mis à mort,
La Liberté non partout recouuree:
Le nouueau Mars par vindicte &
  remort,
Dame par force de frayeur honnoree.

The tyrant Selim will be put to death at the harbor, but Liberty will not be regained. The new war arises from vengeance and remorse. A lady is honored through force of terror.

[1]*Castulon.* A.Pr. Liberty.

At the battle of Lepanto, fought on October 7, 1571, Ali Pasha, the Admiral of Selim II's fleet, was killed onboard ship. Selim's aggression in the Mediterranean was finally quashed by the defeat at Lepanto. However, the crusade by Christian countries to put down Turkish influence did not succeed for some centuries. Line 4 may refer to the fact that the Pope declared that the victory of Lepanto was due to the direct intercession of Our Lady, *Dame.*

Century I

I.XCV

Deuant mouſtier trouué enfant beſſon,
D'heroic ſang de moine & veſtutiſque:
Son bruit par ſecte langue & puiſſance
  ſon,
Qu'on dira fort eſleue le vopiſique.

In front of a monastery the twin son of a monk of illustrious line will be found. His fame, renown and power through sects and speech is such that they will say the living twin is deservedly chosen.

This states that the twin son of a monk will become an important leader. He is unknown. Many commentators refer this quatrain to the Man in the Iron Mask, the possible son of Queen Anne and Cardinal Mazarin. But where is his twin? The whole quatrain is probably erroneous.

Century I

I.XCVI

Celuy qu'aura la charge de deſtruire
Temples, & ſectes, changez par fantaſie:
Plus aux rochiers qu'aux viuans
  viendra nuire,
Par langue ornee d'oreilles refaſſie.

A man will be charged with the destruction of temples and sects, he will be changed by visions. He will harm the rocks rather than the living; ears satiated by ornate speeches.

This may indicate some form of religious revival, whose destiny is concerned with people rather than with the bricks and mortar of the temples of accepted religions. Otherwise it is totally vague.

Century I

I.XCVII

Ce que fer, flamme n'a ſceu paracheuer,
La douce langue au conseil viendra
  faire:
Par repos, ſonge, le Roy fera refuer,
Plus l'ennemy en feu, ſang militaire.

That which neither weapon nor flame could accomplish will be achieved by a sweet speaking tongue in council. Sleeping, in a dream, the king will see the enemy, not in war or of military blood.

Henri III of France was killed, not in battle, but while in council in 1589. A monk, Jacques Clément, came to the king while he was staying at Saint Cloud, saying that he had a secret letter for His Majesty. When granted an audience, Clément leaned towards Henri as though to speak to him confidentially, and stabbed him in the stomach. The king died the next day. It is possible that *douce langue* is a typical Nostradamus deviation on the name of Clément.

What is extremely interesting is that this is a rare example of double precognition. It is well authenticated that Henri had dreamed of his death. Three days earlier the king said that he dreamed that his royal regalia—his blue cloak, two crowns, the scepter, and his sword and spurs, were all trodden underfoot by monks and the populace.

Century I

I.XCVIII

Le chef qu'aura conduit peuple infiny, *Loing de fon ciel, de meurs & langue* * eftrange:* *Cinq mil en Crete & Theffalie finy,* *Le chef fuyant, fauué en marine* * grange.* [1]	*The leader will lead great numbers of people far from their skies, to foreign customs and language. Five thousand will die in Crete and Thessaly, the leader fleeing in a seagoing supply ship.*

During Napoleon's flight from Egypt, 1798–99, he successfully avoided the British Navy to land in France, *le chef fuyant.* He left behind an army of approximately 5,000 men to cope with the Turks. It was they who ruled Thessaly and Crete, and Napoleon did flee in a wooden ship, *marine grange.* This fact alone precludes the prediction from applying to the British Expeditionary Forces in Crete and Thessaly in 1940; ships at that time were made of metal and the numbers of combatants involved were much greater.

Century I

I.XCIX

Le grand monarque que fera * compagnie,* *Auec deux Roys vnis par amitié* *O quel foufpir fera la grand mefgnie,* [2] *Enfans Narbon à l'entour quel pitié.*	*The great king will join with two kings, united in friendship. How the great household will sigh; around Narbonne, what pity for the children.*

I cannot interpret this quatrain.

[1] *grange.* O.F. literally, wooden barn.
[2] *mefgnie.* O.F. household, court.

Century I

I.C

Long temps au ciel fera veu gris oifeau,
Aupres de Dole & de Toufcane terre:
Tenant au bec vn verdoyant rameau,
Mourra toft grand & finera la guerre.

For a long time a gray bird will be seen in the sky near Dôle and the lands of Tuscany. He holds a flowering branch in his beak, but dies too soon and the war will end.

The comte de Chambord, son of the duchess de Berry and last legitimate heir to the French throne, was known at his birth as the dove of peace. Unfortunately, the throne was usurped by the Orléans family and the comte was exiled to Venice, near Dôle and to Modena, near Tuscany, where he married the daughter of the duke of Tuscany in 1846. He died without regaining the French throne, but he and the duc d'Orléans, the pretender, were reconciled when the latter was also sent into exile by the new Republic. It was the death of the comte de Chambord, the dove of peace, which averted the possibility of another war between the monarchists and the Republicans.

Century II

II.I

Vers Acquitaine pars infuls Britaniques
De pars eux mefmes grans incursiôs
Pluyes gelées ferôt terroirs iniques,
Port Selyn fortes fera invafions.

Towards Aquitaine there are assaults by the British, and also great invasions. Rain and frost make the terrain unsafe, against them they make mighty incursions.

This is an important quatrain. When France (Aquitaine) and Britain were deadlocked, *grans incursiôs,* on the Western Front during 1915, Winston Churchill persuaded the Allies to open a new front against Turkey *(Port Selyn).* The general plan was to attack the Dardanelles to reach Constantinople. The weather was dreadful, *Pluyes gelées,* and the troops suffered appallingly from it throughout much of the First World War.

Century II

II.II

La tefte bleu fera la tefte blanche *Autant de mal que France a faict du* *bien,* *Mort à l'anthene grand pendu fus la* *branche,* *Quand prins des fiens le Roy dira* *combien.*	The blue leader will inflict upon the white leader as much damage as France had done them good. Death from the great antenna hung from the branch, when the king will ask how many of his men have been captured.

The blue and white leaders occur several times in the quatrains and appear to apply specifically to the Ayatollah *(la tefte blanche)* who is often referred to as being followed by the Perse *(tefte bleu)*. *Perse* has two meanings in French, blue and Persian. Nostradamus is so ambiguous about this man that he almost certainly envisages both meanings. France's links with the Ayatollah are well known, from the time he was granted freedom there when exiled by the then Shah of Persia, to the French government's general dealings with Iran in both money and arms.

If this is a prophetic quatrain, the Ayatollah's successor is going to deal with France in a far less sympathetic manner. Perhaps he will refuse to allow French prisoners to be redeemed by ransom? Predictive thinking too may be contained in the reference to *l'anthene;* could this refer to an aerial or broadcasting of some kind, which gives or receives messages of death? The information demanded in line 4 may refer to the slaughter of the current Iran-Iraq war, of which then death would indicate that Iraq will be the eventual winner. Since in 1989 Iran has broken diplomatic relations due to the fundamentalist stand of its government against the West, it is possible the quatrain may refer to this.

Century II

II.III

Pour la chaleur folaire fus la mer *De Negrepont les poiffons demi cuits:* *Les habitans les viendront entamer,* *Quand Rhod, & Gennes leur faudra le* *biscuit.*	Because of heat like that of the sun on the sea, the fish around Negrepont will be half-cooked. The local people will eat them when in Rhodes and Genoa there is lack of food.

Such heat exploding upon the sea so that all the fish are dead implies something of far greater strength than a freak heat wave.

Possibly an atomic explosion, somewhere over the Aegean sea, as Negrepont is the Dalian name for the island of Ruboea? The second statement, that people are starving in Italy and other parts of Greece, indicates conditions of famine and possibly war. Nostradamus talks of an explosion over the sea in France in V.XCVIII, where again he describes the fish as being boiled by the heat.

Century II

II.IIII

Depuis Monach iufque aupres de Sicile,	*The coast will remain deserted all along*
Toute la plage demourra defolée	*the coast from Monaco as far as Sicily.*
Il n'y aura fauxbourg, cité ne ville,	*There will be no suburbs, cities or towns*
Que par Barbares pillé foit & vollée.	*which will not have been pillaged and*
	robbed by Barbarians.

This seems to be continuation of the last quatrain, II.III, unusual in Nostradamus as he states that he deliberately confused the time sequence of the quatrains in order to avoid further trouble with the Inquisition.

This therefore foresees the disaster extending through most of southern Europe, from Monaco to Sicily. As to the barbarians who will pillage rich cities and towns, this word contains some difficulty in translation, as it comes from the Greek, *barbar,* meaning, anyone not speaking the Greek tongue. So the identity of the enemies is uncertain.

Century II

II.V

Qu'en dans poiffon, fer & lettres	*When the weapons and documents are en-*
* enfermée,*	*closed in a fish, out of it will come a man*
Hors fortira qui puis fera la guerre:	*who will then make war. His fleet will*
Aura par mer fa claffe bien ramée,	*have voyaged far across the ocean to ap-*
Apparoiffant pres de Latine terre.	*pear near the Italian shore.*

The fish in this quatrain must presumably mean a submarine, since it contains not only documents and weapons as well as carrying a man, one who appears to be responsible for inciting a war. He is described as actually coming out, *hors fortira,* of the machine, exactly as Nostradamus describes the hostile soldiers in I.XXIX. The fleet of the unknown man has apparently traveled a great distance to reach the Italian shores, whether Adriatic or Mediterranean.

It is tempting to link this man with Nostradamus' Third Antichrist, whom he believes will start a Third World War in this present century. Line 1 may contain an astrological meaning, although somewhat tortuous, "When Mars and Mercury are in conjuration in Pisces." According to Norab, the next time this will occur is March 23, 1996. In I.LI, Nostradamus states it may start in 1995, and in II.XLI, 1993, which are close enough to be consistent and disconcerting since it was written over four hundred years ago.

Century II

II.VI

Aupres des portes & dedans deux cités,
Seront deux fléaux & onques n'apperçeu un tel:
Faim, dedans pefte, de fers hors gens boutés,
Crier fecours au grand Dieu immortel.

Near the harbor and in two cities will occur two scourges the like of which have never been seen. Hunger, plague within, people thrown out by the sword will cry for help from the immortal God.

Both Nagasaki and Hiroshima are upon the sea, *portes,* and in 1945 experienced a plague, *fléaux,* such as had never before been seen on earth, that of radiation from the two atomic bombs that were dropped upon both cities. The immediate survivors would have looked similar in many ways to victims of the plague, and remember that Nostradamus was probably the best plague doctor of his time in Europe. Plague turned its victims' bodies black, hence its contemporary name, *le charbon.* Radiation turns victims black too, and there was famine among the miserable survivors who left the cities because of the war, *de fer gens bouté.* The last line implies an immutable, implacable God who does nothing but listen to the victims' helpless cries for mercy.

Century II

II.VII

Entre plufieurs aux ifles deportés,
L'vn eftre nay à deux dents en la gorge:
Mourrant de faim les arbres esbrotés,
Pour eux neuf Roy, nouuel edict leur forge.

Among many people deported to the islands will be a man born with two teeth in his mouth. They will die of hunger, having stripped the trees. A new king will pass new laws for them.

Apart from assuming that the islands referred to are part of the French penal colonies, I cannot decipher this quatrain. The new king who passes new laws may predict the closing of the penal settlements. Most of the tropical ones are already no longer in use.

Many children are born with several teeth already formed. The destiny of the man described here is not made clear, except that he lives during a time of famine, when many die.

Century II
II.VIII

Temples facrez prime façon Romaine,
Reiecteront les goffres fondements
Prenant leur loix premiers & humaines,
Chaffant non tout des faincts les
cultements.

Temples consecrated in the early Roman fashion, they will reject the broken foundations; taking their early human laws, expelling almost all the cults of the saints.

This general quatrain may have been intended for the Huguenots of Nostradamus' time. It predicts a return to simpler religious precepts and practices, and a rejection of the elaborate cult of saints in the Roman Catholic Church.

In this latter prediction he was greatly wrong. During May, 1988, Pope John Paul II consecrated approximately a thousand Vietnamese who had died during the Vietnamese War, and it appears that there is a record number of names waiting for beatification. But it does seem that the influence of the saints upon Roman Catholics is less intense, and worship of individual saints less frequent. However, this ties in with the twentieth century attitude to religion generally among the masses. The division between Church and people has never been stronger.

Century II
II.IX

Neuf ans le regne le maigre en paix
tiendra,
Puis il cherra en foif si fanguinaire:
Pour luy grand peuple fans foi & loy
mourra,
Tué par vn beaucoup plus debonnaire.

For nine years the reign of the slim thing will continue, then it will fall into so bloody a thirst that a great nation will die because of it; killed by a better natured man.

This quatrain seems best to apply to the disease of AIDS, known in Africa, where it originated, as the "slim," a "thin," *"maigre"* disease. It is unclear whether there are nine years before its specific discovery as a disease, or whether the victim can last for as long as nine years.

A 1988 research project in the USA predicted that although the disease may take a long time to emerge, within a decade "99% of those infected will eventually die of AIDS if they do not die from other causes as a result of it."

"A great nation will die of it" seems somewhat overstated, but neither Africa nor America can be ruled out since many in those countries are severely affected by it. Presumably the final cure is found by the better natured man *(debonnaire),* but no date is given as to when that might happen.

Century II

II.X

Auant long temps le tout fera rangé,
Nous efperons un fiecle bien fenestre:
L'eftat des masques & des feuls bien changé,
Peu trouueront qu'à fon rang vueille eftre.

Before long everything will be controlled; we await a very evil century. The state of the masked and the solitary people greatly changed, few will find that they wish to retain their rank.

Some apply this to the French Revolution, 1789, in which the state of the social orders became dangerous and was changed. The two orders most affected were the court, *masques,* and the clergy, *les Seuls*—so called because of their traditional celibacy. Both these classes were abolished in 1790. They obviously suffered financial loss and many were guillotined because of their social rank and function.

However, I wonder whether the first two lines might refer to Russia, after its Revolution in the twentieth century. *Le tout fera rangé* seems to me to smack of the intolerance of the Communist régime of the USSR, and Nostradamus always describes the twentieth century as being a particularly evil one.

Century II

II.XI

Le prochain fils de l'aifnier paruiendra,
Tant esleué iufque au regne des fors:[1]
Son afpre gloire vn chacun la craindra,
Mais fes enfans du regne gettez hors.

The following son will succeed the elder, very greatly raised to a kingdom of privilege. His bitter renown will be feared by all, but his children will be thrown out of the kingdom.

This almost certainly is a quatrain about Napoleon, but it is very convoluted because of the several meanings of *prochain* and *aifnier.* *Prochain* may mean next, nearest, younger, or favorite; and *aifnier*

[1]*fors.* O.F. privileges, dues.

either elder or a falcon, *l'aifnier* conveying the metaphor of a bird of prey similar to Napoleon's eagle. If one accepts that it does refer to Napoleon, the rest of the quatrain falls very neatly into place. He was a second son, elected to an Empire and privilege. He was greatly feared throughout Europe, but after his exile his children were deprived of any rights to kingship by Louis XVIII. However, Napoleon's nephew, Louis-Napoleon, re-established himself as Emperor in 1852 and ruled until the advent of the Third Republic of 1871. Since then France has had no royalty, not even a token figurehead as in some European countries.

Century II

II.XII

Yeux clos, ouuerts d'antique fantafie,	*Eyes unseeing, open to the great myth, the*
L'habit des feuls feront mis à néant:	*habits of priests will be abolished. The*
Le grand monarque chaftiera leur	*great monarch will punish their frenzy,*
frenaifie,	*stealing the treasure from the front of the*
Rauir des temples le trefor par deuant.	*temples.*

Nostradamus was always more concerned with France than any other country in his quatrains, and, whether he was a Crypto-Jew or not, he worried a great deal about the Church because it appeared to him as essential to the basic fabric of society.

From 1789 the wearing of any ecclesiastical costume was banned. The clergy were suppressed during the French Revolution in 1790, and the Cult of Reason was established in 1793. The king can be interpreted either as Louis XVI, who had already helped despoil the monasteries, or Napoleon who continued to do so until the time of his Coronation, when he needed the Pope and found it necessary to restore Roman Catholicism to France. If this is the correct interpretation, it is another example of Nostradamus' failing to confuse the quatrains and it follows straight on from II.XI.

Century II

II.XIII

Le corps fans ame plus n'eftre en	*The body without a soul is no longer at the*
facrifice,	*sacrifice. At the day of death it comes to*
Iour de la mort mis en natiuité:	*rebirth. The divine spirit will make the*
L'esprit diuin fera l'ame felice,	*soul rejoice seeing the eternity of the world.*
Voyant le verbe en fon eternité.	

This seems to be a religious statement in which Nostradamus states he believes in the transmigration of souls, "At death it is brought to rebirth."

Since this doctrine is not Christian or Jewish, he may have been influenced by his predictive faculties. He uses the phrase *esprit diuin* in I.II to describe the spirit which enlightens him. An interesting sidelight on Nostradamus the man.

Century II
II.XIIII

A Tours, Gien, gardé feront yeux penetrans,
Defcouuiront de loing la grand ferine:
Elle & sa fuitte au port feront entrans,
Combat, pouffez, puiffance souueraine.

At Tours and Gienne the watchful eyes will be guarded. They will spy from far off the serene Highness. She and her followers will enter the harbor, combat joined, sovereign power.

Since both Tours and Gien are situated on the Loire, this quatrain is placed firmly in France. It may refer to the Regency of Catherine de' Medicis 1559–89, *la grand ferine*, for she traveled the country continually in an effort to subdue the wars of religion which troubled France from 1542 to 1598. The queen died, lonely and weakened by constant illness, in 1599, having seen all three of her sons predecease her, as predicted.

Century II
II.XV

Vn peu deuant monarque trucidé,[1]
Caftor, Pollux en nef, aftre crinite[2]
L'erain[3] public par terre & mer vuidé,
Pife, Aft, Ferrare, Turin, terre interdicte.

A short while before a king is murdered, Castor and Pollux in the ship, a bearded star. Public treasure plundered on land and sea; Pisa, Asti, Terrara and Turin are forbidden territories.

One can only approach this quatrain through the astrological dating. Castor and Pollux, the twins, stand for Gemini, the ship for Argo and the bearded star, as elsewhere in Nostradamus, is a comet. Linked with this is an assassinated king, a war effort with money being raised on land and sea plus the Italian States being placed *"interdict."*

[1]*trucidé.* L. *trucidare,* to slaughter.
[2]*crinite.* L. *crinitus,* bearded.
[3]*erain.* L. *eranus,* public fund or treasury.

This last event has never occurred and it seems unlikely that it will. A failed quatrain perhaps?

Century II

II.XVI

Naples, Palerme, Sicille, Syaracufes,
Nouueau tyrans, fulgures[1] feux celeftes:
Force de Londres, Gand, Bruxelles, &
   Suses,
Grand hecatombe, triomphe faire feftes.

There are new tyrants in Naples, Sicily, Palermo and Syracuse, thunder and lightning in the skies. An army from London, Ghent, Brussels and Susa; a great massacre, then triumph and festivities.

The new tyrants in the Italian towns were probably Mussolini's *Fascisti*. By extension, the thunder and lightning may stand for the sound of war. London declared war against Italy, allied with Brussels, and after the use of a great force (*grand hecatombe*), eventually wins the war.

Century II

II.XVII

Le camp du temple de la vierge veftale,
Non efloingé d'Ethne & monts
   Pyrenées:
Le grand conduict eft caché dans la
   male,[2]
North[3] getez fleuues & vignes
   maftinées.[4]

The field of the vestal virgin's temple is not far from Ethne and the Pyrenees. They lead the great one, hidden in a trunk; in the north, the rivers overflow and the vines are destroyed.

The key to this quatrain probably lies in the word "*Ethne*," the Greek anagram for Elne, since *the* is one letter in the Greek alphabet. Elne is in the Pyrenees between the rivers Tech and Réart, both of which flow into the Mediterranean. I cannot decipher this quatrain further.

---

[1]*fulgures.* L. *fulgur,* lightning.
[2]*male.* F. 1) *malle,* a trunk, or possibly 2) *mal,* evil.
[3]*North.* one of the rare uses of English in Nostradamus.
[4]*maftiner.* O.F. to bruise, destroy.

Century II

II.XVIII

Nouuelle & pluie fubite impetuefe,
Empefchera fubit deux excercites:
Pierre ciel, feux faire la mer pierreuse,
La mort de fept terre & marin subites.

New, unexpected and heavy rain will suddenly hinder two armies. Stones from the skies will form a stony sea. The death of the seven suddenly by land and sea.

The resolution of this quatrain lies in the word *fept*. It refers to the death of the last of the seven Valois children of Catherine de' Medicis. When Henri III left Paris in 1587, the city was invaded by two armies, *deux excercites*, 35,000 German and Swiss troops. The duc de Guise rushed with his troops of the Huguenot League to Montargis, but the decisive battle was prevented by a violent rainstorm, *pluie fubite*. Henri, the last of the Valois kings, was assassinated in 1589, a direct result of his clash with the Leaguers and the assassination of the two Guise brothers (see I.LXXXV).

Century II

II.XIX

Nouueau venus lieu bafty fans defence,
Occuper la place par lors inhabitable:
Prez, maifons, châps, villes prêdre à
*   plaifance,*
Faim, Pefte, guerre arpen long
*   labourable.*

Newcomers will occupy an undefended place; occupying a place uninhabitable until then. Meadows, houses, fields, towns will be taken at their pleasure. Famine, plague, war (over) much arable land.

I cannot interpret this quatrain.

Century II

II.XX

Freres & soeurs en diuers lieux captifs,
Se trouueront paffer pres du monarque:
Les contempler fes rameaux[1] ententisz,
Defplaifant voir meton, front, nez, les
*   marques.*

Brothers and sisters captive, in varying places, will find themselves passing near the monarch. His attentive offspring will look at them, displeased to see the signs on their chins, foreheads and noses.

Jaubert applies this to an event which occurred soon after publication. In September, 1557, some Huguenots were captured during a raid and Henri II went to see them, taking his children. The king was

---

[1] *rameaux.* F. literally branches, by extension offspring, children.

reportedly angry at seeing so many of the captives wounded and bruised. However, the quatrain is so general that it may apply to many similar events.

Century II

II.XXI

Le camp Ascap[1] de l'Europe partira,
S'adioignant proche de l'isle submergée
D'Arton[2] classe phlange pliera,
Nombril du monde plus grand voix
    subrogée.[3]

The aimless army will depart from Europe and join up close to the submerged island. The NATO (or bread-giving) fleet will fold up its standard in the navel of the world, giving in to a greater voice.

The clue to this quatrain probably lies in the submerged island, *l'isle submergée,* which also occurs in IX.XXXI, where it is ascribed to Britain, the island of St. George. The army is described as aimless—possibly on an exercise, and therefore not acting with warlike intent? The fleet of bread, *Arton* (or possibly an anagram of NATO), folds up its standard for the same reason. The navel of the world is normally applied to Italy, but could be applied here, I think, to the Middle East, the Gulf, near the Garden of Eden where man was metaphorically born.

At the moment, the USA is acting as a protective shield in the Gulf, covering the many tankers (U.S. and foreign) which fly the American flag. But Nostradamus says that this too will be overcome, *plus grand voix subrogée.* Maybe a NATO naval force will take over, particularly since the tragic shooting down of the Iran Airbus July 4, 1988, as the American and other national forces are becoming too intensive a presence in the area.

Century II

II.XXII

L'ambassadeur envoyé par biremes.
A my chemin d'incogneus repoulsez:
De sel renfort viendront quatre triremes,
Cordes & chaines au Negre pont
    troussez.

The ambassador sent by the triremes is repulsed halfway by an unknown man. Four triremes come reinforced with salt. He is bound with cords and chains to the Negroponte.

Biremes are oared galleys with two bridges and triremes larger ones with three. Salt in the *Prophéties* often stands for taxation be-

---

[1]*Ascap.* Gk. *askpops,* incredible, aimless.
[2]*Arton.* Either anagram for NATO or Gk. artos, bread.
[3]*subrogée.* L. *subrogatus,* substitute.

cause of the French salt tax, the infamous *gabelle.* It may also contain the Biblical sense of wisdom. Negroponte is the Italian name for Euboea which belonged to the Turks until 1831, when it became part of Greece.

Century II

II.XXIII

Palais, oyfeaux, par oyfeau dechaffé,
Bien toft apres le prince paruenu:
Combien qu'hors fleuue ennemi repoulfé,
Dehors faifi trait d'oyfeau fouftenu.

The palace, birds, chased out by a bird, very soon after the arrival of the prince. So many of the enemy repulsed beyond the river, the bird in place seized from without by a trick.

The story of a prince, perhaps one who wears highly colorful clothing like a bird, who is captured in his palace through trickery by an upstart. Some commentators translate line 4 as "captured outside, a shaft held by a bird," i.e., an arrow.

Century II

II.XXIIII

Beftes farouches de faim fleuues
  tranner,[1]
Plus part du champ encontre Hifter
  sera.
En caige de fer le grand fera treifner,
Quand rien enfant de Germain
  obferuera.

Beasts wild with hunger will cross the rivers, the greater part of the battlefield will be against Hitler. He will drag the great one in a cage of iron, when the child of Germany observes no law.

One of the remarkable series of quatrains which mentions a German called Hister. There can be little doubt that Hitler is referred to. Until 1936 approximately, all commentators on the Centuries thought that the word referred to the river Danube, the Ister. But there is no doubt in this and later verses that Nostradamus had a person in mind. Ironically by the mid-1930's, Hitler believed these applied to himself and Goebbels made great use of them for propaganda purposes, as did the Allies, especially the British. Evidence of this may be found in Ellic Howe's book *Nostradamus and the Nazis.* During the first years of the Second World War Germany's development depended to a great extent on its armies' crossing the major rivers of Europe in a never-ending stream of manpower and weapons during the early years of the war. This child of Germany obeyed no

---

[1] *tranner.* L. *tranare,* to cross.

law except his own, and his armies' pillaged and looted as they went, *farouches de faim.* (See I.XXXIIII, III.XXXVI, III.LIII, III.LXI, IIII.LX-VIII, V.XXIX, V.XCIIII, VI.LI, IX.XC.)

Century II
II.XXV

La garde eftrange trahira fortereffe,
Espoir & vmbre de plus hault mariage:
Garde deçeue,[1] fort prise dans la preffe,
Loyre, Son, Rofne, Gar. à mort oultrage.

The foreign guard will betray the fortress, the shadowy hope of an important marriage. The guard deceived, the fort captured in crowd. Loire, Saône, Rhône, Garonne outraged unto death.

The defender of a fortress who betrays his trust while chasing the illusion of a higher post, *plus hault mariage,* may be Bazaine, who in 1870 handed over the fortress of Metz and his troops to the Germans. This gave the Germans access to the French interior during the Franco-Prussian war. Much has been written about Bazaine's motives for such an act of treachery, but eventually it seems to boil down to money and the illusory promise of power when the Prussians won the war.

Century II
II.XXVI

Pour la faueur que la cité fera,
Au grand qui toft perdra camp de bataille.
Fuis le rang Pau Thefin verfera.
De fang, feux mors noyés de coup de taille.

Because of the favor that a city will show towards a great man who later loses on the battlefield, the ranks will flee, rushing into the (rivers) Po and Tessin; blood, shooting, dead men drowned and slashed.

Century II
II.XXVII

Le diuin verbe fera du ciel frappé,
Qui ne pourra proceder plus auant:
Du referant[2] le fecret eftoupé,[3]
Qu'on marchera par deffus & deuant.

The divine voice will be struck from heaven and he will not be able to continue further. The secret hidden until the revelation, so that people will walk both above and overhead.

[1]*deçeue.* L. *decisus,* cut down, or F. deceived.
[2]*referant.* L. *reserare,* to lock.
[3]*eftoupé.* O.F. to shut up, imprison.

People walking above indicates that this quatrain may be referring to the grave of a religious man or someone similar *(le diuin verbe)*. To walk *par deffus et deuant* in French means to be confined in an underground cell or to be buried at the foot of a wall. Nostradamus may well be referring to himself. After his death in 1556 his wife buried him, according to his wishes, in the Franciscan monastery at Salon between the great door and the altar of St. Martha. He had requested that he should be buried upright, so that the people of Salon should not walk upon his grave.

During the early part of the French Revolution, however, his body was disinterred by drunken soldiers. Eventually his bones were reburied in the Chapel of Virgin in the Church of Saint-Laurent, where they remain, together with his burial plaque, to this day. An oil painting of him, one of three extant, used to hang above the plaque, but was stolen in the early 1980s.

Century II

II.XXVIII

Le penultiefme du furnom du prophete,
Prendra Diane pour fon iour & repos:
Loing vaguera par frenetique tefte,
Et deliurant vn grand peuple d'impos.[1]

The last but one of the prophet's name will take Monday for his day of rest. He will wander far in his frenzy, delivering a great nation from subjection.

Several ingenious readers have suggested that this quatrain could refer to the Moonies, the cult of Sun Myung Moon, in that Monday was the day of Diana, goddess of the Moon. But I feel that far from rescuing a nation from subjection, this subversive cult does exactly the opposite. Sun Myung Moon is Korean. This may relate to the following quatrain.

Possibly Nostradamus is referring to Mohammed or Mahomet?

Century II

II.XXIX

L'Oriental fortira de fon fiege,
Paffer les monts Apennins voir la
  Gaule:
Tranfpercera le ciel les eaux & neige,
Et vn chafcun frappera de fa gaule.

The Eastern man will come forth from his seat and cross the Apennines to France. He will cross through the sky, the seas and the snows and he will strike everyone with his rod.

[1]*impos.* O.F. *impost,* taxation.

This is a curious verse. The millenniumists of the year A.D. 1000 fully believed that the devil would bring forth his legions from the East at the time of the end of the world. Nostradamus certainly had a strong belief in the second millennium, as is seen in many of the Predictions. The use of the word *fortira* rather than *ira* indicates that this man of the East is leaving his country with deliberate intent, presumably to go to France. France, *La Gaule,* is one of the few countries which still maintains a diplomatic relationship with Iran. The third line clearly indicates Nostradamus' understanding of air travel. The last line is very ambiguous. The word *gaule* also means a stick or rod, it may even be a weapon, and also an indirect reference to de Gaulle, with whom postwar France is linked, just as Churchill is with Great Britain.

Note the curiously threatening tone underlying line 4. Possibly this man from the East is the Third Antichrist, who, elsewhere, Nostradamus states will appear before the second millennium?

Century II

II.XXX

Vn qui les dieux d'Annibal infernaux,
Fera renaiftre, effrayeur des humains:
Oncq' plus d'horreur ne plus dire
  iournaulx,
Qu'auint viendra par Babel aux
  Romains.

A man who is reborn from the infernal Gods of Hannibal, the terror of mankind. Never more horror nor papers tell of worse things than will come to the Romans through Babel.

Taking the eternal gods of Hannibal as the key to this quatrain, meaning North Africa, or the Middle East, there comes forth a man who will bring trouble to the whole world *(Babel).* The word *journeaulx* for the source of information is interesting. In Nostradamus' time this could only have been understood as pamphlets—newspapers did not exist. There is a possibility that the last line may refer to a general worldwide collapse of religions and that the Catholic Church will suffer from it, particularly the *Romains.*

Century II

II.XXXI

En Campanie le Cassilin[1] fera tant,
Qu'on ne verra que d'aux les champs
*   couuers:*
Deuant apres la pluye de long temps,
Hors mis les arbres rien l'on verra de
*   vert.*

In Campanie the (river) Cassilin will grow so much that one will only see fields covered with water. Before and after the long lasting rain, nothing green will be seen except for the trees.

This seems to predict a flood on the Volturno River, perhaps the flooding Capua itself, as the town was built on the ruins of the Roman town of Casilinum. One of a series of quatrains which predict alternating times of flood and drought.

Century II

II.XXXII

Laict, fang grenoilles efcoudre[2] en
*   Dalmatie,*
Conflict donné, pefte pres de Balennes
Cry sera grand par toute Efclauonie,
Lors naiftra monftre pres & dedans
*   Rauenne.*

Milk, blood, frogs will be prepared in Dalmatia; battle engaged, plague near Balennes. A great cry will go up throughout Slavonia; then a monster will be born near Ravenna.

The only clues to this quatrain, apart from the rains of milk, blood, fish and frogs, which are well documented, are the place names. The prediction appears to cover both sides of the Adriatic—Dalmatia is on the eastern Adriatic, Balennes was Trebula Balliensis near Capua, and Ravenna is in central Italy. Slavonia is now part of northern Yugoslavia.

In Birmingham, England, on June 12, 1954, hundreds of frogs were reported falling from the skies, bouncing off witnesses' umbrellas and scaring everyone. On January 2, 1973, the same thing was repeated at Arkansas, Texas, where a shower of frogs was reported "the size of tiny nickels" during a thunderstorm. In Singapore, 1851, an area of approximately fifty acres was found covered by a local species of catfish. In late 1988 in the Australian state of Queensland, Brisbane residents were showered with hundreds of sardines. Scientists said that updrafts probably took the fish from shallow water into the atmosphere. When it rained, they fell.

---

[1]*Cassilin.* town on the Volturno River.
[2]*escoudre.* L. *excudore,* to prepare.

Century II

II.XXXIII

Par le torrent qui defcent de Veronne,
Par lors qu'au Pau guidera fon entrée:
Vn grand naufrage, & non moins en
  Garonne,
Quant ceux de Gênes marcheront leur
  contree.

Through the torrent which pours down
from Verona, where the entrance is guided
to the Po; a great wreck, and not less so
in Garonne, when the people of Genoa
will march against their country.

This quatrain, which may be linked with quatrain II.XXXII, describes three sixteenth-century states—France, Verona and Genoa.
Verona is situated on the river Adige, which enters the Adriatic parallel to the Po about ten miles distant. Nothing really specific.

Century II

II.XXXIIII

L'ire infenfee du combat furieux,
Fera à table par freres le fer luire:
Les, defpartir, bleffé, curieux,
Le fier duelle viendra en France nuire.

In the senseless rage of a furious struggle,
the brothers will draw their weapons at
table. They are separated, wounded and
curious. The proud duel will bring harm
to France.

The duel described here, which occurs between brothers or cousins who were formerly friends (eating at the same table), in some way
causes trouble to France. I am unable to pin down any specific incident, but see II.LV for a possible link and explanation.

Century II

II.XXXV

Dans deux logis de nuict le feu prendra,
Plufieurs dedans eftouffez & roftis:
Pres de deux fleuues pour feul il
  auiendra:
Sol, l'Arq, & Caper tous feront
  amortis.

Fire will take hold in two houses at night,
several people inside suffocated or burnt.
It will definitely happen near two rivers,
when the sun, Sagittarius and Capricorn
are all diminished.

The astrological dating in line 4 occurs every year on December
22nd (Gregorian calendar), for this is the day that the sun moves out
of Sagittarius into Capricorn. All the commentators who wrote from
about 1600 onwards seem to relate the quatrain to a great fire at
Lyons which happened in December, 1582. Lyons is situated at the
mouth of two rivers.

Century II

II.XXXVI

*Du grand Prophete les lettres feront
prinses,
Entre les mains du tyran deuiendront:
Fraudes fon Roy feront fes entreprinfes,
Mais fes rapines bien toft le
troubleront.*

The letters of the great Prophet will be intercepted and fall into the hands of the tyrant. He will make efforts to deceive his king, but soon his thefts will give him trouble.

Abbé Torné, the expansive nineteenth century commentator on Nostradamus, believed this quatrain applied to himself, but gives us no specific reason why it should do so. Nostradamus may be talking of some event in his own life, when he was in Paris advising Catherine de' Medicis and a letter of credit to some friends was stolen (see "The Life and Times of Nostradamus," p. 11).

Century II

II.XXXVII

*De ce grand nombre que lon enuoyera,
Pour fecourir dans le fort affiegez,
Pefte & famine tous les deuorera,
Hors mis feptante qui feront profligez.*[1]

Out of the great number that are sent to relieve the besieged fort, disease and hunger will destroy them all, except seventy who will be killed.

I have no explanation for this quatrain.

Century II

II.XXXVIII

*Des condamnez fera fait vn grand
nombre,
Quand les monarques feront conciliez:
Mais l'vn deux viendra fi malencombre,
Que guere enfemble ne feront raliez.*

There will be a great number of condemned people when the monarchs are reconciled. But one of them will be so unfortunate that they will hardly remain allies.

This may be interpreted as a general quatrain describing the alliance between Hitler and Stalin from the years 1939 to 1941. Others, who apply it to the breakdown of the Yalta conference of 1945, interpret line 1 as referring to the Nuremberg Trials and the "misfortune" as the beginning of the Cold War with Russia.

---

[1]*profligez.* L. *profligare,* to destroy, kill, ruin.

Century II
II.XXXIX

Vn an deuant le conflict Italique,
Germains, Gaulois, Hefpaignols pour le
*   fort:*
Cherra l'efcolle maifon de republicque,
Où, hors mis peu, feront fuffoqué mors.

A year before the war in Italy, Germans,
French and Spanish will be for the strong
one; the schoolhouse of the republic will
crash, where, except for a few, they will be
suffocated to death.

The quatrain appears to apply best to Europe in general during 1939, the year before Italy became involved in the Second World War, declared on June 10, 1940. The Spanish, although technically neutral, backed the German cause, and there was definitely a pro-German element in France, as was proved by the Vichy régime. The strong man at this period must certainly be Hitler. The schoolhouse republic which crushes so many people could refer to either Italy or France, but the adjective *"efcolle"* is difficult to interpret.

This seems to lead on to the following quatrain (II.XL), which claims that after the alliances between Germany, Spain and France, there will be world battles on land and sea—the Second World War.

Century II
II.XL

Vn peu apres non point longue
*   interualle,*
Par mer & terre fera faict grand
*   tumulte:*
Beaucoup plus grande fera pugne[1]
*   naualle,*
Feux, animaux, qui plus feront
*   d'infulte.[2]*

Shortly afterwards, not a very long inter-
val, a great tumult will be raised by land
and sea. The naval battles will be greater
than ever. Fires, creatures which will
make more tumult.

If, as I stated, this is linked with the previous quatrain, the theme of the Second World War continues. The importance of sea domination was obvious; possibly the creatures represent the submarines which came into prominence at this time—Nostradamus has described submarines as fish on various occasions. *Feux* may be translated as firing, or weaponry, which would make the creatures armed ships.

[1]*pugne.* L. *pugna,* battle.
[2]*infulte.* A.Pr. insult or turmoil.

Century II

II.XLI

*La grand' eftoille par fept iours
    bruflera,
Nuée fera deux soleils apparoir:
Le gros maftin toute nuict hurlera,
Quand grand pontife changera de
    terroir.*

*The great star will burn for seven days
and the cloud will make the sun appear
double. The large mastiff will howl all
night when the great pontiff changes his
abode.*

Several popes have changed their abodes—this means surely something more permanent than the summer trips to Castel Gandolfo, or even the present Pope John Paul II's world tours. The most notable examples of this were Pius VI, who died in Valence in France, and Pius VII, who was forcibly detained by Napoleon before returning to Rome.

The reference to the comet may place this quatrain in 1986, the time of Halley's comet and of Pope John Paul II to whom the Irish prophet Malachy allotted the motto *"de laboris solis,"* of the toil of the sun. Perhaps it implies a war towards the end of this century, when the Pope may well have to leave the Vatican, and possibly even Europe. If the seven days stand for seven years, dated from the time of Halley's Comet, we arrive at 1993, near to the date Nostradamus gives elsewhere in the *Prophecies* for the start of a Third World War.

Century II

II.XLII

*Coq, chiens & chats de fang feront
    repeus,
Et de la playe du tyran trouué mort.
Au lict d'vn autre iambes & bras
    rompus,
Qui n'auoit peur mourir de cruelle
    mort.*

*The Cock, cats and dogs will be replete
with blood when a tyrant is found
wounded in the bed of another. Both arms
and legs broken, he, who was not afraid,
dies a cruel death.*

The Cock is the symbol of France, and by extension, the cats and dogs replete with blood might describe the rabble during the Reign of Terror, under the Committee led by Robespierre. Revolutionary fervor grew so out of hand that in sixteen days, July 12–28, 1794, 1,285 victims died on the guillotine. Robespierre was certainly a tyrant but even he took fright at the horrors that were being perpetrated. On July 26 he renewed the Committee of Public Safety. Too late; Robespierre was arrested, but freed by the troops of the Commune who took him to a strange bed in the Hôtel de Ville. The National Guard recaptured him and he was shot in the jaw, not limbs. After a long night of agony he was executed without further trial on July 29 at the Place de la Révolution, now known as the Place de la Concorde.

Century II

II.XLIII

Durant l'eftoille cheuelue apparente,
Les trois grans princes feront faits
ennemis:
Frappés du ciel paix terre tremulente,
Pau, Timbre vndans, ferpent fus le bort
mis.

During the appearance of the bearded star, the three great princes will be made enemies. The tremulous peace on earth will be struck from the skies; the Po, the winding Tiber, a serpent on the shore.

The comet, a hairy star with a tail, was the emblem of Pope Leo XIII and Malachy gave him the motto *"Lumen in Caelo."* The motto seems to be the key to this quatrain because it was during his Papacy that the Triple Alliance, *trois grans princes,* was formed in 1881, with Germany, Austria and Italy allying against France. The tremulous nature of the peace probably refers to the Triple Entente which ultimately led to the First World War. The snake in line 4 is unclear.

Century II

II.XLIIII

L'aigle poufée entour de pauillons,
Par autres oyfeaux d'entour fera
chaffée:
Quand bruit des cymbres tube &
fonnaillons
Rendront le fens de la dame infenfée.

The eagle driven back from circling the tents will be harried by the other birds around him. Then when the cymbals, trumpets and bells sound, sense will be restored to a senseless woman.

The eagle, as always, stands for nineteenth century France and here seems to apply to Napoleon, driven back from Moscow and harried by the other birds of prey, Russia, Austria and Prussia.

The last two lines have two possible interpretations: They may refer to the martial music of the Royalist party, which brings France back to her senses, that is restores the monarchy of Louis XVIII— Nostradamus was a fervent Royalist. Alternatively, they may refer to Napoleon's second marriage, to Marie Louise of Austria, and the grief and distress of the Empress Josephine, *"dame infenfée."* It was a common popular belief that Napoleon's luck deserted him when he discarded Josephine de Beauharnais.

Century II

II.XLV

Trop le ciel pleure l'Androgyn[1] procrée,
Pres de ciel fang humain refpandu:
Par mort trop tard grand peuple recreé,
Tard & toft vient le fecours attendu.

The heavens weep too much at the birth of Androgyn; human blood is spilt near to heaven. It is too late for the great nation to be revived because of the death; the awaited help comes soon, yet too late.

Androgyn implies either an hermaphrodite or, more likely, a victorious king who causes some form of aerial warfare (line 2). The rest is very general.

Century II

II.XLVI

Apres grât troche[2] humain plus grâd
*   s'apprefte.*
Le grand moteur les fiecles renouuelle:
Pluye, fang, laict, famine, fer & pefte,
Au ciel veu feu, courant longue
*   eftincelle.*

After great misery for mankind an even greater one approaches, when the great cycle of the centuries is renewed. It will rain blood, milk; famine, war and disease. In the sky will be seen a fire, dragging a tail of sparks.

Again the great catastrophe of war and plagues which so occupied the millenniumists is linked with a comet appearing towards the end of a century. Comets were believed to have magical properties and to predict events of great import. The last important comet of this decade was Halley's Comet, which appeared in 1986, so presumably we are to understand that this great war shall occur between that time and the end of the century—in keeping with the various dates Nostradamus predicts for the war in the 1990s. Line 1 probably refers to the Second World War, *grât troche humain,* as the earlier appearance of Halley's Comet in this century was 1910, before the Great War.

---

[1]*Androgyn.* Androgens, the son of Minos of Crete, killed at Athens because he won all the prizes in a contest at the Pantheon.
[2]*troche.* Gk. *trikos,* misery.

Century II

II.XLVII

*L'ennemy grand vieil dueil meurt de
  poifon,
Les fouuerains par infiniz fubiuguez:
Pierres plouuoir, cachez foubz la toison,
Par mort articles en vain font alleguez.*

*The great enemy watches with grief the
man dying of poison; the kings are completely overcome. It rains stones, hidden
under the fleece, in vain articles asserted
by the deed.*

I cannot interpret this quatrain.

Century II

II.XLVIII

*La grand copie[1] qui paffera les monts,
Saturne en l'Arq tournant du poiffon
  Mars:
Venins cachés foubz teftes de faulmons,
Leur chief pendu à fil de polemars.[2]*

*The great army will pass over the moun-
tains when Saturn is in Sagittarius and
Mars moving into Pisces. Poison hidden
under the heads of donkeys. Their chief
hung with a cord, during war.*

The conjunction mentioned in line 2 is very rare. It last occurred
on July 17, 1951, and will next happen July 13, 2193. The only clue
in the 3rd line is that *saulmon* in Ancien Provençal means a donkey
head, so perhaps donkeys, but this gets one little further. Line 4 talks
about the hanging of a leader during wartime.

Century II

II.XLIX

*Les confeilliers du premier monopole,[3]
Les conquerants feduits par la Melite:
Rodes, Bifance pour leurs expofant
  pole,[4]
Terre faudra les pourfuiuans de fuite.*

*The counselors of the first conspiracy, vic-
tors won over the part of the Maltese.
Rhodes and Byzantium open their towns
to them, the fleeing pursuers will need
land.*

This probably refers to an obscure incident during the reign of the
Ottoman Empire, given the connection between Istanbul (Byzantium), Rhodes and Malta. The quatrain may well be retrospective.

[1]*copie. copia*, troops.
[2]*polemars*. Gk. *polemardes*, one who leads in war; or A.Pr. twine or thick string.
[3]*monopole*. Gk. *monopulum*, conspiracy.
[4]*pole*. Gk. *polis*, town.

Century II

II.L

Quand ceux d'Hainault, de Gâd & de
  Bruxelles,
Verront à Langres le fiege deuant mis:
Derrier leurs flancz feront guerres
  cruelles
La plaie antique fera pis qu'ennemis.

When the people of Hainault, Ghent and Brussels see siege laid before Langres. Behind their flanks will be dreadful wars, the older wound being worse than the enemies.

Hainault, Flanders (Ghent), and Brabant (Brussels) were the richest provinces of the sixteenth century Netherlands. Nostradamus envisages them in a state of war, besieging Langres, which was an important frontier city during the Hapsburg wars. Thus, line 3 could refer to the uprising of the Netherlands in 1568, two years after Nostradamus' death. But *la plaie antique?* Possibly this refers to some internal dissension?

Century II

II.LI

Le fang du iufte à Londres fera faulte,
Bruflés par fouldres de vint trois les fix:
La dame antique cherra de place haute,
De mefme secte plufieurs feront occis.

The blood of the just will be demanded of London, burnt by fire in three times twenty and six. The ancient lady falls from her high position, and many of the same denomination will be killed.

The only great fire occurring in London in a year '66 (three times twenty plus six) is the Great Fire of London 1666. Neither before nor since has there been anything to equal it. This is an interesting quatrain because the date is definite enough to be checked historically. It was quite common in the 16/17 centuries to leave off the figures denoting the century from a date, i.e., 1666 is written '66. This can be seen on many gravestones in France and England of the period. It may also be a result of Nostradamus' natural caution.

The *dame antique* is usually interpreted as St. Paul's Cathedral, in the City of London, inside whose porch was a large statue of the Virgin Mary. According to the contemporary sources, this fell on people seeking refuge from the fire. Many people rushed to St. Paul's and other stone buildings in an effort to escape the fire. Sadly the heat and smoke were so intense that they did not escape, nor were the buildings unscathed. The *iufte fang* is understood as meaning that the victims of the fire did not deserve their fate. This quatrain is linked with II.LIII by the key words *iufte fang* and *grand dame.*

Century II

II.LII

Dans plufieurs nuits la terre tremblera:	*For several nights the earth will shake; in*
Sur le printemps deux effors fuite:	*the spring, two great upheavals in succes-*
Corinthe, Ephefe aux deux mers nagera,	*sion. Corinth and Ephesus will swim in*
Guerre s'efmeut par deux vaillans de	*the two seas. War will be aroused by two*
luite. [1]	*men, valiant in combat.*

It has been suggested that Corinth and Ephesus represent the United Provinces which were engaged in a naval war with England in 1665–67. However, it takes some stretch of imagination to link Greece with them.

Century II

II.LIII

La grande pefte de cité maritime,	*The great plague in the maritime city will*
Ne ceffera que mort ne foit vengée	*not be stopped until death is avenged by*
Du iufte fang par pris damné fans	*the blood of a just man, taken and con-*
crime,	*demned for no crime. The great lady is*
De la grand dame par feincte	*outraged by the pretense.*
n'outraigée.	

If, as is commonly believed, the death of the just man refers to Charles I's execution in London, the maritime city, this links this quatrain with II.LI, the Great Fire following a year later upon the Great Plague, 1665. The outraged lady, whether the Church itself as designated by St. Paul's Cathedral, or the statue of the virgin, is outraged because soon afterwards Protestantism was re-established in England under William III.

Nostradamus is always hostile to any Protestant beliefs, not, I think because he was that fervent a Catholic, but because the trials and tribulations brought to Europe by Calvin were unforgivable to him. He wanted a secure niche in his society, being of Jewish origin, not the religious wars which persecuted his generation.

---

[1] *luite.* Romance. fight, combat.

Century II

II.LIIII

Par gent eftrange, & Romains
loingtaine,
Leur grand cité apres eaue fort troublee:
Fille fans trop different domaine,
Prins chef, ferreure[1] n'auoir efté riblée.[2]

Far from the Romans, by a foreign people,
their great city will be damaged by water.
A girl of not greatly different estate, taken
by the leader; the lock has not been
removed.

During a time of flooding, Rome will be attacked by a distant enemy. Whether this quatrain is to be understood literally or metaphorically is unclear.

Century II

II.LVI

Que pefte & glaiue n'a fceu definer,[3]
Mort dans le puys fommet du ciel
frappé:
L'abbé mourra quand verra ruiner,
Ceux du naufrage l'efcueil voulant
grapper.

One whom neither plague or sword could
kill, will die on a hilltop, struck from the
sky. The abbot will die when he sees the
people, ruined in the shipwreck, trying to
hold on to the reef.

Someone killed by lightning, having lived a charmed life for many years, together with a shipwreck. I cannot interpret this quatrain.

Century II

II.LVII

Auant conflict le grand tombera,
Le grand à mort, mort, trop fubite &
plainte,
Nay imparfaict: la plus part nagera,
Aupres du fleuue de fang la terre tainte.

Before the battle the great man will fall,
the great one killed, death too sudden and
lamented. Born imperfect, he will go the
greater part of the way: near the river the
ground is stained with blood.

Mort, trop fubite implies a death before it is due, a murder or assassination. *Nay imparfaict* implies someone suffering from some type of deformity. I believe this verse applies to John F. Kennedy's stand against Khrushchev over the Cuban missiles. The Russian fleet certainly came "the greater part of the way," before turning back. It was

---

[1]*ferreure.* Almost certainly a misprint for *serreure,* lock.
[2]*riblée.* O.F. *ribler,* to pillage, rob.
[3]*definer.* O.F. die, finish, decide.

after this confrontation that Kennedy was killed in Dallas *trop subite et plainte*. The infirmity *(nay imparfaict)* may refer to the back trouble he suffered during his Presidency, which was so severe that he normally had to wear a brace all the time for relief. Equally, it might refer to his morals, as Kennedy was a great womanizer.

Century II

II.LVIII

Sans pied ne main dend ayguë & forte,
Par globe[1] au fort de port & lainé nay:
Pres du portail defloyal tranfporte,
Silene[2] luit, petit grand emmené.

Without either foot or hand, strong and sharp teeth, through the crowds to the fortified harbor, with the eldest born. He crosses over near the gates, treacherous. The moon shines little, great pillage.

Some commentators interpret the last line as "the moon shines, the great little man carried off," to mean Napoleon. They apply the same interpretation to *petit grand* in II.LXXXV. But I am not wholly convinced by either quatrain.

Century II

II.LIX

Claffe Gauloife par appuy de grande garde,
Du grand Neptune, & fes tridens fouldars:
Rongée Prouence pour fouftenir grand bande,
Plus Mars Narbon par iauelotz & dards.

The French fleet through the support of the main guard of great Neptune and his trident warriers; Provence ravaged to sustain this great band. Moreover, fighting at Narbonne, with javelins and arrows.

Turkey was the dominant naval power in the Mediterranean during Nostradamus' lifetime, so the "trident troops" are probably the Turks. There does not appear to have been any trouble in Narbonne at this time, so I think this is a failed, or retroactive quatrain, referring to events before Nostradamus' birth.

[1]*globe*. L. *globus*, crowd or throng.
[2]*Silene*. Gk. *selene*, moon.

Century II

II.LX

La foy Punicque en Orient rompue,
Grand Iud[1] & Rofne, Loyre & Tag[2]
  changeront:
Quand du mulet la faim fera repue,
Claffe efpargie,[3] fang & corps
  nageront.

Faith with Africa is broken in the East.
Great Jordan, Rosne, Loire and Tagus
will change. When the hunger of the mule
is slaked, the fleet is scattered and bodies
swim in blood.

This probably refers to the many troubles in Africa—several countries there have strong links with China, the Middle East, *Grand Iud,* and France. Spain and Portugal are less influential there now, but I am still tempted to place this unresolved quatrain in the twentieth century.

Century II

II.LXI

Euge,[4] Tamins,[5] Gironde & la
  Rochele,
O fang Troyen Mort au port de la
  flefche:
Derrier le fleuue au fort mife l'efchele,
Pointes feu grand meurtre fus la
  brefche.

Bravo, men of the Thames, Gironde and
La Rochelle, O Trojan blood, killed by an
arrow at the harbor. Beyond the river the
ladder is put up against the port. Flashes
of fire, great slaughter in the breach.

Nostradamus refers in I.XIX to the legend of the French royal family descending from the Trojans *(fang Troyen),* but this bloodline had finished by the time the English and French fought together on the same side. So it is probably being used to indicate French royalty in a general sense. There is not, however, any record of a prince of the blood being killed or wounded at a harbor.

---

[1]*Iud.* abb. for Jordan.
[2]*Tag.* abb. for Tagus.
[3]*efpargie.* O.F. *espargier,* to sprinkle.
[4]*Euge.* L. bravo, congratulations.
[5]*Tamins.* syncope of *Tamisiens,* people of the Thames.

Century II

II.LXII

Mabus puis toft alors mouera, viendra,
De gens & beftes vne horrible defaite:
Puis tout à coup la vengeance on verra,
Cent, main, foif, faim, quand courra la
    comete.

Mabus will soon die and there will hap-
pen a dreadful destruction of people and
animals. Suddenly, vengeance will ap-
pear, a hundred hands, thirst and hunger,
when the comet passes.

Again Nostradamus mentions a comet together with destruction and war, *la vengeance.* The "hundred hands" is very evocative of the many refugee camps all over the world where people are suffering from famine, "thirst and hunger." When Halley's Comet passed in 1986 there were famines in Africa, the Far East and South America. Is Mabus the name, possibly an anagram, of the Third Antichrist to come? I think it is more likely that he is envisaged as a forerunner, *puis tost alors mourra,* so the time of the Antichrist is still awaited. (See I.LXIII, VIII.LIX, VIII.LXXVII, X.LXXII, X.LXXIIII, X.LXXV.)

Century II

II.LXIII

Gaulois, Aufone[1] bien peu fubiugera,
Pan, Marne & Seine fera Perme l'vrie:
Qui le grand mur contre eux dreffera,
Du moindre au mur le grand perdra la
    vie.

The French will soon subdue Ansonia,
while the world, Marne and Seine will
make Perme drunk. He who raises the
great wall against them, the great one,
will lose his life from the least on the wall.

Perme l'vrie offers a most interesting possibility. In 1590 the duc de Parme was ordered to France from the Netherlands to help the Catholic Leaguers against Henri de Navarre. Parme was defeated by Henri at the Battle of Ivry, 1590. But he did not die until 1592, from wounds received from an unknown soldier in battle. Quite a close quatrain nonetheless.

---

[1]*Aufone,* Ausonia in southern Italy.

Century II

II.LXIIII

Seicher de faim, de foif, gent Geneuoife,
Efpoir prochain viendra au defaillir:
Sur point tremblant fera loy Gebenoife.[1]
Claffe au grand port ne fe peut acuillir.

The people of Geneva will dry up from
thirst and hunger, nearby hope will fail.
The law of the Cévennes will be at breaking point; the fleet cannot be received at
the great harbor.

After the revocation of the Edict of Nantes 1685 by Louis XIV, the
Calvinist people of Cévennes rose in revolt. The fleet may possibly
be trying to take supplies to Lake Geneva and is foiled.

Century II

II.LXV

Le parc enclin grande calamité,
Par l'Hefperie & Infubre fera:
Le feu en nef pefte & captiuité,
Mercure en l'Arc Saturn fenera.

In the feeble lists, great calamity throughout the West and Lombardy. Fire in the
ship, plague and captivity. Mercury in
Sagittarius, Saturn threatening.

This is an astrological dating, sadly not of much use. The commentator Wöllner gives the next date for this configuration as December,
2044. The last was in 1839, when there were no specific dangers to
the West and Italy. Things are no clearer if one takes *Hefperie,* the
West, to mean America.

Century II

II. LXVI

Par grans dangiers le captif eschapé,
Peu de temps grand a fortune changée:
Dans le palais le peuple est attrapé,
Par bon augure la cité assiegé.

The captive having escaped great dangers,
his fortune is greatly changed in a short
time. The people are trapped in the palace;
by good omen, the besieged city.

The captive who escapes great dangers and whose fortunes change
so dramatically in a short time is Napoleon when he escapes from
Elba on March 1, 1815. But this line can also be read inversely,
meaning that the good fortune will soon change back again, as happened at the defeat of Waterloo, 1815. The third line is interesting.
When Napoleon returned victorious to Paris after his escape, the
Parisian mob invaded the palace and court of Louis XVIII, and physi-

[1] *Gebenoife,* Cévennes in Switzerland.

cally carried their hero Napoleon on their shoulders up the stairs to the king's private chamber. The crowd was so enormous that no one could get in or out of the palace for some hours. The final line probably refers to Paris, the city besieged by the Allies, whose monarch will be restored *par bon augure,* which happened to Louis XVIII on July 8, 1815.

Century II

II.LXVII

Le blonde au nez forche viendra
   commettre,
Par le duelle a chassera dehors:
Les exilés dedans fera remettre,
Aux lieux marins commettant le plus
   fors.

The blond man will come into conflict with the hook-nosed one in a duel and will drive him out. He will restore the exiles, placing the strongest in the marine places.

The blond man was understood by authors of contemporary pamphlets to stand for the fair-haired William of Orange, who drove out James II in 1688. The Stuart party, *les exilés,* decided to reinstate James and put all their efforts into a sea battle. James based himself in Ireland and the French fleet came to his aid. In 1690, William and the Allies were badly beaten in a naval battle off Beachy Head, but on the same day William won the Battle of the Boyne. James II was forced to flee to France, from which he never returned. It took another two years for the British to subdue the French and assure maritime supremacy at Cap de la Hague in 1692.

Century II

II.LXVIII

De l'aquilon[1] les effors feront grands.
Sus l'Ocean fera la porte ouuerte:
Le regne en l'ifle fera reintegrand,
Tremblera Londres par voille
   defcouuerte.

In the North the efforts will be great. The harbor will be open across the ocean. The rule on the island will be re-established. London will be afraid of the fleet when it is sighted.

I believe this quatrain continues the action of II.LXVII, despite Nostradamus' claim that he mixed up all the quatrains. If this is the case, the great efforts, *effors feront grands,* in the North, are those of England's invader, William III of Orange. The English fleet, badly commanded at the time by the Earl of Torrington, lost several battles

[1]*aquilon.* L. North Wind, North.

to the French and Stuart fleets, particularly those of Beachy Head and Bounty Bay. It was William III's strength on land, not sea, that kept him on the throne. Line 2 could hold a second interpretation, that the seas were open and undefended, which allowed William III to cross uncontested to England. In line 3, the fact that island, *ifle,* is in the singular, rather than the plural, which Nostradamus always used for Britain, indicates that it means Ireland, where James II took refuge.

Century II
II.LXIX

Le Roy Gaulois par la Celtique dextre,
Voiant difcorde de la grand Monarchie:
Sus les trois pars fera florir fon fceptre,
Contre la cappe[1] de la grand
    Hierarchie.

A Gallic king from the Celtic right, seeing the discord of the great Monarchy will flourish his scepter over the three leopards, against the king of the great Hierarchy.

The key word to this quatrain is in line 3, *pars.* In another of his books, the *Horapollo,* Nostradamus describes three leopards of England in the same manner as the English heraldic lions. So this quatrain too, seems to follow on its two predecessors and continues the theme of the expulsion of James II of England by William III of Orange. William may be understood as the Celtic king from northern Gaul (Holland) who sees England in trouble under James II. It is interesting to note that Nostradamus makes no mention of war. William's was not a bloody invasion, but one of invitation. *Cappe,* as in other quatrains is the usual Nostradamus spelling of Capet, the then French royal line. The French were bitterly opposed to the establishment of the House of Orange in England, and allied themselves with the deposed James II and supplied him with troops and naval aid.

Century II
II.LXX

Le dard du ciel fera fon eftendue,
Mors en parlant: grande execution:
La pierre en l'arbre la fiere gent rendue,
Bruit humain monftre purge expiation.

The arrow from heaven will make its journey. Dead while speaking; a great execution. The stone in the tree, the pond nation brought down. The rumor of a human monster, purge and expiation.

[1]*Cappe.* Capet, one of the names of the French royal line until the last of the Bourbon kings.

Most commentators relate this quatrain to Napoleon, but I think it is too general and lacking in key words to be satisfactory. In theory, the theme is the Battle of Waterloo, 1815, and the arrow from the skies is understood as vengeance from heaven. The *grande execution* refers to the carnage of the battle, and the stone, possibly, to an axe which will cut down the Bonaparte line, *l'arbre*. France surrenders, expiates its guilt and the monster Napoleon is removed to St. Helena. Ingenious, if one can accept it.

Century II

II.LXXI

Les exilés en Sicile viendront,
Pour deliurer de faim la gent eftrange:
Au point du iour les Celtes luy faudront
La vie demeure à raifon: Roy fe range.

The exiles will come to Sicily to deliver the foreign nations from hunger. The Celts will fail them at daybreak. Life is governed by reason: the king joins as an ally.

Reason in line 3 suggests the Age of Reason during the French Revolution. The rest appears incomprehensible.

Century II

II.LXXII

Armée Celtique en Italie vexée,
De toutes pars conflict & grande perte:
Romains fuis, ô Gaule repoulfée,
Pres de Thefin,[1] Rubicon pugne[2]
incerte.

The Celtic Army will be troubled in Italy, great conflict and loss on both sides. O France repelled, flee the Romans. The battle of the Rubicon war (the river), Thessin is uncertain.

This quatrain sounds so specific, yet nothing it contains has happened since it was published in 1566. It is probably a retroactive prophecy. Lines 1–2 could well describe the Battle of Pavia in 1525, line 3 the strategy of the Imperial forces. Even so, Pavia was a definite victory for the Italians, not an uncertain one.

---

[1] *Thefin.* River Ticino, which flows into the Pau near Pavia.
[2] *Pugne.* L. *pugna*, battle.

Century II

II.LXXIII

Au lac Fucin[1] de Benac[2] le riuaige,
Prins du Leman[3] au port de
  l'Orguion:[4]
Nay de trois bras predict bellique image,
Parrois couronnes au grand
  Endymion.[5]

From the shore of Lake Garda to Fucino,
taken from Lake Geneva to the harbor of
Orguion. Born with three arms it predicts
a warlike semblance, through three kingdoms for the great Endymion.

Many wild interpretations have been suggested for this quatrain, including Allen's in 1948, that Endymion (the youth with the gift of eternal sleep) is a metaphor for the USA. I cannot understand this interpretation. Three arms and three kingdoms may refer to the triple tiara of the Pope, thus linking the USA with the Vatican States or an alliance of three Italian States.

Century II

II.LXXIIII

De Sens, D'Autun viendront iufques au
  Rofne,
Pour paffer outre vers les monts
  Pyrenées:
La gent fortir de la Marque d'Anconne,
Par terre & mer suiura à grans
  trainées.

From Sens, from Autun they will come as
far as the Rhône, to cross over the Pyrenees. The people leaving the Marches of
Ancona will follow in great trailing
(hordes) over land and sea.

Yet another confused quatrain. Leoni, 1961, suggests that the Pyrenees are a mistake for the Alps, which would help the geography, as Sens and Autun are in northeastern France, but the Rhône does not fit as it was not on the route to the Alps. If one accepts the mountains as the Alps, the quatrain describes an invasion of Italy; the Marches of Ancona stretch from Rimini to the north of Giulianova. However, even by Nostradamus' standards, to mistake the Alps for the Pyrenees seems rather farfetched. Probably a failed quatrain, as it does not fit into twentieth century geopolitical thought.

[1]*Fucin.* Lake Fucino in Italy, drained in 1876.
[2]*Benac.* Lake Garda, Italy.
[3]*Leman.* Lake Geneva, Switzerland.
[4]*Orguion.* possibly Organ in the south of France or Origano in Italy?
[5]*Endymion.* Gk. The youth loved by Selene, the Moon, who had the gift of eternal sleep.

Century II
II.LXXV

La voix ouye de l'infolit oyfeau,
Sur le canon du refpiral eftage:[1]
Si hault viendra du froment le boiffeau,
Que l'homme d'homme fera
* Antropophage.*[2]

The call of the unwelcome bird is heard on the chimney stack. Bushels of wheat will rise so high. As a result man will devour his fellow man.

The unwelcome bird on the chimney stack is usually interpreted as an owl, which is meant to bring warning of famine. The amassed bushels of wheat, *froment le boiffeau,* which are stacked in storage and not given to the starving bring the famines in Ethiopia and the Sudan in this century to mind. World famine is always Nostradamus' millennium warning as a presage to the Third World War.

Century II
II.LXXVI

Foudre en Bourgongne fera cas
* portenteux,*
Que par engin[3] *oncques ne pourroit*
* faire,*
De leur fenat facrifte fait boiteux.
Fera fçauoir aux ennemis l'affaire.

Lightning in Burgundy will reveal portentous events. Through trickery, a thing (achieved) that could never have been done. The lame priest will reveal affairs of the enemy to the Senate.

Charles Maurice de Talleyrand-Périgord is a suitable candidate for this quatrain. The lame priest, *facrifte fait boiteux,* fits him admirably. He became lame just before his fourth birthday when a chest of drawers fell on his foot, injuring him permanently. Destined by his family for the Church, he took orders in 1778, and the following year was made Bishop of Antin. By 1790 he totally identified with the revolutionaries and he was banned by the Pope in the following year. By 1807, he resigned his position as grand chamberlain to Napoleon because he disapproved of the Emperor's policies.

He secretly advised the Emperor Alexander I of Russia not to pressure Austria, despite Napoleon's wishes to the contrary. When Alexander I stayed at the Hôtel Talleyrand, he was advised by Talleyrand that the only solution for the French was the restoration of the

---

[1] *Sur le canon du refpiral eftage:* literally translated, on the pipe of the breathing floor. Some kind of machinery?

[2] *Antropophage.* Gk. *anthro-phagus,* man-eating.

[3] *engin.* L. *ingenium,* genius, trickery, ruse.

Bourbon kings. On April 1, 1814 Talleyrand convened the Senate, to "reveal affairs of the enemy to the Senat." They pronounced Napoleon to have forfeited his crown.

Century II
II.LXXVII

Par arcs feux poix & par feux
  repouffés,
Cris hurlements fur la minuit ouys:
Dedans font mis par les rampars caffez,
Par cunicules¹ les traditeurs² fuys.

Repulsed by bows, burning pitch and fire, cries and shouts will be heard in the middle of the night. They will get in through the broken defenses. The traitors escape through underground passages.

Too general to be of much interest.

Century II
II.LXXVIII

Le grand Neptune du profond de la
  mer,
De gent Punique³ & fang Gaulois
  meflé:
Les Ifles à fang pour le tardif ramer,⁴
Plus luy nuira que l'occult mal celé.

Great Neptune from the depths of the sea; of mixed African race and French blood, the islands remain bloody because of the slow one. It will harm him more than the badly concealed secret.

This quatrain may refer in part to modern Africa. It is, I think, a split quatrain. Neptune, as used by Nostradamus in II.LIX, refers to the Turkish fleet, a Moslem fleet, and to the Franco-Turkish agreements of Nostradamus' day. The Barbary pirates were based in northern Africa. However, it is possible that the "slow one" affecting the Africans and the French *à fang* may refer to AIDS, which has brought so much harm to Europe from Africa and is still regarded as a plague disease. It has been a "badly concealed secret" for its victims for a long time and with no actual cure to date.

---

¹*cunicules.* L. rabbit, by extension burrow, passage.
²*traditeurs.* L. *traditor,* traitor.
³*Punique.* Carthage in North Africa.
⁴*ramer.* Romance. to remain, stay.

Century II
II.LXXIX

La barbe crefpe & noire par engin,
Subiuguera la gent cruelle & fiere:
Le grand CHIREN oftera du longin[1]
Tous les captifs par Seline[2] baniere.

The man with the curly black beard through his skill will subdue the cruel and proud nation. The great Chiren will take from afar everyone captured under the Turkish banner.

The clue to this quatrain lies in the interpretation of *CHIREN*. All commentators have taken it as an anagram for HENRIC, an alternative spelling of HENRI. If that is so, this verse may be attributed to the Battle of Lepanto, 1571, which forced over 1,500 Christian slaves into the Turkish fleet, *captifs par Seline baniere.* The snag to this is that Charles X was King of France at this time; Henri III did not accede until 1574. Perhaps the word *CHIREN* is used as a symbol for France? It was at Lepanto that the Christians raised their last crusade against the Turks, of the crescent banner, *seline.* Don John of Austria who commanded them was dark and bearded, *barbe crefpe et noir.*

Century II
II.LXXX

Apres conflict du lefé l'eloquence,
Par peu de temps fe trame faint repos:
Point l'on n'admet les grands à
    deliurance,
Des ennemis font remis à propos.

After the battle, the eloquence of the man left behind, brings a short respite for a short time. None of the great will be allowed to go free. They are delivered to their enemies at the proper time.

A quatrain that could apply to many situations.

Century II
II.LXXXI

Par feu du ciel la cité prefque adufte,
L'vrne[3] menace encor Ceucalion,[4]
Vexée Sardaigne par la Punique fufte,[5]
Apres que Libra lairra fon Phaeton.

The city is almost burned to ashes by fire from the sky. Water again threatens Deucalion. Sardinia is vexed by the African fleet after Libra has left Leo.

[1]*longin.* A.Pr. *longinc,* far off, distant.
[2]*Seline.* Gk. *Selene,* moon, crescent.
[3]*Vrne.* Metaphor for water, flooding.
[4]*Ceucalion. Deucalion* in all other editions. Probably a misprint.
[5]*fufte.* L. *fustus,* low oared galley.

This quatrain, with its description of a city destroyed by fire which comes from the air (bombing or something similar), appears to be set in the twentieth century. The devastation is followed by a flood; Deucalion was the equivalent of Noah in Greek mythology. In astrological geography, Libra normally stands for Austria.

Century II

II.LXXXII

Par faim la proye fera loup prifonnier,	*Through hunger the wolf will make the*
L'affaillant lors en extreme detreffe,	*prey prisoner. Then the attacker is in great*
Le nay[1] ayant au deuant le dernier,	*distress, the elder holding the younger in*
Le grand n'efchappe au milieu de la	*front. The great man cannot escape in the*
preffe.	*middle of the crowd.*

It is possible to invert the meaning of line 1, but this does not help to interpret the quatrain.

Century II

II.LXXXIII

Le gros traffic d'vn grand Lyon changé,	*The great trade of great Lyons changed,*
La plus part tourne en priftine ruine.	*the main part falls into early rain. A prey*
Proye aux foldats par pille vendengé:[2]	*to the soldiers pillaging a harvest. Fogs*
Par Iura mont & Sueue[3] bruine.	*through the mountains of Jura and Switzerland.*

Nicollaud interprets this quatrain through the memories of the marquis de Beauregard, who writes that during October, 1795, when the Revolutionary troops were putting down an uprising at Lyons, "we saw large crowds of peasants . . . who with great empty sacks rushed to Lyons to pillage the town." This was the end of a two-month siege and many of the town's inhabitants had been massacred. Fog or mist would have been normal over the mountain areas at that time of year.

---

[1]*Le nay.* Probable corruption of *l'aisné,* elder.
[2]*vendengé.* O.F. harvest, vendage.
[3]*Sueue.* L. *Suevi,* Swiss.

Century II
II.LXXXIIII

Entre Campaigne, Sienne, Flora,
  Tuftie,
Six mois neuf iours ne ploura vne
  goutte:
L'eftrange langue en terre Dalmatie,
Courira fus: vaftant la terre toute.

Between Campania, Sienna, Florence and
Italy there will be not a drop of rain for
six months and nine days. A foreign language will be spoken in Dalmatia. It will
overrun the country devastating all the
land.

This must be a failed quatrain. Such a specific drought has never
been recorded in Dalmatia, which in Nostradamus' time belonged to
the Venetians and was surrounded by the Ottoman Empire. Did
Nostradamus think it would be taken by the Turks, *eftrange langue?*

Century II
II.LXXXV

Le vieux plain barbe foubs le ftatut
  feuere,
A Lyon faict deffus l'Aigle Celtique:
Le petit grant trop outre perfeuere,
Bruit d'arme au ciel: mer rouge
  Lyguftique. [1]

Beneath the severe authority of the old
man with the flowing beard, he is put
above the Celtic Eagle at Lyons. The
small great one presses on too far; noise of
weapons in the sky; the Ligurian sea is
red.

The small great one, *petit grant,* was possibly used to describe
Napoleon in II.LVIII, and the theme may be continued here. The
Celtic Eagle is certainly the eagle of the French; the Hapsburg Imperial Eagle cannot be described as Celtic. But who is the bearded man
who is more important than Napoleon at Lyons?

Century II
II.LXXXVI

Naufrage à claffe pres d'onde
  Hadriatique,
La terre tremble efmeüe fus l'air en
  terre mis:
Egypte tremble augment Mahometique,
L'Herault foy rendre à crier eft commis.

The fleet is wrecked near the Adriatic sea,
the earth trembles, rises into the air and
falls again. Egypt trembles; Mahometan
increase. The herald is sent for to ask for
surrender.

The key words in this interesting quatrain are Adriatic, Egypt and
herald. In 1799, during Napoleon's expedition to Egypt, the British

[1]*Lyguftique,* Ligurian, N.E. Mediterranean.

and French fleets met on the Nile. The French were roundly defeated by Sir Richard Abercromby. From this victory, Napoleon led his troops against the Turks at Acre, but during the siege his men were struck by the plague and so Napoleon decided that he would withdraw back to Egypt if he could not break down the Turkish resistance. A herald was sent to demand the surrender of Acre, but when the Turks refused, Napoleon had to lift the siege.

Century II

II.LXXXVII

Apres viendra des extremes contrees,	*Later a German prince will come from a*
Prince Germain, deffus le throfne doré:	*distant country, to a golden throne. Servi-*
La seruitude & eaux rencontrees,	*tude is accepted from over the seas. The*
La dame ferue, fon temps plus n'adoré.	*lady subordinated, in her time no longer*
	adored.

This quatrain is a perfect description of the accession of George of Hanover to the English throne as George I, in 1714. He came from Germany, a distant country, and was a German Prince. The word *germain* also means "cousin." George was a cousin, a German one, of Queen Anne, so this may well be one of Nostradamus' famous double meanings. The English throne was regarded in Europe as a great prize, *doré*. The great lady, Anne, or Britain, was subordinate in that George was offered the English throne, it was not won in battle. The *dame ferue* may also refer to the old religion, Catholicism, which ceased finally to be the major religion in Britain.

Century II

II.LXXXVIII

Le circuit du grand faict ruineux,	*The completion of a great, disastrous ac-*
Le nom feptiefme du cinquiefme fera:	*tion, the name of the seventh will be that*
D'vn tiers plus grand l'eftrange	*of the fifth. Of the third (name) a greater,*
belliqueux,	*foreign warmonger. Paris and Aix will*
Mouton, Lutece,[1] Aix ne garantira.	*not remain in Aries.*

This is an interesting quatrain and may be one of those that influenced Catherine de' Medicis in her long conversations with Nostradamus concerning the fates of her husband and children. Catherine had seven Valois children, of whom the fifth will be the seventh and last king, Henri III *(tiers)*, whose younger brother, the duc d'Alençon, had died earlier and whose sister Marguerite had

[1] *Lutece.* L. *Lutetia,* Paris.

married a foreigner with the same name as his, Henri de Navarre, *l'eftrange belliqueux.* Henri de Navarre became Henri IV of France through war; he besieged Paris before France capitulated. He started the siege in the sign of Aries (March–April), after the battle of Ivry, 1590. It is therefore reasonable to suppose that line 1 refers to the Massacre of St. Bartholomew, as it was this action that finally sowed the destruction, *circuit ruineux,* of the Valois and one of the reasons, it is claimed, behind the assassination of Henri III by Jacques Clément, which left the throne open for Henri de Navarre.

Century II

II.LXXXIX

Vn iour feront demis les deux grands
    maiftres,
Leur grand pouuoir fe verra augmenté:
La terre neufue fera en fes hauts eftres,
Au fanguinaire le nombre racompté.

One day the two great leaders will be friends; their great power will be seen to grow. The new land will be at the height of its powers. To the man of blood the numbers are reported.

Most editions of this quatrain have the word *demis* written as *d'amis.* I have accepted this version because to understand the word *demis* as meaning "halved" would make nonsense of line 2. The two *grands maiftres* I understand as being the great powers, and line 3, the *terre neufue* of America links these things together. It could possibly mean the New World, but that also implies the USA. The quatrain seems to state that when America is at the height of its powers, it allies with the other great power, Russia. Then, the man of blood, the Third Antichrist, will start to assess his position.

When I translated this quatrain in 1978 I put Russia in inverted commas with a question mark. But now is the age of glasnost and Gorbachev and this seems quite acceptable, but not so good in prediction VI.XXI. Nostradamus also states that the alliance will last only three years and seven months. Will Gorbachev be removed by the other leaders of the Communist party for being too ambitious? We shall see.

Century II

II.XC

Par vie & mort changé regne
   d'Ongrie, [1]
La loy fera plus afpre que feruice:
Leur grand cité d'vrtlemers plaincts &
   crie,
Caftor & Pollux[2] ennemis dans la lice.

Through life and death the rule of Hungary will be changed, the law becoming more bitter than obedience. Their great city calls out with howls and lamentations. Castor and Pollux are enemies in the field.

The life-and-death change in Hungary certainly occurred during the Revolution of 1957 when Premier Nagy renounced the Warsaw Pact on November 1. The Russians advanced into his country on November 4. The violence of the street fighting, the strictness of the new imported régime which followed, from which many thousands escaped to the West, is well documented. The great city of Budapest was occupied and badly damaged. The heavenly twins of the last line, Castor and Pollux, probably stand for the relationship between Russia and its satellite state of Hungary, *ennemis dans la lice.* I do not think that it is an astrological dating.

Century II

II.XCI

Soleil leuant vn grand feu l'on verra,
Bruit & clarté vers Aquilon tendants:
Dedans le rond mort & cris l'on orra,
Par glaiue, feu, faim, mort las
   attendants.

At sunrise a great fire will be seen, noise and light extending towards the North. In the globe death and cries are heard. Death awaits, through weapons, fire and famine.

If one applies this quatrain to the future, it is a very frightening one. It implies that a northern country—either Russia or America—will be bombed at sunrise. In a modern context, this can only mean an atomic explosion of some kind, which will be followed by a period of great devastation.

In I.II and V.LXXV Nostradamus states the destruction will be greater in America, but the victor will be born "on American soil," and therefore, hopefully, sympathetic to the West. (See also VII.XXI, VIII.LXXVII, VIII.LIX, X.LXXVII.)

---

[1]*Ongrie.* Hungary
[2]*Caftor & Pollux.* Gemini, the heavenly twins.

Century II

II.XCII

Feu couleur d'or du ciel en terre veu,
Frappé du haut nay, faict cas
*   merueilleux:*
Grand meurtre humain prinfe du grâd
*   nepeue,*
Morts d'efpactacles efchappe
*   l'orgueilleux.*

From the sky, fire, the color of gold is seen on earth, struck by the high born, a marvelous event. Great slaughter of humanity. A nephew taken from the high born one. Death to the spectator, the proud one escapes.

The probable clue to this quatrain is the word nephew, *nepeue*, in line 3. Nostradamus describes Napoleon III, the nephew of Napoleon, several times in this way. The second line refers to an incident on August 2, 1870, when, during an assassination attempt, a bullet hit the ground by the prince imperial's feet, an event much publicized in the newspapers. The spectator, the prince imperial, was captured during the French capitulation of 1870, but escaped death. He was the last of the French kings and emperors as Louis XVIIII.

Century II

II.XCIII

Bien pres du Tymbre preffe la
*   Lybitine;[1]*
Vn peu deuant grand' inondation:
Le chef du nef prins, mis à la fentine,[2]
Chafteau, palais en conflagration.

Very near the Tiber death hurries, a short while before a great flood. The captain of the ship taken, put into the bilges; the castle and the palace burned down.

Tiber normally stands for Rome, linked here with the captain of the ship (the Barque of St. Peter)? This implies that a pope will come to a dreadful end before a flood. The castle and palace would be Sant' Angelo and the Vatican.

Century II

II.XCIIII

Grand Pau grand mal pour Gaulois
*   receura,*
Vaine terreur au maritin Lyon:
Peuple infiny par la mer paffera.
Sans efchapper vn quart d'vn million.

Great Po will suffer great harm from a Frenchman, a vain terror to the maritime Lion. An infinite number of people will cross the sea and a quarter of a million will not escape.

[1]*Lybitine.* L. *Libitina,* goddess of Death.
[2]*fentine.* L. *sentina,* bilges, dregs.

Italy, the Po, suffered greatly under Napoleonic rule, and Napoleon also terrified the maritime British Lion, but in vain, *vaine terreur*, as he did not manage to invade Britain. Napoleon led a great army across the seas to Europe, and at least a quarter of a million men died either during campaigns or from the plague.

Century II
II.XCV

Les lieux peuplez feront inhabitables:
Pour champs auoir grande diuision:
Regnes liurez à prudents incapables,
Lors les grands freres mort &
  deffention.

The unpopulated lands will become uninhabitable; great disagreement in order to obtain lands. Kingdoms given to a man incapable of prudence. Then for the great brothers, death and dissension.

Some commentators apply this to the present or near future on the strength of line 1. The last line could refer to the three Kennedy brothers, as there has been no other set of important brothers to whom one can relate this line during the last half of the century. (See VIII.LXVII, and VII.LXXVII, also II.XCI.)

Century II
II.XCVI

Flambeau ardent au ciel foir fera veu,
Pres de la fin & principe du Rofne:
Famine, glaiue: tard le fecours pourueu,
La Perfe tourne enuahir Macedoine.

A burning torch will be seen in the sky at night, near the foundation and source of the Rhône. Famine, weapon; help provided too late, Persia will turn and invade Macedonia.

The most specific part of this quatrain is line 4. Nostradamus predicts that the Persians, never part of the Ottoman Empire, would inflict great defeat upon the Turks, Macedonia, in order to open up the Balkans. If the rest is to be accepted, he states that a light in the sky will be seen from the source of the Rhône, at the Furka Pass, as far as the mouth of the river west of Marseilles.

Century II
II.XCVII

Romain Pontife garde de t'approcher,
De la cité que deux fleuues arroufe,
Ton fang viendras aupres de là cracher,
Toy & les tiens quand fleurira la rofe.

Roman pontiff, beware of approaching a city watered by two rivers. You will spit blood in that place, both you and yours, when the roses bloom.

The only pope who suffered in a city between two rivers was Pius VI, who was imprisoned at Valence by the French after they had taken Rome in 1799. The two rivers are the Rhône and the Saône at Lyons. Pius VI died spitting blood, from an attack of acute gastro-enteritis in the summer, *quand fleurira la rofe,* on August 29, 1799. His people *(les tiens)* were the thirty-two priests imprisoned with him. The word *rofe* (red) may have the typical Nostradamus double meaning of the color of the Revolutionaries and of the blood they shed. A convincing quatrain.

Century II

II.XCVIII

Celuy du fang reperfe[1] le vifage,
De la victime proche facrifiée,
Tonant[2] en Leo augure par prefage,
Mis eftre à mort lors pont la fiancée.[3]

His face is spattered with the blood of a newly sacrificed victim. Jupiter and Leo warn through prophecy. He will be put to death for the promised one.

I can find no explanation for this quatrain.

Century II

II.XCIX

Teroir[4] Romain qu'interpretoit augure,
Par agent Gauloyse par trop sera vexée:
Mais nation Celtique caindra l'heure,
Boreas,[5] claffe[6] trop loing avoir pauffee.

Roman land that the augur interprets will be greatly molested by the French nation. But the French will come to dread the time of the North wind, having driven their fleet too far.

The Papal States were enveloped into the French Empire in 1810. But by 1812 Napoleon is suffering from the defeat of his Russian campaign due mainly to the cold weather *(Boreas)* and the folly of his overdeployment of troops. The fleet *"claffe"* may refer to the earlier defeat at Trafalgar.

---

[1]*reperfe.* L. *respergere,* to sprinkle, splash.
[2]*Tonant.* L. *Tonans,* Jupiter, the Murderer.
[3]*fiancée.* R. promise or assurance; L. bride.
[4]*Teroir.* L. *terra,* land.
[5]*Boreas.* L. north wind.
[6]*claffe.* L. *classus,* fleet.

Century II

II.C

Dedans les isles si horrible tumulte,	*Within the islands will be so dreadful a*
Bien on n'orra qu'vne bellique brigue	*tumult although only the warlike party is*
Tant grand fera des predateurs	*heard. So great will be the threat of the*
l'insulte,	*plunderers that they will come to join in*
Qu'on se viendra ranger à la grand	*the great alliance.*
ligue.	

Line 4 gives the clue. It refers to the *Grand Succurso* raised by all the Christian powers sent to Malta in 1565 in order to save Europe. The great alliance is probably the supranational order of Malta's Grand Knights, *les isles,* allied to the Christian forces.

Century III

III.I

Apres combat & bataille nauale,	*After the combat and naval battle, great*
Le grand Neptune à fon plus haut	*Neptune in his highest belfry. The red ad-*
befroy:	*versary will become pale with fear, putting*
Rouge auerfaire de peur viêdra pafle	*the great Ocean into a state of terror.*
Mettant le grand Ocean en effroy.	

This appears to be a failed quatrain. In II.LIX, Nostradamus uses Neptune as a synonym for the Turkish and Algerian fleets who were ravaging the Mediterranean. The Spanish flag is red, they were their adversaries, but of course red can also be understood as "bloodlike." It is here the quatrain fails. The Spanish, far from *viêdra pafle,* won the battle with the Turks at Lepanto in 1571. However, the Barbary Corsairs continued to dominate the Mediterranean for some time to come. This leads into the following quatrain III.II.

Century III

III.II

Le diuin verbe donrra à la fubftance,
Côprins ciel terre, or occult au laict[1]
    myftique:
Corps, ame, efprit ayant toute
    puiffance,
Tant foubz fes pieds comme au fiege
    Celique.[2]

The divine word will give to the substance
(that which) contains heaven and earth,
occult gold in the mystic act. Body, soul
and spirit are all powerful. Everything is
beneath his feet, as at the seat of heaven.

I believe this verse to be an important description of Nostradamus' experiences with the occult, *diuin verbe*, when he is prophesying. The substance is, in this case, the bowl of water on a brass tripod, mentioned in I.I, in which is portrayed the various revelations of the *Prophéties*. The *diuin verbe* may be the incantation used by Nostradamus—his mantra—which makes him all-powerful in body and spirit. The last line could mean that during these sessions Nostradamus felt disembodied, a common enough mystic experience, with everything at his feet and he looking down, "as at the seat of heaven."

Century III

III.III

Mars & Mercure & l'argent[3] ioint
    enfemble,
Vers le midy extreme siccité:
Au fond d'Afie on dira terre tremble,
Corinthe, Ephefe lors en perplexité.

With Mars, Mercury and the Moon in
conjunction towards the South, there will
be a great drought. An earthquake will be
reported from the depths of Asia; both
Corinth and Ephesus then in a troubled
state.

This is the second and only other reference to a linking of Corinth and Ephesus. The first can be found in II.LII, where I interpret them allegorically as standing for England and Holland. When there is a great drought in the south, could Nostradamus mean Africa rather than the conventional interpretation of *midi*, southern France, there will be earthquakes in Asia, and England and Holland will have problems. Possibly the IRA terrorists, and those of many other outlawed organizations, who find a safe house among the Dutch? But if Corinth

[1]*laict.* certainly misprint for *faict,* deed, found in other editions.
[2]*Celique.* O.F. celestial, heavenly.
[3]*argent.* an alchemistic term for the moon, because of its silvery color.

and Ephesus mean Africa Minor, perhaps this quatrain has not been fulfilled. I cannot interpret line 1, although it must be an astrological dating.

Century III
III.IIII

Quand feront proches le defaut des lunaires, *De l'vn à l'autre ne diftant grandement,* *Froid, siccité, danger vers les frontieres,* *Mefme où l'oracle a prins commencement.*	When the downfall of the lunar ones is very close, they will not be very distant from one another. Cold, drought, danger around the frontiers, even where the oracle had its source.

The people of the moon, *lunaires,* are normally described as people of Islam, of the crescent flag. Two Islamic countries who are very close to each other and near a state of collapse are obviously Iran and Iraq, who were at war for close on nine years, and who, certainly more so in the case of Iran, exhausted most of their manpower, and even that of their twelve-year-old boys, who were sent in waves in advance of the more experienced troops, to find any mines, etc., rather in the manner of World War I. As they share a common frontier where there is cold and danger, this seems to strengthen the interpretation. If the oracle has his source here, it may refer to the mysterious Perse, who elsewhere in the quatrains is reputed to be born in the Middle East and will be involved with the coming of the Third Antichrist in some way or another.

Century III
III.V

Pres loing defaut de deux grands luminaires, *Qui furuiendra entre l'Auril & Mars:* *O quel cherté mais deux grans debonnaires,* *Par terre & mer fecourront toutes pars.*	Not long after the eclipse of two great moon signs which will occur between March and April, what a great loss. But two great good influences will help on all sides, by land and sea.

This may follow on the last quatrain. If so, we can expect a cessation of hostilities between Iran and Iraq between March and April, or in the sign of Aries. The two great good influences for peace are presumably America and any of the three European powers trying to keep peace in the Gulf—England, France, and Italy *(par terre & mer)*.

A state of cease-fire has been declared by the United Nations in August, 1988, so perhaps peace will be finalized in March/April of 1989?

Century III

III.VI

Dans temple clos le foudre y entrera,
Les citadins dedans leur fort greuez:
Cheuaux, boeufs hommes, l'ôde mur
  touchera,
Par faim, foif, foubs les plus foibles
  armez.

Lightning will strike inside the closed temple and harm the citizens in their stronghold. Horses, cattle, men, the flood will reach the walls; through hunger and thirst, those armed beneath the weakest.

If the temple stands for a church, nineteenth century commentators accept that this quatrain refers to a famous incident in 1819 at Châteauneuf, when a church was struck by lightning. Nine people were killed and eighty-two injured among the congregation. But this seems rather flimsy to me, and the last line does not fit. I think this is probably a failed quatrain.

Century III

III.VII

Les fugitifs, feu du ciel fus les piques.
Conflict prochain des corbeaux
  s'esbatans,
De terre on crie aide fecours celiques,
Quand pres des murs feront les
  combatans.

The fugitives, the weapons with fire from heaven. The next conflict will be that of the flying crows. They call upon earth and heaven for help, when the aggressors draw near the walls.

This almost certainly describes the fall of France in 1940, when both the French army and multitudes of refugees were driven back in confusion along the roads to Paris. They were strafed and gunned down by German planes *corbeaux s'esbatans*. The crows could also be a literal meaning in that they picked at the bodies of the dead lying on the roadsides. The aggressors are the German forces about to march upon Paris.

Century III
III.VIII

Les Cimbres ioints auecques leurs voifins, *Depopuler viendront prefque l'Efpaigne:* *Gens amaffez, Guienne & Limofins,* *Seront en ligue, & leur feront compaigne.*	*The Cimbrians, allied with their neighbors, will come to ravage almost all of Spain. People gathered in Guienne and Limousin will join in alliance with their company.*

The Cimbrians were a north German tribe who intermixed with the Teutones and vanished around 100 B.C. Therefore this quatrain may describe Germany and her neighbors Prussia and Italy, who supported the Fascist cause of Franco during the Spanish Civil War of 1936–39. The last two lines may refer to the wide support for Nazi policies in France during this period, or to the many French who went to fight for the insurgent armies in Spain. It must also be remembered that after the Spanish Republican army's defeat at Teruel in 1938, its soldiers actually took refuge in France. This was followed by a mass exodus of Spanish refugees into France in 1938 and early 1939. (See IX.XVI.)

Century III
III.IX

Bourdeaux, Rouan, & la Rochelle ioints, *Tiendront autour la grand mer Occeane,* *Anglois, Bretons, & les Flamans conioints,* *Les chafferont iufque au pres de Rouane.*	*Bordeaux, Rouen and La Rochelle allied will hold all around the open seas. The English, Bretons and Flemish together will drive them as far as Roanne.*

Despite the detailed place names and peoples, this quatrain remains completely obscure. Bordeaux and La Rochelle are close to each other, but Rouen is to the north. Roanne is on the upper Loire.

Century III

III.X

De fang & faim plus grande calamité,
Sept fois s'apprefte à la marine plage:
Monech¹ de faim, lieu pris, captiuité,
Le grand mené croc² en ferree caige.

Even greater calamity with blood and
famine. Seven times it approaches the sea-
shore. Monaco captured, in captivity from
hunger. The great golden one caught in
an iron cage.

Monaco was already a semi-independent state under the House of
Grimaldi in Nostradamus' time, but it has never been captured or
besieged. Many readers have written to me saying that they believe
line 4 to refer to Princess Grace of Monaco, she of the golden hair
and film star fame, dying in a car accident with her daughter Princess
Stephanie, *croc en ferree caige.*

Century III

III.XI

Les armes battre au ciel longue faifon,
L'arbre au milieu de la cité tombé:
Verbine,³ rongne, glaiue en face tyfon,
Lors le monarque d'Hadrie fuccombé.

The weapons fight in the sky for a long
time. The tree fallen in the midst of the
city. The sacred branch broken, a sword
opposite Tison, then the King of Hadrie is
fallen.

The first line of this quatrain appears to put it into the twentieth
century, with wars in the air, *armes battre au ciel.* But a far more
interesting legend may relate this quatrain to the assassination of
Henri IV in 1610, a seventeenth century version of the story of the
Angels of Mons of the First World War. Apparently when Henri IV
was assassinated by Ravaillac on May 14 of that year, there appeared
in the *Mercure Français* a story of a ghastly army seen marching in the
skies. Henri is the tree, the fount of his line, chopped down in the
center of Paris. He was the last of the direct Valois line, as he was
descended from Louis XIII, by his second wife, Marie de' Medicis.
Henri is sacred because he was an anointed king. He was actually
stabbed with a knife in the rue Ferroniers, not far from the corner
which branches off the rue Tison. It is this small detail which convinces me of the veracity of the quatrain.

¹*Monech.* L. *Moneceus,* Monaco.
²*croc.* L. *crocens,* yellow; O.F. *croquer,* to crunch; *croc.* Prov. a hook.
³*Verbine.* L. *verbene,* sacred branch.

Century III

III.XII

Par la tumeur de Heb, Po, Tag,
  Timbre, & Rome¹
Et par l'eftang Leman² & Aretin:³
Les deux grands chefs & citez de
  Garonne,
Prins mors noyez. Partir humain butin.

Because of the overflow of the Ebro, Po, Tagus, Tiber and Rhône; by the lakes of Geneva and Arezzo the two great, chief cities of the Garonne taken, dead, drowned. The human booty is shared out.

This is one of the many quatrains describing a flooding so vast it covers most of Europe, Spain and Portugal, Italy and France. Probably another general warning of the millennium, possibly the end result of the ozone gaps over the Arctic pole and the resultant greenhouse effect.

Century III

III.XIII

Par fouldre en l'arche⁴ or & argent
  fondu,
De deux captifs l'vn l'autre mangera:
De la cité le plus grand eftendu,
Quand fubmergee la claffe⁵ nagera.

Through lightning in the ship gold and silver are melted, the two captives will devour each other. The greatest one of the city is stretched when the fleet travels under water.

Line 4 certainly refers to a submarine fleet, and I imagine the lightning in the ship which dissolves metals is probably some form of undersea missile. It is possessed by both sides in the battle and creates mutual destruction, *l'vn l'autre mangera*. However, the quatrain is extremely vague as to actual time, place, etc.

¹*Rome.* misprint for Rhône in most editions.
²*Leman.* L. *Lemannus*, Lake Leman, Lake Geneva.
³*Aretin.* L. *Arentuis*, Arezzo.
⁴*l'arche.* L. *arx*, ship, barque, box.
⁵*claffe.* L. *classus*, fleet.

Century III

III.XIIII

Par le rameau¹ du vaillant perfonnage,
De France infime, par le pere infelice:
Honneurs richeffes, trauail en fon vieil
*   aage,*
Pour auoir creu le confeil d'homme
*   nice.²*

Through the offspring of a valiant personality, of weakened France due to an unfortunate father. Honors, riches and war in
his old age because he believed the counsel
of an inexperienced man.

It was Louis XV, son of the glorious but unfortunate Sun King, who
weakened France. He came to the throne when aged five, and his
Regency was totally governed by the duc d'Orléans. France deteri-
orated into such a poor financial state that it was declared bankrupt
under the banker John Law in 1712. The inexperienced man who
counseled the king badly was Fleury, his tutor and priest, who did not
come to Louis XV's aid until 1726, when he was already seventy-two.
Fleury's inexperience in politics helped towards the general unrest
which led to the attempted assassination of the king by Damiens in
1757. See the following quatrain.

Century III

III.XV

Coeur, vigueur, gloire le regne
*   changera,*
De tous points contre ayant fon
*   aduerfaire,*
Lors France enfance par mort
*   fubiuguera,*
Vn grand regent fera lors plus
*   contraire.*

The heart of the kingdom will change in
vigor and glory. On all sides its adversary
will be opposed. Then through death a
child will rule over France, the great Regent will be much to its detriment.

Yet another of Nostradamus' double quatrains. It continues with
the subject of Louis XV. The kingdom under his uncle, Louis XIV,
one of vigor and glory, will change when a child rules over France.
The great regent, Philippe, duc d'Orléans was the complete opposite
both in private and public life to his late brother, *aduerfaire.* There has
been no other underaged king and male regent of France since the
quatrains were published. The line "then through death a child will
rule over France" may refer to the popular rumor of the time that

¹*rameau.* literally branch, offshoot.
²*nice.* Romance. simple, inexperienced.

both the duc de Burgundy and the duc de Bretagne, Louis XV's grandfather and father, had been poisoned by the regent.

Century III

III.XVI

*Vn prince Anglois Mars à fon coeur de
    ciel,*
Voudra pourfuiure fa fortune profpere:
Des deux duelles l'vn percera le fiel,
Hay de luy, bien aymé de fa mere.

An English prince, Mars to his heart in the heavens, will wish to follow his prospering fortune. In two duels in one he will be pierced in the gallbladder. Hated by him, but well loved by his mother.

Almost certainly an unfulfilled quatrain. No English, nor even Scottish princes satisfy this prediction, and it seems unlikely that duels will take place in the future.

Century III

III.XVII

Mont Auentine brufler nuict fera veu,
*Le ciel obfcur tout à vn coup en
    Flandres:*
*Quand le monarque chaffera fon
    nepueu,*
*Leurs gês d Eglife commettront les
    efclâdres.*

Mount Aventine will be seen burning at night, when suddenly the sky at Flanders will be darkened. When the king drives out his nephew, their churchmen will act scandalously.

Since Mount Aventine is one of the hills of Rome it probably stands for Rome itself. The *ciel obscur* at Flanders may mean an eclipse of the sun, but I am unable to link it with a king. Napoleon however did commit great atrocities against the Roman Catholic Church: he abolished it and later imprisoned the Pope in France. He did not personally drive out his nephew, Napoleon III, but the latter was driven out from Holland as a child when his father King Louis abdicated. Line 1 may then refer to Napoleon's sack of Rome.

Century III

III.XVIII

Apres la pluye laict affés longuette,
En plufieurs lieux de Reims le ciel
  touché:
O quel conflict de fang pres d'eux
  s'apprefte,
Peres & fils Roys n'oferont approcher.

After the rather long milky rain several
places in Reims will be touched by light-
ning. O, what a bloody battle approaches
them, fathers and sons, kings will not dare
approach.

The rain of milk also occurs in the following quatrain, III.XIX.

Century III

III.XIX

En Luques fang & laict viendra
  pluuoir,
Vn peu deuant changement de preteur:[1]
Grand pefte & guerre, faim & foif fera
  voir
Loing où mourra leur Prince recteur.[2]

In Lucca it will come to rain blood and
milk, shortly before a change of governor.
Great plague and war, famine and
drought will appear far from where the
Prince and ruler lies.

Lucca was a duchy between Tuscany and Modena. Together with the rain of milk, we now have a rain of blood, a favorite of Roman historians. This also occurs in modern times, usually when red dust clouds from the Sahara or similar deserts are sucked up into rain clouds, and the resultant raindrops are red. Black rain fell after the atomic bombs were dropped on Japan in 1945. Sadly, the governor and the prince cannot be identified and so the whole quatrain remains an enigma. Some commentators now identify the blood and milk (semen) as indicating AIDS since they are the major source of infection by this disease.

[1]*preteur.* L. *praetor*, governor.
[2]*recteur.* L. leader, ruler.

Century III

III.XX

*Par les contrees du grand fleuue
  Bethique,* [1]
Loing d'Ibere [2] *au royaume de
  Grenade:* [3]
*Croix repouffees par gens
  Mahometiques,*
Vn de Cordube trahira la contrade. [4]

Through the lands of the great Guadalquivir River far from Spain, to the kingdom of Granada. The cross spurned by the Mohammedans, a man from Córdova will betray his country.

This quatrain is preoccupied with Spain. Granada, south of the Guadalquivir River, was the last Moorish outpost of Iberia, conquered in 1492. After its conquest by the Christians, Jews were allowed to remain provided they accepted Christianity. In 1610, the remainder of the Jewish colony were accused by Philip II of a lack of sincerity in their religious practices and turned out of Spain. This was despite the contract drawn up by Ferdinand and Isabella of Spain with Gonsalvo Fernández de Córdova, who had helped to negotiate the treaty. So Nostradamus was wrong in saying that he betrayed his country; his treaty was betrayed. *Cordube* is the key word in this quatrain.

Century III

III.XXI

Au Cruftamin [5] *par mer Hadriatique,
Apparoiftra vn horrible poiffon:
De face humaine & la fin aquatique,
Qui fe prendra dehors de l'amecon.*

Near the Conca by the Adriatic sea will appear a horrible fish with human features and of aquatic purpose; it will be caught without a hook.

Commentators disagree about this obscure quatrain. Garencières (1672) says that a mermaid-type creature, perhaps a manatee or a dugon, was seen near Rome in 1523, and Rondeletius records a similar happening in 1531. Edgar Leoni (1961) states in his commentary that the records of Cattolica, where the Conca flows into the Adriatic, show no such event. This quatrain is one that lends itself to wishful thinking.

[1]*Bethique.* L. *Baetis,* Guadalquivir River.
[2]*Ibere.* Gk. Spaniards, particularly around the Ebro.
[3]*Grenade.* Southern Spain.
[4]*contrade.* Pr. country.
[5]*Cruftamin.* L. *Crustumius,* River Conca.

Century III

III.XXII

Six iours l'affaut deuant cité donné:
Liuree fera forte & afpre bataille:
Trois la rendront & à eux pardonné,
Le refte à feu & fang tranche traille.

For six days the assault is made in front
of the city. It will be freed in a strong and
bitter fight. Three will hand it over, and
they will be pardoned: the rest will go to
the fire, bloody slaughter and slashing.

Another quatrain which is too specific to be of any value.

Century III

III.XXIII

Si France paffes outre mer lyguftique,[1]
Tu te verras en ifles & mers enclos:
Mahommet contraire, plus mer
    Hadriatique,
Cheuaux & d'Afnes tu rongeras les os.

France, if you cross the Ligurian sea, you
will find yourself besieged among islands
and seas. With Mahomet against you,
more so the Adriatic, you will gnaw the
bones of horses and asses.

France will get into difficulties if it marches against Yugoslavia
(across the Ligurian sea). This is probably a prediction of general
disaster for contemporary France and the Ottoman Empire. Nostradamus speaks of France in the singular, affectionate *"tu"* because
it was the country he loved above all.

Century III

III.XXIIII

De l'entreprinfe grande confufion,
Perte de gens, threfor innumerable:
Tu n'y dois faire encore tenfion[2]
France à mon dire fais que fois
    recordable.[3]

Great confusion results from the expedition, immense loss of men and treasure.
You must never attempt to expand there
again. France, take note of my prediction.

This seems to continue on from the previous quatrain and is not
a real prediction but a general warning against the Ottoman Empire.
Note again the use of the familiar tense of the verb *"(tu) fois recordable."*

[1]*lygustique.* L. *ligusticus,* Ligurian.
[2]*tenfion.* L. *tensio,* extension.
[3]*recordable.* O.F. memorable.

Century III

III.XXV

Qui au Royaume Nauarrois
paruiendra,
Quand de Sicile & Naples feront ioints:
Bigore & Landes par Foyx loron
tiendra,
D'vn qui d'Efpaigne fera par trop
conioint.

He who attains the kingdom of Navarre when Sicily and Naples are allies will hold Bigorre and Landes through Foix and Oloran, from one who will be too strongly allied with Spain.

The inheritor of Navarre is Henri IV. Sicily and Naples were joined together sporadically for centuries but this alliance was formalized only twice: first by Philip II of Spain on his marriage to Mary Tudor in 1554 and again by Joseph Buonaparte in the nineteenth century. Henri became king of Navarre in 1562 and king of France in 1594. All of the places in line 3 are situated in Navarre; Bigorre has a double meaning because *Bigorre* was the rallying cry of his Huguenot armies. Possibly the person who is too strongly allied with Spain, *par trop conoint,* may be Henri's cousin Elisabeth, daughter of Henri II of France, who married Philip of Spain in 1559. All the same, it is a rather unsatisfactory quatrain.

Century III

III.XXVI

Des Roys & Princes drefferont
fimulacres,
Augures, creuz efleuez arufpices:[1]
Corne, victime doree, & d'azur, d'acre,
Interpretez feront les extipices.[2]

They will raise up idols of kings and princes, augurers and hollow priests elevated. A victim, its horn gilded with gold and azure, dazzling, the entrails will be read.

I leave the interpretation to the reader.

---

[1]*arufpices.* O.F. auspices.
[2]*extipices.* L. *extispicus,* soothsayer.

Century III

III.XXVII

Prince libinique puiffant en Occident,
François d'Arabe viendra tant
*   enflammer,*
Sçauans aux lettres fera condefcendent,
La langue Arabe en François tranflater.

The Libyan prince will be powerful in the West, the French will be so enamored of Arabia. Learned in letters he will condescend to translate the Arab language into French.

The Libyan Prince who will become powerful in the West is surely President Gadaffi. His terrorist organization, the P.L.O., have strong connections with the French, who have pursued a less severe course with them, despite their being an avowed terrorist organization, than most European countries. The French have also had strong links with North Africa over many centuries. The last line is unclear. The first French-Arabic dictionary came out in 1505, just after Nostradamus was born. I cannot think of any other great works of literary merit translated in the present time which may link line 4 with Gadaffi.

Century III

III.XXVIII

De terre foible & pauure parentele,[1]
Par bout & paix paruiendra dans
*   l'Empire:*
Long temps regner vne ieune femelle,
Qu'oncques en regne n'en furuint vn fi
*   pire.*

A person possessing few lands and of poor parentage through intent and peace will attain to the Empire. For a long time a young woman shall reign; never has so bad an influence been exerted on the kingdom.

This is regarded by most commentators as a split quatrain, referring to two different people and circumstances. I am not certain. The first two lines are related as describing Henri de Navarre, whose court was renowned for its poverty and simplicity.

The second part is described as relating to Elizabeth I of England. However, Henri and Elizabeth only reigned contemporaneously between the years of 1594 and 1601. Henri achieved the kingship of the French empire. Elizabeth's Protestantism would rate the epithet *n'en furuint vn fi pire,* because of Nostradamus' fervent anti-Protestantism. She was a young girl when she acceded to the English throne and reigned for a very long time, nearly half a century. But there is always the possibility that the person of lowly origin, *pauure parentele,* could refer to the comparatively low estate of Anne Boleyn, Elizabeth's mother, and the poverty to which Elizabeth was subjected as a child.

[1]*parentele.* O.F. parentage, family line.

Century III

III.XXIX

Les deux nepueux en diuers lieux
*   nourris:*
Nauale pugne,[1] terre peres tombez:
Viendront fi haut esleuez enguerris,[2]
Venger l'iniure ennemis fuccombez.

He who in a struggle with a weapon in a
warlike deed, will carry off the prize from
one greater than he. Or night, six will
bring harm to his bed; naked, without his
armor, he will suddenly be surprised.

Two nephews will be brought up in different places. A naval battle, fathers
fallen to the ground. They will be greatly
elevated by making war to avenge their
injury; the enemies are overcome.

The nephews may possibly be those of the Constable of France,
Anne de Montmorency, but they were three, not two—Coligny, Châ-
tillon, and d'Audoulet. The question of war and avenging their honor
fits them but partly. This may well be a failed quatrain.

Century III

III.XXX

Celuy qu'en luitte & fer au faict
*   bellique,*
Aura porté plus grand que luy le pris:
De nuict au lict fix luy feront la pique,
Nud fans harnois fubit fera furprins.

He who in a struggle with a weapon in a
warlike deed, will carry off the prize from
one greater than he. Or night, six will
bring harm to his bed; naked, without his
armor, he will suddenly be surprised.

This refers to the sad story of the comte de Montgomery, who was
captain of the Scottish Guard under Henri II. He inadvertently
wounded the king in a festive tournament for the marriage of his
sister and daughter Elisabeth in 1559. Tragically, the king died ten
days later. Henri had given orders that he should be pardoned, but
Catherine demanded his life, determined to avenge her husband's
death. Montgomery fled to England as a Huguenot, and returned
later to Normandy to lead the rebellious Protestants.

After various successes in battle, he was surrounded by the Marshal
at Domfront and forced to surrender. Under the terms of the surrenders, his life was to be spared, but Catherine would have none of that.
Secretly, she sent six men of the royal guard to arrest him. He was
captured in his bed, *de nuict au lict,* on May 27, 1574, and sent under
Catherine's orders to the Conciergerie. It is not known what happened after this nor the manner of his dying. Nostradamus leaves that
out, too.

---

[1]*pugne.* L. *pugna,* battle.
[2]*enguerroir.* O.F. to fight, make war.

Century III

III.XXXI

Aux champs de Mede, d'Arabe &
d'Armenie,
Deux grans copies trois fois
s'affembleront:
Pres du riuage d'Araxes la mefgnie,
Du grand Soliman en terre tomberont.

On the battlefields of Media, Arabia and
Armenia, the two great armies will gather
three times. Near the border of Araxum,
the establishment of great Soliman will
fall to the ground.

Many commentators attribute this quatrain to events which occurred during Nostradamus' lifetime, particularly the Battle of Araxes, 1514. But James Lavers' opinion seems more likely to be correct. He ascribes it to the Battle of Lepanto, 1571, in which Don John of Austria beat Selin II, the son of Soliman. The battle of Lepanto was fought off Cape Papa, then known as Cape Araxum in the Mediterranean.

Century III

III.XXXII

Le grand fepulchre du peuple
Aquitanique,
S'approchera aupres de la Tofcane:
Quand Mars fera pres du coing
Germanique,
Et au terroir de la gent Mantuane.

The huge sepulcher for the French nation,
approaches from the direction of Italy.
When war is near the German corner and
in the hands of the Italian people.

A very good general quatrain on the Second World War, because of Nostradamus' vision of a war killing many Frenchmen, involving both Italy and Germany. Aquitaine stands for France, and Tuscany and Mantua for Italy. The war in the *coing Germanique* is obvious in that the Second World War was started by the Germans' marching into Poland.

Century III

III.XXXIII

En la cité où le loup entrera,
Bien pres de là les ennemis feront:
Copie eftrange grand pays gaftera,
Aux murs & Alpes les amis pafferont.

In the city which the wolf will enter, the
enemies will be very close by. A foreign
army will devastate the great country;
friends will pass by the walls and the Alps.

Unfortunately this quatrain has no link word other than the Alps. If we knew whose foreign army had devastated the unknown country, we might get somewhere. The wolf is presumably a traitor on the side of the enemy.

Century III

III.XXXIIII

Quand le deffaut du Soleil lors fera.
Sur le plain iour le monftre fera veu:
Tout autrement on l'interpretera,
Cherté n'a garde nul n'y aura pourueu.

When there is an eclipse of the sun in broad daylight, the monster will be seen. Many will interpret it in different ways. They will not care about money or make any provision for it.

Another quatrain impossible to interpret, as we are given no dating for the sun's eclipse. Since this is a comparatively common event the quatrain is even harder to decipher. Line 4 indicates an unexpected famine or drought for which no provision will have been made.

Century III

III.XXXV

Du plus profond de l'Occident
d'Europe,
De pauures gens vn ieune enfant
naiftra:
Qui par fa langue feduira grande
troupe,
Son bruit au regne d'Orient plus
croiftra.

From the deepest part of Western Europe a child will be born of a poor family, who will entice many people with his oratory. His reputation will grow even greater in the kingdom of the East.

This is an excellent example of Nostradamus' ambiguous quatrains, those which seem to fit various peoples at varying times. The truism that history repeats itself is made easier by the facts being so general in scope.

Most commentators ascribe the quatrain to either Hitler or Napoleon. I believe it to refer to Hitler, as Austria is better described as in deepest Western Europe *l'Occident d'Europe,* than Corsica, which is nearer the borders of Africa. If Corsica is preferred, *profond* must be translated as lowest.

Both Hitler and Napoleon came from comparatively humble origins. Both were famous for their personal magnetism and powers of oratory. This can be confirmed in Hitler's case by many films of events such as the Nuremberg rallies. But it is line 4 which convinces me most. The Kingdom of the East, Japan, allied with Hitler and fought bravely for him. The nearest Napoleon got to the East was Egypt. (See II.XXXIX.)

Century III
III.XXXVI

Enfeuely non mort apopletique,
Sera trouué auoir les mains mangees:
Quand la cité damnera l'heretique,
Qu'auoit leurs loix fe leur fembloit
   changees.

Burned, apoplectic but not dead, he will
be found to have gnawed his hands. When
the city condemns the heretic, who, it
seemed to them, had changed their laws.

The burned person who is *apopletique* presumably suffered from a stroke, and is buried, presumed dead. This is not an uncommon occurrence, even in the twentieth century with its vast amount of medical knowledge. His hands are hurt, banging against the lid of the coffin when he regains consciousness. Sadly, we are not told if he is rescued. The fact that this occurs when a city revolts against its leader is not specific enough to help identify either event.

Century III
III.XXXVII

Auant l'affaut l'oraifon[1] prononcee,
Milan prins d'aigle par embufches
   deceuz:
Muraille antique par canons enfoncee,
Par feu & fang à mercy peu receus.

A speech is proclaimed before the assault:
Milan, deceived by the ambush, is cap-
tured by the eagle. The ancient walls are
breached by cannon fire. In the fire and
the blood, few receive quarter.

This quatrain can be understood well through the linking of the Eagle, Napoleon, with Milan. Napoleon took the city twice; on May 15, 1796, and on June 2, 1800. It appears to be the first assault that is referred to here. Napoleon made a famous speech which was printed in most of the newspapers of Europe: "Soldiers, you are ill-fed and half-naked. The government owes you much but can do nothing for you . . ." It is said that the speech so rallied his men that the defending Austrians retired without making any further attempts to defend Milan.

It is possible that lines 3 and 4 could apply to the battle of Pavia, soon after the Milan assault, but at Pavia the inhabitants rose up against the French. The city walls were bombarded and breached and the city totally sacked. For *oraifon* see II.XXXV.

[1]*oraifon.* O.F. prayer, speech.

Century III

III.XXXVIII

La gent Gauloife & nation eftrange,
Outre les monts, morts prins &
 profligez:
Au mois contraire & proche de ◦
 vendange,
Par les Seigneurs en accord redigez.

The French people and a foreign nation
beyond the mountains will be captured,
killed and overcome. In a different month,
near harvesttime, by the Lords they will be
put back into order.

Traditionally this quatrain is accepted as describing the peace declared by the Pope and the Spanish in September, 1557, at the time of the grape harvest. Jaubert states that in this treaty the interests of the troops of the duc de Guise, mainly French and Swiss, were totally ignored.

However, it could possibly refer to the Second World War, with the nation over the mountains being either Austria or Italy, both of which suffered as much as France from the Germans, although in Italy's case in rather a different way. The Lords who put things back in order, *en accord redigez,* might be the Lords of Justice at Nuremberg, but the trials were after harvesttime, lasting from November, 1945, to October, 1946.

Century III

III.XXXIX

Les fept en trois mois en concorde,
Pour fubiuguer des Alpes Apennines:
Mais la tempefte & Ligure couarde,
Les profligent en fubites ruines.

The seven are in agreement for three
months to subjugate the Apennines. But
the storm and the cowardly Ligurian destroy them in sudden ruin.

This quatrain seems to refer to one of the leagues of sixteenth century Italy, probably the Holy League of 1576. It implies that the agreement is upset by Genoa (Liguria).

Century III

III.XL

Le grand theatre fe viendra redreffer,
Les dez iettez & les rets ia tendus:
Trop le premier en glaz viendra laffer,
Par arcs proftrais de long temps ia
 fendus.

The great theater will be raised up again,
the dice thrown and the nets already cast.
The leader who tolls the death bell, will
become too tired, destroyed by bows split a
long time ago.

Ancient Rome is conjured up in the first two lines, but the quatrain remains totally obscure.

Century III

III.XLI

Boffu fera efleu par le confeil,
Plus hideux monftre en terre
*   n'apperceu,*
Le coup voulant¹ creuera l'oeil,
Le traiftre au Roy pour fidelle reçeu.

The hunchback will be selected by the council, a more hideous creature never seen on earth. The deliberate shot will pierce his eye; the traitor whom the king received as loyal.

Many commentators have remarked upon the success of this quatrain. It concerns Prince Louis de Condé, a hunchback, and his death on March 13, 1569. Louis de Condé was proclaimed chief of the Huguenot Assembly in 1560. But he was reconciled to the king and Catholicism several times. He even made a public confession of his loyalty to Charles IX in 1560 and again in 1562 but all the while continued to plot against him. He was finally captured at the Battle of Jarnac, March 13, 1569, and, although a prisoner, was deliberately shot through the head, *le coup voulant creuera l'oeil,* and killed.

Century III

III.XLII

L'enfant naiftra à deux dents en la
*   gorge,*
Pierres en Tufcie par pluye tomberont:
Peu d'ans apres ne fera bled ni orge,
Pour faouler ceux qui de faim failliront.

A child will be born with two teeth in his mouth, stones will fall like rain in Tuscany. A few years later there will be neither wheat nor barley, to satisfy those weakened from hunger.

Another general reference to famine together with other phenomena, this time stones falling from the sky in Tuscany. A person born with two teeth is referred to in II.VII. Louis XIV was reputedly born with some teeth fully grown, but this is not uncommon.

---

¹*voulant.* misspelling of *volant,* flying.

Century III

III.XLIII

Gens d'alentour de Tarn Loth, &
  Garonne,
Gardez les monts Apennines paffer:
Voftre tombeau pres de Rome &
  d'Anconne,
Le noir poil crefpe fera trophee dreffer.

People from around the Tarn, the Lot and
Garonne, beware of crossing the Apennine
mountains. Your tomb is near Rome and
Ancona. The man with the dar' curly
hair will set up a trophy.

The man with the dark curly hair, *noir poil crefpe,* is also referred to
in I.LXXIIII and II.LXXIX. He has not been identified, so it is possible these quatrains are still to be fulfilled. The idea of a trophy *(trophee
dreffer)* implies a warlike intent. Perhaps he should be linked with the
Aenobarbe quatrains? The Tarn and the Lot are tributaries of the river
Garonne in France, and Ancona is situated on the eastern coast of
Italy.

Century III

III.XLIIII

Quand l'animal à l'homme domeftique,
Apres grands peines & fauts viendra
  parler,
De fouldre à vierge[1] fera fi malefique,
De terre prinfe & fufpendue en l'air.

When the animal tamed by man begins to
speak after great efforts and difficulty; the
lightning so harmful to the rod, will be
taken from the earth and suspended in the
air.

I wonder if Nostradamus is trying to describe wireless communication and electricity, the animal force *(l'animal)?* He often uses the
word "animal" to describe machines that have lifelike qualities—that
move, make a noise or emit light. Perhaps the tamed animal is the
discovery of sound waves and the wireless a form of communication,
viendra parler. The lightning hostile to the rod could imply that it is
a radio mast or some form of aerial sending out electrical charges.
It might describe a lightning conductor, the principle of which was
discovered in 1752.

[1]*vierge.* O.F. rod or wand.

Century III

III.XLV

Les cinq eftranges entrez dedans le
*   temple*
Leur fang viendra la terre prophaner:
Aux Tholoufains fera bien dur exemple,
D'vn qui viendra ses loix exterminer.

The five foreigners having entered the tem-
ple, their blood will desecrate the land.
The example made of the people of Tou-
louse will be very hard, made by the man
who comes to wipe out their laws.

The five foreigners are understood to be the five great powers who allied against Napoleonic France *(le temple):* England, Austria, Russia, Spain and Prussia. France is desolated by their invasion, much blood is spilled in battle. The battle of Toulouse fought by Wellington in 1814, was regarded as brutal, even by the standards of the time. It is the Allied Powers who wipe out the laws because they are the cause of Napoleon's downfall.

Century III

III.XLVI

Le ciel (de Plancus la cité) nous
*   prefage,*
Par clers infignes & par eftoilles fixes:
Que de fon change fubit s'aproche
*   l'aage,*
Ne pour fon bien ne pour fes malefices.

The heavens foretell (concerning the city
of Plancus), through clear skies and fixed
stars. Suddenly the time of change ap-
proaches, neither for its good nor evil fu-
ture.

Plancus is the city of Lyons, named after its founder Lucius Munatius Plancus in 43 B.C. The general gloom presaged by the stars, astrology, is similar to II.LXXXIII, which also mentions Lyons.

Century III

III.XLVII

Le vieux monarque dechaffé de fon
*   regne*
Aux Orients fon fecours ira querre:
Pour peur des croix ploiera fon
*   enfeigne,*
En Mitylène ira par port & par terre.

The old king chased out of his kingdom
will go to seek help from the people of the
East. For fear of the crosses he will fold his
banner. He will travel to Mitylene by land
and sea.

I thought initially that the old king chased out of his realm might be the Shah of Persia, someone who is not a Christian *pour peur des croix.* But there is no evidence that he ever sought help in the East;

he initially fled to Egypt. But equally he did not go to Mitylene, Lesbos, which became part of Greece in 1913. Could the crosses refer to the swastika, and the help from the East to that of the Japanese? But again, where does Lesbos fit in except as part of the general theater of war between 1940 and 1945?

Century III

III.XLVIII

Sept cens captifs eftachez rudement,
Pour la moitié meurtrir, donné le fort:
Le proche efpoir viendra fi
   promptement,
Mais non fi toft qu'vne quinziefme
   mort.

Seven hundred captives, roughly tied up.
Lots are drawn for half to be murdered.
Sudden hope will come very quickly, but
not fast enough for about fifteen dead.

No definite information has come to light about this very general quatrain, despite the specific number of prisoners and dead.

Century III

III.XLIX

Regne Gaulois tu feras bien changé,
En lieu eftrange eft tranflaté l'empire:
En autres moeurs & loix feras rangé,
Roan, & Chartres te feront bien du
   pire.

Kingdom of France, you will be greatly
changed, the Empire expands to foreign
places. You will be set up with other laws
and customs. Rouen and Chartres will do
their worst towards you.

The key words here are very explicit. France ceases to be a kingdom but becomes an Empire, which occurred under Napoleon. The Code Napoléon gave France *autres moeurs & loix.* It is possible that the last part of this prediction has yet to be fulfilled.

Century III

III.L

La republique de la grande cité,
A grand rigueur ne voudra consentir:
Roy fortir hors par trompette cité.
L'efchelle au mur, la cité repentir.

The republic's government of the great city
will not consent to rigorous suppression.
The king, summoned by trumpets to leave
the city, a ladder at the wall; the city will
repent.

The people's government of a city refers surely to the famous *Journée des Barricades*—May 12, 1588. The Leaguers took Paris the following day and they and the people drove out King Henri III and his followers. Henri retaliated by joining up with Henri de Navarre at St. Cloud, and together they resolved to besiege Paris. But Henri III was assassinated by Jacques Clément in 1589 before this was accomplished. (See I.XCVII.)

Century III

III.LI

Paris coniure vn grand meurtre
   commettre,
Blois le fera fortir en plain effect:
Ceux d'Orleans voudront leur chef
   remettre,
Angiers, Troye, Langres leur feront vn
   meffait.

Paris conspires to commit a great murder. Blois will ensure that it is fully carried out. The people of Orléans will want to replace their leaders. Angers, Troyes and Langres will do them a disservice.

Henri III murdered the two Guise brothers at Blois on December 23, 1588. He had planned the murder in Paris but the duc de Guise had fled to Blois. The duc was killed by the king's bodyguard outside the royal apartments, and the cardinal, his brother, was killed the next day. At this period, the town of Orléans rose up against the governor, Balzac d'Entragues. Charles de Lorraine, a prominent Leaguer and supporter of the Guise cause, took over the rule. The last line is only partially correct. Angers and Langres allied with the Leaguers, but Troyes remained neutral.

Century III

III.LII

En la campaigne fera fi longue pluye,
Et en la Pouille fi grande ficcité:
Coq verra l'Aigle, l'aesle mal accomplie,
Par Lyon mife fera en extremité.

In Campania there will be rain for so long and a very great drought in Apulia. The Cock will see the Eagle, its wing badly damaged, put into difficulties by the Lion.

The Cock stands for France, whether as a kingdom or a republic. The Eagle probably refers to Napoleon. In this case, Nostradamus uses the Lion to symbolize England, rather than his usual use of Léopard, as in I.XXIII. England causes Napoleon's defeat. Rain and drought are not found in contemporary records, but it is possible that the troubles in Italy, Apulia, could refer to the devastation wrought by the Napoleonic campaigns.

Century III

III.LIII

Quand le plus grand emportera le pris,
De Nuremberg, d'Auspourg & ceux de
Bafle
Par Agrippine[1] chef Frankfort repris:
Trauerferont par Flamant ivsqu'en
Gale.

When the greatest man carries off the prize of Nuremberg, Ausburg and those of Basle. Frankfurt is retaken by the leader from Cologne. They will go through Flanders as far as France.

All the place names mentioned have one thing in common, they were part of the Holy Roman Empire. But it might be that this quatrain connects with Hitler through Nuremberg. It was while he held his famous rallies there that he became leader of Germany and his troops did invade France from the north.

Century III

III.LIIII

L'vn des plus grans fuira aux
Efpaignes
Qu'en longue playe apres viendra
faigner:
Paffant copies par les hautes
montaignes,
Deuaftant tout & puis en paix regner.

One of the greatest men will flee to Spain which will bleed with a great wound thereafter. Troops will pass over the high mountains devastating everything. Then he will reign in peace.

This quatrain fits General Franco and the Spanish Civil War (1936–39) very aptly. Franco was exiled from Spain in 1936 and sent to the Canary Islands as military governor. He then went (*fuira*) to Morrocco and back to Spain to incite the rebellion which led to the Civil War. The great wound from which Spain bled, *longue playe,* presumably refers to the appalling number of casualties sustained in the war; the approximate number of dead is given at 611,000. The armies which crossed the Pyrenees, the border, were the 50,000 Italians and 10,000 Germans who fought for Franco's Nationalist party. Also, 20,000 Russian soldiers came to support the Loyalists, the Republicans. It is ironic that the last line talks of peace, but Spain, by remaining neutral throughout the Second World War, did, in a sense, *puis en paix regner.* See IX.XVI where Franco is mentioned by name.

---

[1]*Agrippine.* L. Colonia Agrippina, and Cologne.

Century III

III.LV

En l'an qu'vn oeil en France regnera, *La court fera à vn bien facheux* * trouble:* *Le grand de Bloys fon amy tuera,* *Le regne mis en mal & doubte double.*	*In the year that France has a one-eyed* *king, the court will be in very great trou-* *ble. The great man from Blois will kill his* *friend, the kingdom put into difficulty and* *double trouble.*

This quatrain was believed by Catherine de' Medicis and contemporaries to be linked with I.XXXV, the famous quatrain which predicts Henri II's death in a duel, which happened in 1559. Henri is described as the one-eyed king, *vn oeil en France regnera,* when he was wounded in a duel with his Captain of the Scottish Guard, being pierced in the eye by Montgomery's lance. He died in agony after ten days. His second son, Henri III, assassinated the Guise brothers at Blois—one of the most powerful families in France. This act was followed by general unrest throughout the kingdom. *Doubte double* probably refers to the two factions, the Leaguers and the Catholics, and also to the wars of religion which continued throughout the sixteenth century.

Century III

III.LVI

Montauban, Nifmes, Auignon & Befier, *Pefte tonnerre & grefle à fin de Mars:* *De Paris pont, Lyon mur, Montpellier,* *Depuis fix cens & fept vingts trois pars.*	*Montauban, Nîmes, Avignon and Béziers* *plague, lightning and hail at the end of* *March. Of the bridge at Paris, the wall at* *Lyons and Montpellier, since then six* *hundred and seven, three score pairs.*

If the last line of this quatrain is used to give a date, it is extremely difficult to unravel, as it can be read several ways. It may be 736 or 2031 (1555, date of publication of this part of the *Prophéties* plus 736), or 607 plus 23 pairs, which adds up to 1853, or 2208 if added to the publication date. It is very obscure and may be a failed quatrain. As for the place names, all those in line 1 are situated in the south of France, but the connection between the bridge of Paris, the walls of Lyons and Montpellier as yet makes no sense, except perhaps in the context of modern travel.

Century III

III.LVII

Sept fois changer verrez gent
  Britannique,
Taintz en fang en deux cens nonante
  an:
Franche non point par appuy
  Germanique,
Aries doubte fon pole Baftarnan.

Seven times the British nation will be seen
to change, dyed in blood for two hundred
and ninety years. Not at all free, through
German support, Aries fears for the protectorate of Poland.

Initially this seems a remarkably lucid quatrain. But it is written by
Nostradamus, and in his Centuries little is as it seems. The reader's
problem is to find the date from which the 290 years affecting Britain
starts. If one takes a starting date of 1603 (by working backwards, as
below) the whole verse is comprehensible, including the last line
linking Britain's fate with that of Poland, *Baftarnan,* and a war, Aries.
Nostradamus is saying that there will be a crisis in Polish affairs, the
invasion by the Nazis, at the same time as Britain is facing a warlike
crisis with Germany. It also implies that the present royal line,
George VI and Queen Elizabeth II, will be the start of the last royal
dynasty of any note.

1603. New Stuart monarch, James I of England and III of Scotland.
1649. The execution of Charles I and the declaration of the Com-
monwealth.
1660. The Restauration of the Stuarts under Charles II.
1688. The usurpment of the Stuarts by William of Orange.
1702. The Restauration of the Stuarts under Queen Anne.
1714. The Hanoverian succession starts under George I.
1939. The British declare war after the German invasion of Poland.

I don't find any other commentators reliable, because their excuses
for the last line make no sense. It is valid only in the context of 1939.

Century III

III.LVIII

*Aupres du Rhin des montaignes
  Noriques,
Naiftra vn grand de gens trop tard
  venu.
Qui defendra Saurome & Pannoniques,
Qu'on ne fçaura qu'il fera deuenu.*

*Near the Rhine, from the Norican moun-
tains will be born a great man of the people, came too late. He will defend Poland
and Hungary and they will never know
what became of him.*

Lech Walesa, the founder of the world-famous Solidarity movement in Poland, is the hero of this quatrain. Norican was the Latin
term for Austria and Walesa, *vn grand de gens trop tard venu,* the great
leader who comes too late to save his country, was born in Poland on
the other side of the Austrian mountains. His present battle with the
Polish authorities seems to be losing momentum and credibility, but
one must hope that Solidarity will be accepted by the Polish government.

The Samartians, now southern Russia, was Lithuania in Nostradamus' day, having united with the Crown of Poland in 1447.
Nostradamus implies that either the idea of Solidarity or of free
Trade Unions will move into Hungary as well. The last line cannot
be proven, although it seems extremely likely after the failure of the
dock strike at Gdansk and must still be regarded as futuristic where
Walesa's fate is concerned. I originally thought this quatrain might
apply to Hitler, but this begs line 2, and uses the word "defend" in
the Hitlerian sense of protect by occupation.

Century III

III.LIX

*Barbare empire par le tiers vfurpé,
La plus grand part de fon fang mettra
  à mort:
Par mort fenile par luy le quart frappé,
Pour peur que fang par le fang ne foit
  mort.*

*The barbarian empire is usurped by a
third (party), the greater part of its people
will be put to death. The fourth man,
senile, struck dead by his country, fears
lest his blood line should be extinguished.*

I think that here *tiers* may be accepted as the *Tiers Etat* of the French
Revolution. The rest of the quatrain then proceeds very smoothly.
The word *empire* places it in the time of Napoleon, and *barbare* refers
to the fact that religion was abolished until Napoleon had need of the
Pope for his coronation.

There were three Committees of Public Safety during the Reign of Terror; those of Danton, Robespierre and the Directoire. The fourth man, *par mort fenile frappé*, is Napoleon, who took over from the Directoire in 1799, and eventually died, senile, in St. Helena.

Napoleon had always feared that his line might not be continued, particularly when he realized that his marriage to Josephine was barren. On May 3, 1804, the Tribunal of France declared that "the imperial dignity should be declared hereditary in the line of Bonaparte." He divorced Josephine in 1810 because of her barrenness and married Marie Louise of Austria in the same year, by whom he had an heir, the king of Rome. When Napoleon abdicated on June 22, 1814, Marie Louise was given the Duchy of Parme with her son, the king of Rome. Napoleon abdicated in favor of his son, but realized it was but a formality. He was succeeded in 1808 by Napoleon III, the third son of Napoleon's brother, Louis Bonaparte and Josephine's sister, Hortense de Beauharnais. As a nephew and adopted grandson of Napoleon, he was not a strong contender for the throne. There were also many contemporary rumors that he was illegitimate. Napoleon's fears as to the future of his line were well founded.

Century III

III.LX

Par toute Afie grande proscription,	*Throughout Asia there will be great pro-*
Mefme en Myfie, Lyfie, & Pamphylie:	*scription, also in Mysia, Lycia and Pam-*
Sang verfera par abfolution,	*phalia. Blood will flow because of a young*
D'vn ieune noir remply de felonnie.	*dark man, filled with evil.*

In this quatrain Nostradamus envisages an enormous military callup in the East, in China. All the countries mentioned in line 2 are in Asia Minor. He foresees China as growing in power and influence, *sang verfera,* through war and conquest. The terrible history of Kampuchea may be a warning of future events to come. After all, Nostradamus predicted a rapport between America and the Soviet Union, and that has already come to pass. Asia Minor covers Turkey, Iran and Iraq in modern terms. These countries have now negotiated a cease-fire. Again, we have the young dark-haired man, *ieune noir,* whom I cannot identify. Due to the dating of the Iran-Iraq war, he may be either the Antichrist but more probably his mysterious predecessor. This quatrain is certainly not fulfilled.

Century III

III.LXI

La grande bande & fecte crucigere,
Se dreffera en Mefopotamie:
Du proche fleuue compagnie legiere,
Que telle loy tiendra pour ennemie.

The great following of the sect of the cross,
will arise in Mesopotamia. The light com-
pany (regiment?) at the nearby river will
regard such a law as inimical.

The enigmatic solution to this quatrain lies in the words *fecte cruci-gere*. It could be the swastika—the *croix gammée*, as it was known in France, but I am inclined to place this quatrain in Iraq, as Mesopotamia is now known. The two rivers are the Tigris and the Euphrates. This would then place the quatrain in the war between Iran and Iraq, *tiendra pour ennemie*. Since the Christian cross is straight, we are certainly not dealing with a Christian army. It may even have the convoluted meaning that the followers are totally inimical to the cross.

Century III

III.LXII

Proche del duero par mer Cyrrene clofe,
Viendra perfer les grands monts
    Pyrenées:
La main plus courte & fa percee[1]
    gloze,[2]
A Carcaffonne conduira fes menées.

Near the Douro enclosed by the Cyrenian
Sea he will come to cross the great moun-
tains of the Pyrenees. The shortest route
and his opening noted, he will take his
followers to Carcassonne.

This apparently talks of a leader who will cross the Pyrenees from Spain into France. The river Douro rises in the mountains around Burgos in Spain, and the Cyrenian Sea is the Mediterranean. But who or what this man did is obscure. Line 3 is difficult to translate.

Century III

III.LXIII

Romain pouuoir fera du tout abas,
Son grand voifin imiter les veftiges:
Occultes haines ciuiles & debats,
Retarderont aux bouffons leurs folies.

The power of Rome will be quite cast
down, following the footsteps of its great
neighbor. Secret hatreds and civil disputes
will delay the stupidities of the buffoons.

This is a reasonably accurate description of the state of Italy under Mussolini and its great neighbor, Hitlerian Germany in 1937, in

---

[1]*percee.* O.F. perce, stake, pole, entry.
[2]*gloze.* A.Pr. *gloza*, commentary, notes.

whose footsteps Mussolini tried to follow. The name Mussolini literally means muslin maker, a craft regarded as the lowest of the low, and yet it is this man who becomes the dictator of Italy. The histrionics of both Hitler and Mussolini could certainly qualify them as buffoons *aux bouffons leurs folies,* and the word *folie* also contains the element of failure. The great hatreds and civil disputes, *occultes haines ciuiles & debats,* may also refer to Hitler's certain insanity in later years, and almost certainly that of his second-hand follower, Mussolini.

Century III

III.LXIIII

Le chef de Perfe remplira grande Olchade, *Claffe Trireme contre gent Mahometique:* *De Parthe, & Mede, & piller les Cyclades,* *Repos long temps au grand port Ionique.*	The Persian leader will gather in great Spain. A fleet of triremes (will advance) against the Mohammedans for Parthia and Media. He will take the Cyclades; then a long wait in the great Ionian harbor.

Some Iranians hope that this indicates the revival of a Persian leader to replace the Ayatollah, a theme which occurs several times in Nostradamus. But he would not use the classical *triremes.* Perhaps Nostradamus fails for once to use a word which might describe large ships? The quatrain implies that this man will have help from within Persia: Media and Parthia are part of Iran. It is unclear why he should sack the Greek islands around Delos in the Aegean. The harbor in which he shelters could be anywhere in the Ionian Sea between Greece and Sicily. Possibly an unfulfilled quatrain to date.

Century III

III.LXV

Quand le fepulcre du grand Romain trouué, *Le iour apres fera efleu Pontife:* *Du Senat gueres il ne fera prouué,* *Empoifonné fon fang au facré fcyphe.*	When the tomb of the Great Roman is found, a pope will be elected the following day. He will not be approved by the Senate. his blood poisonous in the sacred chalice.

The dating of this quatrain is found in line 1. A possibly "true" tomb of St. Peter was discovered in 1979, but some doubts remain. Pope John Paul I was elected in the same year, a very unexpected candidate. His death soon afterwards was surrounded by suspicious circumstances. Approximately one month after his election he was invited to dine with his cardinals. He died, unattended, that night. The ensuing scandal in the European newspapers in particular did great harm to the Vatican's reputation. The most suspicious facts were that the nuns who were supposed to attend him that night had been absent for some hours, and his body was cremated at speed, not buried, which is against the Catholic religion.

John Paul I is reputed to have been unpopular with the Curia. However, in my book of 1972 I was skeptical of Nostradamus' prediction of two assassinations of a twentieth century pope. I think he probably referred to this extraordinary situation and also to the attack on Pope John Paul II in May, 1981, by the Turk Mohamet Ali Agça, when he suffered severe injuries. According to Nostradamus, yet another attempt was to come. This happened in Manila in May, 1983, when a news flash on the World Service stated that a priest had tried to assassinate the Pope with a bayonet cut into pieces. It does seem that this prediction has been recently fulfilled.

Century III

III.LXVI

Le grand Baillif d'Orleans mis à mort,
Sera par vn de fang vindicatif.
De mort merite ne mourra, ne par fort,
Des pieds & mains malle faifoit captif.

The great Bailiff of Orleans is condemned to death by a person vindictive for his blood. He will not die a deserved death, nor one by jurors. They will keep him captive (bound) inefficiently by his hand and feet.

The post of the Bailiff of Orléans had been inherited by a member of the Greslot family since 1530, so Nostradamus must have intended this prediction for one of them. A certain Jerôme Greslot was condemned to death for having opened the gates of the town to marauders in 1562, but he was not actually condemned to death for this until 1569. Does Nostradamus mean the gap between his capture and execution was *mal le faifoit captif?*

Century III

III.LXVII

Vne nouuelle fecte de Philofophes,
Mefprifant mort, or, honneurs &
*   richeffes:*
Des monts Germains ne feront
*   limitrophes,*
A les ensuyure auront appuy & preffes.

A new sect of philosophers despising death, gold, honors and riches will not be contained by the German mountains. There will be crowds and support among their followers.

Try as hard as I can, I do not find an easy solution to this quatrain. I think it is probably retroactive, referring to the sect of the Anabaptists, who had been almost wiped out in 1536. It is just possible Nostradamus foresees a revival of these or other Protestant sects from the direction of Germany, but both Luther and Calvin had made their stand before publication.

Century III
III.LXVIII

Peuple fans chef d'Efpaigne & d'Italie,
Morts, profligez[1] dedans le Cherroneffe:[2]
Leur dict[3] trahi par legiere folie,
Le fang nager par tout à la trauerfe.

Leaderless people from Spain and Italy, dead and overcome in the Peninsula. Their leader will be betrayed by stupid folly. Blood will flow everywhere in the area.

This is a quatrain certainly set in the twentieth century, a time when Spain and Italy have elected leaders, *dict,* not being of royal blood. The traitor betrayed is Mussolini and it is possible that by *à la trauerfe* Nostradamus is referring to Mussolini's final death by hanging. *La trauerfe* also means a crossroads, which was the standard site for a gibbet throughout most of Europe. It is possible that perhaps this quatrain is not yet fulfilled.

Century III
III.LXIX

Grand exercite conduict par iouuenceau,
Se viendra rendre aux mains des
  ennemis:
Mais le vieillart nay au demy pourceau,
Fera Chalon & Mafcon eftre amis.

A great army led by a young man will happen to give itself up into the enemies' hands. But the old man, born to the half pig, will make Châlon and Mâcon into friends.

The original half man–half pig occurs in I.LXIIII and as a half man in VIII.XLIIII. Either the man in line 3, *nay au demy pourceau,* is from a generation such as the 1980s when the flier in an oxygen mask is now commonplace, who will fall into enemy hands with the army, through a headstrong young man, or possibly it is derived from the false etymology of the city of Milan itself. According to legend it was derived from the finding of an animal half sheep–half pig at its foun-

[1]*profligez.* L. *profligatus,* vanquished, overcome.
[2]*Cherroneffe.* Gk. peninsula.
[3]*dict.* alternative *duict,* leader.

dation. But the relevance to either interpretation of Châlon and Mâcon, both in Burgundy, escapes me. I lean towards the more modern interpretation.

Century III

III.LXX

La grand Bretaigne comprinfe
  l'Angleterre,
Viendra par eaux fi haut à inonder
La ligue neufue d'Aufonne[1] fera guerre,
Que contre eux ils fe viendront bander.

The whole of Great Britain, including England, will be covered by very deep floods. The new league in Ausonne will declare war so that they will ally against them.

England did not become Great Britain until the unification of the Scottish and English thrones under James I. He assumed the title of King of Great Britain on October 24, 1604. Incidentally, there were great floods covering Bristol and Somerset for an area of thirty miles in 1607, but this is hardly the whole of Great Britain. If we are in the correct period, the last two lines refer to the renewal of the Holy League in 1606, Ausonia standing for Italy. A quatrain that is almost right but leaves one dissatisfied.

Century III

III.LXXI

Ceux dans les ifles de long temps
  affiegez,
Prendront vigueur force contre ennemis:
Ceux par dehors mors de faim profligez,
En plus grand faim que iamais feront
  mis.

Those besieged in the islands for a long time will take strong measures against their enemies. Those who are outside, overcome will die of hunger, by such starvation as has never occurred before.

The blockade of Britain by the German Navy during the Second World War seems clearly described in this quatrain, as are the strong countermeasures taken by the British in opening up Atlantic routes for supplies and troops. It appears that during the siege of Britain there was never more than a six-week supply of food in the country, a fact well hidden from the populace. The final two lines are obvious enough. The British did not starve, but there was appalling famine in occupied Europe. This must refer in particular to the labor camps, so called, of the Nazi régime, where starvation killed off many of the tragic survivors of the gas chambers.

[1]*Aufonne.* Ausonia; southern Italy, especially Naples, but can stand for the whole of Italy.

Century III
III.LXXII

Le bon vieillart tout vif enfeuely,
Pres du grand fleuue par fauffe
foufpeçon:
Le nouueau vieux de richeffe ennobly,
Prins à chemin tout l'or de la rançon.

The good old man is buried while still alive through superstition, near a great river. The newcomer is old, ennobled by wealth, having taken all the ransomed gold on the way.

This obscure quatrain has a counterpart in III.XXXVI, where someone is also buried alive, but nothing else leads to any clue. Probably a failed quatrain.

Century III
III.LXXIII

Quand dans le regne paruiendra le
boiteux,
Competiteur aura proche baftard:
Luy & le regne viendront fi fort
roigneux,
Qu'ains qu'il gueriffe fon faict fera bien
tard.

When the lame man comes into the kingdom, a bastard close to him will compete with him. Both he and the kingdom will be greatly diminished before he recovers; his action will be too late.

This interesting quatrain is full of facts. The heir to King Charles X of France was the duc de Bordeaux, who became lame as the result of a riding accident in 1841. The illegal contender for the throne was the comte de Paris. The trimming away of the kingdom, *fi fort roigneux,* then refers to the Franco-Prussian War. By the time the French came to terms with the duc de Bordeaux, the French had declared France's Third Republic, and both he and the comte de Paris died in exile.

Century III
III.LXXIIII

Naples, Florence, Fauence, & Imole,
Seront en termes de telle fafcherie:
Que pour côplaire aux malheureux de
Nolle,
Plainct d'auoir faict à fon chef
moquerie.

Naples, Florence, Faenza and Imola will come to terms so disagreeable in order to comply with the wretches of Nola, that they complain that their chief had been mocked.

I can make no sense of this quatrain. Faenza and Imola were in the Papal States. Florence is the capital of Tuscany and Naples of the two

Sicilies. Nola is close to Naples in the East. I think this is definitely a failed quatrain.

Century III
III.LXXV

Pau, Verone, Vicence, Sarragouffe,
De glaïues loings terroirs de fang
  humides:
Pefte fi grande viendra à la grand
  gouffe,[1]
Proche fecours, & bien loing les
  remedes.

Pau, Verona, Vicenza, Saragossa, swords dripping with blood from distant lands. A very great plague will come in the great shell, relief near, but the remedies far away.

All the cities here are in Europe and Nostradamus seems to indicate that a devastating plague will afflict them, "within the great shell." This might imply chemical warfare, as used in Iran and Iraq. But I feel the last line is the most important. The *pefte fi grande* may well apply to AIDS. The relief so near for those who suffer it, *proche fecours,* is probably the drug used to contain the HIV-positive condition, which can be maintained and stabilized for as long as five years. But unfortunately the cure for either HIV infection or full-blown AIDS will be a long time arriving, *& bien loing les remedes.* AZT is an example of the drugs used to contain it. Line 2 indicates there may be a war waged against Europe from a distant country. It is impossible to say from where. Nostradamus' guess is China.

Century III
III.LXXVI

En Germanie naiftront diuerfes fectes,
S'approchant fort de l'heureux
  paganifme,
Le coeur captif & petites receptes,
Feront retour à payer le vray difme.

Various sects will arise in Germany which will come near to a happy paganism. The heart is captive, the returns small. They will return to pay the true title.

Although this quatrain can be easily applied as yet another of Nostradamus' obsessions against the many Lutheran, Anabaptist and Calvinist sects which were springing up around him in the sixteenth century and which he cordially disliked, I have the impression that this quatrain actually applies to modern Germany. Under Hitler, before the war of 1939, religion almost disappeared and the Jews

[1]*gouffe.* O.F. shell, husk, scab.

were made to disappear. Hitler, a monomaniac until the very end at the Bunker in Berlin, will soon lose his earlier gains in the war, *petites receptes,* and it was not only he and his followers who will have to repay their dreadful acts, but also a large proportion of the German people.

Century III
III.LXXVII

Le tiers climat fous Aries comprins,
L'an mil fept cens vingt & fept en
  Octobre:
Le Roy de Perfe par ceux d'Egypte
  prins:
Conflit, mort, perte, à la croix grand
  opprobre.

The third climate included under Aries; in the year 1727 in October, the king of Persia will be captured by the people of Egypt. Battle, death, loss, a great shame to the cross.

At first glance this appears to be an extremely correct quatrain. It contains not only the year, but also the month and the place! I can only assume that in some way Nostradamus overlooked these details when he set out to confuse the quatrains. It appears correct in every detail. In October, 1727, a peace was concluded between the Turks and the Persians (Egypt belonged to the Ottoman Empire and represents the Turks).

The loss to Christianity may be explained by the fact that the Shah Ashraf, in return for the recognition of his dynasty, gave the lands of Emvan, Tauris and Hamadam to the Turks, and recognized the sultan as the legitimate successor to the caliph. Ottoman power continued in strength until the twentieth century and the Christians raised no more Crusades.

Century III
III.LXXVIII

Le chef d'Efcoffe auec fix d'Alemaigne,
Par gens de mer Orientaux captif:
Trauerferont le Calpre & Efpaigne,
Prefent en Perfe au nouueau Roy
  craintif.

The leader from Scotland together with six Germans will be captured by Eastern sea warriors. They will go through Gibraltar and Spain and be presented in Persia to the new dreadful king.

From the content, this appears to be a totally failed quatrain. No Scots leader has allied himself with six Germans (although Nazi leader Hess journeyed to Scotland alone to see the duke of Rutland). But then how does the rest of the quatrain fit?

Century III
III.LXXIX

L'ordre fatal fempiternel par chaifne,   The fatal and eternal order of the cycle
Viendra tourner par ordre confequent: will turn in its normal course. The chains
Du port Phocen fera rompue la chaifne,   of Marseilles will be broken, both the city
La cité prinfe, l'ennemy quant &   and the enemy taken at the same time.
   quant.

Chains were used as booms in Marseilles harbor until recently.
Otherwise this is quite obscure.

Century III
III.LXXX

Du regne Anglois l'indigne dechaffé,   The unworthy man is chased out of the
Le confeiller par ire mis à feu: English kingdom. The counselor will be
Ses adherans iront fi bas tracer,   burned through anger. His followers will
Que le baftard fera demy receu.   stoop to such depths that the pretender will
                                                 almost be received.

Charles I, 1600–1649, lost his kingdom mainly due to his own
behavior and his irresponsibility towards Parliament. One of his
counselors, Strafford, was beheaded in 1641 and Archbishop Laud
was burned for treachery in 1645. The followers, ses adherans, who
stooped so low were the Scots, who sold the king back to the English
Parliament in 1646. The Pretender, or bastard (bastard), who is almost received in the kingdom is Oliver Cromwell, the man who was
not born to rule, but who almost achieves kingship as Lord Protector.

Century III
III.LXXXI

Le grand criar fans honte audacieux,   The great speechmaker, shameless and
Sera efleu gouuerneur de l'armee: bold will be elected governor of the army.
La hardieffe de fon contentieux,   The audacity of his contention, the broken
Le pont rompu cité de peur pafmee.   bridge, the city faint from fear.

There is a beautiful clue in this quatrain—the broken bridge, pont
rompu. If this is a typical Nostradamus pun from the Latin pons, a
bridge, and fractus, broken, it stands for Pontefract, the town famous
for holding out for Charles I in two great sieges during the Civil War.
The great speechmaker is Cromwell, for whom Nostradamus had as
little affection as he later shows for the Republican Napoleon.

Century III

III.LXXXII

Freins, Antibor, villes autour de Nice,
Seront vaftees fort par mer & par terre:
Les faturelles terre & mer vent propice,
Prins, morts, trouffez, pillés, fans loy de
　　guerre.

Fréjus, Antibes; the towns around Nice
will be greatly devastated by land and sea.
The locusts over land and sea, the wind
being favorable, captured, dead, trussed
up, plundered without law of war.

Could an invasion of the coast of southern France by air be implied by the quatrain? Nostradamus normally describes modern machines as types of animals. Locusts, read literally, could not cause the death and destruction of line 4.

Century III

III.LXXXIII

Les longs cheueux de la Gaule Celtique,
Accompaignez d'eftranges nations:
Mettront captif la gent Aquitanique,
Pour fuccomber à internitions. [1]

The long-haired person of Celtic Gaul,
joined by foreign nations will capture the
people of Aquitaine, in order that they
should succumb to their plans.

The long-haired person from Celtic Gaul is Louis XVIII of France, known by his contemporaries as *le Chevelu,* his long hair being a great contrast to the short-cropped hair of the Revolutionaries and Bonapartistes. The foreign armies, *Accompaignez d'eftranges nations,* are the Allied armies who helped defeat Napoleon and put Louis on the throne of France. Aquitaine may stand for England: it was English for over three hundred years. (See IX.VI.) But its application to the plans in line 4 is unclear.

Century III

III.LXXXIIII

La grand cité fera bien defolee,
Des habitans vn feul n'y demoura:
Mur, fexe, temple, & vierge violee,
Par fer, feu, pefte, cannon peuple
　　mourra.

The great city will soon be quite deserted,
not a single one of the inhabitants will
remain. Wall, sex, temple and virgin vi-
olated, people will die from the sword; fire,
plague and cannon shot.

If the word sex is an abbreviation of Sextus, this applies to the sack of Rome by Napoleonic troops during the reign of Pius VI, 1775–1799. But many commentators think the city may be Paris.

---

[1]*internitions.* in all other texts read as *"intentions."*

Century III
III.LXXXV

La cité prinfe par tromperie & fraude,
Par le moyen d'vn beau ieune attrappé:
Affaut donné Raubine pres de LAVDE.
Luy & tous morts pour auoir bien
   trompé.

The city is taken by trickery and deceit,
captured by means of a handsome young
man. An assault is made by Raubine near
LAVDE, he and all of them, for having
deceived so well.

The Robine is a tributary of the Aube. Perhaps the city lies upon one of these rivers? There is no clear reason as to why LAVDE should be written in capital letters.

Century III
III.LXXXVI

Vn chef d'Aufonne aux Efpaignes ira,
Par mer fera arreft dedans Marfeille:
Auant fa mort vn long temps languira,
Apres fa mort on verra grand merueille.

A leader from Italy will go to Spain by
sea, and he will make a stop at Marseilles.
He will linger for a long time before dying;
after his death great wonders will be seen.

A ruler of a southern Italian State (or of the Two Sicilies in particular, because that was the home of the Ausones in Roman times), will die a lingering death at Marseilles. This may refer to a member of the Mafia or Cosa Nostra, and may not yet be fulfilled. All the places mentioned are in Mafia country.

Century III
III.LXXXVII

Claffe Gauloife n'approches de
   Corfegue,
Moins de Sardaigne tu t'en repentiras:
Treftous mourrez fruftrez de l'aide
   grogne,
Sang nagera, captif ne me croiras.

French fleet, do not approach Corsica;
even less Sardinia, you will regret it. You
will all die, the help from the Cape
(comes) in vain; captive, swimming in
blood you will not believe me.

In 1655 part of the French fleet, under the command of the chevalier de la Ferrière, was sunk in the Gulf of Lyons while sailing past the islands of Sardinia and Corsica. Many lives were lost because the ships were unable to reach the shelter of the nearby Cap de Porceau. This contains a typical Nostradamus double meaning: grogne could mean either a cape or the snout of a pig. Le Captif in this quatrain becomes a proper name: Jean de Rian, who had earlier been captured and taken as a galley slave by the Algerian corsairs, was the pilot of this tragic fleet. His followers called him *Le Captif.*

Century III

III.LXXXVIII

De Barfellonne par mer fi grand armee,	*From Barcelona, such a great army by*
Toute Marfeille de frayeur tremblera:	*sea, all Marseilles will tremble with ter-*
Ifles faifies de mer ayde fermee,	*ror. The islands seized, help cut off by sea,*
Ton traditeur en terre nagera.	*your traitor will swim on land.*

A very accurate quatrain on the history of Marseilles and the Spanish. On February 17, 1596, Philip of Spain sent his fleet, under the command of Charles Doria, to Marseilles to divide the French interests between the Leaguers and the king. The fleet occupied the islands of Château d'If and Ratonneau and thus prevented help from coming into Marseilles by sea. A certain Charles de Casau tried to betray Marseilles to the Spanish, but was found out and assassinated by Pierre Libertot. He was killed by the sword, drowning in his own blood, literally *en terre nagera,* swimming on land.

Century III

III.LXXXIX

En ce temps là fera fruftree Cypres,	*At that time Cyprus will be deprived of its*
De fon fecours de ceux de mer Egee:	*help from those of the Aegean sea. Old*
Vieux trucidez, mais par mefles[1] &	*men slaughtered; but by cannons and sup-*
lyphres[2]	*plications the king is won over; the queen*
Seduict leur Roy, Royne plus outragee.	*more outraged.*

Could this quatrain refer to the Troubles in Cyprus in the 1950s, when *Enosis,* union with Greece, was the popular demand? The quatrain shows that Cyprus will not obtain complete union with Greece. The Greek king, Constantine, is misled and finally goes into exile. The queen *plus outragee* is his mother, Queen Frederika, who was greatly distressed by the family's enforced exile.

---

[1]*mefles.* O.F. variant of *masle,* cannon ball.
[2]*lyphres.* Gk. *lypros,* supplications, plea.

Century III

III.XC

Le grand Satyre & Tigre d'Hyrcanie,
Don presenté à ceux de l'Occean:
Vn chef de claffe iftra de Carmanie,
Qui prendra terre au Tyrren Phocean.

The great Satyr and Tiger of Hyrcania, a
gift presented to the people of the Ocean.
The leader of a fleet will come forth from
Carmania and land at Phocean Tyre.

Phocea is the Latin name for Marseilles, often used by Nostradamus. But Marseilles is not situated on the Tyrrhenian sea, so Nostradamus is probably thinking of another seaport associated with the Phoenician colonists of Tyre. Both Carmania and Hyrcania were Persian provinces. But unless the events in this quatrain are intended to occur after the building of the Suez Canal, the fleet would have to cross by land. A failed quatrain, I feel.

Century III

III.XCI

L'arbre qu'eftoit par long temps mort
* feché,*
Dans vne nuict viendra à reuerdir:
Cron Roy malade, Prince pied eftaché,
Criant d'ennemis fera voile bondir.

The tree which had been dead and with-
ered for a long time will flourish again in
one night. The Cronian king will be ill;
the Prince have a damaged foot. Fear of
his enemies will make him hoist sail.

The tree which sprouts again miraculously overnight is the family tree of the Bourbons, when the duchesse de Berry gave birth to a son, the duc de Bordeaux, on September 29, 1820, seven months after the assassination of her husband. The duc was a sickly child and injured his foot falling from a horse in Austria, which resulted in his having a permanent limp. He went into exile, *fera voile bondir,* in 1830 with his grandfather Charles X, and despite long negotiations with Republican France, did not succeed in attaining the throne. A satisfactory quatrain.

Century III

III.XCII

Le monde proche du dernier periode,
Saturne encor tard fera de retour:
Tranflat empire deuers nation Brodde,
L'oeil arrache à Narbon par Autour.

The world is near its final period, Saturn
will again be late on his return. The em-
pire will shift to the Brodde nation. An eye
at Narbonne is plucked out by a goshawk.

This astrological quatrain refers to the future of the African nations. *Brodde* in old French means either black or dark brown, and cannot be confused with Nostradamus' vision of Asia and Tuscany. It also contains the meaning of decadent, which certainly applies to the corruption that is rampant in most African states today.

Nostradamus speaks of an *empire tranflaté* when referring to Napoleon. Does he see the beginning of the new power of Africa starting as early as that? He states that more power will be given to the African nations before the final cycle of the world, the second millennium, occurs. He may also contain the meaning that French power will increase in Africa before this time, which it did until France left Algeria. If that is so, we are now approaching the final period.

Century III
III.XCIII

Dans Auignon tout le chef de l'empire	*In Avignon, the leader of all the Empire*
Fera arreft pour Paris defolé:	*will make a stop because Paris is deserted.*
Tricaft[1] tiendra l'Annibalique ire,	*Tricast will contain the African anger; the*
Lyon par change sera mal confolé.	*Lion will be poorly consoled by the change.*

The quatrain hints at a great enemy of France and possibly also of Rome, in that Avignon belonged to the Vatican until 1791. The British Lion will dislike the French presence in Africa. Perhaps one should link this quatrain with those fought by the British in Africa during the Second World War? I feel that I have not properly interpreted this quatrain and that it is of rather greater impact and futuristic. The African quatrains are always difficult. See those on AIDS, World Famine, etc.

Century III
III.XCIIII

De cinq cens ans plus compte l'on tiendra,	*For more than five hundred years they will take notice of him who was the adornment*
Celuy qu'eftoit l'aornement de fon temps:	*of his age. Then suddenly a great revelation will be made which will make the*
Puis à vn coup grande clarté donra,	*people of that century well pleased.*
Que par ce fiecle les rendra tres contens.	

Almost all commentators on Nostradamus' works have seen themselves as the source of the great revelation to be made, *à vn coup grand*

---

[1]*Tricaft.* Tricasses, city of Troyes, southeast of Paris.

clarté donra. Certainly Nostradamus' works have been in print for well over four hundred years. The great revelation I feel is not a commentator but an event which will occur during this century. An as yet unfulfilled quatrain.

Century III

III.XCV

La loy Moricque on verra deffaillir,
Apres vn autre beaucoup plus feductiue:
Borifthenes premier viendra faillir,
Par dons & langue vne plus attractiue.

The Moorish law will be seen to fail, followed by another that is less pleasing. The Dnieper will be the first to give way through gifts and tongues, to another more appealing.

This must forecast the arrival of Communism in northern Europe. The River Dnieper is situated in the USSR. Certainly it is interesting that Nostradamus sees Russia as the first to give way. Gorbachev brought the cutting down of nuclear weapons to Europe. The *dons & langue,* sweet speeches, would apply to the summits in Iceland and Moscow all of which were initiated by the Russians. The tragedy may happen reasonably soon, when these accords break down. See I.XCI, II.LXXXIX, V.LXXVIII, VI.XXI. Nostradamus gives the accord a lifespan of between three years and seven months and thirteen years. If that is so, will Gorbachev be crushed under the machinery of Stalinist Russia? Tragic as it is, Nostradamus seems to foresee the decline of détente and a possible resumption of the Cold War. A worrying quatrain. But in IV.XCV he states the victor will be born "on American soil."

Century III

III.XCVI

Chef de Foffan aura gorge coupee,
Par le ducteur du limier & leurier:
Le faict patré par ceux du mont
   Tarpee,
Saturne en Leo 13. de Feurier.

The leader from Fossano will have his throat cut by the man who exercised the bloodhounds and the greyhounds. The deed will be committed by those of the Tarpeian Rock, when Saturn is in Leo on February 13.

Nostradamus gives us an excellent astrological dating in line 4, Saturn rules Aquarius, so when it is in its opposite sign of Leo it should be considered maleficent. The duc de Berry was stabbed to death on February 13, 1820, when leaving the Opéra.

The reference to Fossano is more difficult. If the quatrain does refer to the duc de Berry, then he has claim to the title of Duc de Fossano through his maternal grandfather who was the duc of Fossano in Sardinia. The rest then fits very well. The assassin was a certain Louvel, who worked in the royal stables, *le ducteur du limier & leurier,* and whose job was to exercise the dogs. He was a Republican, hence the reference to the Tarpeian Rock, from which Republican Rome cast criminals to their deaths (see I.LXXXIIII).

Century III

III.XCVII

Nouuelle loy terre neufue occuper,
Vers la Syrie, Iudee & Paleſtine:
Le grand empire barbare corruer,
Auant que Phebés ſon ſiecle determine.

A new law will occupy a new land around Syria, Judea and Palestine. The great barbarian empire will crumble before the century of the sun is finished.

This is a splendidly vindicated quatrain describing the creation of the state of Israel. Barbarian in Nostradamus' terms means non-Christian. It is implied that Israel will eventually triumph over her enemies before the end of the twentieth century, the century of the sun. King Hussein of Jordan has refused to accept the Gaza Strip as being Palestinian and the Israelis through Mr. Begin have accepted the responsibility of the land they gained in the Six Days' War. This prediction seems well on the way to being fulfilled.

Century III

III.XCVIII

Deux royals freres ſi fort guerroyeront,
Qu'entre eux fera la guerre ſi mortelle:
Qu'vn chacun places fortes occuperont,
De regne & vie fera leur grand
querelle.

Two royal brothers will fight very fiercely, and the feud between them will be so deadly that both will live in fortified places. Their great quarrel will concern their lives and the kingdom.

This prediction is a great example of a prediction which will fit various historical situations. It fits the situation of Henri III, king of France, and the duc d'Alençon, 1574–1584, but it also fits the quarrel between Louis XIII and his brother the duc d'Orléans around 1632. Prophecy, like history, does repeat itself.

Century III

III.XCIX

*Aux champs herbeux d'Alein & du
    Varneigne,
Du mont Lebron proche de la Durance,
Camps de deux parts conflict fera fi
    aigre,
Mefopotamie defaillira en la France.*

*In the green fields of Alleins and Ver-
neques of the Luberon mountains near
Durance, the fighting on both sides of the
armies will be so bitter that Mesopotamia
will cease to be found in France.*

Many commentators, as I have said, take Nostradamus' Mesopotamia to mean Paris, but I must confess I am not too happy with this
interpretation. The villages in line 1 are situated near Nostradamus'
final home in Salon-de-Provence; the Luberon mountains are near
Durance. I can make nothing out of this quatrain.

Century III

III.C

*Entre Gaulois le dernier honnoré,
D'homme ennemy fera victorieux:
Force & terroir en moment exploré,
D'vn coup de traict quand mourra
    l'enuieux.*

*The man least honored among the French
will be victorious over this enemy. He ex-
plores strength and lands in action, when
suddenly the envious one dies from the
shot.*

This quatrain is usually applied to de Gaulle. The man who is
assassinated is identified as Admiral Darlan, who was killed December 24, 1942. *Le traict* is the usual word for an arrow shot, but could,
of course, stand in for gunshot.

Century IV

IV.I

*Cela du refte de fang non efpandu,
Venife quiert fecours eftre donné.
Apres auoir bien long têps attêdu,
Cité liurée au premier cornet sôné.*

*The blood of the just will not be spilled,
Venice seeks for help to be given. Having
waited for a very long time the city is
handed over at the first blast of the trumpet.*

This probably describes the Turkish attack on Cyprus, 1560–73.
Venice asked for but received little help and Cyprus fell to the Turks
after a prolonged siege in 1571.

Century IV
IV.II

*Par mort la France prendra voyage à
   faire,
Claffe par mer, marcher monts
   Pyrénées,
Efpaigne en trouble, marcher gent
   militaire:
Des plus grand Dames en France
   emmenées.*

*Because of a death France will undertake
a journey, marching over the Pyrees, the
fleet at sea. Spain will be troubled, an
army will march; some of the greatest ladies brought into France.*

This is quite a successful quatrain. Philip V, grandson of Louis XIV, inherited the Spanish throne from Charles II in 1700. This was unpopular with Austria, England, Holland, Prussia and Savoy, who formed a coalition to support the pretentions of the Archduke Charles. The French fleet took to sea, and the French Army crossed the Pyrenees. The War of the Spanish Succession lasted for twelve years, 1701–1713, and its cause was two Spanish princesses, *Des plus grand Dames en France emmenées,* who married out of their country into the French royal line, becoming the wives of Louis XII and Louis XIV.

Century IV
IV.III

*D'Arras & Bourges, de Brodes grans
   enfeignes,
Vn plus grand nombre de Gafcons batre
   à pied.
Ceux long du Rofne faigneront les
   Efpaignes,
Proche du mont ou fagonte s'affied.*

*From Arras and Bourges great banners
from the dark ones; a greater number of
Gascons will fight on foot. Those along the
Rhône will make the Spanish bleed, near
the mountain seat of Sagunto.*

Again *Broddes,* the dark ones, appear—these mysterious dark-skinned people whom Nostradamus believed would be part of a disaster in the twentieth century. The last two lines seem to refer to the French invasion of Spain 1701. The import of Sagunto is unclear. Possibly a split quatrain?

Century IV
IV.IIII

L'impotent prince faché, plaincts &
   querelles,
De rapts & pillé, par coqz & par
   Libyques:
Grand eft par terre par mer infinies
   voilles,
Seule Italie fera chaffant Celtiques.

*The powerless prince is angered; com-
plaints and quarrels, rape and pillage by
the cock and the Libyans. He is great on
land, innumerable sails at sea. By Italy
alone will the Celts be driven out.*

The cock is, as always, the symbol of France. If one accepts the
Libyans as the Algerian corsairs who allied with them the prince is
probably a Hapsburg, possibly Duc Cosimo, who was in charge of the
defense of Elba and the surrounding lands. These territories were
razed to the ground in 1555. But this is, in all, an unsuccessful
quatrain. The last line suggests that the French will be defeated by
the Italians but be successful everywhere else. In fact, the reverse
occurred. The French held their own in Italy, but were defeated in
the North. An unsuccessful contemporary quatrain.

Century IV
IV.V

Croix paix, foubz vn accomply diuin
   verbe,
L'Efpaigne & Gaule feront vnis
   enfemble:
Grand clade[1] proche, & combat
   trefacerbe,
Coeur fi hardy ne fera qui ne tremble.

*Cross, peace; under one the divine word
achieved. Spain and Gaul will be united.
A great disaster in close, the fighting very
ferocious. No heart so brave that it will
not tremble.*

This seems yet another quatrain centering upon the Spanish War
of Succession, 1701–1713. Spain and France were united for a short
time when Louis XIV's grandson inherited the Spanish throne. The
revocation of the Edict of Nantes may be hinted at in line 1. Peace
achieved under the *diuin verbe* may refer to the Papal Bull Unigenitus,
issued in 1713, the year the war ended. The great disaster following
the union of the countries is the War of the Spanish Succession. The
last line may be self-explanatory.

[1]*clade.* L. *disaster.*

Century IV
IV.VI

D'habits nouueaux apres faicte la treuue,
Malice tramme & machination:
Premier mourra qui en fera la preuue,
Couleur venife infidiation.

After the truce is made new clothes will be put on; malice, conspiracy and plotting. He who will prove it is the first to die, the color of Venetian treachery.

A very obscure quatrain. Perhaps the new clothes imply a new order of monks, and there is a shade of yellow-brown which is known as Venetian red.

Century IV
IV.VII

Le mineur filz du grand & hay Prince,
De lepre aura à vingt ans grande tache,
De dueil fa mere mourra bien trifte & mince,
Et il mourra là où tombe cher lache.

The younger son of a great and hated Prince will be greatly marked by leprosy by the time he is twenty. His mother will die of grief, very sad and thin, and he will die when the cowardly flesh vanishes (from his bones).

There is no record to date of a younger son of a royal family dying of leprosy.

Century IV
IV.VIII

La grand cité d'affaut prompt & repentin,
Surprins de nuict, gardes interrompus:
Les excubies & veilles fainct Quintin,
Trucidés gardes & les pourtails rompus.

The great city will be surprised at night by a sudden and quick assault. The guards interrupted; the watch and guards of St. Quentin slaughtered, the guards killed and the gates broken down.

St. Quentin is obviously the key word in this quatrain. There was a battle of St. Quentin in 1557 and the city was taken, not in the way Nostradamus described it, but by a seventeen-day siege. At least the prediction of the town's capture is correct. (See IV.III.)

Century IV
IV.IX

Le chef du camp au milieu de la preffe,
D'vn coup de fleche fera bleffé aux
cuiffes,
Lors que Geneue en larmes & detreffe,
Sera trahie par Lozan & Soyffes.

The leader of the army in the middle of the
crowd is wounded in the thighs with an
arrow. When Geneva, troubled and in
distress, is betrayed by Lausanne and the
Swiss.

This is probably another anti-Calvinist tirade by Nostradamus. He
seems to forsee Lausanne and Switzerland returning to the Roman
Catholic faith with only Geneva holding out. A completely mistaken
verse.

Century IV
IV.X

Le ieune prince accufé faulfement,
Mettra en trouble le camp & en
querelles:
Meurtry le chef pour le fouftenement,
Sceptre appaifer: puis guerir efcrouelles.

The young prince, falsely accused, will put
the camp into quarrels and trouble. The
leader is murdered for his support to appease the crown; then he cures the king's
evil.

A pointless quatrain. A leader of an army will support a Prince,
wrongly accused of something, and lose his life as a consequence.
Both French and English kings were reported to be able to cure
scrofula, the king's evil, particularly on the day of their coronation.

Century IV
IV.XI

Celuy qu'aura gouuert de la grand
cappe, [1]
Sera induict à quelque cas patrer: [2]
Les douze rouges viendront souiller la
nappe.
Soubz meurtre, meurtre se viendra
perpetrer.

He who will have government of the Great
Cape will be led to execute them in some
cases. The twelve red ones will come to
spoil the cover, under murder, murder will
be perpetrated.

A detailed quatrain. A pope will be forced into some rash action,
and then be condemned by his twelve cardinals. It is implied that they

[1]*Cappe.* Cloak, cape, standing for the Vatican.
[2]*patrer.* L. *patrare*, to execute, perform.

connive at the Pope's murder. This could possibly refer to Pope John Paul I, who reigned in 1978 for only thirty-four days and died in mysterious circumstances in the Vatican after a meeting with the cardinals of his curia.

John Paul I had determined to look into the scandals of the Vatican connections with the Mafia and the powerful group of Freemasons known as P.2. The night before his death he had given Cardinal Villot a list of those people he wanted removed from positions of power. The cardinal later gave false statements to the police and press about the circumstances of John Paul I's death. The list has not been seen since. Also, hastily, and against all Catholic tradition, the body of the Pope was cremated. If this is the correct interpretation, a good quatrain. (See also X.XII, X.LXV.)

Century IV

IV.XII

Le camp plus grand de route mis en fuite,
Guaires plus outre ne fera pourchaffé:
Oft recampé, & legion reduicte,
Puis hors des Gaules du tout fera chaffé.

The greatest army on the march put to flight, will scarcely be pursued further. The army reassembled and the legion reduced, they will be driven completely out of France.

A general quatrain and the German invasions of the last two wars fit it most accurately. But there is nothing explicit to go on.

Century IV

IV.XIII

De plus grand perte nouuelles raportées,
Le raport fait le camp s'eftonnera:
Bandes vnies encontre reuoltées,
Double phalange grand abandonnera.

News of the great loss is brought; the report will astonish the camp. Bands unite against those who are in revolt, the double phalanx will forsake the great one.

This verse was applied by contemporaries to the 1580's, when a rumor spread through the duke of Parma's army of so great a defeat that they were completely demoralized and this enabled the Dutch to capture Antwerp for a time. A phalanx consisted of 800 men, so double this number are said to have revolted.

Century IV

IV.XIIII

La mort *fubite du premier perfonnage*
Aura changé & mis vn autre au regne:
Toft, tard venu à fi haut & bas aage,
Que terre & mer faudra que on le
   craigne.

The sudden death of the leading personage
will make change, and put another to
rule. Soon, but too late come to high position, of young age. By land and sea it will
be necessary to fear him.

A general prophecy about a young leader who comes to power too
late to alter the status quo of a country. It has fancifully been suggested that it may refer to John F. Kennedy, succeeding old General
Eisenhower, whose politics had been unable to lessen world tension.
During the Cuban Missile Crisis, Kennedy's power was to be feared
by land and sea.

Century IV

IV.XV

D'où penfera faire venir famine,
De là viendra le reffafiement:
L'oeil de la mer par auare canine
Pour de l'vn l'autre donra huyle,
   froment.

From the place where he will think to
bring famine, from there will come help.
The eye of the sea, like a covetous dog. The
one will give oil and wheat to the other.

This verse describes Britain's predicament during the Second
World War, 1939–45, very accurately. The German blockade tried to
starve Britain out (see also III.LXXI), but fortunately she received
large quantities of American aid—*huyle, froment.* The "eye of the sea,
like a covetous dog" is a wonderful description of U-boats, searching
for British convoys through their periscopes, to hunt them down.

Century IV

IV.XVI

La cité franche de liberté fait ferue,
Des profligés & resueurs faict afyle:
Le Roy changé à eux non fi proterue:[1]
De cent feront deuenus plus de mille.

The free city of liberty is enslaved, it
becomes the refuge of profligates and
dreamers. The king changes and is not so
ferocious towards them. From one hundred they will become more than a thousand.

[1]*proterue.* L. *protervus,* violent.

Europe had many free cities when Nostradamus wrote. He may here be referring to Orange, which gave its name to the Dutch royal line, and did not pass to France until 1713. During Nostradamus' time it belonged to William the Silent, and line 2 may refer to it becoming a haven for Protestants, which in fact it did.

Century IV

IV.XVII

Changer à Beaune, Nuy, Chalons &
*   Dijon,*
Le duc voulant amander¹ la Barrée²
Marchant pres fleuue, poiffon, bec de
*   plôgeon,*
Verra la queuë: porte fera ferrée.

Changes at Beaune, Nuits, Chalon and Dijon; the duke wants to improve the Carmelites. Walking near the river, a fish, a diving (bird's) beak, towards the tail. The gate will be locked.

St. Theresa reformed the order of Carmelite nuns in Spain in 1562. I can make nothing of the following lines.

Century IV

IV.XVIII

Des plus lettrés deffus les faits celeftes
Seront par princes ignorans reprouués:
Punis d'Edit, chaffez, comme fceleftes,
Et mis à mort là où seront trouués.

Some of the most learned men in the heavenly arts will be reprimanded by ignorant Princes. Punished by an Edict, driven out as scoundrels and put to death wherever they are found.

Shades of the Inquisition linger over this verse for, in fact, astrologers were never as grossly persecuted after Nostradamus' death as they were before. However, the witch-hunts which bedeviled America and Europe did not occur until a century later.

---

¹*amander.* O.F. to better, to improve.
²*Barrée.* This was the name given to the Carmelite monks and nuns, coming from the O.F. *barré*, motley.

Century IV

IV.XIX

Deuant Rouan d'Infubres mis le fiege,
Par terre & mer enfermés les paffages:
D'Haynault, & Flâdres, de Gâd &
    ceux de Liege,
Par dons laenées[1] rauiront les riuages.

The Insubrians lay siege in front of Rouen, the passages closed by land and sea. By Hainault and Flanders, by Ghent and those of Liege, through hidden gifts they will ravage the shores.

Rouen was first captured by the duke of Parma who was helping the duc de Guise against Henri de Navarre in 1592, but without a long siege. Since Milan was part of Parma's dominions, there could well have been Italians *(Infubres)* among his troops. Rouen has never since been captured by Italians; the Germans captured it in 1870 and 1940, the Americans in 1944. All the other towns mentioned in the quatrain are in the Netherlands and Flanders. Despite all this speculation, it is hard to see that this prophecy has really been fulfilled.

Century IV

IV.XX

Paix vberté[2] long temps lieu louera:
Par tout fon regne defert la fleur de lys:
Corps morts d'eau, terre là lon
    aportera,
Sperants vain heur d'eftre là enfeuelis.

Peace and plenty for a long time will gift the place. The fleur-de-lys is deserted throughout the kingdom. Bodies dead by water will come there to land, hoping in vain for their burial hour.

The fleur-de-lys was not the unique property of the French royal family; it was used by several others, so it is less a clue than it seems. If it does relate to France, the obvious time that it disappears from the kingdom is during the Revolution and Empire. The last two lines seem to be generalities about war and unburied dead.

Century IV

IV.XXI

Le changement fera fort difficile,
Cité, prouince au change gain fera:
Coeur haut, prudent mis, chafsé luy
    habile,
Mer, terre, peuple fon eftat changera.

The change will be very difficult. Both city and province will gain by it. A highly placed, prudent man will be chased out by the cunning one. People will change their estate by land and sea.

[1] *laenées.* L. cloak, mantle; by metaphor, hidden.
[2] *vberté.* L. ubertas, abundance.

If one accepts this quatrain as referring to the fall of France, it could then be applied to Marshal Pétain's policy of "centralized decentralization." The prudent man will then be de Gaulle, chased to England, and the last line would then refer to the general state of the country during the war.

Century IV

IV.XXII

La grand copie[1] qui fera defchafsée,
Dans vn moment fera befoing au Roy,
La foy promife de loing fera faulfée,
Nud fe verra en piteux defarroy.

The great army which will be driven out, will suddenly be needed by the king. The trust, promised from afar, will be broken. He will see himself with nothing, in pitiful disorder.

This is such a general quatrain that these incidents may well have occurred several times. A king quarrels with an ally and suddenly finds he needs its help again. But because one of them breaks faith, the king is left powerless.

Century IV

IV.XXIII

La legion dans la marine claffe,
Calcine,[2] Magnes[3] foulphre, & poix
* bruflera:*
Le long repos de l'affeuree place,
Port Selyn,[4] Hercle[5] feu les confumera.

The legion in the marine fleet will burn, lime, magnesia, sulphur and pitch. There is a long rest in a safe place. Port Selyn, Monaco will be consumed by fire.

This is a strange and interesting quatrain. The second line appears to give us the ingredients for Greek fire, the famous "secret weapon" of the Greeks and the Byzantines. Nostradamus appears to be correct in this. The expert on ancient warfare Lt. Col. H. Hime wrote that it was the presence of quicklime which distinguished Greek fire from all other known incendiaries of the period. The mixture gave rise to heat on contact with water and thus took fire spontaneously when wet and was used with great success in sea battles. On the other hand, if

[1]*copie.* L. *copia,* army, troops.
[2]*Calcine.* L. *calcina,* lime.
[3]*Magnes.* L. lodestone; also an abbreviation of magnesia, the usual description of Greek fire.
[4]*Port Selyn.* Genoa: it was a crescent-shaped republic and *selene* is Greek for crescent.
[5]*Hercle.* L. *Herculeis Monacei,* Monaco.

I am correct in identifying Port Selyn with Genoa, it was attacked in 1684 by the French fleet of Louis XIV, causing considerable destruction in the city.

Century IV

IV.XXIIII

Ouy foubs terre faincte dame voix fainte,
Humaine flamme pour diuine voir luire:
Fera des feuls de leur fang terre tainte,
Et les faincts têples pour les impurs deftruire.

The faint voice of a woman is heard under the holy ground. A human flame lights up for the divine voice. It will cause the earth to be stained with the blood of celibates and destroy the holy temples on behalf of the wicked.

This quatrain is a riddle because of the many possible interpretations of the first line. To which word does *faincte* belong? In other versions *dame* is also given as *d'ame* and *fainte* as *faincte*. The general idea seems to be the persecution of the Church, perhaps as personified by the Holy Lady of line 1. The most probable fulfillment of this quatrain would be the abolition and persecution of the clergy during the French Revolution.

Century IV

IV.XXV

Corps fublimes fans fin à l'oeil vifibles:
Obnubiler viendront par ces raifons:
Corps, front comprins, fens chief &
inuifibles.
Diminuant les facrees oraifons.

The heavenly bodies endlessly visible to the eye come to cloud (the mind) for their own reasons. The body, together with the forehead, senses and head are all invisible, as the sacred prayers recede.

Some commentators believe this quatrain refers to the invention of the telescope, 1610, which will bring in new worlds and concepts hostile to religion. However, I believe this to be one of the "occult" quatrains, where Nostradamus is trying to describe the sensation of bodilessness which he experienced in a predictive trance, when his mind and intellect are used by the heavenly being for its own purposes. The sacred prayers of the last line are the invocations made to the spirit by Nostradamus as he gives up his being to its possession.

Century IV

IV.XXVI

Lou grand eyffame fe leuera d'abelhos,
Que non fauran don te fiegen
*   venguddos:*
De nevch l'êbousĝ, lou gach deffous las
*   treilhos*
Ciutad trahido per cinq lengos non
*   nudos.*

The great swarm of bees will arise but no one will know from whence they have come. An ambush by night, the sentinel under the vines; a city handed over by five tongues, not naked.

This is the only quatrain written entirely in sixteenth century Provençal. It is also amazingly accurate. It describes Napoleon's coup d'état of 1799. The swarm of bees was Napoleon's emblem. They can still be seen on the embroideries in Josephine's house at Malmaison and at Fontainebleau. The five men, literally "babblers" *(lengos non nudos)* who handed Paris over were the members of the Directoire who were bribed, *non nudos,* to give way to Napoleon's Consulate. They were also wearing their official clothes as members of the Directoire, as opposed to their normal apparel, to give authority to their gesture.

The coup was planned the night before its execution. *Las treilhos* is probably an anagram for the Tuileries into which Napoleon moved once he had consolidated his coup. The exact French equivalent is *les treilles.* Close enough in Nostradamus' language to "Tuileries."

Century IV

IV.XXVII

Salon, Manfol, Tarafcon de SEX.
*   l'arc,*
Où eft debout encor la piramide:
Viendront liurer le Prince Dannemarc,
Rachat honny au temple d'Artemide.

Salon, Mansol, Tarascon, the arch of SEX, where the pyramid is still standing. They will come to deliver the Prince of Denmark, a shameful ransom to the temple of Artemis.

The complicated first line refers to St. Rémy-de-Provence where Nostradamus was born, where there stand two great historical monuments: a mausoleum with the inscription SEX. L.M. JUILEI C.F. PARENTIBIS SUIS, next to which still stands a Roman triumphal arch. (It now stands in the middle of a field with cows grazing around it.) *Mansol* is a misprint for Mausole, a priory just outside Saint Rémy. But Dannemarc and the following line I cannot decipher.

Century IV
IV.XXVIII

Lors que Venus du Sol fera couuert,
Soubs l'esplendeur fera forme occulte:
Mercure au feu les aura defcouuert,
Par bruit bellique fera mis à l'infulte.

When Venus will be covered by the sun,
under the splendor will be a hidden form.
Mercury will have exposed them to the fire,
by a rumor of war will be affronted.

I believe that this and four other quatrains IV.XXIX, XXX, XXXI, and XXXIII are hermetic quatrains possibly describing Nostradamus' attempts to isolate and use various materials for his occult practices. They should be read as a sequence.

Century IV
IV.XXIX

Le Sol caché eclipfe par Mercure,
Ne fera mis que pour le ciel fecond:
De Vlcan Hermes fera faicte pafture,
Sol fera veu pur, rutilant & blond.

The hidden Sun eclipsed by Mercury will be placed only second in the heavens. Hermes will be made the food of Vulcan, the Sun will be seen pure, shining and golden.

Hermes is Quicksilver and Vulcan stands for fire.

Century IV
IV.XXX

Plus vnze fois Luna Sol ne voudra,
Tous augmenté & baiffez de degré:
Et fi baf mis que peu or on coudra,
Qu'apres faim, pefte, defcouuert le
*   fecret.*

More than eleven times the Moon will not want the sun, both raised and lessened in degree. Put so low that one will sew little gold. After famine and plague the secret will be discovered.

The Moon here stands for silver and the Sun for gold.

Century IV
IV.XXXI

La Lune au plain de nuict fur le haut
*   mont,*
Le nouueau fophe d'vn feul cerueau l'a
*   veu:*
Par les difciples eftre immortel femond,
Yeux au midy, en feins mains, corps au
*   feu.*

The moon, in the middle of the night over the high mountain; the young wise man alone with his brain has seen it. Invited by his disciples to become immortal; his eyes to the south, his hands on his breast, his body in the fire.

Does the last line suggest that Nostradamus suffers physical pain when making contact with his *diuin verbe*? Note also the position, eyes to the south and hands on his breast. This must be the pose he adopted in his study.

Century IV

IV.XXXII

Es lieux & temps chair au poiſſon donra lieu, *La loy commune fera faicte au contraire:* *Vieux tiendra fort puis ofté du milieu,* *Le Pânta chiona philôn mis fort arriere.*	*In those times and places that meat gives way to fish, the common law will be in opposition. The old (older?) will hold strong, then removed from the scene. Pânta, chiona, philôn, put far behind.*

Pânta chiona philôn is the Greek for "all things held in common among friends." Communism in its most simplistic sense? Nostradamus also describes this in III.XCV, implying that the appeal of the old order will fail. Now we have glasnost, but Nostradamus warns that strong attempts will be made to get Russia to return to its old régime. I originally wrote in 1972, "I wonder whether this means that America and the USSR will ally?" This has now happened. (See V.LXXVIII.)

Century IV

IV.XXXIII

Jupiter ioinct plus Venus qu'à la Lune, *Apparoiſſant de plenitude blanche:* *Venus cachée fouz la blancheur Neptune* *De Mars frappée par la grauée branche.*	*Jupiter joined more to Venus than to the Moon appearing in a white fullness. Venus hidden under the whiteness of Neptune, struck by Mars by the engraved wand.*

Branche is used by Nostradamus in I.II to indicate the wand he uses during his preparatory ritual for prophesying. The rest of his obscure quatrain must be allied with IV.XXVIII, XXIX, and XXX.

Century IV
IV.XXXIIII

Le grand mené captif d'eftrange terre,
D'or enchainé au Roy CHYREN offert:
Qui dans Auftone, Milan perdra la
*   guerre,*
Et tout fon oft mis à feu & à fer.

The great man led captive from a foreign
land, chained in gold, offered to King
Chyren. He who in Ausonia and Milan
will lose the war and all his army put to
fire and the sword.

CHYREN is almost certainly an anagram for the Old French spelling of Henri, Henryc. The problem lies in deciding which Henri the quatrain refers to. Many commentators favor Henri IV; those of the nineteenth century in particular favor a new King Henri to come. The CHYREN quatrains are not particularly favorable to either idea, but it is unlikely that this is still to be fulfilled. It is probably a failed quatrain. (See II.LXXIX, VI.LXX, VIII.LIIII, IX.XXXXI.)

Century IV
IV.XXXV

Le feu eftaint, les vierges trahiront
La plus grand part de la bande
*   nouuelle:*
Fouldre à fer, lance les feulz Roy,
*   garderont*
Etrufque & Corfe, de nuict gorge
*   allumelle.*

The fires put out, the virgins will betray
the greater part of the new band. Lightning in the sword, lances alone will guard
the king. Tuscany and Corsica, at night
throats slit.

During the Empire, Tuscany and Corsica were both troubled by the French.

Century IV
IV.XXXVI

Les ieux nouueaux en Gaule redreffés,
Apres victoire de l'Insubre[1] champaigne:
Monts d'Efperie, les grands liés,
*   trouffés:*
De peur trembler la Romaigne &
*   l'Efpaigne.*

The new games are set up in Gaul after the
victory of the Insubrian campaign. The
mountains of Hesperia; the great ones tied
and bound. Romania and Spain will
tremble with fear.

Romaigne in line 4 stands for the Holy Roman Empire, i.e., Germany. The best interpretation of France's victories in Spain and in the North would be the Napoleonic campaigns.

[1]*Insubre.* L. *Insubria.* Italy, around Milan.

Century IV
IV.XXXVII

Gaulois par faults, monts viendra
penetrer:
Occupera le grand lieu de l'Infubre:
Au plus profond fon oft fera entrer,
Gennes, Monech poufferont claffe rubre.

The Gauls will penetrate the mountains in leaps, they will occupy the great seat of Insubria. He will make his army penetrate deep (into the land). Genoa and Monaco will repulse the red fleet.

In 1800, Genoa was besieged by Austria and surrendered on June 4. The British fleet, which had been helping with the blockade, attacked Monaco on May 23. Earlier that month, Napoleon made his incredible crossing of the Saint Bernard pass with an army of 40,000 men and took Milan *(Insubria)* on June 22. A very satisfactory quatrain.

Century IV
IV.XXXVIII

Pendant que Duc, Roy, Royne
occupera,
Chef Bizant du captif en Samothrace:
Auant l'affault l'vn l'autre mangera,
Rebours ferré fuyura du fang la trace.

While the duke occupies the king and queen, the Byzantine leader is held captive in Greece. Before the attack one will devour the other. The metal reverse will follow the train of blood.

The *rebours ferré*, metal reverse, sounds modern. Otherwise, I cannot decipher this quatrain.

Century IV
IV.XXXIX

Les Rhodiens demanderont fecours,
Par le neglet de fes hoyrs delaifsée:
L'empire Arabe reualera fon cours,
Par Hefperies la caufe redreffée.

The people of Rhodes will demand help, abandoned by the neglect of their heirs. The Arab Empire will assess its course, its cause revived again in the West.

At a time of unrest in Greece the United Arab Emirates will assess its position and be helped in some way by America. The Gulf War springs to mind. America has been selling weaponry to Iraq, and France to Iran. The United Nations, have desperately organized a cease-fire and hopefully end of the war. Probably a twentieth century quatrain.

Century IV

IV.XL

Les forter*es*ses des a*ffieg*és ferrés,
Par poudre à feu profondés en abyfme:
Les prodit*eurs feront tous vifs ferrés,
Onc aux facrif*tes n'aduint fi piteux
   fcifme.

*The fortress of the besieged, closed by gun-
powder, sunk into the abyss. The traitors
will be entombed alive. Never did so pitiful a schism happen to the sextons.*

The clue to this verse lies in the last line. *Sacristes,* sextons, are meaningless in this context. But if Nostradamus means Saxons, the Germans, associated with a schism, the breaking up of a party, this could refer indirectly to Hitler and those pitiful few of his followers who remained with him in the bunker at Berlin which was shelled by the Allies.

Century IV

IV.XLI

Gymnique[1] fexe captiue par ho*ft*age,
Viendra de nuit cu*ft*odes deceuoir:
Le chef du camp deçeu par fon langage:
Lairra à la gente, fera piteux à voyr.

*A female captive, as a hostage, will come
by night to deceive the guards. The leader
of the camp taken in by her words, will
lead her to the people. It will be pitiful to
see.*

Too general a quatrain to be of use.

Century IV

IV.XLII

Geneue & Lâgres par ceux de Chatres
   & Dole,
Et par Grenoble captif au Montlimard:
Seyffett Lofanne par fraudulente dole,
Les trahiront par or foixante marc.

*Geneva and Langres through the people of
Chartres and Dôle captured by Grenoble
at Montelimar. Seysel, Lausanne will betray them by a fraudulent trick for sixty
gold marks.*

There are too many scattered place names in both Switzerland and France to make this clear. A mark was eight ounces of gold.

---

[1]*Gymnique.* misprint for Gk. *gynique,* female.

Century IV
IV.XLIII

Seront ouys au ciel les armes battre:
Celuy au mefme les diuins ennemis:
Voudront loix fainctes iniuftement
    debatre,
Par foudre & guerre bien croyans à
    mort mis.

Weapons will be heard fighting in the skies. In the same year the priests (divines) are enemies. They will want, unjustly, to query the holy laws. Through lightning and war many believers put to death.

The first line definitely indicates an air battle of some kind, which should make this a twentieth century quatrain. Lightning in line 4 is probably a bombardment. But who are the priests and the believers? I don't think this can apply to the Middle East as Nostradamus would never have called Moslems *croyans*. That word is reserved strictly for Christians. This may be linked with the Millennium.

Century IV
IV.XLIIII

Deux gros de Mende, de Roudés &
    Milhau,
Cahours, Limoges, Caftres malo
    fepmano
De nuech l'intrado, de Bourdeaux vn
    cailhau,
Par Perigort au toc de la campano.

The two large ones of Mende, of Rodez and Milhau, Cahors and Limoges, Castres; a bad week. The entry by night. An insult from Bordeaux. Through Perigord at the peal of the bell.

A quatrain of mixed Provençal and French. Unfortunately these seem to disguise little more than the names of various towns in southern France. The toscin singing in line 4 may be an alarm, but against what?

Century IV
IV.XLV

Par conflit Roy, regne abandonnera,
Le plus grand chef faillira au befoing:
Mors profligés peu en rechapera,
Tous deftranchés, vn en fera tefmoing.

Through a battle the king will abandon his kingdom. The greatest leader will fail in time of need. Dead, ruined, few will escape, all cut down save one who will be a witness.

This is a typical prophecy that may refer to several historical events, repeated history as it were, depending upon the reader's viewpoint. Napoleon at Waterloo, Napoleon III and Kaiser Wilhelm II have all been proposed as candidates. The reader can take his choice.

Century IV

IV.XLVI

Bien defendu le faict par excellence,
Garde toy Tours de ta proche ruine:
Londres & Nantes par Reims fera
  defenfe
Ne paffe outre au temps de la bruine.

The deed, through its excellence is strictly forbidden. Tours, beware of your future ruin. London and Nantes will make a defense through Reims. Do not venture further afield at the time of the fog.

I cannot decipher this quatrain.

Century IV

IV.XLVII

Le noir farouche quand aura effayé
Sa main fanguine par feu, fer, arcs
  tendus:
Treftout le peuple fera tant effrayé,
Voir les plus grans par col & pieds
  pendus.

When the ferocious dark one will have exercised his bloody hand through fire, the sword, the drawn bow, all the nation will be so terrified to see the great ones hanging by their neck and feet.

Again we have the mysterious dark-haired man, the *Brodde* of other quatrains, who appears to be terrorizing his people. He has been linked with the advent of the Third World War. I think that this quatrain has yet to be fulfilled.

Century IV

IV.XLVIII

Planure Aufonne fertile, fpacieufe,
Produira taons fi tant de fauterelles:
Clarté folaire deuiendra nubileufe,
Ronger le tout, grand pefte venir
  d'elles.

The plains of Ansonia, rich and wide, will spawn so many gadflies and grasshoppers that the height of the sun will be clouded over. They will devour everything and a great pestilence will come from them.

This may be a futuristic quatrain. At the time of writing, late 1988, there is one of the worst plagues of locusts *(sauterelles)* seen for many years in North Africa and reports have been coming in that they have been found in Sicily and even on the islands off America and England. With the appalling famine in the Sudan, maybe the swarms will turn north to Italy in search of food?

Century IV

IV.XLIX

Deuant le peuple fang fera refpandu,
Que du haut ciel ne viendra efloigner:
Mais d'vn long temps ne fera entendu,
L'efprit d'vn feul le viendra tefmoigner.

Blood will be spilled in front of the people which will not go far from high heaven. But although seen for a long time, it will not be heard. The spirit of a single man will bear witness to it.

Spilled blood is calling to the heavens for vengeance, but the bloody deed which caused it is not clear.

Century IV

IV.L

Libra verra regner les Hefperies,
De ciel & terre tenir la monarchie:
D'Afie forces nul ne verra peries,
Que fept ne tiennent par rang la
*   hierarchie.*

Libra will be seen to reign in the West holding the rule over the skies and earth. No one will see the strength of Asia destroyed until seven hold the hierarchy in succession.

An interesting quatrain. It states that when Libra, the Balance, rules over the Western World and therefore America, that country will be at the height of its powers. But Asian strength will be equally strong until the seventh comes. This does not mean the seventh decade so perhaps it is a seventh ruler, a change of régime? It appears from the last line that a war may occur between East and West once this seventh successor is in power. This should be linked with the quatrains of the Third Antichrist and global war towards the end of the century. "The seven" is one of the portents of the Millennium.

Century IV

IV.LI

Vn Duc cupide fon ennemy enfuyure,
Dans entrera empefchant la phalange:
Haftez à pied fi pres viendront
*   pourfuyure*
Que la iournee conflite pres de Gange.

A duke will enter, eager to follow his enemy, hindering the phalanx. Hurrying on foot they follow so closely that the day of battle is near Ganges.

It is unlikely that *Gange* stands for the river Ganges in India as Nostradamus simply didn't take that country into his calculations, unless it comes under his sweeping term of "Asia and the East." There is a small town named Ganges near Montpellier.

Century IV

IV.LII

En cité obfeffe aux murs hommes &
femmes;
Ennemis hors le chef preft à foy rendre:
Vent sera fort encontre les gendarmes,
Chaffez feront par chaux, pouffiere, &
cendre.

In the besieged city, men and women at the walls, the enemy without, the leader ready to surrender. The wind will drive strongly against the armed men. They will be driven off by lime, dust and cinders.

Another general quatrain about the besieging of a city and its attackers repelled.

Century IV

IV.LIII

Les fugitifs & bannis reuoquez,
Peres & fils grand garniffant les hauts
puits:
Le cruel pere & les fiens fuffoquez,
Son fils plus pire fubmergé dans le
puits.

The fugitives and the banished are recalled, fathers and sons strengthening the deep walls. The cruel father and his followers suffocated. His most wicked son drowned in the well.

Probably a failed quatrain?

Century IV

IV.LIIII

Du nom qui onques ne fut au Roy
Gaulois,
Iamais ne fut vn fouldre fi craintif:
Tremblant l'Italie, l'Efpaigne & les
Anglois,
De femme eftrangiers grandement
attentif.

Holding a name which never belonged to a French king, there was never so fearful a thunderbolt. Italy, Spain and the English tremble. He will be greatly attractive to foreign women.

This is a good quatrain. Napoleon brought the new name of Bonaparte to the ranks of Capet, Valois, and the other French kings. He also brought a new Christian name (there had been six Louises, two Henris, two Charleses and one François since Nostradamus' time). Napoleon caused the great changes that occurred on the map of Europe—to Italy, Spain and England. He was also very enamored of both his foreign wives, Josephine, the Créole, and Marie Louise of Austria. The quatrain may possibly also hint of his Polish mistress,

Marie Walewska. The reference to his name being as dreadful as a thunderbolt should be compared with IV.LXXXII, where Nostradamus refers to Napoleon as "the Destroyer."

Century IV
IV.LV

Quant la corneille fur tout de brique ioincte, *Durant fept heures ne fera que crier:* *Mort prefagee de fang ftatue taincte,* *Tyran meurtri, aux Dieux peuple prier.*	*When the crow will do nothing but croak for seven hours on a tower made of brick, it foretells death. A statue stained with blood, a tyrant murdered, people praying to their Gods.*

Both the crow and the statue weeping blood are common omens of evil or portentous events. However, I cannot pin down anything specific in this stanza.

Century IV
IV.LVI

Apres victoire de rabieufe langue, *L'efprit tempté en tranquil & repos:* *Victeur fanguin par conflict faict harangue,* *Rouftir la langue & la chair & les os.*	*After the victory of the babbling tongue, the spirit is tempted by a tranquil rest. Throughout the battle the bloody victor makes speeches, roasting the tongue, the flesh and the bones.*

I cannot explain this quatrain.

Century IV
IV.LVII

Ignare enuie au grand Roy fupportee, *Tiendra propos deffendre les efcriptz:* *Sa femme non femme par vn autre tentee,* *Plus double deux ne fort ne criz.*	*Ignorant envy, supported by the great king, who will propose that the writings should be forgiven. His wife, who is not his wife, tempted by another. No longer will the double dealing couple protest against it.*

It has been suggested that Nostradamus is referring here to his own writings and to Henri II's cool reception of the *Prophecies*. The second woman would then be Diane de Poitiers, who had such an enormous influence on the king's life. There is a similar reference in VII.IX. The last line is difficult to interpret.

Century IV
IV.LVIII

Soleil ardent dans le gofier coller,
De fang humain arroufer terre
  Etrufque:
Chef feille[1] d'eaue, mener fon fils filer,
Captiue dame conduicte en terre
  Turque.

The burning sun is swallowed in the
throat; the Tuscan land sprinkled with
human blood. The chief with a pail of
water, leads his son away. A captive lady
led into Turkish hands.

I cannot make anything of this, nor the quatrain following
(IV.LIX).

Century IV
IV.LIX

Deux affiegez en ardente ferueur,
De foif eftaincts pour deux plaines
  taffes:
Le fort limé, & vn vieillart refueur,
Aux Geneuois de Nira monftra traffe.

Two besieged in a burning heat, killed by
thirst for want of two full cups. The fort
filed, and an old dreamer will show the
tracks of Nira to the Genevans.

Century IV
IV.LX

Les fept enfans en hoftaige laifsés,
Le tiers viendra fon enfant trucider:
Deux par fon filz feront d'eftoc percés,
Gennes, Florence, los viendra encunder.

The seven children left in hostage, the
third will come to slaughter his child. Two
will be pierced by a hook, because of his
son. He will come to strike Genoa and
Florence.

Usually the seven children in the quatrains refer to those of Catherine de' Medicis, but the rest of the quatrain seems to negate this.

Century IV
IV.LXI

Le vieux mocqué & priué de fa place,
Par l'eftrangier qui le fubornera:
Mains de fon filz mangées deuant fa
  face,
Le frere à Chartres, Orl. Rouan
  trahyra.

The old man is mocked and deprived of his
position by the foreigner who will suborn
him. The hands of his sons are devoured
before his face. He will betray his brother
at Chartres, Orléans and Rouen.

[1]*feille.* O.F. pail, bucket.

During the Second World War, Marshal Pétain, leader of the Vichy government, was nicknamed *Le Vieux;* his position vis-à-vis the Nazis is described clearly in line 2. The hands devoured in front of him are the destroyed forces of his régime. The brother represents the Allies, who simultaneously reached the three towns here mentioned, Chartres, Orléans and Rouen, on August 19, 1944. The régime was betrayed by Pétain to the Germans. He was deported to Sigmaringen on the very day of their liberation.

Century IV
IV.LXII

Vn coronel machine ambition,	*A colonel intrigues through ambition. He*
Se faifira de la plus grand armée,	*will seize the greater part of the army.*
Contre fon prince fainte inuention,	*Against his prince a false invention; he*
Et defcouuert fera foubz fa ramée.	*will be discovered under his flag.*

This quatrain is usually accepted as a general one applying to Oliver Cromwell, who took over the greater part of Charles I's armies and fought with them under the British flag. Cromwell certainly connived in the plotting and accusations laid against the king at his trial and execution. However, it could also be applied very neatly to Colonel Gaddafi, who overthrew King Idris of Libya in 1969.

Century IV
IV.LXIII

L'armée Celtique contre les	*The Celtic army against the people of the*
* montaignars,*	*mountains who will be revealed and*
Qui feront fceuz & prins à la lipee:	*caught in a trap. The fresh bracken will*
Payfans frefz pouferont toft faugnars,	*soon be pressed by the peasants. They will*
Precipitez tous au fil de l'espee.	*all perish on the sword's blade.*

This may well refer to Marshal Villars' wide-ranging battle against the *camisard* rebels of the Cévennes who engaged him in a very efficient form of guerrilla warfare from 1702 to 1704.

Century IV
IV.LXIIII

Le deffaillant en habit de bourgeois,	*The defaulter, dressed as a citizen; the*
Viendra le Roy tempter de fon offence:	*king will come to try his offense. Fifteen*
Quinze fouldartz la plufpart Vstagois,	*soldiers, for the most part outlaws; the end*
Vie derniere & chef de fa cheuance.	*of his life and most of his estate.*

Yet another quatrain still to be unraveled.

Century IV
IV.LXV

Au deferteur de la grand fortereffe,
Apres qu'aura fon lieu abandonné:
Son aduerfaire fera fi grand proueffe,
L'Empereur toft mort fera condamné.

To the deserter of the great fortress after he has abandoned his post, his adversary will display such prowess that the Emperor will soon be condemned to death.

Napoleon III, while still Louis Napoleon, was condemned by the French to life detention in the fortress of Ham, but he escaped from the castle to England on May 25, 1846. Louis Philippe abandoned his position as king of France during the Revolution of 1848 and Louis Napoleon was voted Prince-President in December of that year. He did not, however, display great skills as an Emperor, and his policies were responsible for the Franco-Prussian War with its consequent disaster for the French. He died soon after the war, in 1873. The powerful adversaries are, of course, the Russians.

Century IV
IV.LXVI

Soubz couleur faincte de fept teftes
* rafées*
Seront semés diuers explorateurs:
Puys & fontaines de poyfons arroufées,
Au fort de Gennes humains deuorateurs.

Under the false colors of seven shaven heads several spies will be scattered. The wells and springs will be sprinkled with poisons. At the fort at Genoa they devour human flesh.

Shaven heads is often used as a synonym for the Roundheads by Nostradamus, but the situation in this quatrain does not seem to have occurred. A false prediction.

Century IV
IV.LXVII

L'an que Saturne & Mars efgaux
* combuft,*
L'air fort feiché longue traiection:
Par feux fecrets, d'ardeur grand lieu
* aduft*
Peu pluye, vent chault, guerres,
* incurfions.*

In the year that Saturn and Mars are equally fiery, the air is very dry; a long meteor. From the hidden fires a great place burns with heat. Little rain, a hot wind, wars and raids.

This quatrain gives an astrological dating, common enough in Saturn and Mars. Nostradamus indicates that world drought will escalate at the time of the conjunction. It happened twice in 1985, the Ethiopian famine occurs again in 1987, and also in 1989. This fits in with sunspot activity and appears to indicate that we are approaching the worst famine of this century.

Century IV

IV.LXVIII

En l'an bien proche non efoigné de
  Venus,
Les deux plus grans de l'Afie &
  d'Affrique
Du Ryn & Hifter qu'on dira font
  venus,
Crys, pleurs à Malte & cofté liguftique.

At a nearby place not far from Venus, the two greater ones of Asia and Africa; from the Rhine and Hitler they will be said to have come. Cries and tears at Malta and the Ligurian coast.

Venus, standing for Venice, is the clue to this quatrain as it links Italy, *cofté liguftique,* with Hitler. The two dictators, Hitler and Mussolini, met at the Brenner Pass when they sealed the Tripartite Pact with Asia, that is to say the Japanese. The last line refers to the blockade of Malta by the Italians and the trouble in the Ligurian coast, to the Allied bombing of Genoa and the bombardments by British battleships operating out of Gibraltar.

Century IV

IV.LXIX

La cité grande les exilés tiendront.
Les citadins morts meurtris & chaffés.
Ceulx d'Aquillee à Parme promettront,
Monftrer l'entree par les lieux non
  traffés.

The exiles will hold the great city. The citizens are dead, murdered and driven out. The people of Aquileia will promise Parma to show them the entrance by untrodden paths.

Although Aquileia was a great city in ancient times, by the sixteenth century it was nothing but a village. Parma belonged to the Papacy and became an hereditary duchy for Pope Clement VII's bastard in 1545.

Century IV

IV.LXX

Bien contigue des grans monts Pyrenees,
Vn contre l'aigle grand copie addreffer:
Ouvertes veines, forces exterminees,
Que iufque à Pau le chef viendra
   chaffer.

Very near the great mountains of the Pyrenees a man will raise a great army against the Eagle. Veins will be opened, strength disappears. The leader will chase them as far as Pau.

This quatrain describes Wellington's approach to France through Portugal and Spain where he is to confront the Eagle, Napoleon. The opened veins probably mean the lost supply lines of the French when they were driven back as far as Pau. Despite the French victory at Toulouse, it was of uncertain value to Napoleon.

Century IV

IV.LXXI

En lieu d'efpoufe les filles trucidées,
Meurtre à grand faulte ne fera
   fuperftile:[1]
Dedans le puys veftules inondées,
L'efpoufe eftaincte par haufte
   d'Aconile.[2]

Instead of a bride, girls are slaughtered, murder so wicked there will be no survivors. The Vestals are drowned in the wells, the bride killed by a draught of Aconite.

Aconite is a classic poison distilled from monkshood and wolfsbane. Otherwise the quatrain is completely obscure.

Century IV

IV.LXXII

Les Artomiques par Agen à l'Estore,
A sainct Felix feront leur parlement:
Ceux de Basas viendront à la
   mal'heure,
Saisir Condon et Marsan promptement.

The Artomiques through Agen and Lectoire will hold their parlement at St. Felix. The people of Bazas will arrive at an unfortunate time to seize Condon and Maisan promptly.

What "the Artomiques" means is not certain. *Artos* means bread in Greek, but there is also a strong resemblance to the modern word "atomic."

---

[1] *fuperftile.* misprint for *supersite,* survivor.
[2] *Aconile.* misprint for aconite.

Century IV
IV.LXXIII

Le nepueu grand par forces prouvera,
Le pache fait du coeur pusillanime:
Ferrare & Ast le Duc esprouvera,
Par las qu'un soir fera le pantomine.

The nephew shall prove by great strength the crime committed by a cowardly heart. The duke will test Ferrara and Asti; then, when the comedy takes place in the evening. (See also I.LXXXIIII and III.XCVI.)

The nephew in this case is almost certainly the duc de Berry, who was assassinated when he left the opera on the evening of February 13, 1820. The other nephew who benefits from this deed became Napoleon III, who later succeeded to the French throne because of the death of his cousin, the direct male heir.

Century IV
IV.LXXIIII

Du lac luman & ceux de Brannonices,[1]
Tous affemblez contre ceux d'Aquitaine
Germains beaucoup, encor plus Souiffes,
Seront defaictz auec ceux d'Humaine.[2]

The people of Lake Geneva and Mâcon all gathered against those of Aquitaine. Many Germans, even more Swiss, will be routed together with those of Maine.

It is just possible that with *Humaine* in line 4 Nostradamus is referring to the Humanists, whom he regarded as responsible for the Protestant Reformation in Switzerland. But the variant, *ceux de Maine,* which occurs in many editions does not fit in with this explanation. A confusing quatrain.

Century IV
IV.LXXV

Preft à combatre fera defection.
Chef aduerfaire obtiendra la victoire.
L'arriere garde fera defenfion,
Les defaillans mort au blanc territoire.

He who was ready to fight will desert, the chief adversary will win the victory. The rear guard will raise a defense. The falterers dying in a white country.

Marshal Grouchy is the deserter mentioned in the first line. During the battle of Waterloo, 1815, he was the commander of the French cavalry. His orders from Napoleon were delayed by twelve hours, but

[1]*Brannonices.* L. people from Mâcon and around.
[2]*Humaine.* Variant, *ceux de Maine.*

even when he received them, Grouchy did not obey them. The great adversary of the French is, of course, Wellington. The famous stand of Napoleon's Imperial Guard is described in line three. They fought to the last man. The *blanc territoire* may be an indirect reference to Napoleon's retreat from Moscow in 1812, and also a direct one to the sign of the white cockade of the Bourbons. It was written in contemporary reports that at Napoleon's capture, so many people in Paris sported white cockades that it looked as though there had been a fall of snow.

Century IV
IV.LXXVI

Les Nictobriges[1] par ceux de Perigort,
Seront vexez tenant iufques au Rofne:
L'affocié de Gafcons & Begorne,
Trahir le temple, le prebftre eftant au
    profne.

The people of Agen by those of Périgord will be troubled as far as the Rhône. The association of Gascons and Bigone betrays the Church, while the priest is giving his sermon.

Both Agen and Périgord are about two hundred miles from the Rhône. Bigone is a Gascon town, but also the rallying cry of Henri IV's Huguenots was Bigorre. The verse is probably hinting at the Protestant-Catholic conflict in France during the sixteenth century.

Century IV
IV.LXXVII

SELIN monarque l'Italie pacifique,
Regnes vnis Roy chreftien du monde:
Mourant voudra coucher en terre
    blefique[2]
Apres pyrates auoir chaffé de l'onde.

Selin King, Italy peaceful, kingdoms united by the Christian king of the world. When he dies, he will want to lie in Blois territory having chased the pirates from the sea.

It was upon this quatrain that many nineteenth century Royalists built their hope of a new, great French king who would come and change the face of Europe. The key to the quatrain is the word *SELIN*. It is derived from the Greek *Selene*, meaning the moon or the goddess Diana. I think that Nostradamus and some of his interpreters were completely mistaken about this series of quatrains. Nostradamus probably intended them for Henri II and Diane de Poitiers. Not even prophets are loath to flatter their superiors and Catherine de' Medicis

[1]*Nictobriges.* the people around Agen.
[2]*blefique.* L. *Blesa; Blois.*

would certainly have interpreted this quatrain in her husband's favor. Henri II had adopted the Moon as his device.

Put into a modern context, these predictions seem unlikely to succeed. The notion of a Christian king governing the world seems impossible in modern terms.

Century IV
IV.LXXVIII

La grand armee de la pugne ciuile,
Pour de nuict Parme à l'eftrange
* trouuée,*
Septante neuf meurtris dedans la ville,
Les eftrangiers paffez tous à l'efpee.

The great army of the civil war. Parma taken at night by foreigners. Seventy-nine murdered in the town, the foreigners all put to the sword.

Parma was an Italian Duchy and an ally of the French, so the Spanish are probably the foreign invaders.

Century IV
IV.LXXIX

Sang Royal fuis, Monhurt, Mas,
* Eguillon,*
Remplis feront de Bourdelois les landes,
Nauarre, Bygorre poinctes & eguillons,
Profondz de faim vorer de liege glandes.

Flee, royal blood, Montheurt, Mas and Aiguillon. The Landes will be full of people from Bordeaux. Navarre, Bigorre, points and spurs; deeply hungry they devour the acorns of the cork oak.

These places are all situated in southwest France and probably have some connection with IV.LXXVI. As I mentioned before, *Bigorre* was also the rallying cry of the Huguenot Protestants.

Century IV
IV.LXXX

Pres du grand fleuue grand foffe, terre
* egefte,*
En quinze pars sera l'eau diuifee:
La cité prinfe, feu, fang, cris conflict
* mettre*
Et la plus part concerne au collifee.[1]

Near the river a great trench, earth excavated. The water will be divided into fifteen parts. The city taken, fire, blood, cries and battle given; the greater part concerned with the collision.

James Laver insists that this is the quatrain that persuaded the nineteenth century commentator the Abbé Torné to insist that

---

[1]*collifee.* L. *collisus,* clash.

France erect the infamous Maginot Line, which eventually fell so quickly to the Germans. In the late 1920s the French Minister of Defense decided to build the Line, it is said due to his insistence that the next German invasion would come through Switzerland. The wall cost two million dollars a mile to build. Its existence caused a strong sense of false security in France during the rise of Hitler. The river in the first line is the Rhine. Hitler partially ignored the Maginot Line and advanced from other directions, thus fulfilling lines 3 and 4. The collision becomes the series of battles fought in France during the Second World War.

Century IV

IV.LXXXI

Pont on fera promptement de nacelles,
Paffer l'armee du grand prince
  Belgique:
Dans profondres[1] & non loing de
  Brucelles,
Outre paffés, detrenchés fept à picque.

A bridge will quickly be built from boats to enable the army of a great Belgian Prince to cross. Poured inside, not far from Brussels; having passed over, seven will be out down by a pike.

At the time Nostradamus wrote, the word Belgian was archaic and could only refer to Philip II, who had been given the territory by the Emperor Charles V in 1554. An attack on Northern France, across the river Scheldt (lines 1 and 2), was made in the 1560s.

Century IV

IV.LXXXII

Amas s'approche venant d'Efclauonie,
L'Oleftant vieux cité ruynera:
Fort defolee verra fa Romanie.
Puis la grand flamme eftaindre ne
  fçaura.

A mass (of men) will draw near coming from Slavonia. The Destroyer will ruin the old city. He will see his Romania quite deserted, then will not know how to extinguish the great flame.

This must refer to Napoleon's retreat from Moscow in 1812–13, when the *grande armée* fled during that bitter winter. *Oleftant* means "Destroyer" and Nostradamus refers to Napoleon as this in IV.IIII when he calls him the dreadful thunderbolt, *Vn fouldre si craintif.* The old city is Moscow, razed to the ground by fire. Romania has been used in the *Prophéties* to indicate Rome. Napoleon's younger son had just been made King of Rome and his empire did not last long. Perhaps one may understand the great flame, *grand flamme,* as a meta-

---

[1]*profondres.* L. *profondatus,* poured forth.

phor for the wars initiated by Napoleon and which gathered in momentum to eventually defeat him.

Century IV
IV.LXXXIII

Combat nocturne le vaillant capitaine,
Vaincu fuyra peu de gens profligé:
Son peuple efmeu, fedition non vaine,
Son propre filz le tiendra affiegé.

In a night battle the brave captain is overcome and flees, ruined by a few men. His people are moved, successfully pleading, his own son will keep him besieged.

A quatrain with too many generalities to make it coherent.

Century IV
IV.LXXXIIII

Vn grand d'Auxerre mourra bien
*   miferable,*
Chaffé de ceux qui foubs luy ont efté:
Serré de chaines, apres d'vn rude cable,
En l'an que Mars, Venus & Sol mis en
*   efté.*

An important man from Auxerre will die very wretchedly, driven out by the people under him. Bound in chains, and then with a long-lasting rage in the year that Mars, Venus and the Sun are in conjunction in the summer.

A quatrain with plenty of clues but it is insoluble. Who is the man from Auxerre? This astrological conjunction is very rare, so this quatrain may just possibly be unfulfilled to date.

Century IV
IV.LXXXV

Le charbon blanc du noir fera chaffé,
Prifonnier faict mené au tombereau:
More Chameau fus piedz entrelaffez,
Lors le puifné sillera l'aubereau.

The white charbon is driven out by the black: made a prisoner, led to the tumbril. His feet are tied together like a rogue, when the last born will let stop the falcon.

This is a complicated quatrain. Nostradamus as a plague doctor treated the disease which was known at that time as *le charbon* because of the black pustules it raised on the body and referred to it as such. But many commentators interpret *charbon* as an anagram for Bourbon and *noir* as the usual anagram for king, *roi*. It must be remembered that most anagrams of Nostradamus' period involved an extra letter to further confuse the issue. White was the color of the Bourbon king's standard. Louis XVI was the last Bourbon king before the Revolution. He was imprisoned in the Temple and taken to his death in a cheap carriage. His wife, Marie Antoinette, was dragged through the streets on a tumbril on January 27, 1793. The last line implies that his heir, Louis XVII, about whom there has been so much speculation, may have escaped from his cell in the Temple. For a while the eleven-year-old Louis was placed under the "protection" of Simon the Cobbler who had been given instructions by the *procureur* of the Commune to "humble" the Prince. In December, 1794, Louis was examined by a Dr. Harmand, who noted tumors on his left arm and swollen knees. But when Louis' death was announced in 1795, the body shown to the public was so disfigured that identification was impossible. Louis was the second-born of the family. His elder brother Charles also died in 1795.

Century IV
IV.LXXXVI

L'an que Saturne en eau fera conioinct,
Auecques Sol, le Roy fort & puiffant:
A Reims & Aix fera reçeu & oingt,
Apres conqueftes meurtrira innocens.

In the year when Saturn is in conjunction with Aquarius with the Sun, the very powerful king will be received and anointed at Reims and Aix. After conquests he will murder innocent people.

The astrological conjunction in lines 1 and 2 is reasonably rare. Reims is the traditional site for the coronation of French kings and Aix the coronation site for the German and Holy Roman Emperors. No king has been crowned in both places since Nostradamus wrote this. This is another of the quatrains used by French Royalists to predict the return of the French royal line. (See IV.LXXXVII.) A failed quatrain.

Century IV
IV.LXXXVII

Vn filz du Roy tant de langues aprins,
A fon aifné[1] au regne different:
Son pere beau[2] au plus grand filz
*   comprins*
Fera perir principal adherant.

The son of a king, so many languages learned, is different from his predecessor in the kingdom. His father-in-law, understanding his elder son well, will cause the main adherent to perish.

This quatrain implies that the younger son of a king will take over the kingdom, the elder, legitimate heir having been removed from the succession by his father (in-law?).

[1] *aifné.* elder or predecessor.
[2] *pere beau.* father-in-law or handsome father.

Century IV
IV.LXXXVIII

*Le grand Antoine du nom de faict
fordide
De Phthyriafe à fon dernier rongé:
Vn qui de plomb voudra eftre cupide,
Paffant le port d'efleu fera plongé.*

Anthony, great in name, base in his actions, at the end will be riddled with consumption. One who is eager for lead, passing the harbor will be drowned by the elected one.

In this quatrain we have a specific name and a specific illness. *Phthiriase* is either consumption, *Phthisis,* or *Phthiriasis,* which means someone suffering from lice. Pediculosis is an illness caused by lice. Who the Anthony may be is unclear.

Century IV
IV.LXXXIX

*Trente de Londres fecret coniureront,
Contre leur Roy fur le pont
l'entreprinfe,
Luy, fatalites la mort degoufteront.
Vn Roy efleu blonde, natif de Frize.*

Thirty Londoners will secretly conspire against their king, the enterprise on the sea. He and his followers will not like death. A fair king elected, a native of Friesland.

This is a good prediction of the Glorious Revolution of 1688–89. The Dutch William III insisted that those English lords who supported him should sign a document to ensure their loyalty to him. There were certainly a number of conspirators who crossed the sea to Holland and back before William was prepared to sail with his fleet. Those who dislike death, *la mort degoufteront,* are James II and his supporters, who decide to flee rather than fight it out once the duke of Marlborough, who led the English army, deserted their cause. William III came from Friesland. What makes this prophecy so interesting is that there was no possibility of a Dutch candidate for the English throne while Nostradamus was alive.

Century IV
IV.XC

Les deux copies aux murs ne pourront
ioindre,
Dans cest instant trembler Milan,
Ticin:
Faim, soif, doubtance si fort les viêdra
poindre,
Chair, pain, ne viures n'auront vn seul
boucin.

The two armies cannot join up at the
walls. At that time Milan and Pavia
tremble. Hunger, thirst and drought will
weigh on them so much. They will not
have a scrap of meat, bread nor supplies.

A failed quatrain. It seems unlikely that line 1 could refer to the
twentieth century.

Century IV
IV.XCI

Au duc Gaulois contrainct battre au
duelle,
La nef Mellele monech n'approchera,
Tort accusé, prison perpetuelle,
Son fils regner auant mort taschera.

For the French duke compelled to fight in
a duel, the ship Mellele will not approach
Monaco. Wrongly accused, perpetually
imprisoned, his son will attempt to reign
before his death.

Mellele may be a corruption of Melilla, a Moroccan seaport, but it
does not seem to fit into this context. This quatrain may have a
connection with IV.LXXXIII? The last lines are very similar.

Century IV
IV.XCII

Teste tranchee du vaillant capitaine,
Sera gettee deuant son aduersaire:
Son corps pendu de la classe à
l'antenne,
Confus fuira par rames à vent
contraire.

The head of the brave captain, cut off, will
be thrown down in front of his adversary.
His body hung from the mast of the ship.
Confused, he will flee using oars in a contrary wind.

It is interesting that Nostradamus again uses the word *antenne* instead of *mât,* for the ship's mast. Is he using it to indicate complex
equipment with which he was not familiar? It might possibly be a
radio mast or radar equipment which cover much of the surface of
modern ships.

Century IV
IV.XCIII

Vn ferpent veu proche du lict royal,	A serpent will be seen near the royal bed
Sera par dame nuict chiens	by a lady at night. The watchdogs will not
n'abayeront:	bark. Then in France will be born a prince
Lors naiftre en France vn Prince tant	so royal, that all the princes will see him
royal,	as a gift from heaven.
Du ciel venu tous les Princes verront.	

This quatrain refers to the birth of the comte de Chambord, 1820–83. The duchesse de Berry gave birth to her son seven months after her husband's assassination. The legitimacy of the birth was contested by the duc d'Orléans (the snake), who had right of entry to the duchesse's rooms, so the watchdogs were not alerted. The birth of a grandson to Charles X caused great rejoicing and the child was nicknamed *Dieudonné,* a gift from heaven, as Nostradamus so rightly puts it, *Du ciel venu.*

Century IV
IV.XCIIII

Deux grans freres feront chaffez	Two great brothers will be driven out of
d'Efpaigne,	Spain, the elder beaten beneath the Pyre-
L'aifné vaincu fous les monts	nean mountains. The sea is reddened.
Pyrennees:	Rhône, blood in Lake Geneva from Ger-
Rougir mer, rofne, fang lemam	many. Narbonne and Beziers con-
d'Alemaigne,	taminated by Agde.
Narbon, Blyterre, d'Agath,[1]	
contaminees.	

This detailed quatrain contains five separate predictions:

1. Exile for two Spanish leaders.
2. Defeat for one of them near the Pyrenees.
3. A bloody naval battle.
4. An attack against Geneva from Germany.
5. A possible plague spreading from Agde to local towns. (See VIII.XXI.)

---

[1]*Agath.* L. Agde.

Century IV

IV.XCV

Le regne à deux laiffé bien peu
  tiendront,
Trois ans fept mois paffés feront la
  guerre
Les deux veftales contre rebelleront,
Victor puis nay en Armonique terre.

The rule left to two, they will hold it for
a very short time. Three years and seven
months having passed they will go to war.
The two vestals will rebel against them.
The victor then born on American soil.

If in this quatrain one takes the two rulers to be world powers, it implies that three years and seven months after the final signing of the INF Treaty by the Soviet Union and the USA, an alliance Nostradamus predicts elsewhere, those powers will go to war against Asia. *"Veftales"* in line 3 is probably a corruption of "vassals," two smaller countries who disagree with the treaty and remain neutral. See also III.LX and IV.L for further details and dating. This is also an indirect reference to the age of glasnost.

Century IV

IV.XCVI

La foeur aifnée de l'ifle Britannique,
Quinze ans deuant le frere aura
  naiffance:
Par fon promis moyennant verrifique,
Succedera au regne de balance.

The elder sister of the island of Britain
will be born fifteen years before her
brother. Because of his promise proving to
be true, she will succeed to the kingdom of
the Balance.

Mary was the elder sister of James III, who never came to the English throne. On her accession she was twenty-six, not fifteen years older than her brother. Mary inherited the throne because of promises she and her husband, William of Orange, made to the English Parliament. The Balance is the zodiac sign of Libra, which Nostradamus seems to apply here to England, although many astrologers apply it to Austria and Savoy. But it also governs trading nations, of which Britain was certainly one. It is important to note that Nostradamus speaks of the British isles, *l'ifle Britannique,* which immediately dates the quatrain as after 1603. A satisfactory quatrain.

Century IV

IV.XCVII

L'an que Mercure, Mars, Venus,
   retrograde,
Du grand Monarque la ligne ne faillit:
Efleu du peuple l'vfitant[1] pres de
   Gagdole,[2]
Qu'en paix & regne viendra fort
   enuieiller.

In the year that Mercury, Mars and Venus are retrograde, the family line of the great Monarch will not fail. Elected by the Portuguese people near Cadiz, who in peace will grow very old in his kingdom.

This quatrain may refer to the Portuguese succession and is dated by the conjunction in line 1. It also seems to imply that the Portuguese royal line are elected in Spain, but this never happened. Philip II of Spain seized the Portuguese throne and held it until 1621, followed by his son Philip III, until the Portuguese rose in revolt against the Spanish in 1640.

Century IV

IV.XCVIII

Les Albanois pafferont dedans Rome,
Moyennant Langres demipler[3] affublés,
Marquis & Duc ne pardonnes à
   homme,
Feu, fang, morbilles[4] point d'eau,
   faillir les bleds.

The people of Alba will cross into Rome; by means of Langres the multitude are weakened. The Marquis and the Duke will spare no man. Fire, blood and smallpox, no water, the crops will fail.

The word *Albanois* is hard to interpret here. It probably stands for the troops of the duke of Alba, but Albania is also a possibility. The many disasters are obscure. Langres is in Champagne. (See VII.IIII.)

---

[1]*vfitant.* probable misspelling of *Lusitan,* Portuguese.

[2]*Gagdole.* probable misspelling for *Gades,* Cadiz. The existing reading doesn't even rhyme and is obviously incorrect.

[3]*demipler.* A word invented by Nostradamus. Probably derived from the Greek, *demispleres,* multitude.

[4]*morbilles.* O.F. smallpox.

Century IV

IV.XCIX

L'aifné vaillant de la fille du Roy,
Repouffera fi profond les Celtiques:
Qu'il mettra foudres, combien en tel
  arroy
Peu & loing puis profond és
  Hefperiques.

The brave eldest son of a king's daughter
will drive the Celts back very far. He will
use thunderbolts, so many in such an
array, few and distant, then deep into the
West.

The second part of this quatrain seems to indicate an intercontintal ballistic missile attack which will penetrate deep into the West. Could this be a foretaste of the Third World War?

Century IV

IV.C

De feu celefte au Royal edifice,
Quant la lumiere de Mars defaillira:
Sept mois grâd guerre, mort gent de
  malefice,
Rouen, Eureux au Roy ne faillira.

Fire will fall from the sky on the royal
building when the light of war is weak-
ened. For seven months a great war, peo-
ple dead through evil. Rouen and Evreux
will not fail their king.

During the siege of Paris during the Franco–Prussian War, the royal palace, the Tuileries, was destroyed by cannon fire. The glory of the Bonaparte family was weakened and almost ended by the war. Napoleon III was to die two years later and from then on France remained a Republic. The Franco–Prussian War did last for seven months, July, 1870 to February, 1871, an accurate prediction. The Norman towns in the last line remained loyal to the king and wanted to restore the monarchy through the National Assembly. Successful.

Century V

V.I

Avant venue de ruine Celtique,
Dedâs le têple deux parlementeront
Poignard coeur, d'vn monté au courfier
  & picque,
Sans faire bruit le grand enterreront.

Before the ruin of the Celtish one, two will
talk within the temple. Scarred to the
heart by one riding on a charger with a
lance, they will bury the great one secretly.

There has always been much speculation about the fate of the Celtic French king enclosed within the Temple, Louis XVII, the sec-ond son of Louis XVII and Marie Antoinette. Louis XVI and his family were housed in the Temple in 1792, when the Revolutionary mob appeared to be getting out of control. The fate of the whole royal family was debated by the newly formed French Legislative Assembly, *parlementeront.* It is not known exactly how Louis XVII died. He was put into the charge of a local cobbler and treated very severely, under the orders of the local Commune. But at the time of his supposed death, the body produced to the public could not be identified, even by autopsy. Nostradamus clearly believed Louis died in line 4, *le grand enterreront.* Line 3 seems to describe his killer as a soldier. The young king was treated appallingly while in prison, separated from his mother and sisters and half-entombed for months in the dark, like a wild beast. Some record his body as being found dead among his own excrement. He was declared to be seriously ill in May, 1785, and his death was announced the following June. During the next forty years, several pretenders came forward claiming to be the young prince but if Nostradamus is correct, the prince was buried at the Church of Sainte Marguerite on June 10, as was officially announced, without even a headstone to mark the spot, *sans faire bruit.* A complicated but immensely interesting quatrain.

Century V

V.II

Seps coniurés au banquet feront luire,
Contre les trois le fer hors de nauire:
L'vn les deux claffes au grand fera
    conduire,
Quant par le mail. Denier au front luy
    tire.

Seven conspirators at a banquet will flash their weapons against the three who come from the ship. One of the two will take the fleet to the leader, when the last one will shoot him through the forehead, piercing his armor.

I cannot decipher this quatrain.

Century V

V.III

Le fucceffeur de la Duché viendra,
Beaucoup plus outre que la mer de
    Tofquane:
Gauloife branche la Florence tiendra,
Dans fon giron d'accord nautique
    Rane.[1]

The successor to the dukedom will come from far beyond the sea of Tuscany. A French branch will hold Florence, in its wake an agreement with the nautical force.

[1]*Rane.* L. *rana,* frog. Probably a misprint for *rame,* oar, and by extension, fleet.

This quatrain probably applies to the duc de Lorraine, who was given the Duchy of Tuscany in 1737. Until then it had belonged to Italians, from Alessandro de' Medicis in 1531 to the death of Gian Gastone in 1737. It remained in the Lorraine family until 1859, except during the French Revolution when it belonged to Napoleon and the French. The reference to a nautical force is unclear. If one accepts the translation of *Rane* as frog, it could refer to the myth in which the earliest inhabitants of Tuscany were turned into frogs by Bacchus, which simply reinforces the identity of the particular Duchy referred to in the quatrain.

Century V

V.IIII

Le gros maftin de cité defchaffé,
Sera fafché de l'eftrange alliance,
Apres aux champs auoir le cerf chaffe,
Le loup & l'Ours fe donront defiance.

The great mastiff is driven out of the city, angered by the foreign alliance. Later, having chased the stag to the field, the wolf and the bear will defy each other.

The mastiff in French is also known as *le dogue anglais,* and England is therefore probably intended in line 1. Angered by a foreign treaty, the English chase the stag to the battlefield, where the wolf (Italy, from the legend of Romulus and Remus) and the Bear (Russia) are defying each other. This appears to refer to the Second World War, when the Russians entered the war as British allies.

Century V

V.V

Souz ombre faincte d'ofter de feruitude,
Peuple & cité l'vfurpera luy mefmes:
Pire fera par fraux de ieune pute,
Liuré au champ lifant le faux proefme.

Beneath the faint shadow of removing servitude, the people and the city will usurp power for themselves. He will do worse because of the trickery of a young whore, delivered in the field, reading the false promise.

The shadow or attempt to remove servitude in a city refers to the French Revolution, which started in Paris. However, revolutionary rule was just as authoritative as that of Louis XVI, whom it usurped, albeit in a different way. The people of Paris took over the government of their city after the storming of the Bastille on July 14, 1789. The so-called whore who made things worse is Marie Antoinette, who enraged the populace by her extravagance and in particular by the affair of the diamond necklace, a fraudulent deal of which she was unjustly accused. Although she was certainly innocent of this particular incident, it damaged her popularity beyond repair. When she and Louis were later caught trying to go to Saint Cloud in 1792, the family were turned back by the crowd who said to Louis "we love you alone." The false promises were those given by the king when he promised not to attempt to escape from the Temple where he and his family had been placed to protect them from the wrath of the populace. They attempted to escape to Varennes in 1792 and were caught. (See the remarkable quatrains IX.XX and IX.XXXIIII.)

Century V

V.VI

Au roy l'Augur fur le chef la main
  mettre,
Viendra prier pour la paix Italique:
A la main gauche viendra changer le
  fceptre
De Roy viendra Empereur pacifique.

The Augur will put his hand on the king's head and pray for peace in Italy. The scepter will be changed to his left hand, from the king will proceed a peaceful Emperor.

The Pope, *Augur,* was godfather by proxy to the son of Louis Napoleon, later Napoleon III, who was not popular in his dealings with Italy and the Vatican because the Roman Revolutionaries felt he was too accommodating. The changing of the scepter probably refers to Napoleon III's underhand manipulation of the Revolution in France in 1848 and to the fact that he declared himself Emperor on December 2, 1851. The fact that Nostradamus refers to his being a peaceful Empire ties in well with the famous statement Napoleon III made on attaining power: *"L'Empire, c'est la paix."* The art of Empire is peace. A good quatrain.

Century V

V.VII

Du Triumuir feront trouuez les os,
Cherchant profond threfor
  aenigmatique:
Ceux d'alentour ne feront en repos.
Ce concauer marbre & plomb
  metallique.

The bones of the Triumvir will be found by those searching for a deep and enigmatic treasure. Those around will not be peaceful. The hollow is of marble and metallic lead.

Triumvir is the key word to this quatrain. After the coup d'état of the 18 Brumaire when Napoleon attained power, he reduced the five members of the Directoire to three, and made himself First Consul.

Later, Louis Philippe attempted to revive his waning popularity when he brought back Napoleon's ashes *(les os)* from St. Helena and interred them at Les Invalides. The treasure Louis Philippe was vainly searching for was Napoleon's popular appeal. The restless people are the Bonapartistes, who were politically encouraged by this act and insisted on physically helping in the task of burying the Imperial ashes. The coffin itself was of lead, *plomb metallique.*

Century V

V.VIII

Sera laiffé le feu vif, mort caché,
Dedans les globes horrible
  efpouuentable,
De nuict à claffe cité en poudre lafché,
La cité à feu, l'ennemy fauorable.

There will be let loose living fire and hidden death, fearful, inside terrifying globes. By night the city will be reduced to rubble by the fleet, the city in flames, helpful to the enemy.

This probably refers to the Second World War, rather than Vietnam or Korea, although it might equally be applicable to the Iran-Iraq War or the war in Afghanistan, because of the reference to a city. It almost certainly refers to a war or wars in the twentieth century, characterized by the use of bombs and rocketry, *globes horrible efpouuentable.* Ships are also used in this battle to bombard a city which, when it erupts in flames, is helpful as a target to enemy aircraft.

Century V

V.IX

Iufques au fonds la grand arq demolue,
Par chef captif, l'amy anticipé:
Naiftra de dame front face cheuelue,
Lors par aftuce Duc à mort attrapé.

At the foot of the great fallen arch, by the captured chief the friend forestalled. A woman will bear a son, his face and forehead covered with hair. Through cunning the duke then escapes death.

These first two lines are believed by most commentators to refer to the assassination attempt made upon Napoleon III in 1858. He had been involved in the Italian revolutionary movement as a young man. But after he came to power in France the Italians felt he had betrayed their cause and four of them attempted to assassinate him as he left the Opéra on the night of January 14, 1858. This seems a favorite place for assassinations—see Nostradamus' references to the murder of the Duc de Berry at the Opéra on February 13, 1820 (I.LXXXIIII, III.XCVI, IV.LXXIII). The plot against Napoleon III was led by

Count Orsini. The building was damaged, but did not collapse, although various bystanders were killed. The captured friend was Pieri, a friend of Orsini's, who was arrested before the explosion. Napoleon III was only slightly hurt, *à mort attrapé*. The third line is completely obscure. But line 4 seems to imply that Napoleon III escaped death through foreknowledge, possibly due to Pieri's arrest. The following quatrain appears to follow immediately upon this one.

Century V

V.X

Vn chef Celtique dans le conflict blefsé,	*A French leader wounded in the conflict*
Aupres de caue voyant fiens mort	*sees his subjects struck dead near the thea-*
abbatre:	*ter. Hustled by enemies, with bloody*
De fang & playes & d'ennemis preffé,	*wounds, he will be saved from the four by*
Et fecourus par incognus de quatre.	*unknown people.*

As stated in V.IX there was an attempt to assassinate Napoleon III with a bomb outside the paris Opéra. *Cavea (cave)* is the Latin word for theater. The four conspirators were Orsini, Pieri, Gomez and Rudio. The unknown people *fecourus par incognus* are the innocent bystanders who unwittingly sheltered the king from the blast.

Century V

V.XI

Mer par folaires feure ne paffera,	*Those of the sun will not cross the sea in*
Ceux de Venus tiendront toute	*safety. The people of Venus will hold the*
l'Affrique:	*whole of Africa. Then Saturn occupies*
Lur regne plus Saturne n'occupera,	*their kingdom no longer and a part of*
Et changera la part Afiatique.	*Asia will change.*

The flag of Japan is that of the sun, and the country is known as the Land of the Rising Sun. This quatrain describes Japan's position during the Second World War, between 1941 and 1945. Her ships will not be safe once she enters the war on the side of the Germans and causes a shift in Asian politics, with China joining up with the Allied Powers in 1941. The people of Venice (Venus is a common corruption in the *Prophecies* for the name of this city) stand for Italy and are fighting with Rommel in Northern Africa. The malign influence of Saturn upon Italian affairs causes them to withdraw from the war in 1943.

Century V

V.XII

Aupres du Lac Leman fera conduite,
Par garfe eftrange cité voulant trahir:
Auant fon meurtre à Aufpourg la grand
  fuitte
Et ceux du Rhyn la viendront inuahir.

Near Lake Geneva he will be led by a
woman who wants to betray the foreign
city. Before the death a great retinue will
come to Augsburg. They will come to in-
vade the people of the Rhine.

Augsburg is the key word in this quatrain. The Battle of Augsburg in 1636, during the Thirty Years' War, forced the retreat of Bernhard, duke of Saxe-Weimar, across the Rhine. This left southern and central Germany exposed to the attacks of the Hapsburg armies of the Holy Roman Emperor, Ferdinand II. Augsburg fell to Ferdinand, as did other towns along the Rhine near the Swiss border. The spelling of *Aufpourg* by Nostradamus is a typical pun, containing elements of both the words *Augsburg* and *Hapspurg*. The puzzle is the young woman of line 2.

Century V

V.XIII

Par grand fureur le Roy Romain
  Belgique
Vexer voudra par phalange barbare:
Fureur grinffeant chaffera gent Lybique
Defpuis Pannons[1] iufques Hercules la
  hare.[2]

In a great rage the Roman king will wish
to trouble Belgium with barbarian warri-
ors. In a gnashing fury he will chase the
Libyan people from Hungary as far as
Gibraltar.

This quatrain also applies to the Thirty Years' War. Philip of Spain and the Holy Roman Emperor, Ferdinand II, were allied against Denmark, Saxony and Sweden. In 1648, the Treaty of Westphalia recognized the republic of the United Netherlands, part of which is now modern Belgium. The barbarian *phalange* are the Protestant German powers. The Thirty Years' War started as a revolt in Bohemia and spread as far as Gibraltar when France and Spain refused to recognize the 1648 treaty and continued to fight until the Treaty of the Pyrenees in 1659.

[1]*Pannons.* L. Panonia, now Hungary.
[2]*hare.* misprint for *bare*, pillars (of Hercules), Gibraltar.

Century V

V.XIIII

Saturne & Mars en leo Efpagne
  captifue,
Par chef Lybique au conflict attrapé,
Proche de Malthe, Heredde prinfe viue,
Et Romain fceptre fera par coq frappé.

Saturn and Mars in Leo, Spain is captive, taken in battle by a Libyan leader. Near to Malta (the knights of Rhodes) captured alive, and Roman power smitten by the cock.

This is a mixed quatrain, referring to two separate events. The only time that Spain can really be considered as a captive country was during the Peninsular War of 1807–08 when Napoleon's troops occupied both Spain and Portugal. The resistance of the Spanish patriots led the British to send in an army under Sir Arthur Wellesley, who, after five years of fighting, succeeded in driving out the French. The rest of the quatrain refers to events which occurred ten years earlier. The first action of Napoleon's Egyptian campaign in 1798 was the capture of Malta from the Knights of Rhodes. Finally, at the Treaty of Tolentino the Pope ceded part of the Vatican and Church States to the Cock, the symbol for France.

Century V

V.XV

En nauigant captif prins grand pontife,
Grans aprets faillir les clercz tumultuez:
Second efleu abfent fon bien debife,
Son fauory baftard à mort tué.

While traveling the great Pope will be captured. Great preparations by the troubled clerks will fail. The second elected being absent, his power declines. His favorite bastard put to death.

Pope Pius VII, who had traveled to France in 1804 to crown Napoleon, was taken prisoner by the French in 1808. He was the second Pope to be hurt by Napoleon, the first being Pius VI, who died in exile at Valence. The trouble among the clergy, *clercz tumultuez,* describes the religious discontent in France after the abolition of the established Church. Most commentators interpret the bastard in line 4 as Napoleon, who inherited a crown that was not rightfully his and who, having received favors from the Pope, sacks Rome in 1808, and imprisons the pontiff, although the death of his predecessor, Pius VI, was directly caused by his imprisonment by Napoleon.

Century V

V.XVI

A fon hault pris plus la lerme fabee.
D'humaine chair par mort en cendre
    mettre,
A l'ifle Pharos par croifars perturbee,
Alors qu'à Rodes paroiftra dur efpectre.

The tears of the Sabines will no longer be
of value. Human flesh is put to death
(burned) to ashes. The island of Pharos
disturbed by men of the cross, when at
Rhodes a dreadful sight is seen.

This quatrain appears to implicate Italy with the pogroms against the Jews during the Second World War ("the men of the cross," the swastika). Cremation was anathema to a sixteenth century Jew or Christian. Pharos is an island opposite Alexandria and may be used to indicate Tobruk, which is close by and which Nostradamus mentions in I.XXVIII. Tobruk was troubled several times by the Nazis as the battles in the African desert waged between the Allies and Rommel. The *dur efpectre* at Rhodes would be the invasion of Greece by Mussolini in 1940, followed by the Germans in 1941. Despite British evacuations of Greece, the Germans claimed 270,000 prisoners. About 70,000 people are believed to have been killed.

Century V

V.XVII

De nuict paffant le roy pres d'une
    Andronne,
Celuy de Cipres & principal guette:
Le roy failli la main fuict long du
    Rofne,
Les coniurés l'iront à mort mettre.

The king, passing at night through a narrow lane, the man from Cyprus is the main guard. The king dies, the hand flees the length of the Rhône. The conspirators will put him to death.

Cyprus belonged to Venice until 1571, but the location of this conspiracy is obscure.

Century V

V.XVIII

De deuil mourra l'infelix profligé,
Celebrera fon vitrix l'hecatombe:
Priftine loy franc edict redigé,
Le mur & Prince au feptiefme iour
    tombe.

The wretched man, destroyed, will die of grief. His victorious consort will celebrate the ceremonies. Former laws, free edicts are drawn up. Both the prince and the wall fall on the seventh day.

I cannot decipher this quatrain.

Century V

V.XIX

Le grand Royal d'or, d'aerain augmenté,
Rompu la pache,[1] par ieune ouuerte guerre:
Peuple affligé par vn chef lamenté,
De fang barbare fera couuerte terre.

The great golden royal, augmented by money, breaks the covenant. The war is started by the young man. The people are afflicted by a lamented leader. The land will be covered with barbarian blood.

Another indecipherable quatrain.

Century V

V.XX

Dela les Alpes grand armée paffera,
Vn peu deuant naiftra monftre vapin:
Prodigieux & fubit tournera,
Le grand Tofquan à fon lieu plus propin.

A great Army will cross over the Alps. A short time before a wretched monster will be born. In a strange way, suddenly the great Tuscan will return to his native land.

The great army crossing the Alps is Napoleon III, who achieved this against Austria in 1859. The evil monster would then be, as always in Nostradamus, a Revolution—this time in Italy, led by Garibaldi. It is interesting to note that one of the first results of the 1854 campaign was to drive the grand duke of Tuscany, Leopold II, from Florence. He was a Hapsburg and retired to Austria, *fon lieu plus propin,* to escape the Italians, thus fulfilling the prediction in line 4.

Century V

V.XXI

Par le trefpas du monarque latin,
Ceux qu'il aura par regne fecouruz:
Le feu luyra, diuifé le butin,
La mort publique aux hardis incoruz.

By the death of the Latin king; those whom he will have assisted during his reign. The fire glows, the booty, is shared out. Public death for the bold incursors.

The Latin monarch is difficult to interpret. If it stands for Latium, it represents the Pope. Could Nostradamus be referring to Mussolini and the Fascists?

---

[1]*pache.* A. Pr. treaty, covenant.

Century V

V.XXII

Auant qu'à Rome grand aye rendu l'ame,
Effrayeur grande à larmée eftrangere:
Par Efquadrons, l'embufche pres de Parme,
Puis les deux rouges enfemble feront chere.

Before the great man gives up his soul at Rome, there is much fear among the foreign army. The ambush by the squadrons takes place near Parma. Then the two red ones will feast together.

This seems, together with V.XXIII, to be a futuristic quatrain. Sometime before the death of a pope there will be a war abroad, *eftrangere.* The two red ones who feast together would mean in modern terminology Russia and the People's Republic of China. This may then well occur after the breakdown of the alliance between the USA and the USSR (which Nostradamus tells us will last for three years and seven months). Otherwise the *deux rouges* may refer to terrorist régimes such as that of Colonel Gadaffi, the North Koreans, or even the private army of Abu Nidal, which is an extreme terrorist element supported by Gadaffi.

Century V

V.XXIII

Les deux contens feront vnis enfemble,
Quant la plufpart à Mars feront conioinct:
Le grand d'Affrique en effraieur & tremble:
DVVMVIRAT par la claffe defioinct.

The two contented men are united together when most (planets) are in conjunction with Mars. The African leader trembles in terror. The twin alliance scattered by the fleet.

Nostradamus elsewhere describes the USA and the USSR as *vnis enfemble,* probably while honoring the INF Treaty signed by Reagan and Gorbachev. But war soon breaks out again, possibly the war of the Third Antichrist, the man known as *Brodde,* which troubles even Africa. It appears that naval interference is partly the reason for the breaking of the alliance. Will the American and the Soviet fleets leave the Gulf? It will be interesting to see.

Century V

V.XXIIII

Le regne & loy fouz Venus efleué,
Saturne aura fus Iupiter empire:
La loy & regne par le Soleil leué,
Par Saturnins endurera le pire.

The kingdom and law raised under Venus, Saturn will dominate Jupiter. Law and Empire raised by the Sun will endure the worst through the Saturnine people.

Venus and Saturn dominating Jupiter is obviously yet another astrological dating, but unfortunately Nostradamus is seldom specific enough to enable one to use the astrological clues. The quatrain bears some resemblance to V.XI, but I believe it relates to the preceding quatrain. The Sun might also stand for Charles V or even the Catholic Church. It is a very difficult quatrain to decipher.

Century V

V.XXV

Le prince Arabe Mars, Sol, Venus, Lyon,
Regne d'Eglife par mer fuccombera:
Deuers la Perfe bien pres d'vn million,
Bifance, Egypte, ver. ferp.[1] inuadera.

The Arab Prince, Mars, the Sun, Venus and Leo, the rule of the Church will succumb to the sea. Towards Persia very nearly a million men will invade Egypt and Byzantium, the true serpent.

When Mars, the Sun and Venus are in conjunction with Leo, the following predictions are forecast about the Middle East, Arabia. It will attack Persia (Iran), Egypt, Constantinople and the navies of Christendom. This conjunction last took place on August 21, 1987, so it may well refer to the Gulf wars, and to the various other troubles in the Middle East. The navies would be the U.K., Italian, American and Soviet fleets which are at present patrolling the Gulf. This all occurs at a time when religion is losing its hold upon humanity, although one must not deny the possibility of various Antichrists, the false Messiahs who make claims worldwide.

The total of a million men was an incredible number in Nostradamus' day, when the world population was obviously much smaller. But the Biblical King of the East claims to invade the Soviet Middle East with an army of 2,000,000 men. It is worth noting that in 1961 China's leaders boasted that they could mobilize an army of 2 billion soldiers. An uneasy quatrain.

---

[1]*ver. ferp.* Suggested interpretation, *vera serpens,* true serpent.

Century V

V.XXVI

La gent efclaue par vn heur martial,
Viendra en haut degré tant efleuee:
Changeront prince naiftre vn
    prouincial,
Paffer la mer copie aux monts leuee.

The Slav people, through fortune in war,
will become elevated to a high degree.
They will change their prince, born of the
provinces. An army raised in the mountains to cross over the sea.

The word *efclaue* may mean Slav or slave. The Russians were not
regarded as Slavs in Nostradamus' day; this word was reserved for the
people of the Balkans. The Greeks, who were partially Slav, rose
against the Turks and landed troops at Smyrna in 1919, remaining
there until 1922. They changed their king, as Nostradamus predicted.

King Constantine was exiled in 1917, recalled in 1920 and sent into
exile again in 1922. Although he was born in Athens, he was of
German origin. His rival was Premier Venizelos from Crete. The
same fate was to befall Constantine's son, who is now in permanent
exile in Britain.

Century V

V.XXVII

Par feu & armes non loing de la
    marnegro,
Viendra de Perfe occuper Trebifonde:
Trembler Phatos Methelin, Sol alegro,
De fang Arabe d'Adrie couuert onde.

With fire and weapons, not far from the
Black Sea, he will come from Persia to
occupy Trezibond. Pharos and Mytilene
tremble. The Sun is bright, the Adriatic
Sea covered with Arab blood.

This quatrain appears to link up with V.XXV. What is not clear is
whether the conquerors are the Arabs or the Iranians. In the light of
present events, it appears to be the former, the Iraqis, but the peace
settlement is extremely delicate at this time, with the Iranian army
poised on the border of Turkey, driving the Kurds from Iraq in the
hundreds of thousands who are suffering from the effects of chemical
warfare.

Pharos is an island off Alexandria and Mytilene is the Greek island
of Lesbos. Nostradamus seems convinced in so many quatrains that
Greece will be drawn into this Middle Eastern War.

Century V
V.XXVIII

Le bras pendu & la iambe liée,
Vifaige pafle au feing poignard caché:
Trois qui feront iurez de la meflée,
Au grand de Gennes sera le fer lafché.

His arm hung and leg tied, pale-faced with a dagger hidden in his breast. Three will be sworn in the crowd. Against the great one of Genoa the blade will be drawn.

Genoa is the key word in this quatrain, which speaks of the threat of assassination. King Umberto of Italy (which included Genoa) was assassinated by an unemployed smith named Acciartio on July 29, 1900. But Nostradamus implies that the assassin will be bound up in some way. This was not the case, so it is possible that this refers to some other assassination. The king was stabbed with a dagger.

Century V
V.XXIX

La liberté ne fera recouuree,
L'occupera noir fier vilain inique:
Quand la matiere du pont fera ouvree,
D'Hifter, Venife fafchee la republique.

Liberty will not be regained. It will be occupied by a black, proud, villainous and unjust man. When the subject of the Pope is opened by Hitler, the republic of Venice will be angered.

This quatrain describes Mussolini's intrigues to secure an alliance with Hitler between the years 1934 and 1938. Hitler and Mussolini met at Venice. Notice how accurate the details are in this quatrain. The adjective black can refer both to the Fascisti, the Blackshirts, and to Hitler himself. Both Pope Pius XI and Pius XII played a predominant part in this situation. Pius XI, as secretary of state, played a major part in securing a treaty with Nazi Germany in 1933. He also refused to excommunicate either Hitler or Mussolini. Pius XII continued this policy of remaining on good terms with the Fascists. He refused to condemn Germany's invasion of Poland. The Vatican was known as a notorious escape route for German war criminals. An unpleasant, if accurate, quatrain.

Century V

V.XXX

Tout à l'entour de la grande cité,
Seront foldats logez par champs &
  villes:
Donner l'affaut Paris, Rome incité,
Sur le pont[1] lors fera faicte grand pille.

Soldiers will be billeted in fields and towns all around the great city. Paris will make the assault, Rome incited. There will be great pillage made against the pontiff.

Rome was sacked twice by the French, in 1797 and 1808. The pillage refers to the fact that the Pope was forced to cede part of the Papal States in 1797 which were incorporated into the Republic of France in 1809.

Century V

V.XXXI

Par terre Attique chef de la fapience,
Qui de prefent eft la rofe du monde:
Pont ruiné & fa grand preeminence,
Sera fubdite & naufrage des vndes.

From the land of Attica, source of all wisdom, which presently is the rose of the world. The Pontiff ruined, its great pre-eminence will be subjected and wrecked beneath the waves.

This is the third successive quatrain mentioning Greece, a pope and disaster at sea. It seems to follow the sequence starting at V.XXVII, but I cannot elucidate further.

Century V

V.XXXII

Où tout bon eft tout bien Soleil &
  Lune,
Eft abondant fa ruine s'approche:
Du ciel s'aduance vaner ta fortune,
En mefme eftat que la feptiefme roche.

Where all is good and all abundant, in the Sun and Moon its ruin approaches. It comes from heaven as you boast of your fortune, in the same state as the seventh rock.

James Laver suggests that this refers to the Franco-Prussian War, 1870–1871. Nostradamus applies the singular *ta fortune* only to France. When France is at the height of her fortune (the *Exposition Universelle* in 1867), then the Prussians will gather to declare war. Laver interprets the seventh rock as a reference to the desolation of the seventh rock in the Apocalypse but I feel that it is more likely to

---

[1]*pont.* Normal Nostradamus shorthand for *Pontifex,* Pontiff, Pope.

stand for one of the seven hills of Rome. The difficulty is to fit the Papacy into this interpretation.

Century V

V.XXXIII

Des principaux de cité rebellee,
Qui tiendront fort pour liberté rauoir:
Detrencher mafles, infelice meflee,
Crys hurlemens à Nantes piteux voir.

Some of the principal citizens of the rebellious city, will try hard to regain their liberty. The men are cut up, unhappy confusion. Cries, groans at Nantes, pitiful to see.

The atrocities at Nantes in 1793 were known as the Noyades. They were committed by excessive revolutionaries and are surely the subject of this quatrain. In 1793, the citizens of the town had allied themselves with neighboring districts and declared a Central Assembly of Resistance to Oppression. But the National Convention soon broke up this counterrevolutionary activity. Over one thousand citizens were guillotined, *detrencher mafles,* others were tied, face to face, naked, placed into boats which were rowed to the middle of the river Loire and scuttled. These wretched victims were coolly watched by their killers as they drowned in a threshing mass of bodies.

Century V

V.XXXIIII

Du plus profond de l'occident Anglois.
Où eft le chef de l'ifle Britannique:
Entrera claffe dans Gyronde par Blois,
Par vin & fel, feux cachez aux
*   barriques.*

From the deepest part of the English West where is the leader of the British Isles. A fleet will enter Gironde through Blois, through wine and salt, fires hidden in casks.

The words "British Isles" firmly place this quatrain as later than 1604. The west of England is puzzling. The Duchy of Cornwall belongs, by tradition, to the Prince of Wales, who shall probably become king, although Nostradamus states elsewhere that Prince Charles will be the last of the royal or reigning line. Wine and salt are French metaphors for taxation, especially the latter, known as the *gabelle.* The fires hidden in casks resemble the globes of fire which Nostradamus frequently uses to describe weapons such as bombs or rockets. So this quatrain may possibly have yet to be fulfilled.

Century V

V.XXXV

Par cité franche de la grand mer Seline,
Qui porte encores à l'eftomach la pierre:
Angloife claffe viendra foubs la bruine
I'n rameau prendre, du grand ouuerte
guerre.

For the free city of the great crescent sea
which still carries the stone in its stomach.
An English fleet will come in under the
mist to seize a branch. War started by the
great one.

This quatrain may relate to the preceding one because of the use
of the word English. But an English fleet having a series of protracted
encounters with invaders seems to relate it to the past. The crescent
sea normally stands for the sea of Genoa in Nostradamus, but the
whole quatrain seems improbable.

Century V

V.XXXVI

De foeur le frere par fimulte faintife,
I'iendra mefler rofee en myneral:
Sur la placente[1] donne à vielle tardifue,
Meurt, le gouftant fera fimple & rural.

The sister's brother, through feigned deceit
will come and mix dew with the mineral.
On the cake given to the slow old woman
who dies testing it. She will be simple and
rustic.

A classic case of a woman killed by poison given on a cake. The only
other clue I can offer is that *rofee,* dew, may stand for the Latin *rosarius,*
poison extracted from the laurel rose.

Century V

V.XXXVII

Trois cents feront d'vn vouloir &
accord,
Que pour venir au bout de leur
attaincte:
Vingts mois apres tous & records,
Leur Roy trahi fimulant haine faincte.

Three hundred will be of one accord and
in agreement to arrive at the execution of
their end. Twenty months later, after all
remembrance, their king is betrayed,
feigning a holy hatred.

I cannot decipher this quatrain.

---

[1]*placente.* L. *placenta,* a cake.

Century V

V.XXXVIII

Ce grand monarque qu'au mort
fuccedera,
Donnera vie illicite & lubrique,
Par nonchalance à tous concedera,
Qu'à la parfin faudra la loy Salique.

He who succeeds upon the death of a great king will lead an illicit and debauched life. Through carelessness he will give way to all so that in the end Salic law will fail.

Salic law prevailed in France: it prohibited the accession of women to the throne. Louis XV succeeded his great-grandfather (great in both senses), and led a life of extreme debauchery and irresponsibility. An example of this was his famous seraglio at the Parc des Cerfs, and of course, the influence of Madame de Pompadour. The *Encyclopaedia Britannica* says that it is "difficult to find a European king whose life shows such a record of vulgar vice." His carelessness in state affairs led to the bankruptcy of France and was partially responsible for the trouble which came to a head under the Revolution.

Louis XV was succeeded by his ill-fated son, Louis XVI. Some historians might accept the view that both these French kings were effectively ruled by the women in their life, Louis XV by Mme. de Pompadour and Mme. du Barry; Louis XVI by his wife, Marie Antoinette. I personally think that the latter had little decisive effect upon her weak and inconsiderate husband in his role as king.

Century V

V.XXXIX

Du vray rameau de fleur de lys iffu,
Mis & logé heritier d'Hetrurie:
Son fang antique de longue main tiffu,
Fera Florence florir en l'armoirie.

Issued from the true branch of the fleur-de-lys, placed and lodged as heir to Etruria. His ancient family line woven by many lands will make the armorial bearings of France flower.

The comte de Chambord was the heir to Charles X and his legitimacy was questioned by the duc d'Orléans at his birth. (See IV.XCIII.) His mother, the duchesse de Berry, took her son with her into exile to Venice. Etruria here stands for Italy. In 1846 he married in Venice the daughter of Duke Francis IV of Florence. The fleur-de-lys is part of the arms of the house of Florence as well as the French royal line, and their marriage caused their united family lines to flower. A happy quatrain.

Century V

V.XL

Le fang royal fera si trefmeflé,
Contraint feront Gaulois de l'Hefperie:
On attendra que terme foit coulé,
Et que memoire de la voix foit perie.

The Royal blood will be very mixed, the
French will be restrained by the West.
They will wait until his term of office is
ended and the memory of his voice has
perished.

Line 1 probably indicates that the French royal line will be much diminished, that is, not in power any longer. This brings the quatrain into the twentieth century, which is reinforced by the line *que terme foit coulé,* implying an elected office dependent upon a vote or something similar. The one Frenchman who really interfered effectively with Western politics was, of course, General de Gaulle. Once his term of office and influence ended with his death, his policy, the famous *Non,* was soon forgotten.

Century V

V.XLI

Nay fouz les vmbres & iournee
    nocturne
Sera en regne & bonté fouueraine:
Fera renaiftre fon fang de l'antique
    vrne,
Renouuellant fiecle d'or pour l'aerain.

Born beneath the shadows on a dark day
he will be sovereign both in his rule and
goodness. He will cause his blood to revive
the ancient urn, renewing the century of
gold for one of brass.

Line 4 is the only clue which possibly indicates that this quatrain belongs to the twentieth century, during which all gold coinage disappeared among most nations to be replaced by brass coins. So it is possible that this is a futuristic quatrain.

Century V

V.XLII

Mars efleué en fon plus haut befroy,[1]
Fera retraire les Allobrox[2] *de France:*
La gent Lombarde fera fi grand effroy,
A ceux de l'Aigle comprins fouz la
    balance.

A warlike man raised to the heights will
bring about the return of Savoy to France.
The people from Lombardy will cause such
fear to those of the Eagle, included under
the Balance.

---

[1]*befroy.* literally a belfry.
[2]*Allobrox.* The Allobroges occupied what is present-day Savoy.

Napoleon III and Cavour of Italy agreed between them that in return for French assistance in driving out the Austrians (Libra) from Italy, Savoy should be returned to France. This was done on March 22, 1860. It is the only time that this has occurred since Nostradamus' day.

Century V

V.XLIII

La grande ruine des facrez ne s'efloigne,	The great ruin of the clergy is not far off,
Prouence, Naples, Sicille, Seez &	Provence, Naples, Sicily, Sees and Pons.
Ponce:	In Germany at the Rhine and Cologne;
En Germanie, au Rhin & la Cologne,	vexed to death by those of Maine.
Vexez à mort par ceux de Magonce.[1]	

In this far-reaching quatrain Nostradamus seems to imply that Mainz and the other places mentioned would turn Protestant, possibly because Mainz was the center of Gutenberg's city and the original center of printing with all its inherent dangers as it was still regarded uneasily by the Church. A totally unsuccessful quatrain.

Century V

V.XLIIII

Par mer le rouge fera prins de pyrates,	On the sea the red one will be taken by
La paix fera par fon moyen troublee:	pirates and because of his method there
L'ire & l'auare commettra par fainct	will be a troubled peace. He will reveal
acte	anger and greed through a false act. The
Au grand Pontife fera l'armee doublee.	army of the great pontiff will be doubled.

There is no record of this quatrain's being fulfilled. There has never been a record of a Cardinal, *le rouge,* being captured by pirates. The Pope still had an army in the sixteenth century.

Century V

V.XLV

Le grand Empire fera toft defolé,	The great Empire will soon be desolated
Et tranflaté pres d'arduenne filue:	and changed near the forest of Ardennes.
Les deux baftardz par l'aifné decollé,	The two bastards will be beheaded by the
Et regnera Aenodarb, nez de milue.	oldest. Aenobarbe, the hawk-nosed one,
	will rule.

[1]*Magonce.* L. *Maguntiacum,* Mainz or Mayenze.

The French Empire was lost to the Germans in 1940 and there were bloody battles among the forests of the Ardennes, both then and 1944–45. The two bastards may be the two "unworthy" French generals who let the Germans through after the Battle of Sedan, 1940; they were André Georges Corap of the French Ninth Army and his second-in-command, Henri Giraud, who was taken prisoner. The *aifné*, the commander-in-chief, Maxime Weygand, then took over, but the Allies had already lost. The hawk-nosed man may refer to General de Gaulle, but Nostradamus usually places Aenobarbe with *Brodde* in Africa. De Gaulle, together with the 4th Armored Division, was the only French general who put up any resistance to the Germans at Montcornet. Dunkirk followed upon this crushing defeat. The problem in this quatrain is Aenobarbe. Possibly I am mistaken and this quatrain relates to Africa during the next decade. There are several other quatrains which mention this mysterious Aenobarbe, so far unidentified.

Century V

V.XLVI

Par chapeaux rouges querelles &
    noueaux fcifmes
Quant on aura efleu le Sabinois:
On produira contre luy grans fophifmes,
Et fera Rome lefee par Albanois.

Quarrels and new schisms by those of the red hats when the Sabins will have been elected. They will produce great sophisms against him. Rome will be injured by those of Albania.

In Nostradamus' terminology *chapeaux rouges* always stands for the cardinals of the Roman Catholic Church. He says they will be divided when they elect someone from the Northeast of Rome, *Sabinois*. But the Albanians pose a problem. Albania in the twentieth century is a blocked, Communist state with strong links to the People's Republic of China. Perhaps this is a futuristic quatrain referring to the present Pope or his successor?

Century V

V.XLVII

Le grand Arabe marchera bien auant,
Trahy fera par les Bifantinois:
L'antique Rodes luy viendra au deuant,
Et plus grand mal par auftre
    Pannonois.

The great Arab will march well ahead. He will be betrayed by the Turks. Ancient Rhodes will come forward to meet him and greater harm through the other Hungarians.

This seems another futuristic quatrain. If the great Arab is Gadaffi or his deputy Abu Nidal, they will get into trouble with the Turks. At the moment the Turks are in danger of being dragged into the residue of the Gulf War, with the Iraqis driving the Kurds by the hundred thousand as refugees into Turkey. Again there is this continual complication of Greece which I cannot decipher. The Hungarians, *Pannonois*, stand for the Communist influence in this situation. A quatrain, I imagine, soon to be clarified and fulfilled.

Century V

V.XLVIII

Apres la grande affliction du fceptre,
Deux ennemis par eux feront defaictz:
Claffe d'Affrique aux Pannons viendra
*   naiftre,*
Par mer & terre feront horribles faictz.

After the great affliction of the scepter two enemies will be defeated by them. A fleet from Africa will come forth to the Hungarians. Dreadful deeds will occur on land and sea.

This seems to be a continuation of the last quatrain. Again a fleet, Africa and the Communist satellite countries. Probably a quatrain still to be fulfilled.

Century V

V.XLIX

Nul de l'Efpaigne mais de l'antique
*   France*
Ne fera efleu pour le tremblant nacelle,
A l'ennemy fera faicte fiance, [1]
Qui dans fon regne fera pefte cruelle.

Not from Spain but from ancient France will he be elected for the trembling ship. He will make a promise to the enemy who will cause great devastation during his reign.

This must be a futuristic quatrain if it is correct, because since Nostradamus' time until 1979 when the Polish John Paul II was elected, we have had only Italian popes. When the Church is in a troubled state, *tremblant nacelle*, it appears there will be two main candidates for the Papacy, one Spanish and one French. The French candidate will be elected. He will try to compromise with his enemy, presumably Communism, with remarkably little success.

The Irish prophet Malachy, whose original manuscript works are kept hidden in the Vatican, gives us only two more popes until the Millennium. He ascribes to the next Pope the motto *Gloria Olivae*, The Glory of the Olive. The olive branch is the universal symbol of peace

---

[1] *fiance.* O.F. assurance, promise.

240   *Erika Cheetham*

but presumably in Nostradamus' view, this Pope's essays towards peace will be unsuccessful.

The Benedictines have always claimed through tradition that this next Pope will come from their order. Another name for the Benedictines is the Olevitians. It will be interesting to see. (See also V.XLVI and V.LXXVIII.) It is worth noting that the only Benedictine cardinal in the Curia at the moment is the English Cardinal Hume. The last English Pope was Nicholas Breakspear.

There is a remote chance that this quatrain refers to the present Pope, John Paul II, who was born in southwestern Poland, an area which once formed the boundary of Charlemagne's empire, the outskirts of France. Another of the candidates at his election was from South America, in Nostradamus' time a property of Spain.

It was shortly after John Paul II acceded to the Papacy that AIDS, Auto-Immune Deficiency Syndrome, became a world issue. Perhaps this is the "great plague" and "the enemy within" which Nostradamus refers to repeatedly during this Papacy. He correctly dates John Paul II's accession to the Papacy as during the time of Halley's Comet. (See II.XV, III.LXXV, VI.V, IX.LV.) Nostradamus also predicts that John Paul II will be assassinated. There have so far been two unsuccessful attempts on his life. (See II.XV, II.XCIII.)

Century V

V.L

L'an que les freres du lys feront en aage,
L'vn d'eux tiendra la grande Romanie:
Trembler les monts, ouuert Latin paffage
Pache macher, contre fort d'Armenie.

The year that the brothers of the lily come of age one of them will hold great Romania. The mountains tremble, a Latin passage is opened. A treaty to march against the fort of Armenia.

A difficult quatrain. In V.XCIIII Armenia is connected with Hitler and the Second World War. The rest is unclear.

Century V

V.LI

La gent de Dace,[1] d'Angleterre &
Polonne
Et de Boefme[2] feront nouuelle ligue:
Pour paffer outre d'Hercules la colonne,
Barcins,[3] Tyrrens[4] dreffer crue le
brique.[5]

The people of Dacia, England, Poland
and Czechoslovakia will form a new alliance, in order to pass beyond the Straits of
Gibraltar. The Spanish and the Italians
will hatch a cruel plot.

One of Nostradamus' more interesting predictions. In March,
1939, Britain allied with the Balkan countries. It was the British
support of Poland that sparked off the Second World War in September, 1939. It was essential to keep the Mediterranean, *outre d'Hercules
la colonne,* open for shipping Allied troops and vital supplies. The
Italians were Hitler's natural allies under Mussolini and although
Spain remained technically neutral, she was definitely biased towards
Nazism.

Century V

V.LII

I'n Roy fera qui donra l'oppofite,
Les exilez efleuez fur le regne:
De fang nager la gent cafte[6] hyppolite,[7]
Et florira long temps foubs telle
enfeigne.

There will be a king who will give opposition, the exiles elected over the kingdom.
The chaste, poor ones swim in blood and
he will flourish for a long time under this
standard.

A king who will tyrannize over a rule of bloodshed. Unfortunately
there is nothing specific to work on.

[1] *Dace.* Now part of Romania.
[2] *Boefme.* Modern Czechoslovakia.
[3] *Barcins.* L. *Barcino,* Barcelona, by extension Spain.
[4] *Tyrrens.* L. Tuscans, by extension Italy.
[5] *crue le brique.* printer's error for *cruele brigue.*
[6] *cafte.* L. chaste, pure.
[7] *hyppolite.* Gk. *hyppolitos,* poor, mean, little.

Century V

V.LIII

La loy du Sol, & Venus contendens,	The law of the Sun contending with
Appropriant l'efprit de prophetie:	Venus, appropriating the spirit of proph-
Ne l'vn ne l'autre ne feront entendus,	ecy. Neither the one nor the other will be
Par Sol tiendra la loy du grand Meffie.	understood. The law of the great Messiah
	retained through the Sun.

This relates to Nostradamus' Jewish beliefs, that the law of the Messiah, the Second Coming which was prophesied in the Book of Enoch, will occur in the century of the Sun, the twentieth century. The prophecy referred to is probably Biblical. See the introductory material for a discussion of Jewish influences on Nostradamus' views concerning the Millennium. Most people certainly do not believe in a Second Coming at the end of this century, *Ne l'vn ne l'autre ne seront entendus.* However, it is difficult to reconcile this with Nostradamus' conviction that the Third Antichrist will come before the end of the next decade.

Century V

V.LIIII

Du pont Euxine, & la grand Tartarie,	From beyond the Black Sea and great
Vn roi fera qui viendra voir la Gaule	Tartary, there will be a king who will
Tranfpercera Alane & l'Armenie,	come to see France. He will pass through
Et dans Bifance lairra fanglante	Alania and Armenia, leaving his bloody
Gaule.	rod in Byzantium.

The mention of a man from the East wielding a bloody rod also occurs in II.XXIX. Nostradamus is definite that the Third Antichrist will appear towards the end of this century and that he will come from Asia (beyond Tartary, which is China). His route appears to go through southern Russia (Alania, and Armenia) around the Balkan peninsula to Turkey, Constantinople. The rod may stand for red power or a bloody weapon. Definitely a quatrain of the future.

Century V

V.LV

De la felice Arabie contrade,[1] *Naiftra puiffant de loy Mahometique: Vexer l'Efpaigne conquefter la Grenade, Et plus par mer à la gent Lyguftique.*[2]	*In the fortunate country of Arabia will be born one powerful in the laws of Mahomet. He will trouble Spain and conquer Granada as well as most of the Ligurian nation from the sea.*

This appears to be a failed or retroactive prediction. Granada, Spain, was last lost to the Arabs in 1492. There has never been another conquest of Spain, let alone Italy, by the Arabs since Nostradamus' day.

Century V

V.LVI

Par le trefpas du trefuiellart pontife, Sera efleu Romain de bon aage: Qu'il fera dict que le fiege debiffe, Et long tiendra & de picquant ouurage.	*Through the death of the very old Pope will be elected a Roman of good age. It is said of him that he weakens the (Holy) Seat, but he will hold it with long and painful effort.*

The old Pope who dies is probably Pope John XXIII, a very popular Pontiff. It was under him that the Second Vatican Council was convened. He tried to bring the Church out of its elitist stance and lead it towards a more democratic role. Sadly, he died after only four years in office.

He was succeeded by the worldly, strictly orthodox Pope Paul VI, under whose tenure the Vatican went through a series of severe political and financial scandals, *long tiendra & de picquant ouurage.* Paul VI certainly weakened the Vatican's position when it was revealed that he was a close friend of the Sicilian banker Michele Sindona, believed to be a member of the Mafia, who in fact became an adviser to the Vatican Bank. This led to the scandal of the P2 Freemasons' Lodge and various suicides and murders, perhaps the most well-known being the mysterious death of Roberto Calvi under Blackfriars Bridge, London, in June, 1982. Paul VI died in 1978, to be succeeded for thirty days by Pope John Paul I, whose untimely and mysterious death was almost certainly due to his attempt to rectify the situation created by his predecessor.

[1]*contrade.* A. Pr. *contrada,* country.
[2]*Lyguftique.* The Ligurians came from around Genoa, therefore Italy.

Century V

V.LVII

Iftra du mont Gaulfier & Auentin,
Qui par le trou aduertira l'armée:
Entre deux rocs fera prins le butin,
De SEXT manfol faillir la renommee.

There will go forth from Montgolfier and
Aventine, one who through a hole will
warm the army. The booty will be taken
between two rocks. The renown of Sextus
the Celibate will fail.

This is a gift of a quatrain, which has two unmistakable key words, Montgolfier and Sextus. Montgolfier is remembered in the public mind for only one thing—his invention, together with his brother, of the hot air balloon in 1793 when they made a triumphant ascent over Paris. The following year it was used to help a scouting party, *qui par le trou aduertira l'armée,* at the battle of Fleurus. The French victory at Fleurus, partly based on the Montgolfier's information, was the turning point in the first coalition phase of the Revolutionary Wars, paving the way for the sack of Rome and the Aventine.

The word *manfol* is derived from the Latin *manus solus,* he who remains alone, that is, celibate. Nostradamus elsewhere calls monks and priests *les seuls. SEXT.* is an abbreviation of Sextus, the sixth, and Pius VI, who was in the Vatican at that time, was later captured by Napoleon during the sack of Rome. By the earlier treaty of Tolentino, 1797, Pius VI was deprived of much of his lands, the rocks upon which his power was based, *entre deux rocs fera prins le butin.* A highly elaborate and accurate quatrain.

Century V

V.LVIII

De l'aqueduct d'Vticenfe, Gardoing,
Par le foreft & mont inacceffible:
En my du pont fera tafché au poing,
Le chef nemans qui tant fera terrible.

By the aqueduct of Uzès by Gard, through
the forest and the inaccessible mountain.
In the middle of the bridge he will be cut
in the hand. The chief of Nîmes will also
be very terrible.

The thing for which Uzès is most famed is its Roman aqueduct, which extended from Uzès to Nîmes. In 1627 the duc de Rohan tried to support his fellow Calvinists who were besieged at Nîmes, and he moved in his supporting artillery by means of the aqueduct. Line 3 describes the actions of some of Rohan's soldiers, who cut some of the supports of the aqueduct at Gard to widen the path for the cannon to be brought up. Rohan was put in command when he arrived at Nîmes, *le chef nemans.* An impressive and accurate quatrain.

Century V

V.LIX

Au chef Anglois à Nymes trop feiour,
Deuers l'Efpaigne au fecours
  Aenobarbe:
Plufieurs mourront par Mars ouuert ce
  iour,
Quant en Artois faillir eftoile en barbe.

The English chief stays too long at Nîmes
towards Spain, Aenobarbe to the rescue.
Many will die through war started on that
day when a bearded star falls in Artois.

Again, the ubiquitous and as yet unidentified Aenobarbe, whom elsewhere Nostradamus links with the coming of the Third Antichrist. He is linked with war, the geographical limits are not defined, and with a comet—all standard warnings for the Antichrist and the coming Millennium. An unsolved and futuristic quatrain.

Century V

V.LX

Par tefte rafe viendra bien mal eflire,
Plus que fa charge ne porte paffera:
Si grand fureur & raige fera dire,
Qu'à feu & fang tout fexe trenchera.

Through the shaven heads he will be seen
to be wrongly elected, burdened with a
load he cannot carry. He will be made to
proclaim with such great fury and rage
that all of a sex will be slaughtered into
pieces in fire and blood.

Some commentators apply this quatrain either to Napoleon or to the popes whose heads were shaven as they were monks. But I think it is far more appropriate when applied to Cromwell. As Nostradamus says, Cromwell was elected to power, "wrongly" in that he did not rule by divine right. The fury and rage that cover the population refers to the Civil War between the Cavaliers and the Roundheads, *tefte rafe,* which was a war of both politics and religion. Since fighting armies were composed of men *(fang tout fexe),* great numbers lost their lives during the Protectorate and there were many deaths by fire and beheading, the latter including Charles I, of people who would not change sides and stuck to their beliefs. Comparatively few women and children were victims of these excesses.

246   *Erika Cheetham*

Century V

V.LXI

*L'enfant du grand n'eftant à fa
  naiffance,
Subiuguera les hauts monts Apennis:
Fera trembler tous ceux de la balance,
Et des monts feux iufques à mont Senis.*

The child of the great man, not through
his birth, will subjugate the high Apennine mountains. He will make all those
under the Balance tremble, fire from the
mountains as far as Mount Cenis.

The nearest person who seems to fulfill this quatrain is Eugène de Beauharnais, the son of Josephine and stepson of Napoleon. Nostradamus says that this adopted son of a French ruler will vex the Hapsburgs of Austria (Libra), both in Spain and Italy. In this the prophet was only half correct. Napoleon went forth and conquered and made Eugène ruler of Italy.

Century V

V.LXII

*Sur les rouchers fang on les verra
  plouuoir,
Sol Orient, Saturne Occidental:
Pres d'Orgon guerre, à Rome grand
  mal voir,
Nefs parfondrees & prins le Tridental.[1]*

Blood will be soon to rain on the rocks,
Sun in the East, Saturn in the West. War
near Orgon. A great evil seen near Rome.
Ships sunken and the trident taken.

This must be a futuristic quatrain leading to the Millennium. As I say in my discussion of the Jewish sources for the Millennium, seven great disasters have to accumulate and come together to give warning of its actual coming and of the Third Antichrist. Phenomena such as showers of blood, Saturn in a bad aspect and war together with some great evil affecting the Vatican and the Papacy and a naval war are all portents. Nostradamus intended the reader to take note of these events and try to halt them, but the way the world is going this tragically seems unlikely.

---

[1]*Tridental.* One who holds the Trident, i.e., power of the seas.

Century V

V.LXIII

De vaine emprife l'honneur indue plaincte,
Galiotz errans par latins froit, faim vagues
Non loing du Tymbre de fang la terre taincte
Et fur humains feront diuerfes plagues.

From the useless enterprise honor and undeserved complaint. Boats wandering among the Latins, cold, hunger and waves (storms). Not far from the Tiber the land is stained with blood and there will be several plagues upon mankind.

This quatrain seems in some areas to continue the preceding one, V.LXII. Again we have a fleet in trouble around Italy, the river Tiber stained with blood and plagues throughout the world. At the moment we are cursed with various wars, famine, floods and disease throughout Africa and parts of the East and these troubles seem to be mounting daily. It does seem we are leading up to Nostradamus' vision of the Millennium in every sense. See the introductory material.

Century V

V.LXIIII

Les affemblés par repoz du grand nombre,
Par terre & mer confeil contremandé:
Pres de l'Autonne Gennes, Nice de l'ombre
Par champs & villes le chef contrebandé.

Those assembled through the calm of the great number, countermanded by land and sea. Near Autonne, Genoa, the shadow of Nice. Revolution against the leaders through fields and towns.

Autonne is one of Nostradamus' unsolved anagrams. It is written *Antonne* in some editions. The nearest phonetic equivalents are Nentone or Antipolis (Antibes), but this does not clarify the meaning. It is probably a failed quatrain of events occurring in the nineteenth century.

Century V

V.LXV

Subit venu l'effrayeur fera grande,
Des principaux de l'affaire cachés:
Et dame en braise plus ne fera en veue
Ce peu à peu feront les grans fachés.

Suddenly appeared, the terror will be great, hidden by the ringleaders of the situation. The women on (of) the charcoal will no longer be seen. Thus, little by little, the great ones will be angered.

I cannot decipher this quatrain.

Century V

V.LXVI

Soubs les antiques edifices veftaulx,
Non efloignez d aqueduct ruyne:
De Sol & Lune font les luifans
  metaulx,
Ardante lampe Traian d'or burine.

Under the ancient buildings of the vestals
not far from the ruin of the aqueduct.
There will be glittering metals of the Sun
and the Moon, the golden Trojan lamp,
burning, pillaged.

The commentator Jaubert suggests that this quatrain refers to the convent of St.-Sauveur-de-la-Fontaine, at Nîmes, which was built upon the site of a temple to the goddess Diana, the Moon, and that valuable treasures of gold and silver will be dug up, including a golden lamp. The aqueduct could place the quatrain at Nîmes, but I do not feel able to follow this interpretation further.

Century V

V.LXVII

Quand chef Peroufe n'ofera fa tunique
Sens au couuert tout nud s'expolier:
Seront prins fept faict Ariftocratique,
Le pere & fils mors par poincte au
  colier.

When the great head of Perugia dare not
risk his tunic, without any cover, and strip
himself completely naked. The seven aris-
tocrats will be taken; father and son dead
through a wound in the throat.

The head of Perugia in this case was the Pope, Sixtus V, who had excommunicated Henri de Navarre in 1595, and was reluctant to do the same to Henri III of France and thus risk losing France, *tout nud s'expolier.* The Pope was finally forced to act in 1589, but he did not dare release his Catholic subjects from their oath of allegiance, because the Papacy had already lost the revenues of England and Northern Europe to Protestantism.

The seven are again the children of Catherine de' Medicis. Their father, Henri II, was already dead from a wound in the throat (I.XXXV) and his last ruling son, the sixth Medicis child, Henri III, was to die from stab wounds, but in the stomach, not the throat (see I.XCVII) in 1589. An interesting quatrain, if somewhat convoluted.

Century V

V.LXVIII

Dans le Danube & du Rhin viendra boire,
Le grand Chameau ne s'en repentira:
Trembler du Rofne & plus fort ceux de Loire,
Et pres des Alpes coq le ruinera.

The great Camel will come to drink of the Danube and the Rhine and will not repent of it. Those of the Rhône tremble and even more so those of the Loire. Near the Alps the cock will ruin him.

The great camel, appearing also in IV.LXXV and VI.LV, is a complete enigma. It appears that this person sweeps aside German opposition but gets his comeuppance in France. Shades of Hitler perhaps? I think that this quatrain refers, as do the others, to past events. Nostradamus was wrong in this case.

Century V

V.LXIX

Plus ne fera le grand en faux fommeil,
L'inquietude viendra prendre repoz:
Dreffer phalange d'or, azur, & vermeil,
Subiuguer Affrique la ronger iufques oz.

The great one will remain no longer in a false sleep. Unease will take the place of repose. A phalanx of gold, blue and vermilion will be drawn up to subdue Africa, and gnaw it to the very bone.

Louis Philippe usurped the French crown of his nephew in 1830, having waited for an opportune moment, line 2. He was the first legitimate Bourbon to accept the tricolor of red, white and blue, as the royal standard. The French conquest of Algeria happened in the same year that he snatched the throne. Nostradamus says that the standard is gold, red and blue, line 3. James Laver makes a charming comment: "The old eyes of the prophet may be pardoned for being slightly colour blind." Gold as well was the symbol of royalty and power so perhaps it is understandable.

Century V

V.LXX

Des regions fubiectes à la Balance,
Feront troubler les monts par grande guerre
Captifz tout fexe deu & tout Bifance,
Qu'on criera à l'aube terre à terre.

Some of the regions subject to the Balance will trouble the mountains with a great war. The entire sex will be captured, endebted, with all Byzantium. At dawn they will call from land to land.

The Balance, Libra, stands normally for Austria and Savoy in Nostradamus' writing, and he also applies it to England and trading nations which are governed by Libra. He appears to think that Austria will overthrow the Ottoman Empire. It is possible that the Austrian troubles in the Balkans during the early 1900s are hinted at in this verse.

Century V

V.LXXI

Par la fureur d'vn qui attendra l'eau,
Par la grand raige tout l'exercite efmeu:
Chargé des nobles à dix-fept bateaulx,
Au long du Rofne, tard meffagier venu.

By the fury of one who will wait for the water; by the great rage that moves all the army. Seventeen boats are loaded with nobles. The messenger arrives too late along the Rhône.

This quatrain has been tentatively applied to every would-be invader of Britain *qui attendra l'eau,* who would cross the Channel, including Napoleon, Hitler, etc. I cannot decide to what it actually refers.

Century V

V.LXXII

Pour le plaifir d'edict voluptueux,
On meflera la poyfon dans l'aloy:
Venus fera en cours fi vertueux,
Qu'obfufquera du foleil tout à loy.

For the pleasure of the edict of vice, poison will be mixed with the law. At court, Venus will be so virtuous, that all the glory of the sun will be obscured by it.

A difficult quatrain but possible to solve if one accepts that the glory of the sun refers to the Sun King, Louis XIV, and the Edict of Poitiers, 1577, greatly disapproved of by Nostradamus because it legalized Calvinism and allowed the clergy to marry.

At this time the court of Henri III, Louis XIV's predecessor, was very depraved. His openly flaunted homosexuality and interest in public self-flagellation greatly offended France, and his *mignons* acquired not only power but also great wealth. Henri was reputed to have a familiar sorcerer named Tarragon.

Century V
V.LXXIII

Perfecutee fera de Dieu l'Eglife,
Et les fainctz temples feront expoliez:
L'enfant la mere mettra nud en
* chemife,*
Seront Arabes aux Polons raliez.

The Church of God will be persecuted and
the holy temples will be pillaged. The
mother will put away the child, naked in
a shift. The Arabs will ally with the Poles.

Presumably the clue to this quatrain lies in line 4, but I cannot see either the Polish government or Solidarity linked with the Arabs, who normally stand for terrorism. It may possibly be a futuristic quatrain.

Century V
V.LXXIIII

De fang Troyen[1] naiftra coeur
* Germanique*
Qu'il deuiendra en fi haute puiffance:
Hors chaffera gent eftrange Arabique
Tournant l'Eglife en priftine
* preeminence.*

Of Trojan blood he will be born with a
German heart and will rise to very great
power. He will drive out the foreign Ara-
bic nation and return the Church to her
early glory.

Trojan blood in Nostradamus' predictions stands for French royal blood, a reference to the ancient myth that the line was descended from Priam, king of Troy. But a French king with German ancestry who will control the Arabs and restore the Roman Catholic Church to its former power? Unlikely. A failed quatrain.

Century V
V.LXXV

Montera haut fur le bien plus à dextre,
Demourra affis fur la pierre quarree:
Vers le midi pofé à la feneftre,
Bafton tortu en main, bouche ferree.

He will rise high over his wealth, more to
the right-hand side he will remain seated
on the square of stone. Towards the south,
placed at the window, a crooked staff in
his hand, his mouth sealed.

I cannot help with this quatrain except to mention that a *baston tortu,* a crooked staff, normally refers to a bishop's crook and possibly by extension to that of a pope.

---

[1]*fang Troyen.* The myth by which the French royal line were descended from Francus, son of Priam of Troy.

Century V

V.LXXVI

En lieu libere tendra fon pauillon,
Et ne voudra en citez prendre place:
Aix, Carpen l'ifle volce, mont
  Cauaillon,
Par tous fes lieux abolira fa traffe.

In a free place he will pitch his tent, he will not want to stay in the cities. Aix, Carpentras, L'isle Vaucluse. Montfavet, Cavaillon. In all these places he will abolish his trace.

All the places mentioned are near Nostradamus' home in Salon-de-Provence.

Century V

V.LXXVII

Tous les degrez d'honneur
  Ecclefiaftique,
Seront changez en dial quirinal:
En Martial quirinal flaminique,
Puis vn Roy de France le rendre
  vulcanal.

All degrees of ecclesiastical honor will be changed to Jupiter and Quirinus. A priest of Quirinus in martial guise. Then a king of France will make him a man of Vulcan.

I cannot decipher this quatrain. It implies that Roman ecclesiastical honors revert to paganism. Other than this, I can go no further. It may be linked with the twentieth century decline of religious beliefs.

Century V

V.LXXVIII

Les deux vnis ne tiendront longuement,
Et dans treze ans au Barbare Satrappe:
Aux deux coftez seront tel perdement,
Qu'vn benyra le Barque & fa cappe.

The two will not remain allied for long. Within thirteen years they give into barbarian power. There will be such a loss on both sides, that one will bless the Barque (of Peter) and its leader.

I feel the clue to this quatrain lies in II.LXXXIX when Nostradamus writes of the day the "two great leaders will be friends," and this is reported "to the man of blood," the Antichrist. He gives differing views on the length of the alliance between the two great powers, the USA and USSR, with the commencement of the INF Treaty. In another quatrain he says it will last only "three years and seven months" (IV.XCV). In VIII.LXXVII he states the war which results as the breakdown of this alliance will last for twenty-seven years and will be initiated by the Third Antichrist. This dating would bring us past the Millennium. Nostradamus is somewhat confused as to exact date of the alliance and war, but definite that they will occur. Why the then Pope, the final Pope if we believe Nostradamus and Malachy, should be blessed for his actions remains to be seen, because in other quatrains Nostradamus implies that he will flee Rome.

Century V
V.LXXIX

La facree pompe viendra baiffer les
*   aifles,*
Par la venue du grand legiflateur:
Humble haulfera vexera les rebelles,
Naiftra fur terre aucun aemulateur.

The sacred pomp will come to lower its wings at the coming of the great lawgiver. He will raise the humble and trouble the rebellious. His like will not appear again on earth.

The generalities of this quatrain seem most applicable to Napoleon. He treated both the Church and the Vatican with arbitrary power. He originated France's present legal system, the Code Napoléon. He raised the lowly to aristocracy and was brutal in his stamping out of rebellion. Line 4 is an exaggeration, but he was a great dictator, although different in mold from his successor, Hitler.

Century V
V.LXXX

Logmion grande Bifance approchera,
Chaffé fera la barbarique ligne:
Des deux loix l'vne l'eftinique¹ lachera,
Barbare & franche en perpetuelle
*   brigue.*

Ogmios will approach great Byzantium. The barbarian league will be driven out. Of the two laws the pagan one will fail, barbarian and freeman in perpetual struggle.

Ogmios is the key word in this quatrain, which I cannot decipher in this context. Ogmios was the Celtic Hercules. He appears elsewhere in the quatrains, equally mysterious.

Century V
V.LXXXI

L'oifeau royal fur la cité folaire,
Sept moys deuant fera nocturne augure:
Mur d'Orient cherra tonnerre efclaire,
Sept iours aux portes les ennemis à
*   l'heure.*

The royal bird over the city of the sun will give a nightly warning for seven months. The wall in the East will fall; thunder and lightning. In seven days the enemies (arrive) directly to the gates.

¹*eftinique.* L. *ethnicus,* pagan.

The royal bird is usually an eagle, here flying over either Paris, the City of the Sun, or Rome, the City of Light, as an omen of disaster to come. Earlier commentators have identified the wall in the East as the Maginot Line, the fall of France, and the Blitzkrieg as the seven days (the crucial period of which was June 5–11, 1940). However, it may well refer to the Berlin Wall. Nostradamus indicates that the wall will come down eventually, or allow entry, *aux portes les ennemis,* but that other natural disasters, symbolized by thunder and lightning, will follow in the wake of this event.

Century V

V.LXXXII

Au conclud pache[1] hors de la fortereffe,
Ne fortira celuy en defefpoir mis:
Quant ceux d'Arbois, de Langres, côtre
   Brefse,
Auront mont Dolle, boufcade[2]
   d'ennemis.

At the conclusion of the treaty he will not go outside the fortress, overcome with despair. When the people of Arbois, Langres, against Bresse will have an enemy ambush the mountains of Dôle.

I cannot interpret this quatrain.

Century V

V.LXXXIII

Ceux qui auront entreptins subuertir,
Nompareil regne puiffant & inuincible:
Feront par fraude, nuictz trois aduertir,
Quant le plus grand à table lira Bible.

Those who will have an undertaking to subvert an unparalleled kingdom, powerful and invincible. They will deceive, warn for three nights, when the most important one will read his Bible at the table.

This is a propagandist quatrain and could have many applications since Nostradamus' time. The reference to the Bible probably inclines the prophecy towards the Protestant Huguenots. Otherwise it is too general to place.

[1]*pache.* A.Pr. treaty
[2]*boufcade.* A.Pr. ambush.

Century V

V.LXXXIIII

Naiftra du gouphre & cité immefuree,
Nay de parents obfcurs & tenebreux:
Qui la puiffance du grand roy reueree,
Voudra deftruire par Rouan & Eureux.

He will be born of the gulf and the immeasurable city, born of dark and obscure parents. He will wish to destroy the power of the great, revered king through Rouen and Eureux.

Apart from the fact that Rouen and Evreux are linked in IV.C as loyal to Napoleon III and the monarchy. I cannot decipher this quatrain further.

Century V

V.LXXXV

Par les Sueues[1] & lieux circonuoifins,
Seront en guerre pour caufe des nuees:
Gamp marins locuftes & coufins,
Du Leman fautes, feront bien defnuees.

Through the Swiss and the surrounding areas they will war because of the locusts. A swarm of marine locusts and mosquitoes(?). The faults of Geneva will be laid quite bare.

The Swiss fail, that is the League of Nations (see I.XLVII) and the result is the Second World War. Locusts and their "like" are usually planes or weapons of destruction in Nostradamus' vocabulary, but the geographical location makes it unlikely that one might take them literally, as in this case.

Century V

V.LXXXVI

Par les deux teftes, & trois bras feparés,
La cité grand par eaux fera vexee:
Des grands d'entre eux par exil efgarés,
Par tefte perfe Bifance fort preffee.

Divided by two heads and three arms, the great city will be troubled by water. Some of the great men among them wander in exile. Byzantium is hard pressed by the leader of Persia.

The two heads and three arms probably stand for the river Seine, which troubles the great city of Paris by flooding. This occurred reasonably frequently during the seventeenth and eighteenth centuries, particularly in the earlier part of the former when the Turks (Byzantium) were hard pressed by Persia. There was further fighting

[1]*Sueues.* L. *Suevi,* ancestors of the German Swiss.

in the East during the first part of the eighteenth century. Not a very convincing quatrain in all.

Century V

V.LXXXVII

L'an que Saturne hors de feruage,
Au franc terroir fera d'eau inondé:
De fang Troyen fera fon mariage,
Et fera feur d'Efpaignols circundé.

In the year that Saturn is freed from servitude the Frankish territory will be inundated by water. His marriage will be of Trojan blood and he will be closely encircled by the Spaniards.

The only clear fact here is that Nostradamus foresees someone of French royal blood marrying a Spaniard. I am tempted to think that this is a retroactive quatrain referring to the marriage of Elisabeth, daughter of Henri II and Catherine de' Medicis, to Philip II of Spain, his third wife after Mary Tudor of England. As I have said elsewhere, even prophets needed to be right from time to time in contemporary eyes. There was certainly great flooding in the Midi and around Marseilles in 1554, the worst for many years, possibly linking up with line 2.

Century V

V.LXXXVIII

Sur le fablon par vn hideux deluge,
Des autres mers trouué monftre marin:
Proche du lieu fera faict vn refuge,
Tenant Sauone efclaue de Turin.

Through a dreadful flood a marine monster will be found on the sand from other seas. A refuge will be made near the place, holding Savona slave to Turin.

The only fact I can contribute toward the interpretation of this quatrain is that in 1815 Savona, which was part of the state of Genoa, was given to the house of Savoy, to which Turin also belonged. There is no record of a sea monster. Perhaps it is a metaphor?

Century V

V.LXXXIX

Dedans Hongrie par Boheme, Nauarre,
Et par banniere fainctes feditions:
Par fleurs de lys pays portant la barre,
Contre Orleans fera emotions.

Into Hungary through Bohemia and Navarre, by the banner feigned seduction. The country of the fleur-de-lys carrying the bar. They will cause disturbances against Orléans.

The family whose arms carried the fleur-de-lys with a diagonal bar at each corner were the Bourbons. The junior branches who acquired the throne, such as the Vendômes and the Condés, simply had a diagonal bar in the center of their shields. Nostradamus appears to be describing an expedition into Bohemia and Hungary led by one of the French royal line, possibly a Bourbon Vendôme of Navarre? It is all very obscure and appears to be unfulfilled and probably a failed quatrain.

Century V

V.XC

Dans les cyclades, en perinthe & lariffe,	*In the Cyclades, in Perinthus and La-*
Dedans Sparte tout le Pelloponneff:	*rissa, in Sparta and all of the Pelopon-*
Si grand famine, pefte par faux	*nese, a very great famine, plague through*
conniffe,[1]	*false dust. It will last nine months*
Neuf mois tiendra & tout le cherroneffe.	*throughout the whole peninsula.*

False dust implies a chemical agent of some kind. Is Nostradamus trying to imply here that the plague and famine are artificially introduced? There appears to be a widespread disaster throughout the whole of Greece and the southern Balkans. This quatrain may tie in with those that predict trouble in the Middle East. Perhaps it may be a reference to the deaths of many thousands of Turkish and Iraqi Kurds in 1988.

Century V

V.XCI

Au grand marché qu'on dict des	*At the great market, called that of the*
menfongiers	*liars, all of Torrent and the field of*
Du tout Torrent[2] & champ Athenien:	*Athens. They will be surprised by the light*
Seront fuprins par les cheuaux legiers,	*armed horses, by the Albanians, when*
Par Albanois Mars, Leo, Sat. vn	*Mars is in Leo and Saturn in Aquarius.*
verfien.[3]	

Yet another reference to an unlikely attack from Albania at the conjunction mentioned. This, like most of Nostradamus' astrological datings, is not specific enough to place. Perhaps he was still protecting himself from the French Inquisition. It is very irritating not to be able to be more specific.

---

[1]*conniffe.* Difficult word, possibly from Gk. *konis,* dust, or L. *connissus,* exerted.
[2]*Torrent.* It is unclear whether this is a proper name or not.
[3]*verfien. Verseau,* Aquarius.

Century V
V.XCII

Apres le fiege tenu dixfept ans,
Cinq changeront en tel reuolu terme:
Puis fera l'vn efleu de mefme temps,
Qui des Romains ne fera trop conforme.

After the See (seat) has been held for seventeen years, five will change within the same period of time. Then one will be elected at the same time who will not be too agreeable to the Romans.

Nostradamus says that after a pope has ruled for seventeen years there will be five popes during the next seventeen. If he is slightly out in his calculations, this might apply to Pius XII, who was in the Vatican for nineteen years. Since then we have had John XXIII, 1958–63, Paul VI, 1963–78 and John Paul I, 1978, with Pope John Paul II presently occupying the papal throne. So we have only one more pope to go, the *"Gloria Olivae"* of Malachy. The timing is slightly wrong, but we have had four popes in twenty years, quite a rapid turnover for the Vatican. John Paul II has now been on the papal throne for ten years. It will be interesting to see what his successor may bring.

Century V
V.XCIII

Soubs le terroir du rond globe lunaire,
Lors que fera dominateur Mercure:
L'ifle d'Efcoffe fera vn luminaire,
Qui les Anglois mettra à deconfiture.

Under the land of the round moonlike globe when Mercury is at the height of his powers. The island of Scotland will produce a leader who will put the English into confusion.

Most commentators apply this quatrain to Charles I because he was born in Scotland before the Stuarts came to the English throne. But it seems to me to be more applicable to Bonnie Prince Charlie, who did put the English into confusion for a while when his army marched as far south as Derby.

Century V
V.XCIIII

Tranflatera en la grand Germanie,
Brabant & Flâdres, Gand, Bruges, &
Bolongne:
La traifue fainte, le grand duc
d'Armenie,
Affaillira Vienne & la Coloigne.

He will change into the Greater Germany Brabant and Flanders, Ghent, Bruges and Boulogne. The truce feigned, the great duke of Armenia will assault Vienna and Cologne.

Greater Germany, is, of course, the Third Reich. Hitler assimilated all the countries mentioned during his invasion of Europe. The feigned truce may describe the German invasion of Poland under the guise of help, which elsewhere Nostradamus described as *fimilé fecours*. Armenia is Russia which, once allied with the West, moved troops southwards into Germany. (See I.XXXIIII, III.XXXV, LIII, LXI, IV.XL, LXVIII, IX.XC.)

Century V

V.XCV

Nautique rame inuitera les vmbres,
Du grand Empire lors viendra conciter:
La mer Aegee des lignes les encombres,
Empefchant l'onde Tirreme defflotez.

The nautical oar will invite the shadows and then come to provoke the great Empire. In the Aegean Sea the remains of (bits of) wood obstruct the Tyrrhenian Sea and impede it.

A fleet *(nautique rame)* will trouble an Empire, but whether the French or Roman empire is not clear. The end result is the destruction of the empire in Greek waters.

Century V

V.XCVI

Sur le milieu du grand monde la rofe,
Pour nouueaux faicts fang public
* efpandu:*
A dire vray on aura bouche clofe,
Lors au befoing viendra tard l'attendu.

The rose upon the middle of the world. Because of new deeds public blood is shed. To speak the truth they will have closed mouths. Then, at the time of need the awaited one will come late.

I cannot decipher this quatrain. The key probably lies in line 1.

Century V

V.XCVII

Le nay defforme par horreur fuffoqué,
Dans la cité du grand Roy habitable:
L'edict feuere des captifs reuoqué,
Grefle & tonnerre, Condon ineftimable.

One born deformed, suffocated through honor in the city inhabited by the great King. The severe edict of the captives is revoked, hail and thunder. Condom too powerful.

This quatrain can be dated by line 2 as occurring before the French Revolution. There were no great kings after that. Commentators have suggested it may refer to the mysterious Man in the Iron Mask, the reputed son of the queen and Cardinal Mazarin. But there is no evidence that this mysterious prisoner, in his mask of velvet, not iron, was deformed, or that he was suffocated. Line 3 may refer to the Edict of Nantes, 1598, and be a point for dating the quatrain. Unsatisfactory.

Century V

V.XCVIII

A quarante huict degré climaterique,
A fin de Cancer fi grande feichereffe:
Poiffon en mer, fleuue, lac cuit hectique,
Bearn, Bigorre par feu ciel en deftreffe.

At the forty-eighth degree of the climacteric, the end of Cancer, there is a very great drought. Fish in the sea, river and lake hectically boiled. Bearn and Bigorre in distress from fire in the sky.

The "forty-eighth degree of the climacteric" may mean 48° latitude, which runs through France near Rennes, Orléans and Langres. A drought is predicted as occurring after July 22, when the Sun leaves Cancer. There is another reference to fish cooking in the sea in II.III. Fire in the sky may either be some form of freak electrical storm or Nostradamus' usual reference to an attack by bombs or rockets. Since such a situation seems unlikely to be confined to France alone I think I have probably misinterpreted the 48° of the climacteric. This may well be a futuristic quatrain.

Century V

V.XCIX

Milan, Ferrare, Turin, & Aquillaye,
Capne Brundis vexés par gent Celtique:
Par le Lyon & phalange aquilee
Quant Rome aura le chef vieux
  Britannique.

Milan, Ferrare, Turin and Aqualia, Capua and Brundis vexed by the Celtic nation. By the lion and his eaglelike phalanx, when Rome will hold to old British chief.

Cardinal York, the last of the Stuarts, true heirs to the British throne, died in Rome in 1807. By that time all the places mentioned had been conquered by the Imperial Eagle of France, by Napoleon. A good, simple quatrain.

Century V

V.C

Le boutefeu par fon feu attrapé,	The incendiary trapped in his own fire.
De feu du ciel à Carcas & Cominge:	Fire from the sky at Carcassonne and
Foix, Aux, Mazere, haut viellart	Comminges. Foix, Auch and Mazeres; the
* efchappé,*	important old man escaped, through those
Par ceux de Haffe, des Saxons &	of Hesse, Thuringia and some Saxons.
* Turinge.*	

Yet another reference to fire in the sky, perhaps bombs or rockets, this time in southwestern France. (See V.XCVIII.) Not many of the German forces got this far south even during the Second World War, so this quatrain also may not yet be fulfilled.

Century VI

VI.I

Avtour des môts Pyrenees grâs amas	Around the Pyrenean mountains a great
De gent eftrange fecourir roy nouueau:	throng of foreign people will help the new
Pres de Garonne du grand temple du	king. Near the temple of Mas by the Ga-
* Mas,*	ronne, a Roman leader will fear the one
Vn Romain chef le craindra dedans	on the water.
* l'eau.*	

The Mas d'Agenais has many famous Roman antiquities which Nostradamus would have gotten to know when he lived at Agen with his first wife and as a friend of Scaliger. But the Roman chief fearing a naval commander is unclear.

Century VI

VI.II

En l'an cinq cens octante plus &	In the year five hundred and eighty more
* moins,*	or less, one will await a very strange cen-
On attendra le fiecle bien eftrange:	tury. In the year seven hundred and three,
En l'an fept cens, & trois cieux en	the skies are witness that several king-
* tefmoings.*	doms, between one to five will be changed.
Que plufieurs regnes vn à cinq feront	
* change.*	

This is a daring quatrain in which Nostradamus gives the reader two dates, 1580 and 1703. As I have explained elsewhere, it was common in the fifteenth and sixteenth centuries to give dates leaving out the year 1000. Tombstones of the period give ample evidence of this, both in Britain as well as on the Continent. (See II.LI for the famous quatrain dating the Fire of London in the same manner.)

In 1580, soon after Nostradamus' death, France was torn by yet another civil war, known as the Seventh War, and things looked grim for the country as a whole. But by 1703, Louis XIV was defying Europe and fighting the War of the Spanish Succession. The five kingdoms were probably those of the Two Sicilies, Milan, the Netherlands, the Americas and Spain, the last of which was inherited by a Frenchman, Philip V, the grandson of Louis XIV. A good, realistic quatrain.

Century VI

VI.III

Fleuue qu'efprouue le nouueau nay *Celtique,* *Sera en grande de l'Empire difcorde:* *Le ieune prince par gent ecclefiaftique,* *Oftera le fceptre coronal de concorde.*	*The river is attempted by the newborn French heir. There will be great discord among the Empire. The young prince will remove peace from the crown and scepter because of the ecclesiastics.*

Garencières produces a legend that in former times newborn heirs to the French throne were put on a target and made to swim up the Rhine to see if they were lawfully begotten or not. Unfortunately, I can find no other reference to this tale. The word "Empire" dates the quatrain as post-1798. Napoleon, by his forcing Pope Pius VII to crown him at his coronation and imprisoning his predecessor Pius VI at Valence, may be a more likely interpretation of the last two lines.

Century VI

VI.IIII

Le Celtiq fleuue changera de riuaige, *Plus ne tiendra la cité d'Agripine:*[1] *Tout tranfmué ormis le vieil langaige,* *Saturne, Leo, Mars, Cancer en rapine.*	*The French river will change course and no longer surround the city of Agrippina. All changed except the old language, Saturn in Leo, Mars plundering in Cancer.*

After the Franco-Prussian War and the surrender of Alsace and Lorraine to the Germans, the Rhine, the French river, was no longer the border between France and Germany. The old language that remained must be German. Everything else was changed by the war.

---

[1]*Agripine.* L. *Colonia Agrippina,* now Cologne.

As usual, the astrological dating is not detailed enough to determine the exact time of this quatrain, although Saturn is always a bad aspect and Mars stands for war.

Century VI

VI.V

Si grand famine par vnde peftifere.
Par pluye longue le long du polle
  arctique:
Samarobryn cent lieux de l'hemifphere,
Viuront fans loy exempt de pollitique.

A very great famine (caused) by a plague-ridden wave will extend through long rain the length of the Arctic pole. Samarobrin, one hundred leagues from the hemisphere. They will live without law, exempt from politics.

This quatrain is of great importance. The word *Samarobrin* seems to have two meanings here. Initially I believed it to derive from the Russian words *samo,* self, and *robin,* operator, that is, a self-operating machine in space, such as the Russians' Mir Satellite. But Nostradamus links this with a plague which will cover the earth, in particular the Northern Pole. Two new drugs have appeared which may be helpful in the treatment of the worldwide scourge of AIDS. They are suramin and ribavirin. Together they form a word similar to *Samarobrin.* Perhaps the remedy for AIDS will be produced in a sterile laboratory circling the earth? Certainly AIDS is the plague of the latter half of the twentieth century and the description of a space station can only confirm the dating. The last line is unclear. Does it refer to the victims who are struck down regardless of political stance or to the fact that the astronauts working in the space station are out of the hands of law and politics, in another dimension? A very thought-provoking quatrain.

Century VI

VI.VI

Apparoiftra vers le Septentrion,
Non loing de Cancer l'eftoille cheuelue:
Suze, Sienne, Boece, Eretrion,
Mourra de Rome grand, la nuict
  difperue.

He will appear towards the North, not far from the bearded star in Cancer. Susa, Siena, Boetia, Eretria; the great man of Rome will die, the night dispersed.

One can place this great man of Rome by his successor Pope Leo XIII, whose family's coat of arms contains a bearded star, a comet, *l'eftoille cheuelue.* Leo was also called *"Lumen in Caelo"* by the prophet

Malachy. His predecessor was Pius IX, who died in 1878. I cannot
relate the place names to any particular event.

Century VI

VI.VII

Norneigre & Dace, & l'ifle
  Britannique,
Par les vnis freres feront vexées:
Le chef Romain iffue de fang Gallique
Et les copies aux foreftz repoulfées.

Norway, Dacia and the British Isles will
be troubled by the united brothers. The
Roman leader, sprung from French blood
and the forces thrust back into the forests.

This quatrain strongly resembles V.LI, where Hitler and Mussolini
are described as the united brothers or allies who trouble Norway,
Romania (Dacia) and Great Britain during the Second World War.
The forces in the forests presumably refer to the famous Resistance
movements, the *Maquis,* which caused great trouble for the Nazis.

Century VI

VI.VIII

Ceux qui eftoyent en regne pour fçauoir,
Au Royal change deuiendront apouuris:
Vns exilez fans appuy, or n'auôir,
Lettrez & lettres ne feront à grand pris.

Those who were in the kingdom for knowledge will become impoverished by a royal
change. Some exiled without support,
having no gold, neither learning nor the
learned will be held of much value.

I feel that this is a general comment by Nostradamus on his belief
that learning would decline during a period after his death. Knowledge will not be respected and scholars sent into exile.

Century VI

VI.IX

Aux facrez temples feront faicts
  efcandales,
Comptes feront par honneurs & .
  louanges
D'vn que on graue d'argent, d'or les
  medalles,
La fin fera en tormens bien eftranges.

In the sacred temples scandals will be committed. They will be thought of as honors
and praiseworthy by one whom they en-
grave on silver, gold and medals. The end
will be (achieved) in very strange torments.

John Hogue relates this quatrain to the Papacy but personally I
cannot connect the quatrain with anything to do with the Vatican. I

can see why he wishes to interpret line 1 as the Vatican and line 3 as memorabilia of the Pope, but it does not feel to me to be Nostradamus' line of thought. Also, where does line 4 fit in? The Pope's possible assassination is predicted elsewhere by Nostradamus.

Century VI

VI.X

I'n peu de temps les temples des couleurs
De blanc & noir des deux entremeflée:
Rouges & iaunes leur embleront les
*   leurs*
Sang, terre, pefte, faim, feu d'eau
*   affollée.*

In a short time the colors of the temples, the two will be intermingled with black and white. The red and yellow ones will carry off their (possessions). Blood, earth, plague, hunger, fire, maddened by thirst.

This sounds like a quatrain relating to the Millennium. Religion will become confused, unable to distinguish between right and wrong, *de blanc & noir*. The red and yellow people may well then refer to the Russian Communists and the Chinese who, when they carry the day, bring in their wake all the plagues, famines and wars that are forecast.

Century VI

VI.XI

Des fept rameaux à trois feront reduicts,
Les plus aifnez feront furprins par
*   mort,*
Fratricider les deux feront feduicts,
Les coniurez en dormans sefont morts.

The seven branches will be reduced to three, the elder ones will be surprised by death. Two will be attracted towards fratricide. The conspirators will die while asleep.

This is a good quatrain. The seven children of Catherine de' Medicis were reduced to three in 1575 when only Henri III, the duc d'Alençon and Marguerite de Navarre remained alive. Henri III and his brother were involved in a series of campaigns against the Guises, their first cousins. Finally the duc d'Alençon allied himself with the Guises, hoping to take the throne from his brother *(Fratricider).* Both the Guise brothers, probably the most powerful men in France after the king, were murdered at Blois in the early morning of 1558. (See II.XVIII, III.LI.)

Century VI

VI.XII

Dreffer copies pour monter à l'Empire,
Du Vatican le fang Royal tiendra:
Flamans, Anglois, Espaigne auec
    Afpire,[1]
Contre l'Italie & France contendra.

To raise forces to ascend to Empire the
royal blood of the Vatican will hold fast.
Flemish, English, Spain with Aspire. He
will fight against France and Italy.

This is an extremely interesting quatrain, as Nostradamus visualizes Europe in definitive modern terms, not contemporary ones. Italy did not exist as a cohesive country until 1870. The Flemings were a Hapsburg dependency until the creation of modern Belgium.

This prediction makes three main points: Firstly, there will be an attempt to gain the Imperial throne (Holy Roman Empire?); secondly, a pope, possibly with French blood, which Nostradamus predicts in V.XLIX; whose alliance would be moved to the Vatican against his own country; thirdly, the Hapsburgs and the English will ally against France and Italy. The first and last predictions occurred during the Napoleonic Wars. A succinct commentary about the nineteenth century European political scene.

Century VI

VI.XIII

Vn dubieux ne viendra loing du regne,
La plus grand part le voudra fouftenir:
Vn Capitole[2] *ne voudra point qu'il*
    regne,
Sa grande charge ne pourra maintenir.

The doubtful one will not come far from
the kingdom, the greater part will wish to
support him. A pope will not want him to
reign. He will not be able to bear his great
burden.

Apart from papal interference in European politics, I cannot clarify this. Many commentators apply it to the fall of the House of Savoy, at that time the rulers of Italy.

---

[1]*Afpire.* Uncertain. Possible Speyer or Spires?
[2]*Capitole.* Probably standing for the Pope, as the Capitol was the Roman Citadel.

Century VI

VI.XIIII

Loing de fa terre Roy perdra la
   bataille,
Prompt efchappé pourfuiny fuiuant
   prins,
Ignare prins foubs la doree maille.
Soubs fainct habit & l'ennemy furprins.

Far from his country a king will lose the
battle. Quickly escaped, he is followed and
retaken. The ignorant one taken under the
golden chain mail, under a false garment.
The enemy is surprised.

This is yet another quatrain to support a romantic theory such as V.I, when the king, Sebastian of Portugal, decided to raise a Crusade in 1578, despite the objections of the Pope and the Spanish king.

After all, the age of Crusades was long past. But Sebastian crossed to Morocco in 1578 and attacked the army of the king of Fez and was obliterated at the Battle of Kasr Al-Kabir. He was reported killed but there were strong and persistent rumors that he had escaped. Nostradamus implies he did so by covering his golden chain mail with a more humble garment. Although the Moors discovered this and recaptured him, for political reasons they did not release the information. Nostradamus, for once, gives us a new slant upon history!

Century VI

VI.XV

Deffoubs la tombe fera trouue le Prince,
Qu'aura le pris par deffus Nuremberg:
L'Efpaignol Roy en Capricorne mince,
Fainct & trahy par le grand
   Vvitemberg:

Under the tomb will be found a prince,
who will take him above Nuremberg. The
Spanish king, thin in Capricorn, deceived
and betrayed by the great Wittenberg.

I cannot make head or tail of this quatrain. Wittenberg refers to the first printing of the Bible and Luther but I see no connection with Nuremberg and a Spanish king.

Century VI

VI.XVI

Ce que rauy fera du ieune Milue,
Par les Normans de France & Picardie:
Les noirs du temple du lieu de
   Negrifilue
Feront aulberge & feu de Lombardie.

That which the young hawk will carry off
by the Normans of France and Picardy.
The black ones of the temple of the Black
(forest?) wood, will make an inn and fire
at Lombardy.

The black ones are almost certainly the Benedictines, who were also known as the Black monks. They did have a monastery at Hauenhalb in the Black Forest. But I am afraid the quatrain remains to be deciphered. It may be a failed quatrain.

Century VI
VI.XVII

Apres les limes bruflez les afniers,
Contraints feront changer habits diuers:
Les Saturnins bruflez par les meufniers,
Hors la plufpart qui ne fera couuers.

After the penances are burned the ass drivers will be forced to change into different clothing. Those of Saturn, burned by the milkers. But the greater part excepted, it will not be covered.

I cannot decipher this quatrain.

Century VI
VI.XVIII

Par les phifiques le grand Roy delaiffé,
Par fort non art de l'Ebrieu eft en vie,
Luy & fon genre au regne hault pousé,
Grace donnee à gent qui Chrift enuie.

The great king deserted by the physicians lives through chance, not the skill of the Jew. He and his people placed high in the realm. Pardon given to the race which denies Christ.

This may be one of Nostradamus' very rare revelations about his private life as a crypto-Jewish doctor. He seems to envisage the Jews being restored to their due place in the realm and pardoned. Presumably the latter meant giving them the right to practice the Jewish faith openly. But sadly, the future would bring the Nazis and other similarly thinking political parties, and these prejudices are only now beginning to fade.

Century VI
VI.XIX

La vraye flamme engloutira la dame,
Que voudra mettre les Innocens à feu:
Pres de l'affaut l'exercite s'enflamme,
Quant dans Seuille monftre en boeuf
*   fera veu.*

The true flame will swallow up the woman who wants to put the Innocents to the fire. Near the assault the army is inflamed, when in Seville a gigantic (monstrous) ox will be seen.

The last line may be a reference to the Spanish passion for bull-fighting but the rest of the quatrain remains completely indecipherable.

Century VI

VI.XX

L'vnion faincte fera peu de durée,
Des vns changés reformés la plufpart:
Dans les vaiffeaux fera gent endurée,
Lors aura Rome vn nouueau liepart.

The feigned union will last a short time,
some changed, the greater part reformed.
People will be suffering in the vessels when
Rome has a new Leopard.

In heraldry a Leopard is a lion walking to the left with its head turned left to face the spectator. Possibly the last line is dated to a time when a pope has a leopard in his coat of arms, but since Nostradamus predicts that there will be only one other pope before the Millennium, this is unlikely. The nearest I can come to this is John XXIII, who had a winged leopard on the top of his armorial shield. His dates were 1958–63, so he does not seem to fit into this quatrain. Probably a failed prediction.

Century VI

VI.XXI

Quant ceux du polle artiq vnis
* enfemble,*
En Orient grand effraieur & crainte:
Efleu nouueau, fouftenu le grand
* tremble,*
Rodes, Bifance de fang Barbare taincte.

When those of the Northern Pole are
united together, in the East will be great
fear and dread. A new man elected sup-
ported by the great one who trembles. Both
Rhodes and Byzantium will be stained
with barbarian blood.

This quatrain must be linked with VI.V, which also indicates that the people of the Northern Pole will be united both in the fear and dread of the new twentieth century plague, AIDS. They are united in a search for a cure, possibly through the two anti-virus drugs suramin and ribavirin, which Nostradamus seems to believe will be finally developed in a sterile space station. He is not very optimistic about the length of time this search will take. (See III.LXXV.) "Relief near at hand" is probably AZT, "but remedies far away."

This quatrain may also have a second meaning referring to the new rapprochement between Bush and Gorbachev, *ceux du polle artiq vnis enfemble.*

AIDS started to come to the notice of the world around 1978, when Pope John Paul II was elected, *"Efleu nouuveau."*

The barbarian blood in Greece and Turkey may indicate further wars in the Middle East, possibly the blood of the Kurds who are now fleeing to Iraq in the hundreds of thousands. To Nostradamus they would appear as barbarians. A sobering quatrain.

Century VI

VI.XXII

Dedans la terre du grand temple celique,
Nepeu à Londres par paix faincte meurtry:
La barque alors deuiendra fcifmatique,
Liberte faincte fera au corn & cry.

In the land of the great heavenly temple, a nephew is murdered at London through a false peace. The ship will then be schismatic; false liberty will be shouted abroad.

An odd quatrain. The nephew of a ruler is asked to come to London on a peace treaty and then murdered. This rules out the Scottish pretenders. When this happens there will be a schism at the Vatican. Could this refer to the denounced Archbishop Lefèbvre? It is a most frustrating quatrain, possibly futuristic since Lefèbvre was excommunicated only in 1988.

Century VI

VI.XXIII

D'efprit de regne munifmes defcriées,
Et feront peuples efmeuz contre leur Roy:
Paix, faict nouueau, fainctes loix empirées,
Rapis onc fut en fi tresdur arroy.

Defenses undermined by the spirit of the kingdom, people will be stirred up against their king. A new peace is made, holy laws become worse. Never was Paris in so much trouble.

Rapis is Nostradamus' standard anagram for Paris, and is accepted as such by all commentators. This quatrain is full of generalities, most of which best apply to the French Revolution: new peace, new laws, and the religious element of society controlled rigidly by the state. During the Terror, Paris was in a state of anarchy.

Century VI

VI.XXIIII

Mars & le fceptre fe trouuera conioinct,
Deffoubz Cancer calamiteufe guerre:
Vn peu apres fera nouueau Roy oingt,
Qui par long temps pacifiera la terre.

Mars and the Scepter will be in conjunction, a calamitous war under Cancer. A short time afterwards a new king will be anointed who will bring peace to the earth for a long time.

The scepter here stands for Jupiter and according to Wölner, the only time this conjunction will appear is on June 21, 2002. Before this there will be a dreadful war, probably starting under the sign of

Cancer, June 22 to July 23. But, for the first time in the quatrains, Nostradamus allows that a period of peace may follow the war. If Wölner's dating of the conjunction is correct, there is a future for the world after the Millennium.

Century VI

VI.XXV

Par Mars contraire fera la monarchie,
Du grand pefcheur en trouble ruyneux:
Ieune noir[1] rouge prendra la hierarchie,
Les prodileurs iront iour bruyneux.

With Mars adverse the monarchy of the great fisherman will be in ruinous trouble. The young, red king will take over the government. The traitors will act on a misty day.

The great fisherman is, of course, the Pope, "the fisher of men." This quatrain probably dates to a period when the Vatican had its own army. It was defeated between 1796 and 1815 by Napoleon and was again in trouble in 1860–70. The young king with Socialist leanings, *rouge,* stands for Victor Emmanuel and the ensuing Italian Revolution.

Century VI

VI.XXVI

Quatre ans le fiege quelque peu bien
*   tiendra,*
Vn furuiendra libidineux de vie:
Rauenne & Pife, Veronne
*   fouftiendront,*
Pour efleuer la croix de Pape enuie.

For four years the seat be held for some little good. One will succeed to it who is libidinous in life, Ravenna and Pisa, Verona will support him, desirous of elevating the Papal Cross.

A good pope will after four years be succeeded by a more worldly one. This could most suitably apply to the popular John XXIII, who reigned for less than five years. His successor was the worldly, politically minded Paul VI. Paul gained great support from the main Italian cities, being involved with Michele Sindona, the Sicilian banker who has been linked with the Mafia and the Banco Ambrosiano. The near-collapse of one of Sindona's banks, the Ambrosiano, exposed a vast network of corruption, fraud and murder—all made feasible through Vatican financing. As to Paul VI being *libidineux de vie,* he was widely reputed to have a homosexual lover. He did, however, keep the Papacy for fifteen years, 1963–1978.

[1]*noir.* usual anagram for *roi* and makes much better sense in this context.

Century VI

VI.XXVII

Dedans les ifles de cinq fleuues à vn,
Par le croiffant du grand Chyren Selin:
Par les bruynes de laer fureur de l'vn,
Six efchapés, cachés, fardeaux de lyn.

Within the islands of five rivers to one, by
the crescent of the great Chyren Selin.
Through the mists in the air, the fury of
one. Six escaped, hidden in bundles of
flax.

This must be connected in some way with the other Chyren quatrains, but the text is impenetrable.

Century VI

VI.XXVIII

Le grand Celtique entrera dedans
   Rome,
Menant amas d'exilés & bannis:
Le grand pafteur mettra à mort tout
   homme,
Qui pour le coq eftoient aux Alpes vnis.

The great Celt will enter Rome, leading a
crowd of exiled and banished. The great
pastor will put to death every man who
was united over the Alps for the Cock.

The great Celt, a Frenchman, may be a reference to Napoleon's
conquest of Rome and the subsequent return of Pope Pius VII with
his clergy who had been imprisoned in France. But line 3 is totally
incorrect, as Pius VII was extremely kind to his ex-captors and their
adherents until his death in 1823.

Century VI

VI.XXIX

La vesue faincte entendant les
   nouuelles,
De fes rameaux mis en perplex &
   trouble:
Qui fera duict appaifer les querelles,
Par fon pourchas des razes fera comble.

The holy widow hearing the news of her
offspring in trouble and distress. He who
will be led to calm the quarrels by his
pursuit will make the shaven heads pile
up.

The widow, Catherine de' Medicis, will learn much of the problems
and troubles of her children, in particular of the massacre of Saint
Bartholemew and the murders of the duc de Guise and his brother,
by her son Henri III. All these actions created civil unrest and led to
the eventual religious and civil wars between the Leaguers and the
Huguenots, razes.

Century VI

VI.XXX

Par l'apparence de faincte faincteté,
Sera trahy aux ennemis le fiege:
Nuict qu'on cuidoit dormir en feureté,
Pres de Braban marcheront ceux du
* Liège.*

By the appearance of simulated holiness,
the Seat will be betrayed to the enemies in
the night when they thought to sleep
safely. The people of Liège will march
near Brabant.

Liège was a province east of Brabant in the Netherlands. Normally Nostradamus uses the word Seat to indicate the Papal See, the Vatican, but here it is difficult to be certain.

Century VI

VI.XXXI

Roy trouuera ce qu'il defiroit tant,
Quand le Prelat fera reprins à tort:
Refponce au duc le rendra mal content,
Qui dans Milan mettra plufieurs à
* mort.*

The king will find that which he desires so
greatly, when the Prelate will be wrongly
taken. The reply to the Duce will make
him angry. In Milan he will put several
to death.

The king of Italy, Umberto, achieves his desire when he angers the Duce, Mussolini. The executions at Milan probably refer to the deaths of Ciano and others. The Pope, wrongly taken, might be understood as the Vatican, a neutral city, completely surrounded by a hostile, Fascist Italy during the Second World War.

Century VI

VI.XXXII

Par trahyfon de verges à mort battu,
Prins furmonté fera par fon defordre:
Confeil friuole au grand captif fentu,
Nez par fureur quant Berich viendra
* mordre.*

Beaten to death by rods for treason. Cap-
tured, he will be overcome because of his
disorder. Frivolous advice is handed to the
great captive, when Berich comes to bite
his nose in a rage.

The solution to this quatrain lies in the as yet unsolved *Berich*, probably an anagram.

Century VI

VI.XXXIII

Sa main derniere par Alus fanguinaire,
Ne fe pourra par la mer guarentir:
Entre deux Fleuues craindre main
    militaire,
Le noir l'ireux le fera repentir.

His hand finally through the bloody Alus,
he will be unable to protect himself by sea.
Between two rivers he will fear the mili-
tary hand. The black and angry one will
make him repent of it.

Alus is another unsolved mystery and an interesting one. It (he?)
appears to connect with the fearsome Mabus of II.LXII. Is Alus the
precursor of the Antichrist, whose hand finally acts through the
bloody Alus? There is the repetition of the word *main* in connection
with both. Or it may be an approximation of the Antichrist himself,
tying up with the cryptic quatrain II.XXVIII where Nostradamus
seems to be trying to give the letters which make up the name of the
third Antichrist. See also I.L, II.LXXXIX, VIII.LXXVII and X.LXXII.

Century VI

VI.XXXIIII

De feu volant la machination,
Viendra troubler au grand chef affiegez:
Dedans fera telle fedition,
Qu'en defefpoir feront les profligez.

The machine of flying fire will come to
trouble the great besieged chief. Within
there will be such sedition that those aban-
doned will be in despair.

The first line of the quatrain is very striking; it describes a probable
rocket attack, which places the quatrain in this century. Unfortunately, there are many recent and current situations to which this
prediction could apply and it is too general otherwise to offer a clue.

Century VI

VI.XXXV

Pres de Rion[1] & proche à blanche
    laine,
Aries, Taurus, Cancer, Leo, la Vierge,
Mars, Iupiter, le Sol ardra grand
    plaine,
Bois & citez, lettres cachez au cierge.

Near the Bear and close to the white wool
Aries, Taurus, Cancer, Leo, Virgo, Mars,
Jupiter, the Sun will burn the great plain,
woods and cities. Letters hidden in the
candle.

I wonder whether the white wool might stand for the Milky Way?
Otherwise Nostradamus gives such a plethora of planets and constel-

[1] *Rion.* Misprint for *Trion,* L. *Triones,* the Constellation of the Bear.

lations that it is difficult to know what he intended, other than in line 3, where he predicts extreme drought throughout both city and countryside.

Century VI
VI.XXXVI

Ne bien ne mal par bataille terreftre,
Ne paruiendra aux confins de Perouffe:
Rebeller Pife, Florence voir mal eftre,
Roy nuict bleffé fur mulet à noire
houfe.

Neither good nor evil from the earthly battle will come to the borders of Perugia. Pisa to rebel, Florence seen to be upon bad (times). A king on a mule, wounded by night, to the black cover.

I cannot penetrate the convolutions of this quatrain except to state that all the places mentioned are in Italy or were parts of the Italian States.

Century VI
VI.XXXVII

L'oeuure ancienne fe paracheuera,
Du toict cherra fur le grand mal ruyne:
Innocent faict mort on accufera:
Nocent caiché taillis à la bruyne.

The ancient work will be accomplished and from the roof evil ruin will fall on the great man. Being dead, they will accuse an innocent of the deed. The guilty one hidden in the misty woods.

This detailed prophecy seems likely to have been fulfilled. A great man will be murdered and an innocent person accused of the deed while the guilty person remains hiding out in the woods.

Century VI
VI.XXXVIII

Aux profligez de paix les ennemis,
Apres auoir l'Italie fuperee:
Noir fanguinaire, rouge fera commis,
Feu, fang verfer, eaue de fang couloree.

The enemies of peace, the dissolute ones, having overcome Italy the bloody, black one will be seen red; fire, bloodshed, water colored with blood.

The color red probably stands for blood and revolution, although red did not contain this meaning until late eighteenth century. Before then it was used to refer to the Spanish or to the cardinals of the Catholic Church. Like many of Nostradamus' concepts, this metaphor is surprisingly modern.

Century VI
VI.XXXIX

L'enfant du regne par paternelle prinfe,
Expolié fera pour deliurer:
Aupres du lac Trafimen l'azur prinfe,
La troupe hoftaige pour trop fort
* s'enyurer.*

The child of the kingdom, through his fa-
ther's capture, will be deprived to deliver
him. Near Lake Trasimene the azure cap-
tive, in order that the hostage troop may
become very drunk.

An impenetrable quatrain.

Century VI
VI.XL

Grand de Magonce pour grande foif
* eftaindre,*
Sera priué de fa grand dignité:
Ceux de Cologne fi fort le viendront
* plaindre,*
Que le grand groppe au Ryn fera getté.

To quench the great thirst the great one of
Mainz will be deprived of his great dig-
nity. Those from Cologne will come to
complain so strongly, that the great rump
will be thrown into the Rhine.

The archbishop of Mainz was one of the Electors of the Empire.
Mainz was captured by the French during the Revolution and ceded
by the Treaty of Campoformio to the French. However, the Elector
held his title until the Empire formally ended in 1806. The archbishop of Cologne was also an Elector but his office was abolished
three years earlier, in 1803, so he had every right to complain.

Century VI
VI.XLI

Le fecond chef du regne d'Annemarc,
Par ceux de Frife & l'ifle Britannique,
Fera defpendre plus de cent mille marc,
Vain exploicter voyage en Italique.

The second leader of the kingdom of An-
nemarc, through those of Frisia and the
British Isles will spend more than one
hundred thousand marks, attempting in
vain a voyage to Italy.

A difficult quatrain, but made interesting by the fact that at the time
of Nostradamus' writing, England and Frisia had the same ruler,
Philip II of Spain, husband of Mary Tudor. In IV.LXXXIX Nostradamus foresees William of Orange, a Frisian, attaining the English
throne. This may be a better interpretation since the British Isles, as
opposed to England, did not come into existence until 1604. But a
problem remains with the uninterpreted Annemarc (Denmark?), as
also in IV.XXVII.

Century VI
VI.XLII

A logmyon¹ fera laiffé le regne,
Du grand Selin qui plus fera de faict:
Par les Italies eftendra fon enfeigne,
Regifera par prudent contrefaict.

To Ogmios the kingdom of the great Selin
will be left who will do even more. He will
extend his banner throughout Italy and it
will be ruled by careful forgery.

The enigmatic Ogmios also appears in V.LXXX, VI.LXI, IX.LXXXIX, but his true identity has never been deciphered other than the probability that he was the Celtic equivalent of Hercules.

Century VI
VI.XLIII

Long temps fera fans eftre habitée,
Où Signe & Marne autour vient
  arroufer:
De la Tamife & martiaux tentée,
Deceuz les gardes en cuidant repoufer.

For a long time it will remain uninhabited
around where the Seine and Marne come
to gush forth. Tried by the Tamise and
soldiers, the guards deceived in believing it
rebuffed.

It appears that the city between the Seine and the Marne which Nostradamus envisages here is Paris. The Tamise could mean the Thames in London or a town of the same name near Antwerp.

Century VI
VI.XLIIII

De nuict par Nantes L ris² apparoiftra,
Des artz marins fufciteront la pluye:
Arabiq goulfre grand claffe parfondra,
Vn monftre en Saxe naiftra d'ours &
  truye.

By night the rainbow will appear near
Nantes, the marine arts will raise up rain.
In the Arabian Gulf a great fleet will
flounder. In Saxony, a monster will be
born of a sow and a bear.

This quatrain may apply to the twentieth century for two reasons. In 1947, scientists discovered how to produce artificial rain (line 2); there is no actual Gulf of Arabia but the Gulf War between Iran and Iraq has been raging for most of this decade. The last line remains incomprehensible. It is probably metaphorical.

---

¹*Logmyon.* Misprint for Ogmios, the Celtic Hercules.
²*L ris.* Obvious misprint for *l'iris,* the rainbow.

Century VI

VI.XLV

Le gouuerneur du regne bien fçauant,
Ne confentir voulant au faict Royal:
Mellile claffe par le contraire vent,
Le remettra à fon plus defloyal.

The very learned governor of the kingdom
does not wish to consent to the Royal deed.
The fleet at Melilla by a contrary wind,
will deliver him back to his most disloyal
one.

Melilla is in Spanish Morocco and from this some commentators refer this quatrain to the Spanish Civil War.

Century VI

VI.XLVI

Vn iufte fera en exil renuoyé,
Par peftilence aux confins de Nonfeggle,
Refponce au rouge le fera defuoyé,
Roy retirant à la Rane & à l'aigle.

A just one will be sent back into exile
through pestilence to the confines of Non-
seggle. His reply to the red one will mis-
lead him. The king withdraws to the Frog
and the Eagle.

Nonfeggle remains an unsolved proper name or anagram. The frog also appears in quatrains V.III and V.XCV. It is just possible that the first line may refer to Louis XVIII during the Hundred Days, but the rest remains obscure.

Century VI

VI.XLVII

Entre deux monts les deux grans
  affemblés
Delaifferont leur fimulté fecrette:
Brucelle & Dolle par Langres acablés,
Pour à Malignes executer leur pefte.

The two great ones assembled between two
mountains, will give up their secret quar-
rel. Brussels and Dôle overcome by Lan-
gres in order to execute their pestilence at
Malines.

Brussels, Dôle and Malines were all in the Spanish Netherlands. This quatrain may therefore be a failed prediction in that Nostradamus predicts their being conquered by France (Langres).

Century VI
VI.XLVIII

La faincteté trop faincte & feductiue,
Acccompaigné d'vne langue diferte:
La cité vieille & Parme trop haftiue,
Florence & Sienne rendront plus
defertes.

The holiness, too false and too attractive, is accompanied by an eloquent tongue. The old city, Parma, too hasty. They will make Florence and Siena even more deserted.

I can make nothing of this quatrain.

Century VI
VI.XLIX

De la partie de Mammer grand Pontife,
Subiuguera les confins du Dannube:
Chaffer les croix par fer raffe ne riffe,
Captifz, or, bagues plus de cent mille
rubes.

The great pontiff by the warlike party will subjugate the borders of the Danube. The cross pursued by hook or by crook. Captives, gold, jewels, more than one hundred thousand rubies.

The cross, described by Nostradamus as *ne raffe ne riffe,* is an expression which can mean by hook or by crook, and also by extension crooked. The crooked cross can only be the swastika. Hitler's party originated in Austria, the Danube. Line 4 is horribly reminiscent of the millions of pounds of personal gold, jewelry and possessions which were stolen by the Nazis, particularly when their victims arrived at the concentration camps. The exact meaning of the position of the Pope in line 1 is not clear, but although the Vatican remained technically neutral, it favored the Fascisti under Pius XI and its position on helping the Germans was ambiguous under Pius XII, who was criticized for not excommunicating Hitler and for giving Nazi officers refuge in the Vatican towards the end of the war, and afterwards.

Century VI
VI.L

Dedans le puys feront trouués les oz,
Sera l'inceft commis par la maratre:[1]
L'eftat changé on querra bruict & loz,
Et aura Mars attendant pour fon aftre.

The bones will be found inside the walls. It will be incest committed by the stepmother. The State changed one will seek praise and renown. He will have Mars attendant as his star.

[1]*maratre.* more likely in this concept to mean stepmother than mother, because of the incest theme.

An indecipherable quatrain.

Century VI

VI.LI

*Peuple affemblé, voir nouueau
    expectacle,
Princes & Roys par plufieurs affiftans:
Pilliers faillir, murs, mais comme
    miracle
Le Roy fauué & trente des inftans.*

*The people gathered to see a new sight.
Princes and kings (are) among many on-
lookers. The pillars, walls fall, but as if by
a miracle the king and thirty of those present are saved.*

This is the verse which caused the Swiss astrologer Ernst Krafft, who was working for Goebbels's Propaganda Ministry, to telegraph Hitler that an assassination attempt would be made upon him while he attended a meeting in November, 1939. In fact, it was organized by the party of von Stauffenberg, who was caught and executed when he attempted a similar attempt in 1944. The bomb was hidden in a pillar behind the rostrum and in fact it was by sheer chance that Hitler and some of his party left unexpectedly early. This prediction gained Krafft great credibility at the time, but his refusal to produce interpretations to order ended tragically with his early death in a concentration camp in 1941.

Century VI

VI.LII

*En lieu du grand qui fera condemné,
De prifon hors fon amy en fa place:
L'efpoir Troyen en fix moys ioinct, mort
    nay,
Le Sol à l'vrne feront prins fleuues en
    glace.*

*In the place of the great one who will be
condemned, he is outside the prison, his
friend in his place. The Trojan hope for
six months joined, born dead. The Sun in
Aquarius, the rivers will be frozen.*

This is another of Nostradamus' tantalizing quatrains, in which he contradicts the little that is known of an historical mystery, the fate of the child King Louis XVII (see V.I). Here it is implied that another child died in 1795 and his body was substituted for that of the king. It must be remembered that no certain identification could be made of the corpse, even after an autopsy. The Trojan blood refers, as always, to the French royal line, from the myth that they were descendants of Francis, son of King Priam of Troy. Line 3 is difficult to interpret. Does it refer to the death of the false king after six months, which could have been very possible, or to the death of the real king six months after his escape? The Sun is in Aquarius from mid-February until mid-March. The dauphin's death was officially reported on June 8, 1795, but due to the state of the corpse, it could easily have occurred earlier. An interesting quatrain. Although technically king, the dauphin was never crowned and so was normally referred to by that title.

Century VI
VI.LIII

Le grand Prelat Celtique à Roy fuſpect,
De nuict par cours fortira hors du
regne:
Par duc fertile à ſon grand Roy,
Bretaigne,
Biſance à Cipres & Tunes infuſpect.

The great French prelate suspected by the king, will flee from his realm by night. Through a duke fertile (favorable?) to his great king, Britain Byzantium as far as Cyprus and Tunis are undiscovered.

This confused and probably failed quatrain appears to indicate that a French cardinal or bishop will flee to England and from there to Tunis via Constantinople and Cyprus.

Century VI
VI.LIIII

Au poinct du iour au fecond chant du
coq,
Ceulx de Tunes, de Fez, & de Bugie:
Par les Arabes captif le Roy Maroq,
L'an mil ſix cens & ſept, de Liturgie.

At daybreak at second cockcrow, those of Tunis, Fez and of Bougie. The Arabs captured by the king of Morocco in the year 1607 by the Liturgy.

This quatrain appears to be one of Nostradamus' complete failures, date notwithstanding. He seems to envisage the fall of the Ottoman Empire through a new European king, and in Asia through new Persian and Arab empires. The only enigma is what Nostradamus means by "the Liturgy." It may be an equivalent of Anno Domini, but Nostradamus was usually more convoluted than that.

Century VI
VI.LV

Au chalmé Duc, en arrachant l'efponce,
Voile Arabefque voir, fubit defcouuerte:
Tripolis Chio, & ceux de Trapefonce,
Duc prins, Marnegro & la cité deferte.

The becalmed duke drawing up the contract, an Arabian sail is seen, a sudden discovery. Tripolis, Chios and those from Trabazon. The duke captured, the Black Sea and the city deserted.

The only certainty in this quatrain is that the action takes places in Asia Minor, the Black Sea and the Aegean (Chios).

Century VI

VI.LVI

La crainte armee de l'ennemy Narbon,	The dreaded army of the enemy Narbonne
Effrayera fi fort les Hefperiques:[1]	will greatly terrify the Hesperians. Perig-
Parpignan vuide par l'aueugle darbon,[2]	non is empty through the blind of Arbon,
Lors Barcelon par mer donra les piques.	then Barcelona will take up her weapons
	by sea.

It appears that in this quatrain the Spaniards are being terrified by the French from Narbonne. Narbonne is only forty miles north of Perpignan, while Barcelona, about a hundred miles to the south, is sending supplies and weapons by sea. Perpignan was besieged by the French for a short time in 1597.

Century VI

VI.LVII

Celuy qu'eftoit bien auant dans le regne,	He who was well to the front in the king-
Ayant chef rouge proche à la hierarchie:	dom having a red chief close to the seat of
Afpre & cruel, & fe fera tant craindre,	power. Harsh and cruel, he will make
Succedera à facré monarchie.	himself most greatly feared. He will suc-
	ceed to the sacred monarchy.

A cruel cardinal, or less likely a bishop, will greatly influence his king. He eventually succeeds to the throne. It is difficult to know whom in particular Nostradamus had in mind. Obvious possibilities such as Mazarin and Richelieu do not fit the last line of the quatrain. They were the éminences grises behind the throne. In modern-day context, an unlikely and probably failed quatrain.

Century VI

VI.LVIII

Entre les deux monarques efloignez,	Between the two distant monarchs, at a
Lors que le Sol par Selin clair perdue:	time when the dear Sun is lost by Selin.
Simulté grande entre deux indignez,	Great enmity between two indignant ones,
Qu'aux Ifles & Sienne la liberté rendue.	so that liberty is restored to the islands and
	to Siena.

---

[1]*Hefperiques.* Spanish, Western or American.
[2]*darbon.* of Arbon, possibly somewhere in France or Switzerland.

This quatrain is contemporary with Nostradamus' lifetime. The Sun and the chariot of Apollo were the devices of Philip II of Spain. The moon, *Selin*, was that of Henri II of France, partly to honor his mistress, Diane de Poitiers. Nostradamus seems to envisage that France will conquer the Hapsburgs. All that occurred during this period was that the French held Siena and they were also attempting to conquer Corsica. The restoration of Liberty in line 4 is ambiguous. Does it mean the arrival or the withdrawal of the French? Nostradamus is usually more patriotic than this. If it were not for the first two lines I might be inclined to date this quatrain during the Napoleonic period.

Century VI

VI.LIX

Dame en fureur par rage d'adultere,
Viendra à fon Prince coniurer non de
    dire:
Mais bref cogneu fera le vitupere,
Que feront mis dixfept à martire.

The lady, furious in an adulterous rage, will conspire against her prince, but not speak to him. However, the culprit will soon be known so that seventeen will be martyred.

An incomprehensible quatrain.

Century VI

VI.LX

Le Prince hors de fon terroir Celtique
Sera trahy, deceu par interprete:
Rouan, Rochelle par ceux de
    l'Armorique
Au port de Blaue deceus par moyne &
    prebftre.

The prince, outside his French territory will be betrayed; deceived by the interpreter. Rouen, La Rochelle, by those of Brittany at the port of Blaye deceived by monk and priest.

Nothing remotely relating to this quatrain has occurred to date and I am under the impression that it is a failed quatrain.

Century VI

VI.LXI

Le grand tappis plié ne monftrera,
Fors qu'à demy la plufpart de l'hiftoire:
Chaffé du regne loing afpre apparoiftra
Qu'au faict bellique chafcun le viendra
croire.

Folded, the great carpet will not show except by halves the greater part of its history. Driven far out of the kingdom he will appear harsh, so that each one will believe in his warlike act.

Yet another quatrain I cannot unravel.

Century VI

VI.LXII

*Trop tard tous deux les fleurs feront
    perdues,
Contre la loy ferpent ne voudra faire:
Des ligueurs forces par gallots[1]
    confondues,
Sauone, Albingue par monech grand
    martyre.*

Too late, both of the flowers will be lost,
the snake will not want to act against the
law. The forces of the Leaguers, con-
founded by the French. Savona, Albenga,
great martyrdom through Monaco.

Yet another erroneous quatrain. Nostradamus seems to envisage
a League conspiring against the French, but the French emerge victorious. But Monaco was bound to the Spanish by treaty and Savona
and Albenga belonged to Genoa. The League was probably one of
the sixteenth century Italian Leagues, but none of this happened.

Century VI

VI.LXIII

*La dame feule au regne demeuree,
L'vnic eftaint premier au lict
    d'honneur:
Sept ans fera de douleur exploree,
Puis longue vie au regne par grand
    heur.*

The lady left alone in the kingdom, her
only (spouse) first dead on the bed of
honor. For seven years she will weep with
grief, then a long life for the good fortune
of the kingdom.

Nostradamus may have been somewhat prejudiced in this quatrain
as he knew Catherine de' Medicis well and their relationship continued until his death in 1566. But the queen certainly lived for the
good of her adopted country. Every time the king, or his sons, were
in need of money, it was Catherine who was sent to beg for it from
the Parlement de Paris, and she was always successful. It was she, too,
who recognized and tried to avert the terrible religious wars that
racked France during the reigns of her three sons. She was a far better
political animal than any of the Valois.

She left off mourning for her late husband, Henri II, on August 1,
1566, after seven years. She acted as regent under François II and
Charles IX, but age and illness reduced most of her power during the
reign her third son, Henri III.

[1]*gallots.* O.F. a Gallic or French man.

Century VI
VI.LXIIII

On ne tiendra pache aucune arrefté,
Tous receuans iront par tromperie:
De paix & trefve, terre & mer protefté,
Par Barcelone claffe prins d'induftrie.

They will not keep any peace agreed upon, all the receivers will go through deceit. In peace and truce, land and sea having protested, the fleet is seized with skill by Barcelona.

I know of no fleet seized in these circumstances in Barcelona.

Century VI
VI.LXV

Gris & bureau[1] demie ouuerte guerre,
De nuict feront affaillis & pillez:
Le bureau prins paffera par la ferre,
Son temple ouuert, deux au plaftre
  grillez.

Gray and brown in half declared war at night they will be besieged and pillaged. The captured, brown one will pass through the prison, his temple opened, two shipped in the plaster.

It is likely that here Nostradamus was describing a feud between two monastic orders, *gris & bureau*. Some of the Franciscans wore brown habits, although many their subsidiary orders wore gray, as did the Dominicans. The last line appears incomprehensible.

Century VI
VI.LXVI

Au fondement de la nouuelle fecte,
Seront les oz du grand Romain trouués,
Sepulchre en marbre apparoiftra
  couuerte,
Terre trembler en Auril, mal enfouetz.

At the founding of a new sect the bones of the great Roman will be found. A sepulcher, covered in marble will appear. The earth will quake in April, badly buried.

The great Roman is presumably a pope, and in this context the bones probably refer to the tomb of Saint Peter. Nostradamus says it will be found in April. (See III.LXV.) Some sixty-five years ago a grave was found and declared to be that of Saint Peter, but many people remain unconvinced, as indeed, does Nostradamus. There is a very old legend that Peter actually died in Alexandria, Egypt.

---

[1]*bureau.* O.F. variant of *burel*, brown.

Century VI

VI.LXVII

Au grand Empire paruiendra tout vn
aultre
Bonté diftant plus de felicité:
Regi par vn iffu non loing du peaultre,
Corruer regnes grande infelicité.

Quite a different man will attain to the
great Empire, distant from kindness, more
so from happiness. Ruled by one not long
raised from his bed, the kingdom rushes to
great misfortune.

Line 3 may be interpreted in two ways. Either the Emperor is but
a very young child, not long having left the cradle, or he is a man who
lived a very debauched life, as *peaultre* also means a brothel. It just
possibly may refer to Napoleon, ruled by his Empress Josephine. He
certainly put France into dreadful difficulties.

Century VI

VI.LXVIII

Lors que foldatz fureur feditieufe,
Contre leur chef feront de nuict fer
luire,
Ennemy d'Albe foit par main furieufe,
Lors vexer Rome & principaux feduire.

When the soldiers rise up in a treacherous
fury at night to fight against their leader.
The enemy of Alba with furious hand,
then troubles Rome and wins over the
Principals.

This prediction was probably meant for the near future, the sixteenth century and the duke of Alva (Alba). Nostradamus correctly
foresees him trying to suppress a revolt in the Spanish army, which
he did soon afterwards in the Netherlands.

Century VI

VI.LXIX

La pitié grande fera fans loing tarder,
Ceux qui dônoient feront contrains de
prêdre,
Nudz affamez de froit, foif, foy bander,
Les monts paffer commettant grand
efclandre.

A very great sadness will arrive before
long. Those who give will be forced to
take. Naked, starving with cold and
thirst, they band together to cross the
countries causing a great scandal.

France disbanded and disestablished the Catholic clergy in 1792,
which left many priests in really wretched circumstances. Instead of
supporting themselves through their duties to their parishioners,
they were constrained to beg to stay alive. Many of them did join up
in a band and crossed the Alps to ask help from the Vatican. Their
plight was scandalous by any standards.

Century VI
VI.LXX

Au chef du monde le grand Chyren fera,
Plus oultre[1] apres aymé, craint, redoubté:
Son bruit & loz les cieux furpaffera,
Et du feul titre victeur fort contenté.

The great Chyren will be chief of the world after "plus oultre," loved, feared and dreaded. His fame and praise go beyond the heavens and he will be greatly satisfied with the sole title of victor.

Here again we have the enigmatic Chyren, the anagram of the older French spelling of Henri, Henryc. This quatrain implies that Chyren will be even greater than the Emperor Charles V. It is tempting to equate Chyren with Henri IV de Navarre but some of the other Chyren quatrains will not support this interpretation. Perhaps Nostradamus saw several kings called Henri? Until Chyren is satisfactorily explained, these quatrains are impenetrable.

Century VI
VI.LXXI

Quand on viendra le grand roy parenter
Auant qu'il ait du tout l'ame rendue:
Celuy qui moins le viendra lamenter,
Par lyons, d'aigles, croix, couronne vendue.

When they will come to give the last rights to the great king before he has quite given up his soul. He will come who will lament him least, through lions the cross and the crown of the Eagles sold.

This general quatrain description could apply to the death of any king not much lamented by his heir. Possibly the last line indicates armorial bearings, but *"lyons"* were also a form of currency, so it seems more likely that the heir sold much of the regalia.

Century VI
VI.LXXII

Par fureur faincte d'efmotion diuine,
Sera la femme du grand fort violee:
Iuges voulans damner telle doctrine,
Victime au peuple ignorant imolee.

Through feigned fury of a divine emotion the wife of the great one will be badly violated. The judges wishing to condemn such a doctrine, the victim is sacrificed to the ignorant people.

[1] *"Plus oultre Carol Quint"* was the device of the Emperor Charles V. *Plus oultre* is printed in capitals in the 1605 edition, which clarifies Nostradamus' meaning.

Many modern commentators see in this verse a reference to the manner in which Rasputin dominated the wife of the last czar. Although Rasputin's sexual prowess was legendary, the word "violates" here should, I feel, be taken metaphorically, although rumors certainly went round the Russian court that he was the czarina's lover. The whole Russian royal family became victims of their vast, ignorant populace when they refused to try to understand the new doctrines of the times. This led to their eventual, tragic deaths.

Century VI
VI.LXXIII

En cité grande vn moyne & artifan,
Pres de la porte logés & aux murailles:
Contre Modene fecret, caue difant,
Trahis pour faire fouz couleur
    d'efpoufailles.

In a great city a monk and an artisan are lodged near the gate and the walls. Speaking vainly and secretly against Modena; betrayed for acting under the guise of marriage.

I cannot decipher this quatrain.

Century VI
VI.LXXIIII

La defchaffee au regne tournera,
Ses ennemis trouués des coniurés:
Plus que iamais fon temps triomphera,
Trois & feptante à mort trop affeurés.

She who was cast out will return to reign, her enemies found among conspirators. More than ever will her reign be triumphant. At three and seventy death very sure.

Elizabeth I of England was certainly rejected for most of her childhood and then became the victim of conspirators during the reign of her sister, Mary Tudor. England rose to great heights during the Elizabethan period. Elizabeth died in her seventieth year, in 1603. Most commentators insert a comma between *trois & feptante,* thus indicating the first number as the year she died and the second as her age. An interesting conundrum. I leave it to the reader.

Century VI
VI.LXXV

Le grand pilot par Roy fera mandé,
Laiffer la claffe pour plus haut lieu
    attaindre:
Sept ans apres fera contrebandé,
Barbare armée viendra Venife craindre.

The great pilot will be commissioned by the king to leave the fleet to attain to higher rank. Seven years later he will be in rebellion, Venice will come to fear the barbarian army.

Gaspard de Coligny was made Henri II's Admiral of the Fleet, *grand pilot,* in 1552 but resigned the post seven years later (after the king's death in 1559) to join up with the Calvinist party. He was one of the principal initiators of the Huguenot Catholic Wars in France, *fera contrebandé.* These events occurred at the same time that Venice, line 4, was attacked by the Sultan Selim II, who took Cyprus from them in 1570. A good and accurate quatrain.

Century VI

VI.LXXVI

La cité antique d'antenoree[1] forge,	The ancient city created by Antenor is no
Plus ne pouuant le tyran fupporter:	longer able to support the tyrant. A false,
Le manchet[2] fainct au temple couper	one-armed man in the temple will cut his
gorge,	throat. The people will come to put his
Les fiens le peuple à mort viendra	followers to death.
bouter.	

Padua *(Antenoree)* belonged to Venice which, as I have mentioned earlier, was governed by an hereditary office of podestas. But I cannot find any record of a murder committed in the church there, followed by further killings of followers.

Century VI

VI.LXXVII

Par la victoire du deçeu fraudulente,	Through the fraudulent victory of the de-
Deux claffes vne, la reuolte Germaine:	ceived, two fleets in one, the German re-
Le chef meurtry & fon filz dans la	volt. The chief murdered with his son in
tente,	a tent. Florence and Imola pursued into
Florence, Imole pourchaffés dans	Romania.
Romaine.	

There were numerous revolts during the sixteenth and seventeenth centuries against the Holy Roman Emperor. *Romaine* is most likely to stand for either Romania, the Holy Roman Empire, or the Papal States.

---

[1]*Antenoree.* Antenor was the legendary founder of Padua.
[2]*manchet.* O.F. one-armed.

Century VI

VI.LXXVIII

Crier victoire du grand Selin croiffant,
Par les Romains fera l'Aigle clamé:
Ticcin, Milan, & Gennes n'y confent,
Puis par eux mefmes Bafil grand
  reclamé.

To shout aloud the victory of the great
crescent moon, the Eagle will be proclaimed by the Romans. Pavia, Milan
and Genoa will not agree to it. Then the
great Lord is claimed by themselves.

This quatrain is obviously a retroactive one, involving the Ottoman
and the Holy Roman empires, whose particular emblems were the
crescent moon and the Eagle. The sultan was known in Europe as the
Grand Seignior, *Basil,* but not one has been captured by the Roman
Empire since Nostradamus' day. The last was the Sultan Jem, captured in the fifteenth century.

Century VI

VI.LXXIX

Pres du Tefin les habitans de Loyre,
Garonne & Saonne, Seine, Tain, &
  Gironde:
Outre les monts drefferont promontoire,
Conflict donné Pau granci, fubmergé
  onde.

Near the Ticino the inhabitants of the
Loire, Garonne, the Seine, Tain and Gironde. Beyond the mountains they will
build a promontory. Conflict engaged.
Pau seized, submerged by the wave.

Many commentators accept the word *"Pau"* in line 4 as a shortened
version of Napoléon (see also VIII.I). If this is so, the quatrain is a
very precise description of an accident which befell Napoleon during
the Battle of Lodi, 1796. While the bridge over the Adda was being
stormed Napoleon fell into the water, *"fubmergé onde,"* but was pulled
out before he could drown. The places in lines 1 and 2 are areas
which suffered from the French campaigns.

Century VI

VI.LXXX

De Fez le regne paruiendra à ceux
  d'Europe,
Feu leur cité, & lame trenchera:
Le grand d'Afie terre & mer à grand
  troupe,
Que bleux, pers,[1] croix, à mort
  dechaffera.

From Fez the kingdom will stretch out to those of Europe. The city blazes, the sword will slash. The great man of Asia with a great troop by land and sea, so that the blues, perse, will drive out the cross to death.

Nostradamus says in VI.LIIII that the king of Fez will be captured by the Arabs. I think, however, that the rest of this quatrain belongs to a more modern context. Together with the Third Antichrist, "the great man of Asia," we have wars on land and sea and fascinatingly enough Perse is mentioned again, as the man whom Nostradamus believes will succeed the Ayatollah Khomeini. The Persians (Iranians) are not a Christian country, and they will persecute those who are not followers of Islam.

Century VI

VI.LXXXI

Pleurs, crys & plaincts, hurlement
  effraieur,
Coeur inhumain, cruel, noir, & tranfy:
Leman, les ifles de Gennes les maieurs,
Sang efpancher, frofaim[2] à nul mercy.

Tears, cries and wailing, howls and terror, an inhuman heart both black and cold. Lake Geneva, the Islands, most of the people of Genoa. Blood pours, hunger for wheat, mercy to none.

This may continue the horrors depicted in the last quatrain, with the war spreading through Switzerland, Italy and the Mediterranean. War and injury, famine and terror, all caused by the inhuman beast "both black and cold." I wonder if there is any connection with the hitherto undeciphered Aenobarbe?

---

[1]*pers.* either a shade of royal or dark blue, or Persian.
[2]*frofaim.* a concocted word. Probably from *froment-faim,* a hunger for wheat.

Century VI
VI.LXXXII

Par les defers de lieu, libre, & farouche,
Viendra errer nepueu du grand Pontife:
Affommé à fept auecques lourde fouche,
Par ceux qu'apres occuperont le cyphe.

Through the deserts of the free wild place,
the nephew of the Great Pontiff will wan-
der. Killed by seven with a heavy club, by
who will afterwards occupy the chalice.

Several clues, such as the nephew of the Pope who is killed by people who soon afterwards take part of the Holy Sacrament. But, unfortunately impossible to place.

Century VI
VI.LXXXIII

Celuy qu'aura tant d'honneur &
  careffes,
A fon entree de la Gaule Belgique:
I'n temps apres fera tant de rudeffes,
Et fera contre à la fleur tant bellique.

He will have so much honor and affection
at his entry into Belgian Gaul. A while
later he will act so crudely and will be very
bellicose towards the flower.

When Charles V abdicated, Philip of Spain was well received in the Netherlands *(Gaule Belgique)* until his bigotry alienated the people to such a degree that they rose up in revolt in 1558. The duc François d'Alençon was invited by the Netherlands to become their Protector in 1580, but stupidly he attempted to regain control of Antwerp and lost the loyalty of his subjects. The flower in line 4 would be the fleur-de-lys of France led by Henri IV, against whom Philip went to war from 1589 to 1598.

Century VI
VI.LXXXIIII

Celuy qu'en Sparte Claude[1] ne peut
  regner,
Il fera tant par voye feductiue:
Que au court, long le fera araigner,
Que contre Roy fera fa perfpectiue.

The lame man who could not rule in
Sparta will do much with his seductive
ways. So that, by the long and short of it
he will be accused of aiming his objectives
against the king.

Line 1 probably merely refers to the fact that the Spartans killed all children born imperfect and many girls by leaving them exposed to the elements. As for famous men in history, Nostradamus writes

[1]*Claude. L. claudus,* lame.

in detail of Talleyrand, lame from childhood, but perhaps this could refer to Lord Byron, who suffered from a clubfoot and worked with the Greek freedom fighters. That would fulfill line 4.

Century VI
VI.LXXXV

La grand cité de Tharfe par Gaulois
Sera deftruite, captifz tous à Turban:
Secours par mer du grand Portugalois,
Premier d'efté le iour du facre Vrban.

The great city of Tarsus will be destroyed by the Gauls, all captured at Turban. Help from the sea from the great Portuguese. The first day of summer, Urban's consecration.

There are two major saints named Urban, whose feasts are celebrated on May 25 and January 23. The former is most likely the one referred to in this context, as summer begins on June 1. There are, incidentally, twelve other minor saints of the same name.

Nostradamus seems to envisage a French army capturing Tarsus in Asia Minor and continuing on to Asia. Portugal was one of the greatest sea powers in Nostradamus' day and he envisages them as allies of the French. A failed quatrain in the main essentials.

Century VI
VI.LXXXVI

Le grand Prelat vn iour apres fon
fonge,
Interpreté au rebours de fon fens:
De la Gafcogne luy furuiendra vn
monge,
Qui fera eftire le grand Prelat de Sens.

One day the great prelate, after his dream is interpreted opposite to its meaning, a monk from Gascony will come to him who will cause the great prelate of Sens to be elected.

Too many prelates and nothing more specific than a misinterpreted dream.

Century VI
VI.LXXXVII

L'election faite dans Frankfort,
N'aura nul lieu Milan s'opposera:
Le fien plus proche femblera fi grand
fort
Que outre le Rhyn és marefchz chaffera.

The election made in Frankfurt will not be valid. Milan will oppose it. The closest follower will seem so very strong that he will drive him out beyond the Rhine into the marshes.

The election at Frankfurt was probably that of the coronation of Ferdinand as Holy Roman Emperor, which took place in 1558. Philip, who was Ferdinand's rival, had already been given Milan by his uncle, Charles V, before his death in 1542. Philip tries to drive Ferdinand out of Germany in line 4, and into the Netherlands. He was not at all successful in this but continued to intrigue against Ferdinand for the succession until 1562.

Century VI
VI.LXXXVIII

Vn regne grand demourra defolé,
Aupres del Hebro fe feront affemblees:
Monts Pyrenees le rendront confolé,
Lors que dans May feront terres
   tremblees.

A great kingdom will remain desolate. Near the Ebro they will be gathered in assemblies. The Pyrenean mountains will console him when in May there will be earth tremors.

The last line is the only one that I can relate to here. Elsewhere Nostradamus refers to a great earthquake that will take place in May, which he tentatively places on the west coast of America during the next decade, certainly some time before the Millennium. The European side of the quatrain is not clear.

Century VI
VI.LXXXIX

Entre deux cymbes piedz & mains
   eftachés,
De miel face oingt & de laict fubftanté:
Guefpes & mouches, fitine[1] amour
   fachés,
Poccilateur faucer, Cyphe tempté.

Feet and hands bound between boots, the face anointed with honey and touched with milk. Wasps and flies, fatherly love angered, the cupbearer lies, the goblet tried.

The fact that the face of the victim is anointed with milk and honey indicates that the person referred to was a crowned king, for this anointment was part of the coronation service. The wasps and flies may stand for the angry populace. With hands and feet bound it seems as though this quatrain refers to Louis XVI on the way to his execution. (See I.LVII.)

---

[1]*fitine.* Gk. *phitus,* father.

Century VI
VI.XC

L'honniffement puant abhominable
Apres faict fera felicité,
Grand excufé, pour n'eftre fauorable,
Qu'à paix Neptune ne fera incité.

The stinking and abominable shame, after the deed he will be congratulated. The great one is excused for not being favorable, so that Neptune cannot be tempted towards peace.

Someone gets away with a deed of such skulduggery that it is almost incredible. Yet he is unsuspected and congratulated despite the fact he cannot arrange for a naval peace. He was presumably in communication with the enemy.

Century VI
VI.XCI

Du conducteur de la guerre nauale,
Rouge effrené, feuere horrible grippe,
Captif efchappé de l'aifné dans la bafte:
Quant il naiftra du grand vn filz
   Agrippe.

Of the leader of the naval war, the red one unbridled, a severe, horrible quarrel. Captive, escaped from the older one in the saddle, when the great Agrippa bears a son.

The naval commanders in Nostradamus' time were the baron de la Garde and M. de la Molé. The rest of the quatrain is obscure unless the "red one" is a Communist leader creating great trouble in more modern times.

Century VI
VI.XCII

Prince de beauté tant venufte,
Au chef menee, le fecond faict trahy:
La cité au glaiue de poudre face aduste,
Par trop grand meurtre le chef du Roy
   hay.

A prince of such handsome looks intrigues against his person, betrayed to the second rank. The city put to the sword, consumed with a powder that burns. By this, so great a murder, the head of the king is hated.

Louis XVI was considered to be very handsome as a youth but many intrigues, *menees,* were directed against him, and he was deposed to the "second rank" of a Constitutional monarch. Then he was betrayed by the Revolution. The line *poudre face adufte* has been most cleverly interpreted by James Laver from the Latin *fax,* a torch and *adustus,* burned or consumed by a powder that burns. After his execution on the guillotine the king's head was taken from the wicker basket into which it had fallen, and placed in quicklime. Line 3, *cité au glaiue,* is an excellent description of Revolutionary Paris.

Century VI
VI.XCIII

Prelat auare d'ambition trompé.
Rien ne fera que trop viendra cuider:
Ses meffagiers, & luy bien attrapé,
Tout au rebours voir, qui le bois
  fendroit.

The great prelate deceived by ambition will think nothing is too great (for him). He and his messengers, completely trapped. The man who cuts the woods sees everything in reverse.

I can make nothing of this quatrain.

Century VI
VI.XCIIII

Vn Roy iré fera aux fedifragues,[1]
Quant interdicts feront harnois de
  guerre:
La poifon taincte au fuccre par les
  fragues[2]
Par eaux meurtris, mors, difant ferre
  ferre.

A king will be angry with the sedifrages when warlike arms are prohibited. The poison tainted with sugar in the strawberries. Murdered by water, death saying close, close.

Those who break the Seat, *fedifragues,* probably refers to the various Protestant sects who helped break up the unity of the See of Rome.

Century VI
VI.XCV

Par detracteur calumnié à puis nay.
Quant iftront faicts enormes &
  martiaux:
La moindre part dubieufe à l'aifnay,
Et toft au regne feront faicts partiaux.

Calumny against the younger born by the detractor, when enormous, martial deeds will occur. The least part doubtful for the elder one. Soon in the kingdom there will be partisan actions.

I cannot make anything of this quatrain.

---

[1]*fedifragues.* a compound word Nostradamus invented, probably from L. *sedem frangere,* which taken literally means to break a seat.
[2]*fragues.* L. *fraga,* strawberries.

Century VI

VI.XCVI

Grande cité à foldatz abandonnée,
Onques n'y euft mortel tumult fi proche,
O quel hideuse calamité s'approche,
Fors vne offence n'y fera pardonnée.

A great city abandoned to the soldiers,
there was never a mortal tumult so close.
Oh what dreadful calamity approaches.
Except for one offense it will not be for-
given.

This quatrain is so general that it could apply to the sack of any city, St. Quentin in 1557, or Paris during the Revolution. But I believe that line 3 predicts the Millennium. A very interesting new theory has just been published by the Oxford astrophysicist Dr. Victor Cube. He suggests that the earth is bombarded by comets about every one thousand years, and that the time is now ripe for another comet storm, which would cause a "nuclear winter." He suggests that an earlier attack might have been responsible for the Ice Age and have caused the Medieval Church to believe that the Millennium, Judgment Day, would arrive around A.D. 1000.

Century VI

VI.XCVII

Cinq & quarante degrés ciel bruflera,
Feu approacher de la grand cité neufue,
Inftant grand flamme efparfe fautera,
Quant on voudra des Normans faire
preuue.

The sky will burn at forty-five degrees.
Fire approaches the great New City. Im-
mediately a huge scattered flame leaps up
when they want to have proof of the Nor-
mans.

New York City lies between 40 and 45 degrees parallel in the USA. It is often referred to by Nostradamus as the *Cité neufue,* which was its contemporary name during Nostradamus' lifetime. It appears that the attack on the city is widespread, *instant grand flamme efparfe fautera.* It is certainly a futuristic quatrain. Where and how France is involved is unclear—by 1992 it will stand after all for the European Community—but it is also involved in similar quatrains. (See X.XLIX, I.XLI and IX.XLII.)

Century VI
VI.XCVIII

Ruyne aux Volfques¹ de peur fi fort
  terribles,
Leur grand cité taincte, faict peftilent:
Piller Sol, Lune & violer leurs temples:
Et les deux fleuues rougir de fang
  coulant.

Ruin for the Vocae, so very terrible with
fear, their great city stained by a pestilen-
tial deed. To plunder the Sun and Moon,
violate their temples and redden the two
rivers running with blood.

The plundered sun and moon stand for gold and silver. The capital
city of Languedoc is probably Toulouse. It seems as though a state
of general insurrection occurs there. Unlikely to be a successful prediction now.

Century VI
VI.XCIX

L'ennemy docte fe tournera confus,
Grâd camp malade, & de faict par
  embufches,
Môts Pyrenees & Poenus luy ferôt faicts
  refus,
Proche du fleuue defcouurât antiques
  oruches.

The learned enemy will turn around confused, the great camp sick and defeated in
the ambushes. Both the mountains of the
Pyrenees and the Pennines will be refused
to him. Near the river discovering ancient
urns.

I cannot decipher this quatrain.

Century VI
VI.C

LEGIS CANTIO CONTRA
  INEPTOS CRITICOS,

INCANTATION OF THE LAW
AGAINST INEPT CRITICS

Quos legent hofce verfus maturè
  cenfuncto,
Profanum vulgar & infcium ne
  attractato:
Omnesq; Aftrologi Blenni,² Barbari
  procul funto,
Qui alter facit, if ritè, facer esto.

May those who read this verse think upon
it deeply. Let the profane and ignorant
herd keep away. Let all astrologers, idiots
and barbarians stay far off. He who does
otherwise, let him be priest to the rite.

¹*Volfques.* People of Languedoc, southern France.
²*Blenni.* Gk. *Blennos*, simpleton, idiot.

This quatrain of doggerel verse in medieval Latin gives the reader a good idea of the type of construction and vocabulary used by Nostradamus when writing Latin as he would have done throughout his professional life as doctor and philosopher. The inclusion of astrologers in this verse must mean those who did not make it a lifetime study, as did Nostradamus. Or perhaps it is just an attempt to bluff the authorities. Line 4 sounds vaguely like a threat: Let no one study Nostradamus' work lightly.

Century VII

VII.I

L'Arc du threfor par Achilles deçeu,	The arc of the treasure deceived by
Aux procreés[1] fçeu la quadrâgulaire:	Achilles; the quadrangle known to the
Au faict Royal le côment fera fçeu,	procreators. The intention will be manifest
Cors veu pêdu au veu du populaire.	by a royal deed. A corpse seen hanging in
	the sight of the populace.

There are only two well-known Achilles in French history. The first was Achille de Harlay, Président of the Parlement de Paris, who contributed to the downfall of Catherine de' Medicis' favorite, Concini. He was eventually assassinated in 1617. The other was the Marshal of France, Achille Bazaine, whose incapacity and defeatism led to the fall of France in 1870.

However, I wonder whether this quatrain has magical overtones? Was Nostradamus trying to raise the spirit of the Greek hero Achilles through *la quadrâgulaire,* possibly at the wish of Catherine de' Medicis, who certainly dabbled with the occult during the first ten years of her marriage before she conceived her first child. It is believed, incidentally, that the fault for this infertility lay with the king. He had an operation in adulthood and Catherine then conceived seven children who survived childbirth. It is quite possible that the corpse seen was someone hanged for one of the many capital offenses that existed at the time, or maybe a hanged man was necessary to the ritual. I leave this to the reader.

[1]*procreés.* Other mss. offer the variant *procès* which would offer the better reading "in the documents."

Century VII

VII.II

Par Mars ouuert Arles ne donra guerre,
De nuict feront les foldartz eftonnés:
Noir, blanc à l'inde diffimulés en terre,
Souz la faincte vmbre traiftres verez &
    fonnés.

Arles opened up by war will not offer resis-
tance, the soldiers will be overcome by
night. Black & white concealing indigo
on land. Under the false shadow you will
see traitors assessed.

An unintelligible quatrain. What or who are the black, white and indigo?

Century VII

VII.III

Apres de France la victoire nauale,
Les Barchinons, Saillinons,[1] les
    Phocens,
Lierre d'or, l'enclume ferré dedans la
    bafle,
Ceux de Ptolon[2] au fraud feront
    confens.

After the naval victory of France the peo-
ple of Barcelona, the Saillinons and those
of Marseilles. The robber of gold, the the
anvil enclosed in the ball. The people of
Ptolon will be party to the fraud.

It is impossible to fix the dating of the French naval battle from the remaining material of the quatrain. The Barchinons may come from Barcelona. Both the Saillinons and Ptolons are unclear.

Century VII

VII.IIII

Le duc de Langres affiegé dedans Dolle,
Accompaigné d'Oftun & Lyonnois:
Geneue, Aufpour, ioinct ceux de
    Mirandole,
Paffer les monts contre les Anconnois.

The duc de Langres besieged at Dôle, ac-
companied by people from Autun and
Lyons. Geneva, Augsburg allied to those
of Mirandola, to cross the mountains
against the people of Ancona.

This complicated quatrain describes the duc de Guise (Langres), together with soldiers from Autun and Lyons, besieged at Dôle during an attack on the Spanish. At the same time armies of the Empires from Geneva, Augsburg and northern Italy will invade the Papal States. Ancona belonged to the Pope.

[1] *Saillinons.* Not identified.
[2] *Ptolon.* Either Egypt, the land of Ptolemy or Acre, which was normally known as *Ptolemais.*

Century VII

VII.V

V'in fur la table en fera refpandu,
Le tiers n'aura celle qu'il pretendoit:
Deux fois du noir[1] de Parme defcendu,
Petoufe à Pize fera ce qu'il cuidoit.

Some of the wine on the table will be spilled, the third will not have that which he claimed. Twice descended from the black one of Parma. Perouse will do to Pisa that which he believed in.

Century VII

VII.VI

Naples, Palerme, & toute la Secille,
Par main barbare fera inhabitee,
Corficque, Salerne & de Sardeigne l'ifle,
Faim pefte, guerre fin de maux
*   intemptee.[2]*

Naples, Palermo and all of Sicily will be uninhabited through barbarian might. Corsica, Salerno and the island of Sardinia; hunger, plague, war, the end of extended evils.

This is probably a retroactive quatrain. It predicts in general terms the invasion of Sicily and southern Italy as well as of Corsica and Sardinia. There were many such raids made by Barbary pirates both before and during the sixteenth century, when Nostradamus wrote the *Prophecies.*

Century VII

VII.VII

Sur le combat des grans cheuaux legiers,
On criera le grand croiffant confond.
De nuict tuer monts, habits de bergiers,
Abifmes rouges dans le foffé profond.

Upon the struggle of the great. Light horses it will be claimed that the great crescent is destroyed. To kill by night, in the mountains, dressed in shepherd's clothing, red gulfs in the deep ditch.

The crescent moon was the symbol of the Turks and of Islam. Apparently Nostradamus sees them as suffering a great defeat, probably from a cavalry attack, line 1. The red gulfs are probably rivers of blood resulting from the slaughter. A graphic quatrain, but irritating as it is so unspecific.

---

[1]*noir.* The usual anagram for *roi* may be permissible here.
[2]*intemptee.* L. *intentatus,* extended, stretched.

Century VII

VII.VIII

Flora fuis, fuis le plus proche Romain,
Au fefulan fera conflict donné:
Sang efpandu les plus grans prins à
*   main,*
Temple ne fexe ne fera pardonné.

Florence flee, flee the nearest Roman. At
Fiesole will conflict be exchanged. Blood
shed, the greatest ones taken by the hand.
Neither temple nor sex will be forgiven.

A failed quatrain. It appears to predict that Florence will suffer a severe attack by Vatican troops. As Fiesole is only a few miles away, it would naturally suffer the same fate.

Century VII

VII.IX

Dame à l'abfence de fon grand
*   capitaine,*
Sera priee d'amours du l'iceroy,
Faincte promeffe & malheureufe
*   eftraine,*
Entre les mains du grand prince
*   Barroys.*

The lady, in the absence of her great mas-
ter will be begged for love by the viceroy.
Feigned promise and misfortune and love,
in the hands of the great prince of Bar.

France has never had a viceroy, the only comparable offices being those of the constable of France or the lieutenant general, an office held by the Guises when Nostradamus wrote. There is no question that this quatrain could apply to India, as it is a country ignored by Nostradamus, for whatever reason.

The title of the duc de Bar was given to the eldest son of the duc de Lorraine. As the duke was a minor there was no duc de Bar during that period. It is unlikely that *Dame* refers to the queen, Catherine de' Medicis, but it may well refer to Henri II's mistress Diane de Poitiers, who would at this time be in her late fifties. She never allowed any portraits of her to be painted after the age of twenty, in order to preserve her search for youth in her face.

Century VII

VII.X

Par le grand prince limitrophe du
    Mans,
Preux & vaillant chef de grand exercite:
Par mer & terre de Gallotz &
    Normans,
Cafpre paffer Barcelone pillé ifle.

By the great Prince bordering Le Mans,
the brave and valiant leader of the great
army. By land and sea with Bretons and
Normans, to pass Gibraltar and Barcelona to pillage the island.

Le Mans used to be the principal city of Maine in northwest France; Mayenne, the next in importance, belonged to the Guise family. During Nostradamus' lifetime Le Mans was held by Claude, the marquis of Mayenne and duc d'Amale. He fought at Metz in 1552 and later at Calais, Saint Denis, Dreux and Montcoeur, but he never invaded Spain or North Africa. Nostradamus seems to have foreseen a much greater future for him in the Mediterranean basin than ever occurred, so this quatrain is, in part, a failure.

Century VII

VII.XI

L'enfant Royal contemnera la mere,
Oeil, piedz bleffés, rude, inobeiffant,
Nouuelle à dame eftrange & bien
    amere,
Seront tués des fiens plus de cinq cens.

The royal child will scorn his mother; eye,
feet wounded, rude, disobedient. Strange
and very bitter news to the lady. More
than five hundred of her people will be
killed.

This quatrain seems to refer to the quarrel of a queen with her son. Since Nostradamus' lifetime there has been only one notable example of this, between Louis XIII and his mother Marie de Medicis. Garencières says that more than five hundred of the queen's supporters were killed in the dispute. A satisfactory quatrain.

Century VII

VII.XII

Le grand puisné fera fin de la guerre,
Aux dieux assemble les excusés:
Cahors, Moissac iront long de la serre,
Reffus Lestore, les Agenois razés.

The great younger one will make an end
of the war. He assembles those pardoned
before the gods. Cahors and Moissac will
go far from the prison. A refusal at Lectoure, the people of Agen shaved.

The younger brother of a ruling king or the descendant of a younger brother of the king was known as the Cadet branch. However this quatrain is unclear. The last line describes what sounds like retribution, as for example when the French shaved the heads of any person they found collaborating with the Nazis and the Nazis did the same to the Jews in the concentration camps.

Century VII
VII.XIII

De la cité marine & tributaire,
La tefte raze prendra la fatrapie:
Chaffer fordide qui puis fera contraire,
Par quatorze ans tiendra la tyrannie.

From the marine tributary city, the shaven head will take up the satrapy to chase the sordid man who will then be against him. For fourteen years he will hold the tyranny.

Bonaparte, of the shaven head, will retake Toulon, the marine city, from the English in 1793, from the English military led by Sir Arthur Wellesley, who had made the city a tributary. Napoleon then goes on to overthrow the Directoire *fordide,* and put an end to the Republic. He did enjoy absolute power *(la tyrannie)* for fourteen years (November, 1799 to April, 1814). Le Pelletier in his commentary believes that the sordid one *(fordide)* referred to the English but otherwise roughly agrees with this interpretation.

Century VII
VII.XIIII

Faux expofer viendra topographie,
Seront les cruches des monumens
     ouuertes:
Palluler fecte saincte philofophie,
Pour blanches, noires, & pour antiques
     vertes.

He will come to oppose the false topography, the urns of the tombs will be opened. Sect and holy philosophy to thrive; black for white, the new for the old.

On December 22, 1789, the National Assembly changed the ancient regional districts of France into Départements. Nostradamus feels that the tombs of the French kings, traditionally interred at St. Denis, will be violated and their ashes scattered. This is, together with the antireligious bias of the quatrain, just a general comment upon the extremes of the Revolution.

Century VII

VII.XV

Deuant cité de l'Infubre[1] contree,
Sept ans fera le fiege deuant mis:
Le tref grand Roy y fera fon entree,
Cité puis libre hors de fes ennemis.

Before the city of the Insubrian lands the siege will be laid for seven years. A great king enters then the city is free, away from its enemies.

Probably a failed quatrain. Nostradamus seems to predict a very long drawn-out siege of Milan *(Insubre)* which will last for seven years. The liberating king will free Milan from its Spanish masters. This belongs to the seventeenth or eighteenth centuries and is unlikely to be fulfilled now.

Century VII

VII.XVI

Entree profonde par la grand Royne
*   faicte*
Rendra le lieu puiffant inacceffible:
L'armee des troys lyons fera deffaite,
Faifant dedans cas hideux & terrible.

The profound entry made by the great queen will make the place powerful and inaccessible. The army of the three lions will be defeated, causing within a thing hideous and terrible.

The great queen, Mary Tudor, held Calais "engraved upon her heart" until it was recaptured for the French by the duc de Guise in 1558. At this period, England was an ally of Spain, due to Mary's marriage to Philip. The three lions are part of the English standard. A comparatively successful quatrain.

Century VII

VII.XVII

Le prince rare de pitié & clemence,
Viendra changer par mort grâd
*   cognoiffance:*
Par grand repos le regne trauaillé,
Lors que le grand toft fera eftrillé.

The prince who has little pity or mercy will come through death to change (becoming) very knowledgeable. The kingdom will be attended with great tranquillity, when the great one will soon be passed.

Again, a quatrain I cannot decipher.

[1]*Infubre.* L. *Insubria,* the area around Milan.

Century VII
VII.XVIII

Les affiegés couloureront leurs paches,
Sept iours apres feront cruelle iffue
Dans repoulfés feu, fang. Sept mis a
*   l'hache*
Dame captiue qu'auoit la paix tiffue.

The besieged will color their pacts, but
seven days later they will make a cruel
exit. Thrown back inside, fire and blood.
Seven put to the axe the lady who had
woven the peace is captive.

This is an obscure quatrain describing a treacherous enemy who, while besieged, pretends to sue for peace but seven days later makes a disastrous attempt to escape. Line 4 could well refer to Nostradamus' period. The Peace of Cambrai, instigated in 1529, was known as the Ladies Charter because it was negotiated *(tiffue)* by the mother of François I and the aunt of Charles V.

Century VII
VII.XIX

Le fort Nicene ne fera combatu,
Vaincu fera par rutilant metal
Son faict fera vn long temps debatu,
Aux citadins eftrange efpouuantal.

The fort at Nice will not engage in combat, it will be overcome by shining metal.
This deed will be debated for a long time,
strange and fearful for the citizens.

Nice has been captured twice since Nostradamus wrote the *Prophecies,* in 1705 and 1891, both times by the French.

Century VII
VII.XX

Ambaffadeurs de la Tofcane langue,
Auril & May Alpes & mer paffer:
Celuy de veau¹ expofera l'harangue,
Vie Gauloife ne venant effacer.

Ambassadors of the Tuscan language will
cross the Alps and the sea in April and
May. The man of the calf will deliver an
oration, not coming to wipe out the French
way of life.

The good relations which existed between Napoleon III and the Pope were spoiled when Cavour arrived in Paris in 1854 to plead the cause of Italian unity. The Congress at Paris took place during the months Nostradamus predicted, April and May. The reason for naming Cavour the man of the calf *(celuy de veau)* is obscure but

¹*de veau.* Some commentators think this should read *de Vaud,* a Swiss canton; but I quite like my interpretation of Nostradamus' puns in the second meaning of Cavour.

fascinating. It is a typical Nostradamus contortion of the facts. Cavour was the envoy of Turin and *Torino* means the city of the bull. It was known as *Augusta Taurinorium* by the Romans, so Cavour is thus the offspring of the calf.

Century VII

VII.XXI

Par peftilente inimitié Volficque,	By the pestilential enmity of Languedoc
Diffimulee chaffera le tyran:	the dissimulated tyrant will be driven out.
Au pont de Sorgues fe fera la traffique,	The bargain will be made on the bridge at
De mettre à mort luy & fon adherant.	Sorgues to put to death both him and his
	follower.

This is probably the bridge at Sorgues, the main town on the river of the same name. It belonged to the Vatican State in 1791. Languedoc is a large province to the west of the Rhône. Otherwise an irritating, vague quatrain.

Century VII

VII.XXII

Les citoyens de Mefopotamie,[1]	The citizens of Mesopotamia are angry
Yrés encontre amis de Tarraconne,[2]	with the friends from Tarraconne. Games,
Ieux, ritz, banquetz, toute gent endormie	rites, banquets, everyone invited. The
Vicaire au Rofne, prins cité, ceux	vicar at Rhône, the city taken and those
d'Aufone.[3]	of Ausonia.

In this quatrain Nostradamus does not seem to use the word Mesopotamia as modern Iraq and he is probably using the word to describe a European town. The Venassin between the Rhône and the Durance at Avignon makes a great deal of sense in this context. The Vicar (of Rome) was Pope Pius VI, whom Napoleon had captured and imprisoned at Valence in 1799. The second part of line 4 describes how a French army led by General Championnet recaptured Rome and then went on to take Naples in 1799.

---

[1]*Mefopotamie.* Either modern Iraq, or the Venassin between the Rhône and the Durance at Avignon or Paris between the Seine and Marne.

[2]*Tarraconne.* L. *Tarroca,* Tarragona in Catalonia, Spain, or less likely *Tarraconensis,* the northeastern part of Roman Iberia.

[3]*Aufone.* Southern Italy, probably Naples.

Century VII

VII.XXIII

Le Royal fceptre sera contrainct de
  prendre,
Ce que fes predeceffeurs auoient engaigé:
Puis que l'aneau on fera mal entendre,
Lors qu'on viendra le palays faccager.

The royal scepter will be forced to take that which his predecessor had pledged. Because they do not understand about the ring when they come to sack the palace.

Hugh Allen, at best an unreliable commentator on Nostradamus, wrote categorically in 1943 that the scene of this pawnbroking of royal jewels would take place in Buckingham Palace! The ring and the scepter are part of the royal regalia at most coronations. But otherwise a very frustrating quatrain.

Century VII

VII.XXIIII

L'enfeuely fortyra du tombeau,
Fera de chaines lier le fort du pont:
Empoyfonné auec oeufz de Barbeau,
Grand de Lorraine par le Marquis du
  Pont.[1]

He who was buried will come out of the tomb, he will free the strong one from the bridge to be bound with chains. Poisoned with the roe, or eggs of a barbel, the great one from Lorraine by the Marquis du Pont.

The barbel is a freshwater fish found throughout Europe. What is symbolized here is unclear. The grand one from Lorraine is probably the duke, Charles III, who was taken from his family to be reared in the French court. Later the marquisate of Bar passed to the sons of the House of Lorraine. Nostradamus predicts that the duc is to be poisoned by the marquis, one of the younger sons. A failed quatrain.

---

[1]*Marquis du Pont.* The younger son of the House of Lorraine had the title of Marquis du Pont à Mousson.

Century VII
VII.XXV

Par guerre longue tout l'exercice expuifer, *Que pour fouldartz ne trouueront pecune:* *Lieu d'or d'argent, cuir on viendra cufer,*[1] *Gaulois aerain, figne croiffant de Lune.*	*Through the long war all the army exhausted, so that they do not find money for the soldiers. Instead of gold or silver they will start to coin leather. Gallic brass and the crescent sign of the moon.*

The quatrain refers to the dreadful battles of the First World War which ranged across hundreds of miles, and killed millions of soldiers each week. Many commentators believe this may refer to battles such as Gallipoli. To the east the Allies were fighting on the hills of the Dardanelles and falling before the lethal gunfire of the Turks, *figne croiffant.* I do not understand the reference to payment by leather instead of coinage, but it might refer to barter among the soldiers on the battlefield.

Century VII
VII.XXVI

Fuftes & galees autour de fept nauires, *Sera liuree vne mortelle guerre:* *Chef de Madric receura coup de vires,*[2] *Deux efchapees & cinq menees à terre.*	*Foists and galleys around seven ships, a mortal war will be let loose. The leader from Madrid will receive a wound from two arrows; two escaped and five brought to land.*

In November, 1555, some privateers attacked a Spanish fleet in the Channel. *Vires* should be read as *virer,* a nautical verb, to attack. The privateers concentrated upon the admiral's ship and succeeded in capturing it, together with four other ships which came to its aid, *cinq menees à terre.* They were towed victoriously to Dieppe. An excellent quatrain, but it may be retroactive due to the date, the same as that of the publication of the first part of the *Prophecies.*

---

[1]*cufer.* L. *cusare,* O.F. *cudere,* to mint money.
[2]*vires.* alternative *vires,* arrows, or *virer,* a nautical word, to attack.

Century VII

VII.XVII

Au cainct[1] de Vaft[2] la grand caualerie,
Proche à Ferrage empefchee au bagaige:
Prompt à Turin feront tel volerie,
Que dans le fort rauiront leur hoftaige.

At the wall of Vasto the great cavalry are
impeded by the baggage near Ferrara. At
Turin they will speedily commit such robbery that they will ravish their hostage in
the fort.

There are nine villages in France named Vast, plus a monastery near Arras and a harbor near Cherbourg. None of these seem to help. Alternatively, the quatrain may refer to Alphonso II, marquis de Vasto, 1502–1544, who was governor of Milan from 1537 onwards. He retired to Asti in 1554 and this may stand for Ferrara as it was a duchy in the House of Este, seized by the Papal States in 1547. An unsatisfactory quatrain nevertheless, unlikely to be fulfilled in the future.

Century VII

VII.XXVIII

Le capitaine conduira grande proye,
Sur la montaigne des ennemis plus
    proche,
Enuironné, par feu fera tel voye,
Tous efchappez or[3] trente mis en
    broche.

The captain will lead a great herd on the
mountain closest to the enemy. Surrounded by fire he forces such a route, all
escape except for thirty put on the spit.

Most commentators understand "put on the spit," *mis en broche,* as meaning that the unlucky victims were run through. However, I think that Nostradamus is describing them as being roasted alive. Apart from that, the quatrain could refer to many possible events either in war or peacetime. I can make nothing further of it.

[1]*cainct.* O.F. belt or waist. Possibly used here to mean encircling.
[2]*Vast.* uncertain meaning, see commentary.
[3]*or.* misprint for *hors* in other editions, without, except for.

Century VII

VII.XXIX

Le grand Duc d'Albe fe viendra rebeller
A fes grans peres fera le tradiment:
Le grand de Guife le viendra debeller,
Captif mené & dreffé monument.

The great one of Alba will come to rebel,
he will betray his great forebears. The
great man of Guise will come to vanquish
him, led captive, with a monument
erected.

At first sight a very clear quatrain, but sadly it is not accurate. The duke of Alba was in charge of all the Spanish forces and the duc de Guise of the French. But de Guise never triumphed over Alba, let alone took him captive. Perhaps Nostradamus foresaw Alba crossing over to the French, which he did from 1555–57, to fight against the Vatican States. Probably wishful thinking on the prophet's part.

Century VII

VII.XXX

Le fac s'approche, feu, grand fang
 efpandu
Po, grand fleuues, aux bouuiers¹
 l'entreprinfe,
De Gennes, Nice, apres long attendu,
Fouffan, Turin à Sauillan la prinfe.

The sack approaches, fire and great blood-
shed. Po, the great rivers, the enterprise
for the clowns. After a long wait from
Genoa and Nice, Fussana, Turin; the
capture at Savigliano.

Another infuriating quatrain, with lots of names and no real facts. Fossano, Turin and Savigliano were all in Piedmont, but Nice had been lost to the House of Savary. Genoa at this time was an independent state under the Hapsburgs.

Century VII

VII.XXXI

De Languedoc, & Guienne plus de dix,
Mille voudront les Alpes repaffer:
Grans Allobroges² marcher contre
 Brundis
Aquin & Breffe les viendront recaffer.

From Languedoc and Guienne more than
ten thousand will want to cross the Alps
again. The great Sayoyards march
against Brindisi. Aquino and Bresse will
come to drive them back.

The action in this quatrain is unclear. The place names are all so separate. Languedoc and Guienne were in southwest France, Bresse

---

¹*bouuiers.* O.F. clowns or cowherds.
²*Allobroges.* L. the inhabitants of Savoy.

belonged to Savoy until 1601. Brindisi is in southern Italy and along with Aquino, was a vassal of the Two Sicilies. I get very frustrated with quatrains in the Seventh Century, unfinished as it is. Maybe the reason the verses are so obscure is quite simply that Nostradamus had not gone over them properly before his death, and his pupil Chavigny did not have the courage to shape them into more interesting material.

Century VII
VII.XXXII

Du mont Royal naiftra d'vne cafane,[1]
Qui caue, & compte viendra tyrannifer
Dreffer copie de la marche Millane,
Fauene, Florence d'or & gens efpuifer.

From the bank of Montereale will be born someone who is both calculating and boring, becoming a tyrant. To raise a force in the Marches of Milan, to drain Faenza and Florence of gold and men.

The Medici family came from the area of Florence called Montereale. Could this be a warning to Catherine concerning her family? Apart from this, one has the usual geographical chaos. Milan belonged to the Hapsburgs, Faenza was part of the Papal States and Florence, as I have said, belonged to the Medicis. Obviously a failed quatrain.

Century VII
VII.XXXIII

Par fraude regne, forces expolier,[2]
La claffe obfeffe, paffages à l'efpie:
Deux fainctz amys fe viendront rallier,
Efueiller hayne de long temps affoupie.

The kingdom stripped of its forces by fraud, the fleet blockaded, passages for the spy. Two false friends will come to rally (round), awakening a hatred dormant for a long time.

This is a typical Nostradamus prediction which may have been fulfilled several times since it was written. It is usually interpreted as describing the Fall of France in 1940. Line 3 would apply to the Germans and the Russians and line 4 to the Anglo-French connections. The following quatrain seems to continue this theme.

---

[1]*cafane.* Low L. *casana,* bank.
[2]*expolier.* O.F. plunder, strip, despoil.

Century VII
VII.XXXIIII

En grand regret fera la gent Gauloife,
Coeur vain, legier croira temerité:
Pain, fel, ne vin, eaue: venin ne
  ceruoife,
Plus grand captif, faim, froit, neceffité.

The French nation will be in great grief,
vain and lighthearted they will believe
rash things. No bread, salt, wine nor
water, venom nor ale. The greater one
captured. Hunger, cold and want.

This quatrain seems to follow upon VII.XXXIII and is yet a further description of the appalling deprivations suffered by the French under German occupation. Bread, salt, wine and water would be considered by Nostradamus as the basics of life. "The greater one captured." I am not certain whom this refers to, certainly not Hitler in this context, although the cold and want (*faim, froit*) continued for some years after the war.

Century VII
VII.XXXV

La grande pefche viendra plaindre,
  plorer
D'auoir efleu trompés feront en l'aage:
Guiere auec ceux ne voudra demourer,
Deçeu fera par ceux de fon langaige.

The great fish will come to complain and
weep for having made his choice, deceived
concerning his age. He will hardly want
to remain with them, deceived by those of
his own tongue.

Henri III, the third son of Catherine de' Medicis and Henri II, was elected king of Poland in the unrestrained manner used at the time, *pesche,* which also implies a lottery. He hated it and on the premature death of his brother Charles IX, he managed to escape from the Polish court and retain his claim to the French throne. This upset the political arrangements of both Poland and France to found new dynasties. Henri III was deceived, *deçeu,* by a fellow Frenchman, Jacques Clément, who also managed to assassinate him. A good, factual quatrain.

Century VII
VII.XXXVI

Dieu, le ciel tout le diuin verbe à
*   l'vnde,*
Porté par rouges sept razes à Bizance:
Contre les oingz trois cens de
*   Trebisconde,*
Deux loix mettront, & horreur, puis
*   credence.*

God, the heavens, all the divine words on the waves, carried by seven red-shaven heads to Byzantium. Against the anointed three hundred from Trebizond will make two laws; first horror, then trust.

The seven red heads are almost certainly cardinals of the Roman Catholic Church, who not only wear red robes but red skullcaps. But what are they doing going to Constantinople? Trying to convert the sultan? I can find no record of any incident similar to this so conclude it is a failed quatrain.

Century VII
VII.XXXVII

Dix enuoyés, chef de nef mettre à mort,
D'vn aduerty, en claffe guerre ouuerte:
Confufion chef, l'vn fe picque & mord,
Leryn, ftecades[1] nefz cap dedans la
*   nerte.[2]*

Ten sent to put the captain of the ship to death are warned by one, that there is open revolt in the fleet. Confusion; the leader and the man stab and bite each other at Lerins and Hyères. Ships, prow into the darkness.

This dramatic quatrain heralds the unsuccessful attempted assassination of a naval commander. There is no clue as to whom he might be. The Isles de Lerins are off Cannes and those of Hyères off Toulon. Probably an unsuccessful quatrain.

Century VII
VII.XXXVIII

L'aifné Royal fur courfier voltigeant,
Picquer viendra, fi rudement courir:
Gueulle, lipee, pied dans l'eftrein
*   pleignant*
Trainé, tiré, horriblement mourir.

The elder Royal on a frisky horse will spur it so fiercely that it will bolt. Mouth, mouthful, foot complaining in the embrace. Dragged, pulled, to die horribly.

[1]*ftecades.* L. *Stoechadef.* the Islands of Hyères.
[2]*nerte.* O.F. black. Possibly Gk. *nerthe,* underneath.

The only French prince of the royal line who was killed in a riding accident was Crown Prince Ferdinand in 1842. He was the heir of Louis Philippe and his untimely death caused dynastic problems. A good quatrain.

Century VII
VII.XXXIX

Le conducteur de l'armé Françoife,
Cuidant perdre le principal phalange;
Par fus paire de l'auaigne & d'ardoife,
Soy parfondra par Gennes gent
* eftrange.*

The leader of the French army will expect to lose the main phalanx. Upon the pavement of oats and slate the foreign nation will be undermined through Genoa.

I can make nothing of this quatrain apart from the fact that a French leader will lose an important part of his army.

Century VII
VII.XL

Dedans tonneaux hors oingz d'huile &
* greffe,*
Seront vingt vn deuant le port fermés,
Au fecond guet par mort feront proueffe:
Gaigner les portes & du guet affommés.

Within casks anointed outside with oil and grease, twenty-one will be shut before the harbor at the second watch. Through death they will do great deeds to win the gate and be killed by the watch.

It appears that Nostradamus is attempting to describe a seaport being captured rather in the manner of Ali Baba and his Forty Thieves! Apparently they succeed in entering the town but are killed by the guards. A failed quatrain.

Century VII
VII.XLI

Les oz des piedz & des mains enferrés,
Par bruit maifon long temps inhabitee:
Seront par fonges concauant deterrés,
Maifon falubre & fans bruyt habitee.

The bones of the feet and the hands are locked up. Because of the noise the house is uninhabited for a long time. Digging in dreams they will be unearthed, the house healthy and inhabited without noise.

This is certainly a description of the exorcism of a haunted house which seems to quiet down when the bones of a victim are removed. Perhaps line 3 indicates that the source of the skeleton was discovered in a dream? Exorcism was a ceremony greatly practiced by the

Catholic Church in Europe in Nostradamus' time and the seventeenth century.

Century VII

VII.XLII

Deux de poifon faisiz nouueau venuz,
Dans la cuifine du grand Prince verfer:
Par le fouillard tous deux au faict
* congneux,*
Prins qui cuidoit de mort l'aifné vexer.

Two newly arrived have seized the poison
to pour it in the kitchen of the great prince.
Both are caught in the act by the scullion,
taken, he who thought to trouble the elder
with death.

This is a specific quatrain but with no facts behind it. Two conspirators on a prince's kitchen staff try to poison him. They are caught red-handed by the kitchen boy *le fouillard,* but as only one is reported captured, it is possible his accomplice got away.

Century VII ends abruptly here. Neither Nostradamus nor his disciple Chavigny give any reason for this. It seems unlikely that the quatrains were suppressed, more probable that Nostradamus had not written the full thousand he intended to do before his death.

Century VIII

VIII.I

PAV, NAY, LORON plus feu qu'à
* fang fera.*
Laude nager, fuir grand aux furrez.
Les agaffas[1] entree refufera.
Pampon,[2] Durance les tiendra enferrez.

PAY, NAY, LORON will be more fire
than blood. Swim in praise, the great one
to flee the confluence (of rivers). He will
refuse entry to the magpies. Pampon and
the Durance will keep them confined.

Although the names in line 1 are all small towns in western France, Nostradamus does seem to be talking about a person, not places. The capital letters further indicate their importance; By anagram *PAV NAY LORON* becomes *Napaulon Roy,* Napoleon the King. The varied spelling of Napoleon's name with an *au* instead of an *a* was commonplace even in the nineteenth century and one must also remember Nostradamus' personal and extremely unordothox orthography. The *agassas,* magpie or *Pie,* Pius, would refer to both Pius VI and VII, who were imprisoned by Napoleon. The confluence of rivers would then

---

[1] *agaffas.* A.Pr. *aggasa,* a magpie, also known as *pie,* which is the French spelling of Pius. A Nostradamus pun.
[2] *Pampon.* Doubtful, possibly Gk. *pamponeros,* depraved?

refer to Valence, where the rivers Rhône and Isère meet and where Pius VI died in 1799. Pius VII was taken first to Savoa and then on to Fontainebleau in 1872. Therefore, neither was imprisoned near the Durance. A small error in such an otherwise accurate quatrain. But on the other hand, Durance is near Avignon, which belonged to the Papacy until 1791. Both the Rhône and the Durance meet at the Papal City.

Century VIII

VIII.II

Condon & Aux & autour de Mirande	*Condom and Auch and around Mirande,*
Le voy du ciel feu qui les enuironne.	*I see fire from the sky which encompasses*
Sol Mars conioint au Lyon puis	*them. The Sun and Mars conjoint in Leo.*
marmande	*Then at Marmande, lightning, great hail,*
Fouldre, grand grefle, mur tombe dans	*a wall falls into the Garonne.*
Garône.	

This is another irritating quatrain with many clues but none that seem to relate to given fact. It is just possible that line 2 indicates the quatrain is futuristic, but personally I doubt it. All the towns mentioned are in the Département of Gers in the southwest, except for Marmande, which is about fifty miles north. It is not possible to find a place where a wall has fallen along the length of the Garonne.

Century VIII

VIII.III

Au fort chafteau de Viglanne[1] &	*Within the strong castle of Vigilance and*
Refuiers	*Resviers the younger born of Nancy will*
Sera ferré le puifnay de Nancy:	*be shut up. In Turin the first ones will be*
Dedans Turin feront ards[2] les premiers,	*burned, when Lyons will be transported*
Lors que de dueil Lyon fera tranfy.	*with grief.*

The names in the first line of this quatrain are difficult to decipher, but the best combinations are in Italy. There is a castle built by the Scaligers of Verona at Malescino. There is also a monastery founded by Saint Francis in Lake Garda between San Vigilio and the Riviera. Nancy is the capital of Lorraine, and the cadet a brother or younger branch of the family, most likely refers to Nicolas, duc de Mercoeur,

---

[1]*Viglanne.* Probably San Vigilio and the Riviera, but might stand for Rubberia and Vignola.
[2]*ards.* L. *audere,* to burn.

the father-in-law of Henri III, who did not die until 1577. But despite all this detail, a failed quatrain. The duc was never imprisoned in a castle on Lake Garda. (Turin, line 3, belonged to the French at the time of Nostradamus' writings.)

Century VIII

VIII.IIII

Dedans Monech¹ le coq fera receu,	The Cock will be received into Monaco.

Dedans Monech¹ le coq fera receu,
Le Cardinal de France apparoiftra
Par Logarion² Romain fera deceu
Foibleffe à l'aigle, & force au coq
   naiftra.

The Cock will be received into Monaco.
The cardinal of France will appear. He
will be deceived by the Roman legation.
Weakness to the Eagle, strength will be
born in the Cock.

This was a totally misleading quatrain. If one reads *legation* for *Logarion,* in fact exactly the opposite occurred. The quatrain speaks of the struggle for power in the Mediterranean between the French and the Spanish. Monaco had nominal independence under the Grimaldis but was bound by treaty to help Spain. Nostradamus predicts that this protection refers to Charles, second Cardinal of Lorraine (1524–1547). There were two legates in France, the Vice Regal legate and the papal legate, both at Avignon. Nostradamus describes one of these legates deceiving the French, Hapsburg power declining, and that of the French expanding. In fact, this is the opposite of what happened. Monaco became a close ally of France and the French were driven out of Italy in 1559.

Century VIII

VIII.V

Apparoiftra temple luifant orné,
La lampe & cierge à Borne & Bretueil.
Pour la lucerne le canton deftorné,
Quand on verra le grand coq au
   cercueil.

There will appear a shining ornate tem-
ple, the lamp and the candle at Borne and
Breteuil. For the canton of Lucerne will be
turned aside, when one will see the great
cock in his shroud.

Nostradamus predicts that a great French king will die at the same time as the canton of Lucerne will be conquered. This has never happened and is unlikely to happen in the future. A totally failed quatrain.

¹*Monech. Monaceis,* Monaco.
²*Logarion.* Other texts print *legation,* which is a better reading in the context.

Century VIII
VIII.VI

Clarté fulgure à Lyon apparante
Luyfant, print Malte fubit fera eftainte,
Sardon,[1] *Mauris*[2] *traitera decepuante,*
Geneue à Londes à coq trahyfon fainte.

Lightning and brightness are seen shining at Lyon, Malta is taken and will be suddenly extinguished. Mauris will act deceitfully, Geneva to London, feigning treason towards the cock.

Malta was an independent state until the French Revolution. The Turks attacked it in 1565. Mauris, possibly Maurice, according to legend was leader of a Theban religion whose adherents were annihilated because they refused to murder Christians. His cult is still strong in Switzerland and Savoy. If Sardon stands for Sardinia, it belonged to the House of Savoy after 1720. Nostradamus indicates that Savoy stands for both regions, which means the quatrain predates 1720. The involvement between Geneva and London probably describes Elizabeth I's involvement with Calvin in the Conspiracy of Amboise, 1566.

Century VIII
VIII.VII

Verceil, Milan donra intelligence,
Dedans Tycin[3] *fera faite la paye.*[4]
Courir par Siene eau, fang, feu par
  Florence.
Vnique choir d'hault en bas faifant
  maye.[5]

Vercelli, Milan will give the news, the wound will be inflicted at Pavia. To run through the waters of the Seine, blood and fire through Florence. The unique one falling from high to low calling for help.

An obscure quatrain. Vercelli and Pavia belonged to the Duchy of Milan and were taken over by the Hapsburgs until the nineteenth century.

---

[1]*Sardon.* The most probable interpretation for this is Sardinia.
[2]*Mauris.* St. Maurice, the patron saint of much of the French Alps and Savoy.
[3]*Tycin.* L. *Ticinium,* Pavia.
[4]*la paye.* O.F. wound, but possible misprint for the plague.
[5]*maye.* O.F. a kneading-trough. Alternatively a misreading of *"ma'aie,"* Help me!

Century VIII

VIII.VIII

Pres de linterne¹ dans de tonnes fermez,
Chiuaz² fera pour l'aigle la menee,
L'efleu caffé luy fes gens enfermez,
Dedans Turin rapt efpoufe emmenee.

Near Focia, enclosed in some barrels Chi-
vasso will plot for the eagle. The elected
one driven out, he and his people shut up.
Rape within Turin, the bride led away.

An irritating quatrain. The village of Focia occupies the old site of Linternum, but is not likely to be the subject of this verse. Chivasso, a few miles northeast of Turin, was occupied by the French, but Nostradamus sees it plotting on behalf of the Emperor (Napoleon?). Unclear.

Century VIII

VIII.IX

Pendant que l'aigle & le coq à Sauone
Seront vnis Mer Leuant & Ongrie,
L'armee à Naples, Palerne, Marque
    d'Ancone
Rome, Venife par Barb'³ horrible crie.

While the eagle is united with the cock at
Savona, the Eastern sea and Hungary.
The army at Naples, Palermo, the mar-
ches of Ancona, Rome and Venice. A great
outcry by the barbarian.

At Savona Nostradamus foresees an alliance between the Emperor and the French. Both the Levant and Hungary belonged to the Turks except for the small area retained, and paid for, by the Hapsburgs. Both Naples and Palermo belonged to the Hapsburg Kingdom of the Two Sicilies and Ancona belonged to the Papal States. Nostradamus appears to envisage a Moslem invasion of Italy, possibly just feasible, but it seems unlikely that these remaining Christian forces would align against it. On balance, a quatrain belonging to Europe of the past few centuries, and as such, a failure.

---

¹*Linterne.* now Focia, near Naples.
²*Chiuaz.* Chivasso in Italy.
³*Barb'.* F. shortened form of barbarian, but just possibly refers to the enigmatic Aenobarbe.

Century VIII

VIII.X

Puanteur grande fortira de Laufanne,
Qu'on ne faura l'origine du fait,
Lon mettra hors toute la gent loingtaine
Feu veu au ciel, peuple eftranger
  deffait.

A great stench will come from Lausanne but they will not know its origin. They will put out all the people from different places; fire seen in the sky, a great foreign nation defeated.

The stench from Lausanne is probably Nostradamus' graphic reference to the Calvinists in general and in particular to Calvin's second-in-command, de Bèze, who taught in Lausanne during the second half of the sixteenth century. Some later commentators refer this quatrain to the meetings of the early Marxists. Line 4 gives this view some credence.

Century VIII

VIII.XI

Peuple infiny paroiftra à Vicence
Sans force feu brufler la Bafilique
Pres de Lunage deffait grand de
  Valence,
Lors que Venife par more prendra
  pique.

A multitude of people will appear at Vincenza, without force, fire to burn the Basilica. Near Lunage the great one of Valenza defeated at the time when Venice takes up the quarrel through custom.

At the present time the site of Valentinois is held by Prince Albert of Monaco, son of Prince Rainier and the late Princess Grace. During Nostradamus' lifetime it belonged first to Diane de Poitiers, and then to the Grimaldis of Monaco. As to the place names, Vincenza was in the Republic of Venice, Valenza belonged to the Hapsburgs, Milan and Valence were in France. These geopolitical place names make this appear to be a retroactive quatrain.

Century VIII

VIII.XII

Apparoiftra aupres de Buffalorre
L'hault & procere entré dedans Milan
L'abbé de Foix auec ceux de faint
  Morre
Feront la forbe abillez en vilan.

He will appear near to Buffalora, the highly born and tall one entered into Milan. The Abbé of Foix with those of Saint-Maur will cause damage dressed up as serfs.

Buffalora is a tiny village west of Milan, so small that it is unlikely Nostradamus would have known of it, unless he passed through it on his Italian wanderings. The people of St. Mark are the Benedictines, the connection being that St. Maurus founded the Order in France. The Abbey at Foix belonged to the Benedictines. But it is difficult to imagine quite what Nostradamus envisaged in line 4.

Century VIII
VIII.XIII

Le croifé frere par amour effrenee	The crusader brother through impassioned
Fera par Praytus Bellerophon mourir,	love will cause Bellerophon to die through
Claffe à mil ans la femme forcenee	Proteus. The fleet for a thousand years.
Beu le breuuage, tous deux apres perir.	The maddened woman, the potion drunk, both of them die.

This story of poisoning is based on the myth of Bellerophon and Proteus, king of Argus, whose wife was furious when her advances to Bellerophon were refused. Queen Anteia persuaded Proteus to send Bellerophon on a mortal mission which was concealed in a sealed message to Lebates, king of Lycia. Lebates therefore sent Bellerophon to kill the monster Chimera, which he succeeded in doing with the help of his flying horse, Pegasus. Nostradamus perceives the cuckold husband will be poisoned as well as his wife.

But what relevance this has to the sixteenth century or later is completely impossible to interpret. I sometimes wonder if Nostradamus liked to amuse himself when considering the credulity of the reader. However, this in no way diminishes the serious, specific aspect of many of his predictions.

Century VIII
VIII.XIIII

Le grand credit d'or, d'argent l'abondance	The great credit of gold and abundance of silver will cause honor to be blinded by
Fera aueugler par libide honneur	lust. The offense of the adulterer will
Sera cogneu d'adultere l'offense,	become known, which will occur to his
Qui paruiendra à fon grand deshonneur.	great dishonor.

This quatrain appears to indicate a general condemnation of the great riches which flowed from the Spanish-American mines into Europe, causing great financial inflation throughout the sixteenth century. Lines 3 and 4 seem to show that Nostradamus connects monetary lust with sexual lust, a concept not unknown to the twentieth century!

Century VIII
VIII.XV

*Vers Aquilon grands efforts par
  hommaffe
Prefque l'Europe & I'vniuers vexer,
Les deux eclypfes mettra en telle chaffe,
Et aux Pannons vie & mort renforcer.*

*Great exertions toward the North of a
man-woman to vex Europe and almost all
the universe. The two eclipses will be put
into such a rout that they will reinforce life
or death for the Hungarians.*

This quatrain must certainly tie up with Nostradamus' predictions concerning the great expansion of the German Empire. The *hommaffe* is applied by most commentators as Germania, and thus the quatrain refers to Nazi Germany. However, apart from the troubles suffered by the Hungarians, and the reference to problems in the whole of Europe (line 1), it remains a rather unsatisfactory quatrain.

Century VIII
VIII.XVI

*Au lieu que HIERON feit fa nef
  fabriquer,
Si grand deluge fera & fi fubite,
Qu'on n'aura lieu ne terres s'atacquer
L'onde monter Fefulan Olympique.*

*At the place where HIERON builds his
ship, there will be such a great and sudden
flood. No one will have a place or land to
fall upon. The waters rise to the Olympic
Fesulan.*

I cannot discover the meaning of the anagram *HIERON*. It does not occur elsewhere in the quatrains. Some commentators believe it to be an anagram of *JASON,* which would fit the atmosphere of the latter part of the quatrain. It is difficult to find any connection between Greece and Fesulan (Fiesole) in central Italy. As to the question of flooding, Fiesole stands only 970 feet above sea level, whereas Mount Olympus rises 9,570 feet above it.

Century VIII
VIII.XVII

*Les bien aifez fubit feront defmis
Par les trois freres le monde mis en
  trouble,
Cité marine faifiront ennemis,
Faim, feu, fang, pefte, & de tous maux
  le double.*

*Those at ease will suddenly be cast down,
the world put into trouble by three brothers. Their enemies will seize the marine
city. Hunger, fire, blood, plague; all evils
doubled.*

This is a splendid Millennium quatrain. Line 4 gives all the ingredients needed. The mention of the three brothers who will put the world into trouble helps give us a dating. When three brothers are in positions of power during a century, world troubles will start to erupt.

The only well-known three brothers "in power" towards the Millennium are the Kennedys. Tragically, two of them have been assassinated. It seems unlikely that the youngest brother, Edward Kennedy, will now attain any position of power; he is what one might term a "psychological assassinee." During the lifetimes of these three brothers, America will suddenly find itself in trouble. Could the marine city be Hong Kong, due to be handed back to the Chinese in 1997?

Century VIII
VIII.XVIII

De Flora iffue de fa mort fera caufe,
Vn temps deuant par ieufne & vieille
  bueyre
Par les trois lys luy feront telle paufe,
Par fon fruit fauue comme chair crue
  mueyre.

The reasons for her death will be issued from Florence, it will be drunk once by both young and old. Through the three great lilies they will give her a great pause (become thoughtful). Saved through her offspring as raw meat is dampened.

Florence belonged to the de' Medicis family for several centuries, and two of the Medicis daughters married into the royal line, *les trois lys,* of France: Nostradamus' protector Catherine and later Marie de' Medicis.

Catherine was saved from a possible divorce from her husband, Henri, the dauphin, when after ten barren years she bore him seven children. But the last part of line 4, *chair crue mueyre,* remains obscure.

Century VIII
VIII.XIX

A foubftenir le grand cappe troublee,
Pour l'efclaircir les rouges marcheront,
De mort famille fera prefque accablee.
Les rouges rouges le rouge affomeront:

To support the great troubled Cappe the reds will march in order to clarify it. A family will almost be overcome by death. The bloody red ones will knock down the red.

Cappe is probably Nostradamus' shortened form of *Capet,* the name of the French royal line. The French certainly marched against Louis XVI and Marie Antoinette at the time of the Revolution. Republicans marched against them so that the family had to take enforced refuge in the Temple. The royal family was almost destroyed *prefque accablee*. The only certain survivor was the king's sister, Elisabeth, and possibly Louis XVII, his eldest son (see V.I.). Then the extremists will guillotine the more moderate revolutionaries, the Girondins. It is possible that Robespierre is also hinted at in the last line.

Century VIII
VIII.XX

Le faux meffaige par election fainte
Courir par vrben, rompue pache arrefte,
Voix acheptees, de fang chapelle tainte,
Et à vn autre l'empire contraicte.

The false message about the rigged election to run through the city, stopping the broken pact. Voices bought, a chapel stained with blood, the empire contracted to another one.

Possibly a Holy Roman Emperor who uses bribery, *voix acheptees*, to attain his ends. This false election will be followed by a short war which ends when the Pretender is murdered. I think this is a failed quatrain.

Century VIII
VIII.XXI

Au port de Agde trois fuftes entreront
Portant l'infect non foy & peftilence
Paffant le pont mil milles embleront,
Et le pont rompre à tierce refiftance.

Three foists will enter the port of Agde carrying the infection and pestilence, not the faith. Passing the bridge they will carry off a million. The bridge is broken by the resistance of the third.

The enormity of the number of deaths from the plague makes the figures suspect. They are more suitable for the twentieth century. Agde is a seaport.

Century VIII
VIII.XXII

Gorfan, Narbonne, par le fel aduertir
Tucham, la grace Parpignam trahye,
La ville rouge n'y vouldra confentir.
Par haulte vol drap gris vie faillie.

Coursan, Narbonne through the salt (marsh?) to warn Tuchan, the grace of Perpignan betrayed. The red town will not wish to consent to it. A high flight, a gray flag, life ended.

Line 4 is a good example of Nostradamus' convoluted style when it is hard to get any meaning from the words at all. A difficult quatrain. Communists have a surprisingly strong hold in present-day France, particularly outside Paris. But who or what is Tucham?

Century VIII

VIII.XXIII

Lettres trouuees de la royne les coffres,
Point de fubfcrit fans aucun nom
   d'hauteur
Par la police feront cache les offres.
Qu'on ne fcaura qui fera l'amateur.

Letters are found in the queen's chests. No signature and no name of the author. The government will conceal the offers, so that they will not know who the lover is.

There is no definitive link word that I can pursue in this quatrain, but if Nostradamus did not meet Mary, Queen of Scots, wife of Catherine's son, he certainly knew a great deal about her. She spent most of her childhood years in France with the Guise family, to whom she was related.

The Casket Letters, as they later became known, were documents pertaining to the murder of Darnley, Mary, Queen of Scots' husband, and the events of 1567, a year after Nostradamus' death. These documents were produced by the earl of Moreton, in front of commissions of London and York. The "originals" disappeared after 1584 and their authenticity has always been in dispute.

Century VIII

VIII.XXIIII

Le lieutenant à l'entree de l'huys,
Affomera le grand de Parpignan,
En fe cuidant fauluer à Montpertuis.
Sera deceu baftard de Lufignan.

The lieutenant at the door of the house will knock down the great man of Perpignan. Thinking to save himself at Montpertius, the bastard of Lusignan will be deceived.

The Lusignan family died out before Nostradamus' time. It ruled Jerusalem and Cyprus until 1489, and its titles passed to the House of Savoy. One of Nostradamus' patrons was the comte de Tende, governor of Provence, who was the son of the great Bastard of Savoy. If this is so, then Montpertius almost certainly stands for the Perthus Pass in the Pyrenean mountains. Nostradamus must have envisaged Tende or one of his descendants trapping the Spanish around Roussillon. An unlikely quatrain.

Century VIII

VIII.XXV

Coeur de l'amant ouuert d'amour
fertiue
Dans le ruyffeau fera rauyr la Dame,
Le demy mal contrefera laffiue.
Le pere à deux priuera corps de l'ame.

The heart of the lover, awakened by furtive love, will ravish the lady in the stream. She will shyly claim to be half injured. The father of each will deprive the body of its soul.

A possible history of incest and rape? The plot may be clear but the references are too general to be of any use.

Century VIII

VIII.XXVI

De Caron es¹ trouues en Barfellonne,
Mys defcouuers lieu terrouers & ruyne,
Le grâd qui tient ne tient vouldra
Pamplonne.
Par l'abbaye de Monferrat bruyne.

The bones of Cato found in Barcelona, placed, discovered, the site found again and ruined. The great one who holds, but does not hold, wants Pamplona. Drizzle at the Abbey of Montserrat.

None of Cato's famous family died at Barcelona and only Caius Pacius Cato died in Spain. Technically this is an unfulfilled quatrain.

Century VIII

VIII.XXVII

La voye auxelle l'vne fur l'autre forniz²
Du muy defer hor mis braue & geneft,
L'efcript d'empereur le fenix³
Veu en celuy ce qu'à nul autre n'eft.

The auxiliary way, one arch upon another. Le Muy deserted except for the brave one and his twin. The writing of the emperor of the phoenix seen by him, but to no other.

An impossible quatrain, probably set in Provence. The aqueduct may be the one that runs from the river Saigne to Fréjus. A jennet *(geneft)* is a small, black horse. But who is the Phoenix Emperor?

---

¹*es.* alternative reading *os*, bones. O.F. *ez* means planks or boards.
²*forniz.* A.F. an arch or brothel. I take it in the first meaning.
³*fenix.* Phoenix or Phoenecian.

Century VIII
VIII.XXVIII

Les fimulachres d'or & d'argent enflez,
Qu'apres le rapt au lac furent gettez
Au defcouuert eftaincts tous & troublez.
Au marbre efcript prefcripz intergetez.

The copies of gold and silver inflated
which after the theft never thrown into the
lake. At their discovery all is exhausted
and dissipated by the debt. All scrips and
bonds will be wiped out.

Could this quatrain possibly describe monetary inflation? In Nostradamus' day only gold, silver and copper was used as coinage. Paper money, _les fimulachres d'or & d'argent enflez,_ did not exist. How well this quatrain applies to the twentieth century.

Century VIII
VIII.XXIX

Au quart pillier lon facre[1] à Saturne.
Par tremblant terre & deluge fendu
Soubz l'edifice Saturnin trouuee vrne,
D'or Capion rauy & puis rendu.

At the fourth pillar which they dedicate to
Saturn, split by earthquake and by blood.
Under Saturn's building an urn is found.
Gold carried off by Caepio and then re-
stored.

This is an odd quatrain. Saturn's building presumably means a temple dedicated to him, or possibly the famous church of Saint Saturnin (Sernin) at Toulouse. Caepio was a Roman consul involved in the sacking of Toulouse in 106 B.C. The treasure he found never reached Rome, for which reason Caepio was impeached and expelled from the Senate. Does Nostradamus indicate that he knows where the treasure really ended up?

Century VIII
VIII.XXX

Dedans Tholoze non loing de Beluezer
Faifant vn puys loing, palais
_   d'efpactacle_
Trefor trouué vn chacun ira vexer,
Et en deux locz tout & pres del
_   vafacle.[2]_

In Toulouse, not far from Beluzer, mak-
ing a deep pit, a palace of spectacle. The
treasure found will vex everyone in two
places, near the Basacle.

[1] _facre._ O.F., to dedicate.
[2] _vafacle._ Basacle is the name of mill section of Toulouse and also the castle which protects the main bridge and gate to the city.

Beluzer is as yet unidentified by all of Nostradamus' commentators. Does this quatrain, again with the theme of treasure, follow upon VIII.XXIX? It is just possible that these two quatrains may still be unfulfilled.

Century VIII

VIII.XXXI

Premier grand fruit le prince de Pefquiere *Mais puis viendra bien & cruel malin,* *Dedans Venife perdra fa gloire fiere* *Et mys à mal par plus ioyue Celin.*	*The first great fruit of the prince of Peschiera; then will come a cruel and wicked man. In Venice he will lose his proud glory and is led into evil by the younger Selin.*

When Mussolini led the Fascists in revolt in Italy the first prize that fell to him was the prince of Peschiera, Victor Emmanuel himself, who there performed one of the most honorable acts of his reign. The prince had gone to the front after Caporetto, taking command in person, rejecting all proposals of surrender and determined to fight it out. Their council of war was also held at Peschiera. The cruel one is Mussolini, who will lose his glory in Venice and be delivered to the hands of the younger Selin. Selin normally means crescent or moon. If Nostradamus foresaw some connection between Italy and Islam after the time of Mussolini, he is wrong. But the rest of the quatrain fits nicely.

Century VIII

VIII.XXXII

Garde toy roy Gaulois de ton nepueu *Qui fera tant que ton vnique filz* *Sera meurtry à Venus faifant voeu,* *Accompaigné de nuict que trois & fix.*	*French king, beware of your nephew who will intrigue so much that your only son will be murdered while making his vows to Venus. Accompanied at night by thousand and six.*

An apparently clear quatrain, but I think a failed one. It seems unlikely to belong to the future.

Century VIII

VIII.XXXIII

Le grand naiftra de Veronne &
  Vincence,
Qui portera vn furnom bien indigne.
Qui à Venife vouldra faire vengeance,
Luy mefme prins homme du guet &
  figne.

The great one who will be born of Verona and Vincenza carries a very unworthy surname. He who at Venice will wish to take vengeance, himself taken by a man of the watch and sign.

   This quatrain seems to follow, partly at least, from the last. Northern Italy is indicated by the names of Verona and Vincenza. The one born *vn furnom bien indigne* is Mussolini; the word literally means muslin-maker, one of Italy's more lowly professions. The vengeance he desired was against those powers who frustrated his dream of *Mare Nostrum.*

Century VIII

VIII.XXXIIII

Apres victoire du Lyon au Lyon
Sus la montaigne de IVRA Secatombe[1]
Delues[2] & brodes[3] feptieme million
Lyon, Vlme à Maufol mort & tombe.

After the victory of the Lion over the Lion there will be great slaughter on the mountains of Jura. Floods, and dark-skinned people, the seventh million. Lyons, Ulm, at the mausoleum death and the tomb.

   The Jura mountains run through Franche-Comté. It belonged to the Hapsburgs until 1674. But the key word *brodes,* the dark-skinned people, the people of Africa, brings this quatrain into the twentieth century. The appalling flooding throughout Sudan, Bangladesh and Ethiopia during 1988 may well eventually leave a total death roll of seven million. Concomitant with floods is disease and this too will decimate the afflicted peoples. Nostradamus, the doctor, would know that well. The last line is unclear.

---

[1] *Secatombe.* a misprint for *hecatombe,* a tomb.
[2] *Delues.* possibly from L. *diluvis,* flood, destruction.
[3] *brodes.* O.F. *brode,* black, brown, decadent.

Century VIII

VIII.XXXV

Dedans l'entree de Garonne & Bayſe
Et la foreſt non loing de Damazan
Du marfaues[1] gelees, puis greſle & bize
Dordonnois gelle[2] par erreur de mezan.[3]

At the entrance to Garonne and Baise, the forest not far from Damazan. Discoveries of the frozen sea, then hail and north winds. Frost in the Dardonnais through the mistake of the month.

I cannot decipher this quatrain. It describes cold and unseasonable weather.

Century VIII

VIII.XXXVI

Sera commis conte oingdue aduché[4]
De Saulne & fainct Aulbin &
Bell'oeuure[5]
Pauer de marbre de tours loing eſpluché
Non Bleteram reſiſter & chef d'oeuure.

It will be committed against the anointed bought from the Saulnier, Saint Aubin and Bell'oeuvre. To pave with marble taken from distant towers, not to resist Bleteram and his masterpiece.

Bleteram is yet another of the so-far uncoded Nostradamus words, unless it stands for Bletterans, again in the Franche-Comté belonging to the Hapsburgs until 1674. (See VIII.XXXIIII.) An enigmatic, difficult quatrain.

Century VIII

VIII.XXXVII

La forterefſe aupres de la Tamiſe
Cherra par lors le Roy dedans ferré,
Aupres du pont fera veu en chemiſe
I'n deuant mort, puis dans le fort
barré.

The fortress near the Thames will fall when the king is locked up inside. He will be seen in his shirt, near the bridge, one facing death, then barred within the fortress.

This is one of Nostradamus' more exciting quatrains and a reasonably exact one too. After his defeat in 1648, Charles I was taken captive to Windsor Castle, overlooking the Thames. He remained there until January 9, 1649. The castle did fall, in a sense, because

---

[1]*marfaues.* compound word. O.F. *mar,* sea and O.F. *saue,* discovery
[2]*gelle.* O.F. frost.
[3]*mezan.* L. *mensa,* a month, by metathesis.
[4]*aduché.* A.Pr. *aducha,* bought.
[5]*Bell'oeuure.* an enigmatic place name or just literally a "beautiful work."

it came into the hands of the Parliamentarians. After his trial, Charles was beheaded, dressed in a white shirt, on January 30, 1649. The nearest bridge would be London Bridge, as Westminster Bridge was not built at that time. This quatrain connects with IX.XLIX.

Century VIII
VIII.XXXVIII

Le Roy de Bloys dans Auignon regner
Vne autre foys le peuple emonopolle,[1]
Dedans' le Rofne par murs fera baigner
Iufques à cinq le dernier pres de Nolle.[2]

The king of Blois will reign in Avignon;
once again the people covered with blood.
In the Rhône he will swim near the walls.
Up to fire, the last one near Nolle.

I leave this one to the reader. A king of all France will cause war and bloodshed. But I cannot connect this with the last two lines.

Century VIII
VIII.XXXIX

Qu'aura efté par prince Bizantin,
Sera tollu par prince de Tholoze.
La foy de Foix par le chief Tholentin,
Luy faillira ne refufant l'efpoufe.

He who will have been for the Byzantine
priest will be taken away by the prince of
Toulouse. The faith of Foix through the
leader of Tolentino will fail him, not
refusing the bride.

The difficulty here is to identify the people in this quatrain. The Byzantine priest may be either a sultan, or a Moslem leader. The prince of Toulouse may be its archbishop, or any number of the hereditary Montmorency family. As Tolentino is part of the Papal States, the leader may be the Pope. Foix belonged to the house of Navarre.

---

[1]*emonopolle.* A compound word of Nostradamus' invention. Probably derived from *aimopnoos,* bloodthirsty, or *aimatopotes,* blood-drinker.

[2]*Nolle.* a proper name? Possibly Nola in Italy, but it does not seem to fit the context.

Century VIII

VIII.XL

Le fang du Iufte par Taurer la
   daurade,[1]
Pour fe venger contre les Saturnins[2]
Au nouueau lac plongeront la
   maynade,[3]
Puis marcheront contre les Albanins.[4]

The blood of the just for Taur and la Dorade, in order to avenge itself against the Saturnins. They will immerse the band in the new lake. Then they will march against Alba.

If one accepts that these two churches stand for Toulouse, the quatrain seems to imply that the inhabitants are fighting both Calvinism as well as a Spanish attack led by the duke of Alba. An unsatisfactory quatrain.

Century VIII

VIII.XLI

Efleu fera Renad ne fonnant mor,
Faifant le faint public viuant pain
   d'orge,[5]
Tyranniser apres tant à vn cop[6]
Mettant à pied des plus grans fus la
   gorge.

A fox will be elected without speaking one word, appearing saintly in public. Living on barley bread afterwards he will suddenly become a tyrant, putting his foot on the throats of the greatest men.

Napoleon III was known as *le Taciturne* when elected president, and was certainly as cunning as a fox. He fulfills line 3 when he executed his coup d'état in December, 1851, to make way for the Second Empire. He used his power in the way described in lines 3 and 4.

---

[1] *Taurer la daurade.* Two churches in Toulouse, Notre Dame du Taur and Notre Dame la Daurade?

[2] *Saturnins.* Those of Saturn or of St. Sernin.

[3] *maynade.* A.Pr. *marinada,* a) band of people, b) household, servants

[4] *Albanins.* Probably the troops of the duke of Alba, or just possibly Albanian mercenaries.

[5] *viuant pain d'orge.* This has a secondary meaning, to feather one's nest, very appropriate in this context.

[6] *cop. coup. à un coup,* at a blow.

Century VIII

VIII.XLII

*Par auarice, par force & violence
Viendra vexer les siens chiefz d'Orleans,
Pres faint Memire affault & refiftance.
Mort dans fa tante diront qu'il dort
    leans.*

*Through avarice, through force and vio-
lence the chief of Orléans will come to vex
his supporters. Near St. Memire, assault
and resistance. Dead in his tent, they will
say he is asleep inside.*

If one can read St. Memire as St. Merri—it is otherwise unidentifi-
able—Louis Philippe d'Orléans will engage in combat around Saint
Merri. That Nostradamus reached the title of Orléans is interesting
because the founder of the house was the brother of Louis XIII, born
long after Nostradamus' death. The cryptic last line may just mean
he slept like the dead in his tent after the battle, or possibly something I cannot decipher.

Century VIII

VIII.XLIII

*Par le decide[1] de deux chofes baftars
Nepueu du fang occupera le regne
Dedans lectoyre feront les coups de dars
Nepueu par peur pleira l'enfeigne.*

*Through the fall of the two bastards crea-
tures the nephew of the blood will occupy
the throne. Within Lectoure there will be
blows of lances, the nephew, through fear
will fold up his standard.*

Yet again the nephew. The only important nephew in French history appeared over 300 years after Nostradamus' death. He was Louis
Napoleon, son of King Louis of Holland, who was the brother of
Napoleon I. The two bastards who fall may be the governments of
Louis Philippe and that of the Second Republic. *Lectoyre* may be an
anagram of *Le Torcey,* a suburb of Sedan, where, in 1870, Louis
Napoleon was defeated by the Germans and Prussians. He ordered
a flag of surrender to be hung on Sedan's church and then on its
citadel, *par peur pleira l'enfeigne,* after which the emperor formally
surrendered to the Germans at Douchery, two miles from Le Torcey.

[1]*decide.* L. *decidere,* to fall.

Century VIII

VIII.XLIIII

Le procrée naturel dogmion,[1]
De fept à neuf du chemin deftorner
A roy de longue & amy aumi hom,
Doit à Nauarre fort de PAV profterner.

The natural offspring of Ogmios will turn off the road between seven and nine. To the king, long friend of the half-man, Navarre must destroy the fort at Pau.

Ogmios turns up in various quatrains but has never been properly identified in other than his classical form. An unclear quatrain.

Century VIII

VIII.XLV

La main efcharpe & la iambe bandee,
Longs puis nay de Calais portera
Au mot du guet la mort fera tardee,
Puis dans le temple à Pafques faignera.

With his hand in a sling and his leg bandaged, the younger brother of Calais will reach far. At the word of the watch, death will be delayed. Then he will bleed at Easter in the Temple.

I cannot make anything of this quatrain.

Century VIII

VIII.XLVI

Pol menfolee mourra trois lieuës du Rofne,[2]
Fuis les deux prochains tarafc deftrois:
Car Mars fera le plus horrible trofne,
De coq & d'aigle de France freres trois.

Paul the Celibate will die three leagues from Rome, the two nearest flee the oppressed monster. When Mars will take up his horrible throne, the Cock and the Eagle, France and the three brothers.

Pope Paul VI died at his villa exactly three miles from Rome in 1978. The linking with a pope and three brothers helps place this quatrain in the second half of this century. Wars will be raging which Nostradamus seems to feel will become worldwide, *Car Mars fera le plus horrible trofne.* This appears to indicate a leading up to the Millennium (see also V.LXXVIII). Apparently, France, the *coq,* will have an important rôle to play. The Eagle here seems to stand for the USA through the linkage with the three brothers. (See I.XXVI, II.LCV.)

---

[1]*dogmion.* Ogmios, the Celtic Hercules.
[2]*Rofne.* Misspelling of Rome or Rhône.

Century VIII

VIII.XLVII

Lac Trefmenien portera tefmoignage,
Des coniurez ferez dedans Peroufe,
I'n defpolle contrefera le fage,
Tuant Tedefq de fterne & minufe.

Lake Trasimene will bear witness of the
conspirators locked up in Perugia. A fool
will imitate the wise one, killing the Teu-
tons, destroying and cutting to pieces.

I can offer no explanation for this quatrain.

Century VIII

VIII.XLVIII

Saturne en Cancer, Iupiter auec Mars,
Dedans Feurier Chaldondon[1] faluaterre.
Sault Caftallon[2] affailly de trois pars,
Pres de Verbiefque[3] conflit mortelle
guerre.

Saturn in Cancer, Jupiter with Mars in
February,   Chaldondon   Salvatierra.
Sierra Morena besieged on three sides near
Verbiesque, war and mortal conflict.

An incomplete astrological dating with two undeciphered names,
Chaldondon and Verbiesque. A very difficult verse.

Century VIII

VIII.XLIX

Satur. au beuf ioue en l'eau, Mars en
fleiche,
Six de Feurier mortalité donra,
Ceux de Tardaigne[4] à Bruges fi grand
breche,
Qu'à Ponterofo[5] chef Barbarin mourra.

Saturn in Taurus, Jupiter in Aquarius,
Mars in Sagittarius. The sixth of February brings death. Those of Tardaigne, so
great a breach at Bruges, the barbarian
chief will die at Ponteroso.

According to Wöllner this conjunction occurred in 1736 and will
not happen again in the foreseeable future. But McCann (1942) says
that it occurred on February 6, 1971, so Nostradamus seems to have
been wrong on both counts.

[1]Chaldondon? L. Chaldons. soothsayer, otherwise incomprehensible.
[2]Sault Caftallon. L. Saltus Castulonensis, Sierra Morena.
[3]Verbiefque. an unsolved name.
[4]Tardaigne. Misspelling of Sardaingne, Sardinia.
[5]Ponterofo. Unidentified—may mean the red bridge.

Century VIII

VIII.L

La peftilence l'entour de Capadille,
Vn autre faim pres de Sagont
  s'apprefte:
Le cheualier baftard de bon fenille,
Au grand de Thunes fera trancher la
  tefte.

The plague around Capellades, another
famine is near Sagunto. The knightly bastard of the good old man will cause the
great one of Tunis to lose his hand.

This quatrain, despite its apparent confusion, is a very successful hit for Nostradamus. In 1573, Don John of Austria, the bastard son of the old Charles V, recaptured Tunis for his half brother, Philip of Spain. Although there is no definite record of a famine, Spain was suffering from sporadic outbursts of endemic plague from 1570 to 1574.

Century VIII

VIII.LI

Le Bizantin faifant oblation,
Apres auoir Cordube à foy reprinfe:
Son chemin long repos pamplation, [1]
Mer paffant proy par la Colongna [2]
  prinfe.

The Byzantine makes an oblation after
having taken back Córdoba. Long rest on
his road, the vines cut down, at sea the
passing prey captured near the pillar.

In this quatrain Nostradamus appears to predict that the leader of Constantinople will invade Spain near Córdoba. Córdoba belonged to the Arabs until 1031 and then to the Moslems until 1236. Line 4 seems to suggest that this Turkish (?) leader will be caught near the Pillars of Hercules, Gibraltar. A retroactive quatrain.

[1] *Pamplation.* dubious. Possibly L. *pampinatio,* to cut vines.
[2] *Colongna. Collones d'Hercule,* Gibraltar.

Century VIII

VIII.LII

Le roy de Bloys dans Auignon regner,
D'amboife & feme¹ viendra le long de
Lyndre
Ongle à Poytiers fainctes aefles ruiner
Deuant Boni.²

The king of Blois to reign in Avignon,
from Amboise and Seme, the length of the
Indre. Claws at Poitiers, holy wings
ruined before Boni . . .

Line 1 is identical to the first line of VIII.XXXVIII. The unfinished last line suggests that this is probably another quatrain "rescued" by Chavigny, following upon the unfinished version of Century VII. Alternatively it may have been cut by a censor as heretical, but this seems less likely. Without the final version it is difficult to learn much from this quatrain.

Century VIII

VIII.LIII

Dedans Bolongne vouldra lauer fes
fautes,
Il ne pourra au temple du foleil,
Il volera faifant chofes fi haultes
En hierarchie n'en fut oncq vn pareil.

Within Boulogne he will want to wash
away his misdeeds which he cannot (do)
at the temple of the Sun. He will fly away
doing very great things. In the hierarchy
he never had an equal.

Many commentators apply this to Napoleon by reading Bolongne as Boulogne, but there is just a possibility that it may mean Bologna in the Papal States. Tradition held that Westminster Abbey, which Napoleon was unable to enter by right of conquest, was built on the Temple of Apollo, destroyed by an earthquake in A.D. 154. Napoleon flew so high as to think of taking both England and Russia. He had no equal during his lifetime.

Century VIII

VIII.LIIII

Soubz la colleur du traicte mariage,
Fait magnanime par grand Chyren
felin,
Quintin, Arras recouurez au voyage
D'efpaignolz fait fecond banc macelin.

Under the color of the marriage treaty, a
magnanimous act by the Chyren Selin. St.
Quentin and Arras recovered on the journey. By the Spanish a second butcher's
bench is held.

¹*feme.?* the Seine. Otherwise not identified.
²*Boni . . .* incomplete line.

I cannot explain this quatrain nor the mysterious reference to Chyren Selin.

Century VIII

VIII.LV

Entre deux fleuues fe verra enferré,
Tonneaux & caques vnis à paffer outre,
Huict pontz rompus chef à tant enferré
Enfans parfaictz font iugutez en
   coultre. [1]

He will find himself shut in between two rivers, casks and barrels joined to cross beyond. Eight bridges broken, their chief run through so many times. Children's throats slit by the knife.

I cannot decipher this quatrain.

Century VIII

VIII.LVI

La bande foible le terre occupera
Ceux du hault lieu feront horribles crys,
Le gros troppeau d'eftre coin troublera,
Tombe pres D. nebro defcouuers les
   efcris.

The weak band will occupy the land. Those of high places will make dreadful cries. The large herd of the outer corner troubled, near Edinburgh it falls, discovered by the writings.

D. nebro is taken as meaning Edinburgh through the phonetic pun "Edinbro." If so, this quatrain describes the Battle of Dunbar, which took place twenty-five miles east of the city. Charles II landed in Scotland in 1650. The Highlanders, line 1, were more numerous than the Cromwellians, but their position was weaker. The phrase *eftre en coin* is interesting because before the battle the Scots boasted that they had the Cromwellians cornered "in a pound." The Cromwellians routed the Scots on September 3, 1650. Could line 4 be explained by the fact that Cromwell took possession of all the papers in the Scottish War Office?

[1] *coultre.* O.F. knife.

Century VIII
VIII.LVII

De fouldar fimple paruiendra en empire,
De robe courte paruiendra à la longue
Vaillant aux armes en eglife ou plus
  pyre,
Vexer les preftres comme l'eau fait
  l'efponge.

From simple soldier he will attain to Em-
pire, from the short robe he will grow into
the long. Brave in arms, much worse to-
wards the Church, he vexes the priests as
water fills a sponge.

This quatrain is an excellent description of Napoleon's career. From a simple lieutenant he attained to government of the French Empire. He exchanged his short robe of Consul for the long robes of Imperial Majesty. But, although brave in battle, he mishandled the Church and troubled the priests by the abolition of the clergy. An explicit quatrain.

Century VIII
VIII.LVIII

Regne en querelle aux freres diuifé,
Prendre les armes & le nom
  Britannique
Tiltre Anglican fera tard aduifé,
Surprins de nuict mener à l'air
  Gallique.

A kingdom divided by two quarreling
brothers to take the arms and the name of
Britain. The Anglican title will be advised
to watch out, surprised by night, led into
the French air.

Since Nostradamus' death there have been no brothers fighting for the English throne with the loser fleeing to France. The nearest this quatrain has come to fulfillment was when James II and his Anglican son-in-law, William of Orange, came to open disagreement in 1668. The Anglican Church may have exerted its influence upon James II. He certainly did flee to France to "take the Gallic air."

Century VIII
VIII.LIX

Par deux fois hault, par deux fois mis à
  bas
L'orient auffi l'occident foyblira
Son aduerfaire apres plufieurs combats,
Par mer chaffé en befoing faillira.

Twice put up and twice cast down the
East will also weaken the West. Its adver-
sary, after several battles, chased by sea
will fail at time of need.

This quatrain seems to describe the geopolitical situation of the twentieth century better than any other. It appears that the man of the East, possibly the Third Antichrist, will make two violent attacks on Western powers, but finally the East will prove the weaker at sea against the West. Certainly a futuristic quatrain.

Century VIII

VIII.LX

Premier en Gaule, premier en Romanie,
Par mer & terre aux Angloys & Parys
Merueilleux faitz par celle grand mefnie
Violant terax perdra le NORLARIS.

First in Gaul, first in Romania, over land and sea against the English and Paris. Marvelous deeds by that great violent troop, the wild beast will lose Lorraine.

Napoleon III was the only French leader to lose the Lorraine, but the rest of the quatrain does not fit him very well. James Laver ascribes it to Napoleon I saying that he can be described as the first in France and Rome. Perhaps this is a split quatrain or Nostradamus confused the two men, seeing them as one?

Century VIII

VIII.LXI

Iamais par le descouurement[1] du iour
Ne paruiendra au figne fceptrifere[2]
Que tous fes fieges ne foyent en feiour,
Portant au coq don du TAG[3] amifere.

Never by the revelation of daylight will he attain the mark of the scepter bearer. Until all his sieges are at rest, bringing to the Cock the gift of the armed legion.

The Cock bearing the gift of arms symbolizes France, although it was an obscure symbol until adopted by the Revolutionaries. Most commentators apply this quatrain to Napoleon III. Although I am not happy with this interpretation, I can find none better.

Century VIII

VIII.LXII

Lors qu'on verra expiler[4] le faint temple,
Plus grand du rofne leurs facrez prophaner
Par eux naiftra peftilence fi ample,
Roy fuit iniufte ne fera condamner.

When one sees the holy temple plundered, the greatest of the Rhône profaning their sacred things. Because of them a very great pestilence will appear. The king, unjust, will not condemn them.

---

[1]*descouurement.* O.F. discovery.
[2]*fceptrifere.* L. scepter-bearing, royal.
[3]*TAG.* variant in other editions, *tagma,* a body of soldiers.
[4]*expiler.* L. *expilare,* to rob, plunder.

A very general quatrain which I cannot relate to anything specific.

Century VIII
VIII.LXIII

*Quant l'adultere bleffé fans coup aura
Meurdry la femme & le filz par defpit,
Femme affoumee l'enfant eftranglera:
Huit captifz prins, s'eftouffer fans
   respit.*

When the adulterer wounded without a blow will have murdered his wife and son out of spite. His wife knocked down he will strangle the child. Eight captives taken, choked beyond help.

Again, too general a quatrain to identify.

Century VIII
VIII.LXIIII

*Dedans les Ifles les enfans tranfportez,
Les deux de fept feront en defefpoir,
Ceux du terrouer¹ en feront fupportez,
Nom pelle² prins des ligues fuy l'efpoir.*

The infants transported to the islands two out of seven will be in despair. Those of the soil will be supported by it. The name pelle taken, the hope of the leagues fails.

Most twentieth century commentators apply this to modern Britain besieged by the Nazis in the Second World War. But this does not really explain the seven satisfactorily, nor the undeciphered *pelle*.

Century VIII
VIII.LXV

*Le vieux fruftré du principal efpoir,
Il paruiendra au chef de fon empire:
Vingt mois tiendra le regne à grand
   pouuoir,
Tiran cruel en delaiffant vn pire.*

The old man disappointed in his main hope will attain to the leadership of his Empire. Twenty months he will hold rule with great force, a cruel tyrant, giving way to one worse.

The twenty months seem to be the key to this quatrain. If the reader accepts, as I do, that most of Nostradamus' general quatrains refer to France, this may well refer to that country in 1940. In July of that year a rump session of the French Assembly invested Pétain with plenary powers until a new constitution could be formed. After increasing pressure from the Germans to collaborate, he handed over most of his powers to Laval twenty months later, in April 1942.

¹*terrouer*. O.F. soil, land, ground.
²*pelle*. This has never been deciphered. Perhaps Garencières got closest with his suggestion of Montpellier.

Century VIII

VIII.LXVI

Quand l'efcriture D.M.[1] trouuee,
Et caue antique à lampe defcouuerte,
Loy, Roy, & Prince Vlpian[2] efprouuee,
Pauillon Royne & Duc fous la
* couuerte.*

When the inscription D.M. is found in the ancient cave, revealed by a lamp. Law, the king, and Prince Ulpian tried, the queen and duke in the pavilion under cover.

Many commentators have suggested ingenious solutions for D.M. but, as I say in the footnote, it is simply the equivalent of "Here lies . . ." on any English tombstone, "In the hands of the Gods." James Laver takes it to mean *du manuscript.* This probably ties in with the puzzling quatrain of IX.LXXXIV.

Century VIII

VIII.LXVII

PAR. CAR. NERSAF, à ruine grand
* difcorde,*
Ne l'vn ne l'autre n'aura election,
Nerfaf du peuple aura amour &
* concorde,*
Ferrare, Collonne grande protection.

PARIS, CARCASSONNE, FRANCE ruined in great disharmony, neither one nor the other will be elected. France will have the love and good will of the people. Ferrara, Colonna, great protection.

PAR. and *CAR.* probably stand for Paris and Carcassonne but *NERSAF* is not a very good anagram for France. Although Ferrara was joined with the Franco-Papal troops fighting Spain in 1557, Colonna was always firmly pro-Spanish. The key to this quatrain lies in the word *NERSAF.*

Century VIII

VIII.LXVIII

Vieux Cardinal par le ieufne deceu,
Hors de fa charge fe verra desarmé,
Arles ne monftres double foit aperceu,
Et Liqueduct & le Prince embaufmé.

The old cardinal is deceived by the young one, he will find himself disarmed, out of his position. Do not show, Arles, that the double has been understood. Both Lique-duct and the prince embalmed.

---

[1]*D.M.* Probably stands for the Latin inscription *Diis Manibus,* which was put on many Roman tombstones.
[2]*Vlpian.* Ulpius is a Roman name.

This is an excellent quatrain of which the key word is *Liqueduct*. Cardinal Richelieu was supported by the young Cinq Mars, lost the favor of Louis XIII and had to resign. But at Arles, says the quatrain, he will receive a copy of the treaty with Spain signed by Cinq Mars and the king's brother in 1642. Richelieu tells the king of this treachery. Although very ill, he travels to Paris on a barge, *Liqueduct,* led on the water. The cardinal died at the end of 1642 and the king five months later. As Nostradamus says, both bodies were embalmed.

Century VIII

VIII.LXIX

Aupres du ieune le vieux ange baiffer,
Et le viendra furmonter à la fin:
Dix ans efgaux au plus vieux rabaiffer,
De trois deux l'vn l'huitiefme feraphin.

Beside the young one the old angel falls and will come to rise above him at the end. Ten years equal to most, the old one falls again, of three, two, one, the eighth seraphim.

This obscure quatrain seems to describe the rivalry of favorites.

Century VIII

VIII.LXX

Il entrera vilain, mefchant, infame
Tyrannifant la Mefopotamie,
Tous amys fait d'adulterine d'ame.
Tertre horrible noir de phifonomie.

He will enter, wicked, unpleasant, infamous, tyrannizing over Mesopotamia. All friends made by the adulterous woman. The land dreadful and black of aspect.

Mesopotamia is often used to describe Avignon, also between two rivers, at the confluence of the Rhône and the Durance. If this is so, the villain of this obscure quatrain would be the cardinal legate in Avignon, governing as the Pope's deputy.

Century VIII

VIII.LXXI

Croiftra le nombre fi grand des
   aftronomes
Chaffez, bannis & liures cenfurez,
L'an mil fix cens & fept par facre
   glomes
Que nul aux facres ne feront asseurez.

The number of astrologers will grow so great that they will be driven out, banned, and their books censored, in the year 1607 by sacred assemblies, so that none will be safe from the holy ones.

This dating appears totally successful when reading other commentators who apply it to a Council of Malines of 1607, which was said to have banished astrology. But I can find no record of this council at all. I think this is a case of prophecy fulfilling itself. It was invented to meet the prediction. Therefore, despite the dating, this quatrain is a failure.

Century VIII
VIII.LXXII

Champ Perufin d'lenorme deffaite
Et le conflit tout au pres de Rauenne,
Paffage facre lors qu'on fera la fefte,
Vainqueur vaincu cheual manger la
    venne.

Oh, what a great defeat on the battlefield of Perugia; the conflict very close to Ravenna. A holy passage when they will celebrate the feast, the conqueror banished to eat horse meat.

This is probably a retrospective quatrain, describing an event which had already occurred when Nostradamus wrote the *Prophéties*. Both Perugia and Ravenna were Papal States and this quatrain describes accurately enough the victory of Gaston de Foix at Ravenna in 1512.

Century VIII
VIII.LXXIII

Soldat Barbare le grand Roy frappera,
Iniuftement non eflongné de mort,
L'auare mere du fait caufe fera
Coniurateur & regne en grand remort.

The king is struck by a barbarian soldier unjustly, not far from death. The greedy ones will be the cause of the deed, conspirator and realm in great remorse.

If used correctly, *barbare* refers to the pirates of Barbary, Algeria, but Nostradamus used it frequently to denote Moslems and others not of the Christian faith. It is otherwise unclear.

Century VIII
VIII.LXXIIII

En terre neufue bien auant Roy entré
Pendant fubges luy viendront faire
    acueil,
Sa perfidie aura tel recontré
Qu'aux citadins lieu de fefte & recueil.

Far before a king enters into a new land, the subjects will come to bid him welcome. His treachery will have such an effect that to its citizens it is a reception instead of a festival.

The new land, *terre neufue,* is an interesting phrase because it was one of the names for the newly found land of America in Nostradamus' day. If the USA is indicated, this verse indicates that a world leader comes to that country and is given an excellent reception, whereas the whole time the guest is planning treachery.

Could this refer to Gorbachev? Or is it still a futuristic quatrain?

Century VIII

VIII.LXXV

Le pere & filz feront meurdris enfemble *Le prefecteur dedans fon pauillon* *La mere à Tours du filz ventre aura* *enfle.* *Caiche verdure de feuilles papillon.*	The father and son will be murdered together, the leader within his pavilion. The mother at Tours will have her belly swollen with a son. A verdure chest with little pieces of paper.

The first line of this quatrain is quite definite: A father and son will be murdered together. It cannot apply to France, as no French king and dauphin have been assassinated together. In the case of Louis XVI, there was a space of over two years between the king's death and the presumed death of his young son. Neither was there any pregnant widow at Tours involved with the family. The most important father and son assassination outside France occurred in 1908 when Carlos I and Louis Philippe of Portugal were killed. But the rest of the quatrain still remains unexplained.

Century VIII

VIII.LXXVI

Plus Macelin que roy en Angleterre
Lieu obfcur nay par force aura
    l'empire:
Lafche fans foy fans loy faignera terre,
Son temps s'approche fi pres que ie
    foufpire.
	More of a butcher than a king in England, born of obscure rank he will gain empire through force. Coward, without faith, without law, he will bleed the land. His time approaches so near that I could sigh.

Nostradamus' idea of cosmic time was pretty exact when he predicted the advent of Cromwell (1599–1656), thirty years after his own death. Cromwell's description as "more of a butcher than a king" is very apt when one considers the bloodshed of the Civil War. He was a Protestant so Nostradamus regards him, as always, as a heretic. Cromwell came from comparatively humble origins and attained his position through military force, *par force aura l'empire.* The reference to his being a coward *(lafche)* is interesting. Cromwell was so afraid of being assassinated that he was reported to wear an undervest of chain mail.

Century VIII

VIII.LXXVII

L'antechrift trois bien toft anniehiliez,
Vingt & fept ans fang durera fa
*   guerre.*
Les heretiques mortz, captifs, exilez,
Sang corps humain eau rogie grefler
*   terre.*

The Third Antichrist soon annihilates everything, twenty-seven years of blood his
war will last. The unbelievers dead, captive, exiled with blood, human bodies,
water and red hail covering the earth.

Nostradamus envisages three separate Antichrists. The first appears to be Napoleon, the second Hitler and the Third is still to come. Line 1 has an ambiguous reading: It may be interpreted as "the third Antichrist" or the "Antichrist soon annihilates the three." Presumably the three are the Kennedy brothers, two of whom are already dead. Perhaps the third, Edward Kennedy, is a psychological assassinee. With his removal from state politics I now consider that it is unlikely that he is considered as a political person of great depth or importance. Does it make more sense in this context to think that the Third Antichrist is a way of life? I think that Nostradamus believed it to be an actual person.

The war mentioned in the quatrain seems to be one of attrition. After the bombing of Nagasaki and Hiroshima large "black raindrops fell, full of dust," as recorded by survivors. So perhaps Nostradamus is not so far out when he speaks of *eau rogie,* the rain of blood. This last war appears to be the worst in this century and there is less than a decade before we can expect it to start. Another Millennium quatrain.

Century VIII

VIII.LXXVIII

Vn Bragamas[1] auec la langue torte
Viendra des dieux le fanctuaire,
Aux heretiques il ouurira la porte
En fufcitant l'eglife militaire.

A soldier of fortune with twisted tongue
will come to the sanctuary of the gods. He
will open the door for heretics and raise up
the Church militant.

This general quatrain could be applied either to France during the Wars of Religion 1542–98, or to Germany during the Thirty Years' War 1618–48.

---

[1]*Bragamas.* O.F. broadsword or A. Pr. *Briamanso,* a soldier of fortune.

Century VIII
VIII.LXXIX

Qui par fer pere perdra nay de
  Nonnaire[1]
De Gorgon fur la fera fang perfetant[2]
En terre eftrange fera fi tout de taire,
Qui bruflera luy mesme & fon enfant.

He who loses his father by the sword, born in a nunnery, upon this Gorgon's blood will conceive anew. In a strange land he will do everything to be silent, he who will burn both himself and his child.

The legendary Gorgon was a monster who turned everyone who gazed upon her into stone. Hugh Allen, in his book on Nostradamus (1943) applies this quatrain to himself (page 12). I can make no sense of it.

Century VIII
VIII.LXXX

Des innocens le fang de vefue & vierge.
Tant de maulx faitz par moyen fe
  grand Roge
Saintz fimulachres trempez en ardant
  cierge
De frayeur crainte ne verra nul que
  boge.

The blood of innocents, widow and virgin so many evils committed by the great Red one. Holy images placed over burning candles, terrified by fear more will be seen to move.

The great Red one of line 2 must stand for a revolution, but it is difficult to decide whether it refers to the French or Russian revolution. I am inclined to accept the latter, as Nostradamus describes the French Revolution elsewhere by the "tricolor." Line 1 would therefore refer to the deaths of the czar, czarina, and their children. Line 3 hints vaguely at the influence of the Orthodox Church through Rasputin.

Century VIII
VIII.LXXXI

Le neuf empire en defolation,
Sera changé du pole aquilonaire.
De la Sicile viendra l'efmotion
Troubler l'emprife à Philip tributaire.

The new empire in desolation will be changed from the Northern Pole. From Sicily will come such trouble that it will bother the enterprise tributary to Philip.

[1]*Nonnaire.* Low L. *nonneria,* nunnery.
[2]*perfetant.* L. *(super) fetens,* to conceive while pregnant.

The first two lines of this quatrain sound contemporary by the sheer scope of their context. A ravaged empire moves itself and its civilization southwards. Could this be after the war in the North mentioned in previous quatrains? But the last two lines take us back to sixteenth century Europe. Nostradamus seems to see a Hapsburg civil war between Philip and Ferdinand over the division of Charles V's empire. It predicts the uprising against Philip as starting in Sicily.

Century VIII
VIII.LXXXII

Ronge long, fec faifant du bon valet,	Thin, tall and dry, playing the good valet
A la parfin n'aura que fon congie, [1]	in the end, will have nothing but his dis-
Poignant poyfon & lettres au collet	missal. Sharp poison and letters in his
Sera faifi efchappé en dangie. [2]	collar, he will be seized escaping into dan-
	ger.

Apparently a valet tries to poison his master, is caught and dismissed.

Century VIII
VIII.LXXXIII

Le plus grand voile hors du port de Zara,	The largest sail set out of the port of Zara near Byzantium, will carry out its enter-
Pres de Bifance fera fon entreprinfe,	prise. There will not be loss of family nor
D'ennemy perte & l'amy ne fera	friend; a third will turn on both with great
Le tiers à deux fera grand pille & prinfe.	pillage and capture.

This is another retroactive prophecy describing the atrocities of the Fourth Crusade in 1202. Venice agreed to cross to Egypt with the Crusaders for a large sum of money and half the plunder. The Crusaders could not raise the money so they captured Zara (then in Hungary, now in Yugoslavia). The Pope then excommunicated the whole Crusade, whereupon they sacked Constantinople (Byzantium) and set up Romania, the Roman Empire of the East.

---

[1] *congie.* F. dismissal.
[2] *dangie. dangier,* shortened for rhyme.

Century VIII
VIII.LXXXIIII

Paterne orra de la Sicile crie,
Tous les aprefts du goulphre de Triefte,
Qui s'entendra iufque à la trinacrie.[1]
De tant de voiles fuy, fuy l'horrible
   pefte.

Paterno will hear the cry from Sicily, all
the preparations in the Gulf of Trieste. It
will be heard as far as Sicily. Flee, oh flee,
so many sails, the dreaded pestilence.

This is probably a continuation of VIII.LXXXI. The Spanish Empire of the Two Sicilies owned Catonia and Paternum, and Trieste belonged to the Hapsburg branch in Venice.

Century VIII
VIII.LXXXV

Entre Bayonne & à faint Iean de Lux
Sera pofé de Mars la promottoire
Aux Hanix[2] d'Aquilon Nanar[3] hoftera
   lux,
Puis fuffocqué au lict fans adiutoire.[4]

Between Bayonne and as far as Saint
Jean de Luz will be placed the promontory
of Mars. To the Hanix of the North
Nanar will remove the light, then suffo-
cate in bed without assistance.

Nostradamus foresees a war or a war zone (Mars) between Bayonne and Saint-Jean-de-Luz in southwest France. The difficulty in interpretation lies in the words *Hanix* and *Nanar*. Another suggestion is that the promontory is Biarritz where Napoleon III, like Mars, the God of War, retired into the arms of various loving women when the north wind ceased to blow. *Hanix* might then come from the Greek, *anscisus,* without force. Napoleon died from the operation for a kidney stone, but his physical condition was weak due to his various debaucheries, and may have made him much frailer than was thought.

---

[1] *trinacrie.* Trinicia, poetic name for Italy.
[2] *Hanix.?* Gk. *anikatos,* unconquerable. Or L. *Hamaxaeci,* nomads of Northern Europe.
[3] *Nanar.* L. *nonaria,* prostitute?
[4] *adiutoire.* O.F. assistance, aid.

Century VIII

VIII.LXXXVI

Par Arnani Tholofer ville franque,
Bande infinie par le mont Adrian,
Paffe riuiere, Hurin,[1] par pont la
  planque
Bayonne entrer tous Bihoro[2] criant.

Through Emani, Tolosa and Villefran-
che, an infinite band through the moun-
tains of Adrian. It passes the river, com-
bat over the bridge for a plank. Bayonne
will be entered, all crying Bigorre.

The three towns in line 1 and the mountain of Adrian in line 2 are all close together in the southwestern tip of the Spanish Pyrenees. The only river to the north between them and Bayonne is the Bidassoa. As I have said before, *Bigorre* was the battle cry of the Huguenots of Navarre. Originally, Navarre covered the area south of the Pyrenees and north into France. It became a separate state in 1515 and was reunited with France at the accession of Henri de Navarre to the French throne, after Nostradamus' death.

Century VIII

VIII.LXXXVII

Mort confpiree viendra en plein effect,
Charge donnee & voiage de mort,
Efleu, crée, receu par fiens deffait.
Sang d'innocence deuant foy par
  remort.

A death conspired will come to its full
effect, the charge given and the voyage of
death. Elected, created, received; defeated
by his followers. With remorse, the inno-
cent blood before him.

The conspiracy by the French Revolutionaries to rob Louis XVI of both his crown and his life is successfully carried off. The change of his position to constitutional monarch and his flight to Varennes, *"the voyage of death,"* will be the cause of his death. He will be defeated by his own nation which had earlier elected him. His innocent blood will be a source of remorse to the French.

[1]*Hurin.* O.F. dispute, combat.
[2]*Bihoro. Bigorre,* the battle cry of the Huguenots of Navarre.

Century VIII
VIII.LXXXVIII

Dans la Sardeigne vn noble Roy viendra
Que ne tiendra que trois ans le royaume,
Plufieurs coulleurs auec foy coniondra,
Luy mefmes apres foin fomeil marrit[1] scome.[2]

A noble king will come to Sardinia who will rule for only three years in the kingdom. He will join several colors to himself. He himself, after taunts, care spoils slumber.

When the French Republic took most of his lands, King Charles Emmanuel IV retired to Sardinia where he reigned for only three years, *que trois ans le royaume.* He then abdicated in favor of his brother, Victor Emmanuel I. He then went on to Rome, humiliated and unhappy. He joined the Jesuits and stayed with them until his death in 1819. This was one of the few times in modern history that Sardinia had its own king and not a titular one.

Century VIII
VIII.LXXXIX

Pour ne tumber entre mains de fon oncle,
Qui fes enfans par regner trucidez[3]
Orant[4] au peuple mettant pied fur Peloncle[5]
Mort & traifné entre cheuaulx bardez.

In order not to fall into the hands of his uncle who slaughtered his children so that he could reign. Pleading with the people, putting his foot on Peloncle, dead and dragged between armored horses.

The key word to this quatrain is *Peloncle,* which so far remains indecipherable.

---

[1]*marrit.* O.F. to afflict, spoil.
[2]*scome.* L. *scoma,* scoff, taunt, jeer.
[3]*trucidez.* L. *trucidare,* to slaughter.
[4]*Orant.* L. *orans,* praying.
[5]*Peloncle.* Doubtful. Possibly Pellonia, the goddess who put enemies to flight?

Century VIII

VIII.XC

Quand des croifez vn trouué de fens
  trouble
En lieu du facre verra vn boeuf cornu
Par vierge porc fon lieu lors fera
  comble,
Par roy plus ordre ne fera fouftenu.

When those of the cross are found, their senses troubled, in place of a sacred thing he will see a horned bull. Through the virgin the place of the pig will be filled. Order will no longer be maintained by the king.

The men of the cross are either Crusaders or Nazis. The bull may stand for Taurus and the virgin for Virgo, but the rest means very little. An indecipherable quatrain.

Century VIII

VIII.XCI

Frymy[1] les champs des Rodanes[2] entrees
Ou les croyfez feront prefque vnys,
Les deux brafsieres[3] en pifces
  rencontrees
Et vn grand nombre par deluge punis.

Entered among the fields of those of the Rhône where those of the cross are almost united. Two lands meeting in Pisces and a great number punished by the flood.

Yet again, as in the last quatrain, people of the cross. The astrological conjunction here is Pisces with Venus, at a time when the Rhône is in flood.

Century VIII

VIII.XCII

Loin hors du regne mis en hazard
  voiage
Grand oft duyra pour foy l'occupera,
Le roy tiendra les fiens captif oftrage
À fon retour tout pays pillera.

Far from his kingdom sent on a dangerous journey. He will lead a great army and will hold it for himself. The king will keep his people captive and hostage. He will plunder the whole country on his return.

I had earlier thought that this quatrain was indecipherable, but now believe it may apply to Mao Tse-tung. In the 1930s Chiang Kai-Shek's Nationalist Army had tried to annihilate the Chinese Red Army. But

---

[1] *Frymy.* misprint for *parmi* in other editions, among.

[2] *Rodanes.* L. *Rhodanus,* the Rhône.

[3] *Brafsieres.* lead strings—possibly standing for Venus, who was bound to Mars by an unbreakable thread forged by Vulcan.

Mao Tse-tung led his Communist followers on the Long March, an enormous trek through the hinterlands of China. Later, he put himself in command of the Red Army and defeated the Nationalist Chinese in 1949. In the 1960s, under the title of the Cultural Revolution, he threw the whole country into disarray, *à fon retour tout pays pillera.*

Century VIII
VIII.XCIII

Sept moys fans plus obtiendra prelature
Par fon deces grand fcifme fera naistre:
Sept moys tiendra vn autre la preture
Pres de Venife paix vnion renaiftre.

For seven months, no longer, he will hold the office of prelate. Through his death a great schism will arise. For seven months another acts as prelate near Venice. Peace and union are reborn.

The only popes (*"prelature"*) to live for less than seven months after election have been Sixtus V; Urban VII, who died after two weeks; and Gregory XIV, who died after ten months, all in 1590. An interesting quatrain, but unfortunately there is no record of a schism.

Century VIII
VIII.XCIIII

Deuant le lac ou plus cher fut getté
De fept mois, & fon hoft defconfit
Seront Hyfpans par Albannois gaftez
Par delay perte en donnant le conflict.

In front of the lake where the dearest one was destroyed for seven months, his army routed. The Spaniards will be devastated by means of Alba. Through delay in giving battle, loss.

Ward applies this quatrain to the English attack on Cadiz by Essex, Howard and Raleigh in June, 1596. The word *cher* in line 1 then becomes treasure or valuables. Their ships were heavy with booty on their return from a seven-month voyage. Cadiz Bay is called a lake by Nostradamus because the root word *Gaddir,* from which Cadiz is derived, means an enclosed space. During the attack by the English, forty galleons and thirteen warships were destroyed.

What makes this quatrain so interesting is that Nostradamus foresaw the war between Spain and England, but when he wrote the countries were allies because England's queen was Mary Tudor, wife of King Philip of Spain.

Century VIII

VIII.XCV

Le feducteur fera mis en la foffe,
Et eftaché iufques à quelque temps,
Le clerc vny le chef auec fa croffe[1]
Pycante droite attraira[2] les contens.

The seducer will be placed in a ditch and will be tied up for some time. The scholar joins the chief with his cross. The sharp right (one) will draw the contented ones.

I have no interpretation for this quatrain.

Century VIII

VIII.XCVI

La fynagogue fterile fans nul fruit
Sera receu entre les infideles
De Babylon la fille du porfuit
Mifere & trifte luy trenchera les aifles.

The sterile synagogue without any fruit will be received by the infidels. The daughter of the persecuted one of Babylon. Miserable and sad they will clip her wings.

This quatrain probably describes the Jews' attitude towards Moslem countries between 1550 and 1566, which means these events mostly occurred during Nostradamus' lifetime. After the wave of persecution suffered by the Jews during this period in Christian countries, the sultan of Turkey, Suleiman the Magnificent, offered hospitality to any Jews who settled in his country, particularly in Constantinople and Salonika. One such emigré became very powerful. In 1566, the year of Nostradamus' death, Don Joseph Nassi was created duke of Naxos and became the principal adviser to Selim I.

Century VIII

VIII.XCVII

Au fin du VAR changer le pompotans,
Pres du riuage les trois beaux enfans
  naiftre.
Ruyne au peuple par aage competans
Regne au pays changer plus voir
  croiftre.

At the end of the Var the great powers change. Near the bank three beautiful children are born. Ruin to the people when they are of age. In the country the kingdom is seen to grow and change greatly.

In X.C *pompotans* stands for England, but probably does not so in this case. The river Var flows into the Mediterranean between Cannes and Nice and was the approximate border of Savoy in Nostradamus'

---

[1]*croffe.* O.F. abbey or cross?
[2]*attraira.* O.F. to draw, attract.

time. The three beautiful children may be a reference to the three Kennedy brothers who bring *ruyne,* scandal, to the USA, linking up with the other quatrains on this subject. Certainly the USA changed its power basis, Korea, withdrawal from Vietnam, etc., during their lifetimes and now its growing influence has made it one of the great world powers. Possibly the quatrain is only partially fulfilled to date?

Century VIII

VIII.XCVIII

Des gens d'eglife fang fera efpandu,
Comme de l'eau en fi grande
  abondance:
Et d'vn long temps ne fera reftanché
Ve ve[1] au clerc ruyne & doleance.

Of the churchmen the blood will pour forth as abundantly as water. For a long time it will not be restrained. Woe, woe, ruin and grief for the clergy.

Possibly another quatrain about the persecution of the clergy in France in 1792. The last line does have Jewish linguistic overtones.

Century VIII

VIII.XCIX

Par la puiffance des trois rois temporelz,
En autre lieu fera mis le faint fiege:
Où la fubftance de l'efprit corporel,
Sera remys & receu pour vray fiege.

Through the powers of the temporal kings the sacred seat will be put in another place where the substance of the body and spirit will be restored and received as a true seat.

The only occasion to date since Nostradamus' writing when the Papal See has been moved from the Vatican was when Pope Pius VI was removed by Napoleon to Valence, and died there. But there are hints in Malachy that a pope towards the end of this century will be forced from the Vatican, probably due to the advent of a World War or the coming of the Third Antichrist. Lines 3 and 4 seem to indicate a revival of religious fervor. Possibly a futuristic quatrain?

[1]*Ve ve.* L. *Vae,* alas, woe.

Century VIII

VIII.C

Pour l'abondance de larme refpandue	By the great number of tears shed, from
Du hault en bas par le bas au plus	top to bottom and from the bottom to the
hault	very top. A life is lost through a game with
Trop grande foy par ieu vie perdue,	too much faith. To die of thirst through a
De foif mourir par habondant deffault. [1]	great deficiency.

I cannot decipher this quatrain.

Century IX

IX.I

Dans la maifon du traducteur de	In the house of the translator from Bourg
Bourc [2]	letters will be found on the table. One-
Seront les lettres trouuees fus la table,	eyed, red and white haired will hold the
Bourgne, roux, blanc chanu tiendra de	course which will change for the new con-
cours,	stable.
Qui changera au nouueau conneftable.	

This is a fascinating quatrain. One of the best-known sixteenth century French scholars was Etienne de la Boétie. If *Bourc* stands for *Boétie,* then the prophecy makes some kind of sense in that the latter had a famous quarrel with the then-Constable of France, Anne de Montmorency, over the publication of a book, *La Servitude Volontaire.* Nostradamus seems to foresee that Boétie would have even more trouble with the Constable's successor, Henri de Montmorency. But this did not occur, as Boétie died four years before Anne de Montmorency in 1563. (See also IX.LXXXI.)

---

[1]The whole of line 4 is difficult to interpret. It probably means drowned, or even to drink oneself to death.

[2]*Bourc.?* Bourg, north of Bordeaux.

Century IX

IX.II

Du hault du mont Auentin voix ouye,
Vuydez vuydez de tous les deux coftez,
Du fang des rouges fera l'ire affomye, [1]
D'Arimin Prato, Columna [2] *debotez.* [3]

A voice is heard from the top of the Aven-
tine Hill. Go away, go away, on both
sides! The anger will be appeased by the
blood of the red ones. From Rimini and
Prato, Colonnna expelled.

This is yet another quatrain centered around the feuds of the Vatican States with the great Italian families, like the Colonnas and the Orsinis. In Nostradamus' time, they were allied to the Spanish and thus got deeply involved with the anti-Spanish policies of Pope Paul IV.

Century IX

IX.III

La magna vaqua [4] *à Rauenne grand*
  trouble,
Conduictz par quinze enferrez à Fornafe
A Rôme naiftre deux monftres à tefte
  double
Sang, feu, deluge, les plus grands à
  l'efpafe.

The magna vaqua near Ravenna in great
trouble, led by fifteen shut up at Fornese.
At Rome two monsters with double heads
are born. Blood, fire, floods the greatest
(hanging) in the air.

This quatrain is similar to its predecessor, with the added enigma of the *magna vaqua,* literally, the great cow. It too seems to be involved with the Papal States and the Vatican, together with a hanging and the production of two double-headed monsters. Probably a failed quatrain.

---

[1] *affomye.* O.F. to appease.
[2] *Columna.* original spelling of the Colonnas of Rome.
[3] *debotez.* O.F. *debouter,* to expel, drive out.
[4] *magna vaqua.* possibly the port Magna Valca between Ravenna and Ferrara, or an unsolved word.

Century IX

IX.IIII

L'an enfuyuant defcouuertz par deluge,
Deux chefs efleuz le premier ne tiendra
De fuyr vmbre à l'vn d'eux le refuge,
Saccagee cafe¹ qui premier maintiendra.

The following year revealed by a flood two leaders elected, the first will not hold on. For one of them, refuge in fleeing shadows. The victim plundered who maintained the first.

Yet another failed quatrain combining a discovery of treasure and vague threats.

Century IX

IX.V

Tiers doit du pied au premier femblera.
A vn nouueau monarque de bas hault
Qui Pyfe & Lucques Tyran occupera
Du precedant corriger le deffault.

The third toe will look like the first one of a new king, of low height he will occupy as a tyrant Pisa and Lucca to correct the fault of his predecessor.

The third estate, established for a second time in 1848, will seem no more than the toe of the first, i.e., very insignificant. Louis Napoleon found it easier to deal with than did Napoleon I. In 1831 Louis Napoleon was involved with Italian revolutionaries and helped to seize the Civita Castellana, which is in Tuscany as are Pisa and Lucca. The fault of Louis Napoleon's predecessor, Napoleon II, was his failure to obtain real power.

Century IX

IX.VI

Par la Guyenne infinité d'Anglois
Occuperont par nom d'Anglaquitaine
Du Languedoc Ifpalme² Bourdeloys.
Qu'ilz nommeront apres Barboixitaine.³

A great number of English in Guienne will occupy it, calling it Anglaquitaine. Of Languedoc, Ispalme, Bordelais which they will name after Barboxitaine.

The English occupied Guienne, the Languedoc and Bordelais steadily between the twelfth and fifteenth centuries, but not since Nostradamus' lifetime. Bordelais was one of the centers of English

---

¹*cafe.* A.Pr. *casa,* the hunt, or victim of a hunt.
²*Ifpalme.* unidentified place name.
³*Barboxitaine.* Possibly derived from *Barbe-Occitanie?* *Barbe* may refer to the enigmatic Aenobarbe and *Occitanie* was the medieval name for the Mediterranean coast.

dominance in southern France. Possibly Ispalme is a misprint for Lapalme near Narbonne? Barboxitaine seems to stand for "the beard's southwestern France" and the beard may refer to the strange character which haunts the quatrains, Aenobarbe, who brings war and tragedy in his wake (see V.LIX). Not a successful quatrain on the whole.

Century IX

IX.VII

Qui ouurira le monument trouué,
Et ne viendra le ferrer promptement.
Mal luy viendra & ne pourra prouué,
Si mieux doit eftre roy Breton ou
    Normand.

The man who opens the tomb when it is found and who does not shut it immediately, evil will come to him. No one will be able to prove it. It might have been better were he a Breton or a Norman king.

Yet another quatrain about the discovery of a tomb. The last line is suitably enigmatic. Nostradamus' tomb was opened by drunken soldiers during the Revolution.

Century IX

IX.VIII

Puifnay Roy fait fon pere mettre à
    mort,
Apres conflit de mort tres inhonefte:
Efcrit trouué foubfon donra remort,
Quand loup chaffé pofe fus la couchette.

The younger son will put his father the king, to death after the quarrel, to a death very dishonest. Writings found, suspicion will bring remorse, when the chased wolf lies on the bedcover.

Although the event of a younger son taking over his father's throne through murder has happened many times in history it is hard to find any definite fulfillment of this since Nostradamus' lifetime, nor of the strange details of the last two lines.

Century IX

IX.IX

Quand lampe ardente de feu
  inextinguible
Sera trouué au temple des Veftales,
Enfant trouué feu, eau paffant par
  trible:[1]
Perir eau Nymes, Tholofe cheoir les
  halles.

When the lamp burning with eternal fire will be found in the temple of the Vestals. A child found in the fire, water passing through the sieve. Nîmes to perish in water, the markets will fall in Toulouse.

Nostradamus may have cheated over this verse because in 1557 there was an enormous cloudburst over Nîmes. This was popularly held to be the site of the Temple of Diana, tended by her Vestal Virgins. The water fell to over six feet deep in some places and many antique monuments were discovered. But, against this, nothing of note happened at Toulouse at this time. Probably a failed quatrain. (But see V.VI.)

Century IX

IX.X

Moyne moyneffe d'enfant mort expofé,
Mourir par ourfe & rauy par verrier.[2]
Par Fois & Pamyes le camp fera posé.
Contre Tholofe Carcas dreffer forrier.

The child of a monk and a nun will be exposed to die, killed by a she-bear and carried off by a boar. The army will be camped near Foix and Pamiers. Carcassonne will raise the pillage against Toulouse.

An indecipherable quatrain set in southwestern France.

Century IX

IX.XI

Le iufte à tort à mort lon viendra
  mettre
Publiquement & due millieu eftaint:
Si grande pefte en ce lieu viendra
  naiftre,
Que les iugeans[3] *fouyr feront conftraint.*

They will come to put the just man wrongfully to death. He is killed publicly in their midst. So a great plague will be born in this place that the judges will be forced to flee.

[1] *trible*. possibly Fr. *crible*, a sieve.
[2] *verrier*. possibly a word Nostradamus concocted from the Latin *verez*, a boar.
[3] *iugeans*. judges, a Nostradamus word.

This quatrain is generally understood to apply to England and in particular to the unjust death *(à tort à mort)* of Charles I, his execution. His death was followed by the Great Plague of London, 1655–56.

Century IX
IX.XII

Le tant d'argent de Diane & Mercure
Les fimulachres au lac feront trouuez,
Le figulier cherchant argille neufue
Luy & les fiens d'or feront abbreuez.

The great amount of silver of Diana and Mercury, the images will be found in the lake. The sculptor looking for new clay, both he and his followers will be soaked in gold.

Another treasure quatrain. Does it relate to VIII.XXVIII and VIII.XXX?

Century IX
IX.XIII

Les exilez autour de la Soulongne
Conduis de nuit pour marcher à
*   Lauxois,*
Deux de Modene truculent[1] de Bologne,
Mys defcouuers par feu de Burançoys.

The exiles around Sologne, led by night to march into Anxas. Two from Moderna for the cruel one of Bologna; put discovered, by the fire of the Buzançais.

I cannot find the key word to this quatrain. The place names have no logical sequence.

Century IX
IX.XIIII

Mys en planure chaulderons
*   d'infecteurs,[2]*
Vin, miel & huyle, & baftis fur
*   fourneaulx*
Seront plongez fans mal dit mal
*   facteurs*
Sept fum extaint au canon des
*   borneaux.*

The dyers' caldron put in a flat place, wine, honey and oil, built over furnaces. They will be drowned without saying or doing an evil thing. Seventh of Borneaux, the snake extinguished at the cannon.

A typically unintelligible Nostradamus quatrain, of which there seem to be quite a few in Century IX.

[1]*truculent.* L. *truculentus,* ferocious, hard, cruel.
[2]*infecteurs.* L. dyers.

Century IX

IX.XV

Pres de Parpan les rouges detenus,
Ceux du milieu parfondrez menez loing:
Trois mis en pieces, & cinq mal
*   fouftenus,*
Pour le Seigneur & Prelat de
*   Bourgoing.*

The red ones detained near Perpignan,
those in the middle ruined, led far away.
Three cut into pieces and five badly supported for the Lord and Prelate of Burgundy.

Perpignan belonged to Spain until 1659, and red was the Spanish national color. Nostradamus appears to foresee a Franco-Spanish struggle around the Pyrenees. The governor of Burgundy in Nostradamus' time, the duc d'Aumale, died in 1573. The country had four, not five, bishops under him.

Century IX

IX.XVI

De caftel[1] Franco fortira l'affemblee,
L'ambaffadeur non plaifant fera fcifme:
Ceux de Ribiere feront en la meflee,
Et au grand goulphre defnier ont
*   l'entree.*

From Castille Franco will bring out the
assembly. The ambassadors will not agree
and cause a schism. The people of Riviera
will be in the crowd. The great man will
be denied entry to the Gulf.

One of Nostradamus' best quatrains with the names of two principal personages given to us. Rivera was the dictator of Spain, Primo de Rivera, and Franco is Francisco Franco, who helped depose him. Franco was exiled to Morocco but returned triumphantly to Spain when his party came to power. The last line is understood to refer to Franco's exile when he was not able to cross the Mediterranean, *goulphre,* to his native Spain. *Caftel* should read *Castille* (see III.VIII).

Century IX

IX.XVII

Le tiers premier pys que ne feit Neron,
Vuidez vaillant que fang humain
*   refpandre:*
R'edifier fera le forneron,
Siecle d'or, mort, nouueau roy grand
*   efclandre.*

The third one does firstly worse than Nero;
go, flow, brave human blood. The furnace
will be rebuilt, a golden century, Death, a
new king and great scandal.

[1]*Caftel.* Castille.

"The third" in Nostradamus seems always to refer to the Third Estate, whose first effort was its National Convention in Revolutionary France. The prophet refers to it as being worse than Nero's reign, with blood flowing from the guillotines. The guillotine was placed in the Place de la Révolution (now the Place de la Concorde) opposite the Tuileries, where formerly the furnaces for the tile kilns stood. The golden century of the kings (Louis XIV–XVI) is over. Perhaps the great scandal is an indirect reference to the killing of the royal family, treason. (See also III.LIX)

Century IX

IX.XVIII

Le lys Dauffois portera dans Nanfy
Iufques en Flandres electeur de l'empire,
Neufue obturee au grand Montmorency,
Hors lieux prouez deliure à clere peyne.

The lily of the dauphin is taken as far as Nancy, the Elector of the Empire as far as Flanders. A new prison for the great Montmorency, not in the usual place, delivered up to Clerepeyne.

Louis XIII was the first bearer of the lilies of France and the title of Dauphin since Nostradamus' death. He entered Nancy in September, 1633. The city of Treves had been recovered a year earlier by the Maréchal d'Estrées, who re-established the authority of the Elector. However, in 1633, the Elector was carried off by the Spanish and taken as a prisoner to Brussels *(Flandres)*. At the same time in 1632, a revolt was led in southern France by the great Montmorency, who was captured. His family pleaded in vain for his release: instead they obtained for him the doubtful privilege of execution by a private, rather than a public executioner. He was beheaded in the court of the prison, the Hôtel de Ville, which had recently been built, *hors lieux. Deliure à clere peyne* may contain two meanings: It means delivered to clear punishment, but some commentators state that Clerepeyne was the name of the executioner. I have not been able to verify this. It first appears in a commentary by Jaubert in 1656.

Century IX

IX.XIX

Dans le milieu de la foreft Mayenne,
Sol au lyon la fouldre tombera,
Le grand baftard yffu du gran du
* Maine,*
Ce iour fougeres pointe en fang entrera.

In the middle of the Mayenne forest, the Sun in Leo, the lightning will fall. The great bastard born of the great man of Maine, on that day a point will enter the blood of Fougères.

Mayenne, in northwestern France, has a large forest west of the city. Fougères is about twenty miles further west, the seat of a great family name which died out in the thirteenth century. The title of the Mayennes was used in the fifteenth century by Henri II's mistress, Diane de Poitiers, and also by Henri III while he was duc d'Anjou. No other great families are connected with the house, unfortunately for Nostradamus. As for the dating of the Sun in Leo, it is not specific enough.

Century IX

IX.XX

De nuit viendra par la foreſt de Reines,
Deux pars vaultorte Herne[1] la pierre
   blanche,
Le moine noir[2] en gris dedans Varennes
Eſleu cap cauſe tempeſte feu, ſang
   tranche.
	By night will come through the forest of
	Reines, two partners, by a roundabout
	way. The queen, the white stone. The
	monk-king dressed in gray at Varennes.
	The elected Capet causes tempest, fire and
	bloody slicing.

This is one of Nostradamus' more remarkable quatrains, describing the flight to Varennes by Louis XVI and Marie Antoinette in 1791. The royal couple, having fled from the Tuileries through a secret door in the queen's apartment, travel through the forest of Reims. This happened, and they also lost their way and chose an extremely bad route, *vaultorte*. The *pierre blanche* probably refers to the affair of the diamond necklace, which finally demolished Marie Antoinette's fragile popularity with the French populace. It may also refer indirectly to the fact that her lady in waiting reported that on capture the queen's hair turned white overnight and that she usually wore white dresses. The king was wearing a simple gray suit when they entered Varennes. It is possible that the word "monk" refers to his impotence earlier in his marriage. He was a Capet, the first elected king of France, and as Nostradamus states, was the cause, the final symptom of a revolution and the shedding of blood. *Tranche* as a verb means to slice, particularly apposite in the context of the guillotine. A really fascinating quatrain with facts and places.

[1]*Herne.* possible anagram for *Reine.*
[2]*noir.* usual anagram for *roi,* king.

Century IX

IX.XXI

Au temple hault de Bloys facre Solonne,
Nuict pont de Loyre, prelat, roy
    pernicant[1]
Curfeur[2] victoire aux mareftz de la
    lone[3]
Dou prelature de blancs à bormeant.[4]

At night, the high temple of Blois at Sacré
Solonne. A priest in the Loire bridge a
king dying. A messenger, victory for the
marshes on the water. Destruction for a
priestly gift from the whites.

This quatrain is a repetition of Nostradamus' strongly held belief that France would gain a king from Blois. Sacré Solonne is the Church of Saint Solonne, the Cathedral at Blois. Unfortunately, this gets us no further.

Century IX

IX.XXII

Roy & fa court au lieu de langue
    halbe,[5]
Dedans le temple vis à vis du palais
Dans le iardin Duc de Mantor &
    d'Albe,
Albe & Mantor poignard langue &
    palais.

The king and his court in the place of the
clever tongue, in the temple facing the palace. In the garden the duke of Mantua
and Alba, Alba and Mantua, dagger,
tongue and the palace.

The key to this quatrain lies in the identity of Alba and Mantua, which had been joined together in 1536 by Charles V. Their ruler from 1550 to 1587 was Gonzaga, who did suffer an assassination attempt but at Casale, not at Blois. But the famous Château de Blois does not face the Cathedral. An irritating quatrain.

Century IX

IX.XXIII

Puifnay iouant au frefch deffouz la
    tonne,
Le hault du toict du milieu fur la tefte,
Le pere roy au temple faint Solonne,
Sacrifiant facrera fum de fefte.

The younger son playing outdoors under
the arbor, the top of the roof on the middle
of his head. The father king in the Temple
is solemn, sacrificing. He will consecrate
the smoke of the feast.

[1]*pernicant.* L. *pernecare,* to kill, or *pernix,* swift.
[2]*Curfeur.* O.F. runner or messenger.
[3]*lone.* A.Pr. *lona,* a pool, still water.
[4]*à bormeant.* L. *aboriri,* to miscarry. A.Pr. *abouriment,* destruction.
[5]*halbe.* O.F. *habler,* to talk.

The younger son is the second son of Louis XVI and his wife, who was allowed out to play in the Temple Gardens while Louis was imprisoned in a tower, away from the rest of the family, as stated in line 3. The quatrain continues to describe the solemn future of the king, sacrificed to the Revolution on the guillotine.

Century IX
IX.XXIIII

Sur le palais au rochier¹ des feneſtres
Seront rauis les deux petits royaux,
Paſſer aurelle² Luthece³ Denis cloiſtres,
Nonain, mallods⁴ aualler verts noyaulx.

At the palace from the balcony of the windows, two little royal ones will be carried off. To pass Orléans, Paris and the cloisters of Saint Denis, a nun; the flies devouring the green pits.

An incomprehensible quatrain.

Century IX
IX.XXV

Paſſant les pontz venir pres des roſiers,⁵
Tard arriué pluſtoſt qu'il cuydera,⁶
Viendront les noues⁷ eſpaignolez à
*   Beſiers,*
Qui icelle chaffe emprinſe⁸ caffera.

Crossing the bridges to come near the Rosiers, sooner than he thought he arrived late. The new Spaniards will come to Beziers, so that this chase will break the enterprise.

The interesting points in this quatrain are Nostradamus' new Spaniards, *noves eſpaignolez*. Béziers was on the Spanish invasion route to France about fifty miles northeast of the pre-1659 border. Otherwise, the quatrain remains obscure.

---

¹*rochier.* rock. In the context of windows, probably means a balcony.
²*aurelle.* L. *Aurelianum,* Orléans.
³*Luthece.* L. *Lutecia,* Paris.
⁴*mallods.* O.F. *malots,* flies? *malois,* wicked? or L. *malum,* apple?
⁵*roſiers.* either Rosiers, or rosebushes.
⁶*cuydera.* O.F. to think.
⁷*noues.* O.F. new.
⁸*emprinſe.* O.F. enterprise.

Century IX

IX.XXVI

Nice fortie fur nom[1] des letres afpres,
La grande cappe[2] fera prefent son fien,
Proche de vultry aux murs de vertes
*   capres*
Apres plombin[3] le vent à bon effien.

Departed from the name of Nice through bitter letters, the great cappe will present his own thing. Near Voltai at the wall of the green columns, after Piombino the wind in good earnest.

I cannot interpret this quatrain.

Century IX

IX.XXVII

De bois la garde vent cloz rond pont
*   fera,*
Hault le receu frappera le Daulphin,
Le vieux teccon[4] boix vnis paffera,
Paffant plus oultre du duc le droit
*   confin.*

The guardian of the forest, the wind will close around the bridge. Received highly he will strike the dauphin. The old craftsmen will pass through the woods in company, going far beyond the known borders of the duke.

It is just possible that this quatrain may be yet another continuing the description of escape of the dauphin, son of Louis XVI, who was reported dead in June, 1795. It implies that the boy is taken out of France, but the method is obscure. (See V.I.)

Century IX

IX.XXVIII

Voille Symacle[5] port Maffiliolique,[6]
Dans Venise port marcher aux
*   Pannons:*
Partir du goulfre & finus[7] Illirique
Vaft[8] à Socile, Ligurs coups de canons.

The allied fleet from the port of Marseilles, in the Venetian harbor to march against Hungary. To leave from the gulf and the bay of Illyria. Devastation in Sicily, for the Ligurians, cannon shot.

Geographically this quatrain covers a lot of ground: Panonia, Hungary, Marseilles, the Gulf of Illyria. But despite all these clues, I cannot decipher it.

[1]*fur nom.* Either surname, or "under the name of."
[2]*cappe.* The Pope, cape, O.F. *cape* or *Capet,* then the French royal line.
[3]*plombin.* Piombino or L. leaden, of lead.
[4]*teccon.* O.F. A game played with a ball. Possibly from Gk. *tekton,* a craftsman.
[5]*Symacle.* Gk. *symmachos,* auxiliary, allied with.
[6]*Maffiliolique.* L. *Masilioticus,* of Marseilles.
[7]*finus.* L. a bay.
[8]*Vaft.* L. *vastum,* destruction, devastation.

Century IX

IX.XXIX

Lors que celuy qu'à nul ne donne lieu,
Abandonner vouldra lieu prins non
*   prins:*
Feu nef par faignes, bitument[1] à
*   Charlieu,*
Seront Quintin Balez[2] reprins.

When the man will give way to none he will wish to abandon a place taken, yet not taken. A ship on fire through the swamps. Bitumen at Charlieu. Saint Quentin and Calais will be recaptured.

The last line of this quatrain is interesting. The unexpected fall of Calais, so regretted by Mary Tudor, occurred on January 6, 1558, when the duc de Guise recaptured it. Calais was the last bastion of the English in France. After that St. Quentin was given back to the French in the general settlement of 1559.

Century IX

IX.XXX

Au port de POVLA & de faint Nicolas,
Perir Normande au goulfre
*   Phanaticque,[3]*
Cap.[4] de Bifance raues crier helas,
Secors de Gaddes[5] & du grand
*   Philipique.*

At the port of PUOLA and Saint Nicolas a Normand will punish in the Gulf of Quaerno. Capet cries alas in the streets of Byzantium. Help from Cadiz and the great Philip.

All the places mentioned in this quatrain except Cadiz are in Yugoslavia. If Philip in line 4 was intended to be Philip II, Nostradamus predicted a Franco-Turkish attack on the Hapsburgs in the south, with the Spaniards helping the French. This never took place. A failed quatrain.

[1]*butiment.* O.F. *butimen,* asphalt. pitch.
[2]*Balez.* anagram of Calais?
[3]*phanaticque.* ? L. Sinus Flanaticus, the Gulf of Quaerno.
[4]*Cap.* probably the usual apocope of Capet, the French royal line.
[5]*Gaddes.* L. Gadez, Cadiz.

Century IX
IX.XXXI

Le tremblement de terre à Mortara,[1]
Caffich[2] faint George[3] à demy
perfondrez,
Paix affoupie, la guerre efueillera,
Dans temple à Pafques abifmes
enfondrez.

The trembling of the earth at Martara,
the tin island of Saint George half sunk.
Drowsy with peace, war will arise at
Easter. In the temple abysses opened.

This is another earthquake quatrain, but it is difficult to relate it to the British Isles. Earthquakes occur there, but not of such a dimension that half the land would be destroyed. An earthquake in Martara would mean a disturbance over 1,000 miles from Britain. But the quatrain should not be totally dismissed. Geoffrey Goldman, an expert on earthquake, stated recently that "we are the earthquake generation" and he seems to foresee that the earthquakes will cover a far larger area than the so-called earthquake zone. Easter fits comparatively well with the great earthquake Nostradamus foresees in the west coast of America in mid-May.

Century IX
IX.XXXII

De fin porphire profond collon trouuee
Deffoubz la laze[4] efcriptz capitolin:[5]
Os poil retors Romain force prouuee,
Claffe[6] agiter au port de Methelin.

A deep column of fine porphyry is found,
inscriptions of the Capitol under the base.
Bones, twisted hair. The Roman strength
tried, the fleet is stirred at the harbor of
Mitylene.

Yet another difficult quatrain.

[1]*Mortara.* probably misprint for Martara.
[2]*Cassich.* Gk. *Cassitorides,* the tin islands, a name given to Cornwall and the Scilly Islands.
[3]*faint George.* probably England, as George was adopted as its patron saint in the fourteenth century.
[4]*laze.* Gk. *laz,* foot or base.
[5]*capitolin.* belonging to the capitol of Rome, i.e., Roman, Latin.
[6]*claffe.* L. *classus,* fleet.

Century IX

IX.XXXIII

Hercules Roy de Romme & *d'Annemarc,[1]* *De Gaule trois Guion[2] furnommé,* *Trembler l'Itale & l'vude de fainct* *Marc,[3]* *Premier fur tous monarque renommé.*	Hercules, king of Rome and of Annemarc. Of Gaul three times the leader will be so called. Italy will tremble and the waters around Saint Mark, the first to be re- nowned over all kings.

A reference to de Gaulle? For Annemarc see IV.XXVII.

Century IX

IX.XXXIIII

Le part soulz mary fera mittré, *Retour conflict paffera fur le thuille:* *Par cinq cens vn trahyr fera tiltré,* *Narbon & Saulce par coutaux auons* *d'huille.*	The partner, solitary but married will be mitred; the return, fighting will cross over the Tuileries. By five hundred one traitor will be ennobled. Narbonne and Saulce, we will have oil for knives.

This is again a riveting quatrain following directly upon IX.XX. When Louis XVI and Marie Antoinette were stopped at Varennes they passed the night at the house of a man named Saulce, line 4. The Sauces (modern spelling), have been chandlers and *marchands-épiciers* at Varennes since the sixteenth century, and Nostradamus is able to give us their name! The statement that the king above is mitred *(soulz mary fera mittré)* refers to Louis' return to the Tuileries on June 20, 1792, when the mob invaded the palace and the king was forced to wear the revolutionary cap of liberty, which looks very much like a mitre. It is thought that *coutaux* in line 4 should read as *quartants,* which means oil sold at retail, which was exactly what the eighteenth century M. Saulce did. In Thiers' *History of France* he comments that when the king and queen returned to the Tuileries for the second time *retour . . . thuille,* the mob murdered five hundred people.

A convincing quatrain.

---

[1]*Annemarc.?* Hungary and Bohemia, Moravia.
[2]*Guion.* O.F. guide, leader, chief.
[3]*fainct Marc.* Venice, of whom St. Mark is the patron.

Century IX

IX.XXXV

Et Ferdinand blonde fera defcorte,[1]
Quitter la fleur fuyure le Macedon.[2]
Au grand befoing defaillira fa routte,
Et marchera contre le Myrmidon.[3]

And the fair-haired Ferdinand will disagree, to abandon the flower and follow
the Macedonian. In great need his course
will fail him and he will march against
the Myrmidons.

This could possibly be a quatrain relating to the Second World War, describing the situation of King Ferdinand of Bulgaria.

Century IX

IX.XXXVI

Vn grand Roy prins entre les mains
    d'vn Ioyne,
Non loing de Pafque confufion coup
    cultre:[4]
Perpet.[5] captifs temps que fouldre en la
    hufne,
Lors que trois freres fe blefferont &
    murtre.

A great king captured by the hands of a
young man, not far from Easter. Confusion, a state of the knife. Everlasting captives, times when the lightning is on top,
when three brothers will be wounded and
murdered.

Here again is the theme of the three brothers, which I have tentatively interpreted as the Kennedys, the three brothers from the *Nouvelle Lande,* America. In this verse Nostradamus indicates that all three brothers will be murdered and this may happen around Easter. Since John F. Kennedy was killed in November, 1963, and his brother Robert Kennedy on June 6, 1968, maybe another assassination is to be expected around Easter (April, May), with possibly a storm thrown in *(fouldre en la hufne).* But equally, the lightning may refer to a gun on the top of a tall building, which recalls Dallas in 1963. As I have said, I regard Edward Kennedy as possibly a psychological assassinee. This is possibly partly futuristic, but definitely a quatrain of the twentieth century.

[1]*defcorte.* O.F. disagreement, detached.
[2]*Macedon.* The Greeks?
[3]*Myrmidon.* The tribe of Achilles, renowned for their obedience to commands.
[4]*cultre.* L. *coulter,* knife.
[5]*Perpet.* apocope of L. *Perpetulialis,* everlasting.

Century IX

IX.XXXVII

Pont & molins en Decembre verfez,
En fi haut lieu montera la Garonne:
Murs, edifices, Tholofe renuerfez,
Qu'on ne fçaura fon lieu autant
matronne. [1]

The entry at Blaye for la Rochelle and the
Bridges and mild overturned in December,
the Garonne will rise to a very high level.
Walls, buildings, Toulouse overthrown,
so that none will know his place before
Matronne.

An unintelligible quatrain. The key word probably lies in *Matronne*.

Century IX

IX.XXXVIII

L'entree de Blaye par Rochelle &
l'Anglois,
Paffera outre le grand Aemathien, [2]
Non loing d'Agen attendra le Gaulois,
Secours Narbonne deceu par entretien.

The entry at Blaye for la Rochelle and the
English. The great Macedonia will pass
beyond. Not far from Agen the Gaul will
wait, [3] help from Narbonne misled by a
conversation.

Century IX

IX.XXXIX

En Arbiffel à Veront [4] *& Carcari,*
De nuict conduitz pour Sauonne
attrapper,
Le vifz Gafcon Turbi, & la Scerry
Derrier mur vieux & neuf palais
gripper.

In Albisola to Veront and Carcara led by
night to seize Savona, the swift Gascon,
La Turbie and l'Escarene. To seize both
the old and new palace behind the wall.

A quatrain with too many place names and nothing upon which to
hang them for an interpretation.

---

[1]*Matronne.* May be a disguised place name?
[2]*Aemathien.* L. *Emathia,* a poetic name for Macedonia and Thessaly.
[3]Alternative reading, "he will wait for the Frenchman."
[4]*Veront.* Probably not Verona, as all the other places mentioned are close to Albisola.
An unsolved place name?

Century IX

IX.XL

Pres de Quintin dans la foreft bourlis,[1]
Dans l'abbaye feront Flamens ranches,[2]
Les deux puifnais de coups my eftourdis
Suitte oppreffee & garde tous aches.

Near Saint Quentin deceived in the forest,
in the Abbey the Flemish will be cut up.
The two youngest half stunned by blows,
their followers crushed and the guard all
cut to pieces.

Could this refer to the Battle of Saint Quentin in 1557? Before the battle, the Spaniards seized the Abbey of Vermondois. But even that information leaves us still unclear as what to Nostradamus was aiming at.

Century IX

IX.XLI

Le grand Chyren[3] foy faifir d'Auignon,
De Romme letres en miel plein
    d'amertume
Letre ambaffade partir de Chanignon,[4]
Carpentras pris par duc noir rouge
    plume.

The great Chyren will seize Avignon, from
Rome will come honeyed letters full of bit-
terness. The letter and embassy to leave
from Chanignon. Carpentras taken by the
black duke with a feather.

Nostradamus seems to envisage Henri II as capturing Avignon, which at that time belonged to the Papacy. Unfortunately Avignon did not come into French hands properly until 1791, although it was occupied by the French in 1663–64 and 1768–74. Presumably the letters are dispatches from an irate Vatican. *Chanignon* is still undeciphered. Carpentras is near Avignon and part of the papal lands.

Century IX

IX.XLII

De Barfellonne, de Gennes & Venise,
De la Secille pefte Monet[5] vnis,
Contre Barbare claffe prendront la vife,
Barbar, poulfe bien loing iufqu'à
    Thunis.

From Barcelona, from Genoa and Venice,
from Sicily a pestilence allied with
Monaco. They will take aim against the
barbarian fleet. The barbarian driven
back as far as Tunis.

[1] *bourlis.* Possible derivative of *boucle*, deceived, or an untraceable word.
[2] *ranches.* Error for *tranches* in all other editions.
[3] *Chyren.* The usual anagram for Henryc, Henri.
[4] *Chanignon.* An unsolved place or proper name.
[5] *Monet.* an unusual spelling for *Monech*, Monaco.

This prediction was well fulfilled in 1571 at the Battle of Lepanto when the allied fleets of the Papacy, Venice and Spain were crushed by the Turks at Lepanto. By 1573, Don John of Austria, the leader of the expedition, had gone on to recapture Tunis. Much of the Turkish fleet was composed of ships from their ally the Algerian Barbary pirates. A successful quatrain.

Century IX

IX.XLIII

Proche à defcendre l'armee Crucigere[1]
Sera guettee par les Ifmaëlites[2]
De tous cottez batus par nef Rauiere,[3]
Prompt affaillis de dix galeres eslites.

Ready to land the army of the Cross will be watched for by the Ismaelites. Struck from all sides by the ship Raviere. Quickly attacked by ten chosen galleys.

I think this is probably a continuation of IX.XLII.

Century IX

IX.XLIIII

Migres migre de Genefue treftous,
Saturne d'or en fer fe changera,
Le contre RAYPOZ[4] exterminera tous,
Auant l'a ruent le ciel fignes fera.

Leave, leave Geneva everyone. Saturn will change from gold into iron. Those against RAYPOZ will all be exterminated. Before the rush the sky will show signs.

Geneva was famous in Nostradamus' time as the Protestant equivalent of the Vatican because Calvin made it his center. Is Nostradamus warning the inhabitants of a Calvinist purge or of an attack by Philip II? Could *RAYPOZ* stand for a traitor? (See footnote.) An intriguing quatrain.

---

[1]*Crucigere.* bearing a cross, a Crusader.
[2]*Ifmaëlites.* biblical name for the Arabs.
[3]*Rauiere.* O.F. impetuosity, or an unidentified place name.
[4]*RAYPOZ.* an unsolved anagram except for one suggestion, Zopyre who betrayed Babylon to Darius.

Century IX

IX.XLV

Ne fera foul iamais de demander,
Grand Mendofus[1] obtiendra fon empire
Loing de la cour fera contremander,
Pymond, Picard, Paris, Tyrron[2] le pire.

There will never be a single person to ask,
great Mendosus will attain his empire.
Far from the court he will countermand
Piedmont, Picardy and Paris. Tuscany is
the worst.

Mendosus is accepted by most commentators as an anagram for the family of Vendôme, of which the earlier spelling was Vendosme. If this is the case, the quatrain may describe either Henri IV or his father Antoine de Navarre, duc de Vendosme. But despite this excellent lead the rest of the quatrain is very obscure. Piedmont was Italian and belonged to Savoy, Picardy is a Normandy province of France. A disappointing quatrain.

Century IX

IX.XLVI

Vuydez, fuyez de Tholofe les rouges
Du facrifice faire expiation,
Le chef du mal deffouz l'vmbre des
*   courges*
Mort eftrangler carne omination.[3]

Begone, the red ones, flee from Toulouse,
make expiation to the sacrifice. The main
course of evil in the shadow of the gourds.
Dead, to strangle the prognostication of
flesh.

Century IX

IX.XLVII

Les foulz fignez d'indigne deliurance,
Et de la multe auront contre aduis,
Change monarque mis en perille pence,[4]
Serrez en caige fe verront vis à vis.

The undersigned to an infamous delivery
receiving contrary advice from the crowds.
A monarch changes, thoughts are put in
danger. Shut in a cage they will see each
other face to face.

This quatrain could be applied to François II, 1559–1560, but it is still very vague.

[1]*Mendofus.* an anagram for *Vendosme*, the Bourbon branch of the French royal family who won the throne in 1594.

[2]*Tyrron.* probably from the L. *Tyrrheni*, the Etruscans.

[3]*omination.* probably derived from *carne ominato*, prognostic of flesh.

[4]*pence.* This probably comes from F. *penser*, to think, but possibly from the English, *pence.*

Century IX
IX.XLVIII

La grand cité d'occean maritime,　　　The great city of the maritime ocean, sur-
Enuironnee de maretz en criftal:　　　rounded by a swamp of crystal. In the
Dans le folftice hyemal[1] & la prime,[2]　winter solstice and the spring (he) will be
Sera temptee de vent efpouuental.　　tried by a dreadful wind.

This quatrain is interpreted by Allen (1943) as the destruction of
Central Park in New York and by Boswell (1941) as the destruction
of Tokyo by Russian chemical bombs. The latter was almost correct
in his prediction. Nagasaki and Hiroshima were destroyed by atomic
(chemical?) bombs in 1945. A curious quatrain.

Century IX
IX.XLIX

Gand & Bruceles marcheront contre　　Ghent and Brussels march against Ant-
　Enuers　　　　　　　　　　　　　werp. The Parliament of London will put
Senat de Londres mettront à mort leur　their king to death. The salt and wine will
　roy　　　　　　　　　　　　　　oppose him. Because of them he will have
Le fel & vin luy feront à l'enuers,　　the kingdom in trouble.
Pour eux auoir le regne en defarroy.

Line 2 is the obvious clue to this quatrain, describing the death of
Charles I. The king was executed in 1649 by the new-style calendar,
in 1648 by the old-style calendar that Nostradamus used, when New
Year's Day was on March 25.

Philip IV had made great attempts to reconquer the Netherlands
but by 1648 they were anxious to get the Dutch out of the war and
ceded several key towns to them. This may indicate that Nostradamus
saw lines 1 and 2 as simultaneous. When Philip had achieved this he
closed the Scheldt, which ruined Antwerp. It is interesting to note
that the quatrain is numbered XL.IX, and Charles was executed in
1649. (See VIII.XXXVII.)

---

[1]*hyemal.* L. *hiemalus.* (of) winter.
[2]*prime.* O.F. springtime.

Century IX

IX.L

Mendofus tost viendra à fon hault
  regne
Mettant arriere vn peu de Norlaris:
Le rouge blaifme, le mafle à
  l'interregne,
Le ieune crainte & frayeur Barbaris.

Mendosus will soon come to his great reign, somewhat putting aside the Norlaris. The pale red one, the one in the interregnum, the frightened young man and the fear of the Barbaric ones.

As was seen in IX.XLV and X.XVIII, *Mendosus* is an anagram of Vendosme and *Norlaris* an anagram of Lorraine, the home of the Guise family. This quatrain states that Vendosme, Henri IV, will soon come to the throne and relegate the House of Guise to the wings, which indeed happened. The *rouge blaifme* probably stands for the old cardinal of Bourbon, red in his cardinal's robes and pallid with age. He was actually proclaimed Charles X in 1589, but died the following year. The *mafle* may stand for the duc de Mayenne, who was lieutenant general during the interregnum. The young man *(le ieune crainte)* would then be the duc de Guise and *Barbaris* stands for Philip II of Spain, who claimed the throne of France through his daughter Isabella, his wife having been a sister of Henri II of France. A satisfactory quatrain.

Century IX

IX.LI

Contre les rouges fectes fe banderont,
Feu, eau, fer, corde par paix fe
  minera,[1]
Au point mourir ceux qui machineront
Fors vn que monde fur tout ruynera.

Against the red ones sects will unite. Fire, water, iron, the rope, will weaken through peace. Those who plot are at point of dying except one who above all will ruin the world.

This quatrain must have a twentieth century interpretation. The Reds fit here as Communist countries in a modern politico-social setting. The conditions described in lines 1 and 2 existed between the two World Wars with Fascism, Communism, Nazism and line 2 obviously refers to the *Cordon Sanitaire.* Line 3 describes Western statesmen, mostly appeasers like Chamberlain and Pétain. Their exception is Hitler, in line 4, who attempted to rule the world.

---

[1]*minera.* O.F. *miner,* to ruin, destroy.

Century IX

IX.LII

La paix f'approche d'vn costé, & la
  guerre
Oncques ne feut la pourfuict fi grande,
Plaindre hôme, fême, fang innocent par
  terre
Et ce fera de France à toute bande.

Peace approaches from one side. Never
was the pursuit of war so great. Men and
women moan, innocent blood on the land
and this will be throughout the whole of
France.

On April 13, 1559, the king of France declared in the Peace of
Cateau-Cambrésis that he would stop fighting the Spanish and would
turn his attention to liquidating heretics in France. The declared
peace between France and Spain sparked the Civil War between the
Catholics and Huguenots, a time of bloodshed for all France, which
indeed happened. A good general quatrain.

Century IX

IX.LIII

Le Neron ieune dans les trois cheminees
Fera de paiges vifz pour ardoir[1] getter,[2]
Heureux qui loing fera de telz menees,
Trois de fon fang le feront mort guetter.

In three chimneys the young Nero will
throw out to burn the living pages. He is
happy who will be far from such happenings. Three of his family will ambush him
to death.

Rafael Sabatini, the well-known novelist, wrote in one of his historical novels of a young man being thrown into a fireplace. Otherwise
I can offer no clue.

Century IX

IX.LIIII

Arriuera au port de Corfibonne,
Pres de Rauenne qui pillera la dame,
En mer profonde legat de la Vlisbonne
Souz roc cachez rauiront feptante ames.

There will arrive at Porto Corsini near
Ravenna, one of whom will plunder the
lady. The legate in Lisbon in the deep sea.
Hidden under the rock they will carry off
seventy souls.

Perhaps the Dome stands for the Catholic Church to be plundered
at Porto Corsini, which is eight miles north of Ravenna.

[1]*ardoir.* O.F. to burn.
[2]*getter.* O.F. for jeter, to throw.

Century IX

IX.LV

L'horrible guerre qu'en l'occident
  s'aprefte
L'an enfuiuant viendra la peftilence,
Si fort horrible que ieune, vieulx, ne
  befte,
Sang, feu, Mercure, Mars, Iupiter en
  France.

*The dreadful war which is prepared in the
West, the following year the pestilence will
come, so very dreadful that young nor old
nor animal (will survive). Blood, fire,
Mercury, Mars, Jupiter in France.*

This quatrain is generally applied to the First World War, which
was followed by the dreadful influenza epidemic of 1917–18 governed by the conjunction of Mercury, Mars and Jupiter always one
indicating disaster. However it may equally well apply to AIDS, the
plague of the last decades of this century. Nostradamus' mention of
animals is interesting. One theory of the origin of AIDS holds that
the disease mutated from the Green Monkey of Africa to human
beings. Certainly Africa is the source of the AIDS epidemic. This is
also a good Millennium quatrain with the prime ingredients of disease, war and fire. Possibly a quatrain that has not yet been completely fulfilled.

Century IX

IX.LVI

Camp pres de Noudam paffera Gouffan
  ville,
Et à Maiotes[1] laiffera fon enfeigne,
Conuertira en instant plus de mille,
Cherchant les deux remettre en chaine
  & legne.[2]

*The army near Noudan will pass Gous-
sainville and will leave its scar at Maiotes. In an instant more than a thousand
will be converted, looking for the two who
will put back chain and wood.*

A difficult quatrain. Both Noudan and Goussainville are to the west
of Paris, but Maiotes is unsolved and I am unclear as to the exact
meaning of *legne* in line 4.

---

[1]*Maiotes.* a place name, Mantes? or possibly Gk. *memaotes,* soldiers.
[2]*legne.* A.Pr. *legna,* firewood.

Century IX

IX.LVII

Au lieu de DRVX¹ vn Roy repofera,
Et cherchera loy changeant d'Anatheme,
Pendant le ciel fi tres fort tonnera,
Portee neufue Roy tuera soymesme.

In the place of DRVX a king will rest and look for a law to change Anathema. While the sky thunders so loudly the king will kill himself at the new gate.

The clue to this unsolved quatrain must be *DRVX*.

Century IX

IX.LVIII

Au cofté gauche à l'endroit de Vitry
Seront guettez les trois rouges de
France,
Tous affoumez rouge, noir non murdry,
Par les Bretons remis en affeurance.

To the left side of the place of Vitry the three red ones of France will be watched. All those killed are red, the black not murdered. Reassured in safety by the Bretons.

The red ones of France are probably Revolutionaries, all of whom are killed with their followers. Like the following quatrain this is practically unintelligible.

Century IX

IX.LIX

A la Ferté prendra la Vidame
Nicol tenu rouge qu'auoit produit la
vie.
La grand Loyfe naiftra que fera
clame.²
Donnant Bourgongne à Bretons par
enuie.

At the Ferté Vidame he will take Nicol the red, who had produced life. To the great Louis who acts secretly one will be born, who gives Burgundy to the Bretons through envy.

A quatrain about a mythological illegitimate child born to someone called Louis who has some connection with Burgundy and the Bretons.

---

¹*DRVX.* possibly an anagram for Dreux?
²*clame.* L. *clam.* secretly.

Century IX

IX.LX

Conflict Barbar en la Cornere noire.
Sang efpandu trembler la d'Almatie,
Grand Ifmaël[1] mettra fon promontoire,
Ranes[2] trembler fecours Lufitanie.

In a black headdress the Barbarian fights,
blood shed, Dalmatia trembles. The great
Ismaël will wake his promontory. Frogs
tremble under aid from Portugal.

I can make nothing of this quatrain.

Century IX

IX.LXI

La pille faite à la cofte marine,
La cita noua & parenz amenez
Plufieurs de Malte par le fait de
  Meffine,
Eftroit ferrez feront mal guerdonnez.

The plunder taken on the sea coast, in the
new city and relations brought forward.
Several of Malta will be closely shut up,
through the deeds of Messina, poorly re-
warded.

I am unable to decipher this quatrain.

Century IX

IX.LXII

Au grand de Cheramon agora
Seront croifez par ranc tous attachez,
Le pertinax[3] Oppi,[4] & Mandragora,[5]
Raugon[6] d'Octobre le tiers feront
  lafchez.

To the great one of Cheramon agora will
all the crosses by rank be attached. The
long lasting Opium and Mandrake, the
Raugon will be released on October the
third.

This is a very odd quatrain. Cheramon Agora was actually the name of a town in Asia Minor, believed to be present-day Usak. Both opium and the mandrake root had mysterious virtues and were used in occult practices. But what this has to do with a town in Asia Minor, I cannot tell.

---

[1]*Ifmaël.* the Arab nation.
[2]*ranes.* L. *rama,* a frog.
[3]*pertinax.* L. long-lasting.
[4]*Oppi.* Gk. opium.
[5]*Mandragora.* Gk. mandrake.
[6]*Raugon.* An unsolved place name?

Century IX
IX.LXIII

Plainctes & pleurs crys & grands
  vrlemens
Pres de Narbon à Bayonne & en Foix
O quel horrible calamitz changemens,
Auant que Mars reuolu quelques foys.

Complaints and tears, cries and great
howls, near Narbonne, Bayonne and in
Foix. Oh, what dreadful calamities and
changes, before Mars has revolved a few
times.

Each revolution of the planet Mars lasts 687 days. The only definite fact one can glean from this quatrain is that a calamity will occur, probably war *(Mars)* after a certain number of revolutions. But there is no date to start the time factor so the quatrain remains obscure.

Century IX
IX.LXIIII

L'Aemathion[1] paffer montz Pyrennees,
En Mars Narbon ne fera refiftance,
Par mer & terre fera fi grand menee.
Cap.[2] n'ayant terre feure pour
  demeurance.

The Aemathian will cross the Pyrenees in
March. Narbonne will not make any resistance. He will carry on a very great
intrigue by land and sea. Cap having no
land in which to stay safely.

For line 1 see IX.XXXVIII. *Cap.* is Nostradamus' usual shortening of the Capet name, the French royal line. But on occasions he has used *Cappe* to mean cape and even the Pope. Probably a failed quatrain about sixteenth century politics.

Century IX
IX.LXV

Dedans le coing de luna viendra rendre,
Ou fera prins & mys en terre eftrange,
Les fruitz immeurs feront à grand
  efclandre
Grand vitupere à l'vn grande louange.

He will be taken to the corner of Luna
where he will be placed on foreign land.
The unripe fruit will be the subject of great
scandal. Great blame, to the others great
praise.

If Luna is to be understood as the moon, this quatrain is surprisingly good. The Americans landed on the moon led by Captain Armstrong in 1969. The "unripe fruit which causes great scandal" is the tragic explosion of the Space Shuttle Challenger in 1986. The

---

[1]*Aemathion.* either Macedonian or from Thessaly.
[2]*Cap.* Capet, Nostradamus' usual abbreviation of the French royal line.

great praise goes to the others, the Russians, who have satisfactorily installed their space station, the MIR, which is in continual use.

Century IX

IX.LXVI

Paix, vnion fera & changement,
Eftatz, offices bas hault, & hault bien
*   bas.*
Dreffer voiage le fruict premier torment,
Guerre ceffer, ciuil proces debatz.

There will be peace, union and change, estates and offices low (become) high, those high very low. To prepare for a journey torments the first child. War to cease, legal processes debates.

This quatrain could apply to any postwar period because of the inevitable changes that follow war, both for the victors and the vanquished.

Century IX

IX.LXVII

Du hault des montz à l'entour de Lizer
Port à la roche Valen cent affemblez
De chafteau neuf pierre late en donzere,
Contre le creft Romans foy affemblez.

From the top of the mountains around Isère a hundred assembled at the gate to the Vatican rock. From Châteauneuf, Pierrelatte in Danzère. Against the Crest, Romans assembled in faith.

This quatrain implies religious troubles especially in line 4, with those of Rome assembled against the Moslem *creft*, crescent. Almost certainly a failed quatrain.

Century IX

IX.LXVIII

Du mont Aymar[1] fera noble obfcurcie,
Le mal viendra au ioinct de fonne &
*   rofne*
Dans bois caichez foldatz iour de
*   Lucie,[2]*
Qui ne fut onc vn fi horrible throfne.

The noble of Mont Aymar will become obscure the evil will come at the junction of the Saone and the Rhône. Soldiers hidden in the woods on (Saint) Lucy's day, there was never so horrible a throne.

This last line is horribly reminiscent of another quatrain where Nostradamus describes war "on its dreadful throne," VIII.XLVI.

[1]*Mont Aymar.* Montélimar? or "by the mountains of slaughter."
[2]*Lucie.* St. Lucy's day, December 13.

This one probably describes the sack of Lyons, between the junction of the rivers, in 1793. It was done by soldiers of the Revolutionary forces and there was great bloodshed. The key word, *mont Aymar,* is still undeciphered.

Century IX

IX.LXIX

Sur le mont de Bailly & la Brefle
Seront caichez de Grenoble les fiers,
Oultre Lyon, Vien. eulx fi grande grefle,
Langoult[1] en terre n'en reftera vn tiers.

On the mountain of Sain Bel and l'Arbesle the proud people of Grenoble will be hidden. Beyond Lyons at Vienne there will be such great hail. Locusts on the land, not a third of it will remain.

A quatrain with lots of place names and a swarm of locusts but I cannot interpret it.

Century IX

IX.LXX

Harnois trenchant dans les flambeaux
 cachez
Dedans Lyon le iour du Sacrement,[2]
Ceux de Vienne feront treftous hachez
Par les cantons Latins Mafcon ne
 ment.

Sharp armor hidden in the torches at Lyons on the day of the sacrament. All those of Vienne will be cut to pieces by the Latin cantons. Mâcon does not lie.

Century IX

IX.LXXI

Aux lieux facrez animaux veu à trixe,[3]
Auec celuy qui n'ofera le iour:
A Carcaffonne pour disgrace propice,
Sera posé pour plus ample feiour.

Animals with hair seen at the holy places with one who does not dare (to face) the day. Carcassonne is suitable for the disgrace and will be left for a longer stay.

A complicated quatrain without any apparent meaning.

[1] *Langoult.* O.F. *langouste,* a locust, not crayfish, as in modern French.
[2] *Sacrement.* Understood as Corpus Christi, the first Thursday after Trinity Sunday.
[3] *trixe.* Gk. *thrix,* hair or wool. Perhaps sheep in this context?

Century IX

IX.LXXII

Encor feront les faincts temples pollus,
Et expillez par Senat Tholoffain,
Saturne deux trois cicles reuollus,
Dans Auril, May, gens de nouueau
    leuain.

Again the holy temples will be polluted
and plundered by the Senate of Toulouse.
Saturn having completed two or three cy-
cles in April and May, there will be people
of a new leaven.

A cycle of Saturn lasts for 29.5 years. Presumably these "two or three" cycles follow the sack of Toulouse. Nostradamus appears to fear that the Calvinists will take over and despoil the churches. It is also possible that line 3 may mean two times three cycles of Saturn, i.e., six, which would total 177 years, a figure also mentioned by Nostradamus in his preface.

Century IX

IX.LXXIII

Dans Fois entrez Roy ceiulee Turbao,
Et regnera moins reuolu Saturne,
Roy Turban blanc Bizance coeur ban,
Sol, Mars, Mercure pres la hurne.

The king enters Foix wearing a blue tur-
ban, he will reign for less than a revolu-
tion of Saturn. The king with the white
turban, his heart banished to Byzantium,
Sun, Mars and Mercury near Aquarius.

This quatrain, because of the turbans, apparently describes a Moslem or Eastern invasion. Foix is understood to belong to a blue-turbaned man who rules for less than one cycle of Saturn, 29.5 years. In other quatrains the Ayatollah, the man of the white turban, is described as being followed by the "man in blue, perse." McCann (1942) dates this quatrain as February 18, 1981, but I think it is still unfulfilled. The Perse may be the precursor of the Antichrist or the Antichrist himself.

Century IX

IX.LXXIIII

Dans la cité de Fertfod[1] homicide,
Fait & fait multe beuf arant ne
macter,[2]
Retour encores aux honneurs
d'Artemide,
Et à Vulcan corps morts fepulturer.[3]

In the homicidal city of Fertsod again and again many oxen plow, not sacrificed. Again a return to the honors of Artemis. To Vulcan the corpses of the dead for burial.

Fertfod is obviously the clue to this quatrain but unfortunately it has not been deciphered as yet.

Century IX

IX.LXXV

De l'Ambraxie & du pays de Thrace,
Peuple par mer mal & fecours Gaulois,
Perpetuelle en Prouence la trace,
Auec veftiges de leur couftume & loix.

From Arta and the country of Thrace, people ill by sea, help from the Gauls. In Provence their perpetual trace, remnants of their customs and laws.

This quatrain appears to describe the Greeks returning to ask aid from southern France, and particularly Provence, of which their early colonial settlers were particularly fond.

Century IX

IX.LXXVI

Auec le noir[4] Rapax & fanguinaire,
Yffu du peaultre[5] de l'inhumain Neron,
Emmy[6] deux fleuues main gauche
militaire,
Sera murtry par Ioyne chaulueron.[7]

With the rapacious and bloody king, sprung from the pallet of the inhuman Nero. Between two rivers, the military on the left, he will be murdered by a bald young man.

I cannot interpret this quatrain.

[1]*Fertfod.* La Ferté? Sodom?
[2]*macter.* L. *mactare,* to slaughter.
[3]*fepulturer.* O.F. *sepultrer,* to bury.
[4]*noir.* usual anagram for *roi.*
[5]*peaultre.* pallet, brothel, rudder (Laver).
[6]*Emmy.* O. F. in between.
[7]*chaulueron.* Diminutive of *chauve,* bald.

Century IX

IX.LXXVII

Le regne prins le Roy conuiera,
La dame prinfe à mort iurez à fort,
La vie à Royne fils on defniera,
Et la pellix[1] au fort de la confort.

The kingdom taken, the king will plot, the
lady taken to death by those sworn by lot.
They will refuse life to the queen's son and
the mistress suffers the same fate as the
wife.

For once a good, clear quatrain describing the fates of Marie Antoinette and Mme. du Barry. After the royal family's imprisonment,
Louis XVI was executed in January, 1793. He was condemned by the
Convention who elected their powers to itself. However, the queen,
who was not executed until the following October, was judged by a
newly created revolutionary tribunal with a jury elected by lot. This
was an institution unknown to the France of Nostradamus' day. The
third line tells of the fate of their son, Louis XVII, his kingdom was
denied to him. The last line is the most interesting of all. While the
queen was imprisoned in the Conciergerie the mistress of Louis XV,
Mme. du Barry, was held in the prison of Sainte-Pélagie. An impressive quatrain.

Century IX

IX.LXXVIII

La dame Grecque de beauté laydique,[2]
Heureufe faicte de procs innumerable,
Hors tranflatee au regne Hifpanique,
Captiue prinfe mourir mort miferable.

The Greek woman of the beauty of Lais
is made happy by innumerable suitors.
Transferred out to the Spanish kingdom
she is captured, taken to die a wretched
death.

Several modern commentators interpret the lady as Democracy,
which originated in Greece and which started to die out in Europe
beginning with the Spanish Civil War, 1936.

---

[1]*pellix.* L. *pelex*, concubine.
[2]*laydique. Lais* was the most beautiful woman in Corinth, but possibly this is derived
from the opposite meaning, *laid*, ugly.

Century IX

IX.LXXIX

Le chef de claffe par fraude ftratageme,
Fera timides fortir de leurs galleres,
Sortis murtris chef renieur de crefme,
Puis par l'embusche luy rendront les
  faleres.

The leader of the fleet through deceitful trickery will make the scared come out of their galleys. Having come out, murdered, the leader to renounce the holy oil. Then through an ambush they give him his just deserts.

The holy oil in line 3 smacks of the oil used in the coronation of kings, but otherwise this is completely obscure.

Century IX

IX.LXXX

Le Duc voudra les fiens exterminer,
Enuoyera les plus forts lieux eftranges,
Par tyrannie Pize & Luc ruiner,
Puis les Barbares fans vin feront
  vendanges.

The duke wants to kill his followers. He will send the strongest to the most alien places. Through tyranny he ruins both Pisa and Lucca then the Barbarians will harvest grapes without wine.

I cannot decipher this quatrain.

Century IX

IX.LXXXI

Le Roy rufé entendra fes embufches
De trois quartiers ennemis affaillir,
Vn nombre eftrange larmes de
  coqueluches[1]
Viendra Lemprin[2] du traducteur faillir.

The crafty king will understand his ambushes from three sides the enemies threaten. A large amount of strange tears from the hooded ones. The splendor of the translator will fail.

Could the translator of line 4 be the same as the one in IX.I who also gets into trouble with Church and State?

---

[1]*coqueluches.* hooded men, probably monks.
[2]*Lemprin.* Gk. *lampros,* splendor.

Century IX
IX.LXXXII

Par le deluge & peftilence forte
La cité grande de long temps affiegee,
La fentinelle & garde de main morte,
Subite prinfe, mais de nul oultragee.

By the flood and the great plague the great
city is besieged for a long time. The sentry
and guard killed by hand, suddenly captured but none wronged.

Yet another vague, generalized quatrain. A great city, troubled by
floods and the plague, is besieged and vanquished. Probably a failed
quatrain.

Century IX
IX.LXXXIII

Sol vingt de taurus fi fort terre
  trembler.
Le grand theatre rempli ruinera,
L'air, ciel & terre obfcurcir & troubler,
Lors l'infidelle Dieu & fainctz voguera.

The sun in twenty degrees of Taurus there
will be a great earthquake. The great theater, full, will be ruined. Darkness and
trouble in the air, sky and land when they
call upon the faithless God and the Saints.

This quatrain is a typical description of an earthquake. Nos-
tradamus gives the day but not the year of its happening. *Sol vingt de
Taurus* means twenty days after the sun moves into Taurus, giving us
either I May by the old Julian calendar, or May 21 by the present one.
This seems to link with the general quatrains of doom around the
Millennium. Even God appears to have failed mankind. See quatrains
I.LXXXVII and X.XLIX for other general disasters of this type and
period.

Century IX
IX.LXXXIIII

Roy expofé parfaira L'hecatombe,
Apres auoir trouué fon origine,
Torrent ouurir de marbre & plomb la
  tombe
D'vn grand Romain d'enfeigne
  Medufine.

The king exposed will complete the slaughter once he has found his origin. A torrent
to open the tomb of marble and lead, of a
great Roman with the Medusine motto.

The key to this quatrain lies in the word *Medufine.* If it is an anagram
of *Deus in Me,* this would indicate that the tomb uncovered acciden-
tally in a flood is the real tomb of St. Peter, as that was his device.
This would mean that the one uncovered some years ago is not that
of St. Peter, but of another early pope.

Century IX

IX.LXXXV

Paffer Guienne, Languedoc & le Rofne,
D'Agen tenens de Marmande & la
    Roole,
D'ouurir par foy par roy[1] Phocé[2] tiêdra
    fon trofne
Conflit aupres faint Pol de Maufeole.[3]

To pass Guienne, Languedoc and the
Rhône from Agen, holding Marmande
and La Réole. To open the wall through
the king. Marseilles will hold its throne.
A battle near St. Pol-de-Mausole.

Apart from the fact that Nostradamus knew Agen, Marseilles and St. Pol-de-Mausole, there is no cohesive factor in this quatrain.

Century IX

IX.LXXXVI

Du bourg Lareyne paruiêdront droit à
    Chartres
Et feront pres du pont Authoni panfe,[4]
Sept pour la paix cautelleux comme
    martres
Feront entree d'armee à Paris claufe.

From Bourg-la-Reine they will go directly
to Chartres, they will pause near the Pont
d'Anthony. Seven for peace, as crafty as
martens, they will enter a closed Paris
with weapons.

The "seven for peace," the seven allied nations who joined against Napoleon and entered Paris on July 3, 1815, were Austria, England, Prussia, Portugal, Sweden, Spain and Russia. The city was stripped of its troops when the French army was evacuated to Chartres, taking up positions on their way to the Loire, passing through Bourg-la-Reine and the Pont d'Anthony, under which they are reputed to have camped. A good quatrain.

Century IX

IX.LXXXVII

Par la foreft du Touphon[5] essartee,
Par hermitage fera pofé le temple,
Le duc d'Eftampes par fa rufe inuentee,
Du mont Lehori prelat donra exemple.

In the cleared forest of Touphon the temple
will be placed near the Hermitage. The
duc d'Etampes, through the ruse he in-
vented, will give an example to the priest
of Mont Lehori.

---

[1]*par roy.* possibly O.F. *parroi,* wall?
[2]*Phocé.* Marseilles.
[3]St. Pol-de-Mausole. A convent, then an asylum where Van Gogh stayed, outside St. Rémy-de-Provence.
[4]*panfe.* misprint for *paufe,* to rhyme with line 4.
[5]*Touphon.* doubtful. Possibly Gk. *tophion,* a plaster quarry, or F. *touffe,* a clump.

The clue to this quatrain probably lies in line 3. Three mistresses of French kings held the title d'Estampes. First Anne de Pisselieu, then Diane de Poitiers and later Henri IV's mistress, Gabrielle d'Estrées. But I cannot decipher *mont Lehori* in line 4.

Century IX

IX.LXXXVIII

Calais, Arras fecours à Theroanne,
Paix & femblant fimulera lefcoutte,[1]
Soulde[2] d'Alabrox[3] defcendre par
    Roâne
Deftornay peuple qui deffera la routte.[4]

Calis and Arras, help to Thérouanne, the spy will simulate peace and semblance. The soldiers of Savoy go down by Roanne. Those who would stop the rout are turned away.

This quatrain must refer to incidents before 1558, when Calais fell to the French. Both Arras and Thérouanne belonged to Spain. When Calais fell, Philip II, husband of the English queen, lost all rights to Calais. On February 5, 1556, the Treaty of Vaucelles was declared between France and Spain. Therefore, this quatrain was probably written between the truce and the Spanish attack of 1557. Savoy *(Alabrox)* was almost completely occupied by the French during this period, so it is possible that a garrison of soldiers was sent there after St. Quentin. The borders of Savoy were only thirty-five miles from Roanne.

Century IX

IX.LXXXIX

Sept ans fera Philip, fortune profpere,
Rabaiffera des Arabes l'effaict,
Puis fon mydi[5] perplex rebors affaire
Ieufne ognyon[6] abyfmera fon fort.

Fortune will favor Philip for seven years, he will cut down again the exactions of the Arabs. Men in the middle of a perplexing, contrary affair, young Ogmios will destroy his stronghold.

The first seven years of Louis Philippe's reign, 1830–38, were extremely fortunate. He managed to subdue the Arabs *(Rabaiffera des Arabes l'effaict)* and to consolidate the French occupation of Algeria.

[1]*lefcoutte.* O.F. spy, scout.
[2]*Soulde.* O.F. pay or mercenaries.
[3]*Alabrox.* classical inhabitants of Savoy.
[4]*routte.* either O.F. *route,* a rout, or *route,* a road?
[5]*fon mydi.* either in middle age, or to the South?
[6]*ognyon.* The Celtic Hercules.

In the middle of his reign, 1838–40, he will be troubled by the Eastern question and the result shames both him and France. Finally, in 1848, the French dethrone him and keep him under guard.

Century IX

IX.XC

I'n capitaine de la grand Germanie
Se viendra rendre par fimulé fecours
I'n Roy des roys ayde de Pannonie,[1]
Que fa reuolte fera de fang grand
   cours.

A captain of Greater Germany will come to deliver false help. King of Kings. To support Hungary. His war will cause great shedding of blood.

The Greater Germany sounds uncannily like the *Grossdeutschland* of Hitler's Germany, the Third Reich. The second line of the quatrain is excellent. Hitler annexed Poland under the pretext of feigned help, as Nostradamus says in I.XLV. For a time Hitler was almost all-powerful in Europe, Russia and Asia, truly a king of kings, Lord of all he surveyed. He also captured Hungary, line 3, and the war he started killed about fourteen million people among the soldiers of both sides and according to some estimates as many again among the civilian population and the concentration camps.

Century IX

IX.XCI

L'horrible pefte Perynte[2] & Nicopolle,[3]
Le Cherfonnez[4] tiendra & Marceloyne,[5]
La Theffalie vaftera l'Amphipolle,[6]
Mal incogneu & le refus d'Anthoine.

The dreadful plague at Perinthus and Nicopolis will take the Peninsula and Macedonia. It will lay waste Thessaly and Amphibolis, an unknown evil, refused by Anthony.

Here we have a plethora of place names ranging throughout Greece and parts of Turkey but there seems no linking factor save that of the plague. Anthony may stand for Antoine de Navarre, father of Henri IV, but the whole quatrain seems extremely unlikely.

---

[1]*Pannonie.* Panonia, classical Hungary.
[2]*Perynte.* Modern Eski Eregli.
[3]*Nicopolle.* Modern Preveza.
[4]*Cherfonnez.* Either the Gallipoli Peninsula (Cheronese) or the Peloponnesus.
[5]*Marceloyne.* probable error for Macedoine.
[6]*Amphipolle.* near modern Salonika.

Century IX

IX.XCII

Le Roy vouldra dans cité neufue entrer
Par ennemys expugner[1] lon viendra
Captif libere faulx dire & perpetrer,
Roy dehors eftre, loin d'ennemys
    tiendra.

*The king will want to enter the new city,
they will come to subdue it through its
enemies. A captive, falsely faced to speak
and act. The king to be outside he will stay
far from the enemy.*

The *cité neufue* may refer to New York (as in VI.XCVII) being
actually attacked during a war. This has not happened to date, so this
quatrain must be regarded as futuristic and probably a Millennium
quatrain as well. See X.XLIX where Nostradamus sees New York as
being attacked through its water supply. The king outside (*Roy dehors
eftre*) may refer to the President of the United States and other essential staff, holed up in a secret underground bunker away from the city,
from which they will continue to direct the war.

Century IX

IX.XCIII

Les ennemis du fort bien eflongnez,
Par chariots conduict le baftion,
Par fur les murs de Bourges efgrongnez,
Quand Hercules battra l'Haemathion.[2]

*The enemies are very far from the strong
man, the bastion is brought by wagons.
Above, the crumbled walls of Bourges,
when Hercules strikes the Macedonian.*

This quatrain describes Aemathion, who in this context can stand
for Louis XIV, pushing back his enemies and consequently enlarging
the borders of France. Bastions of earth were constructed at the
fortification by Vauban. It was during his time that Bourges fell into
ruin. The final line refers to a labor worthy of Hercules, the construction of the lengthy Languedoc Canal. It was started in 1666 and
finished in 1681 at the cost, at that time, of 34,000,000 francs and it
was the wonder of the age. This new route freed the French from
dependency on the western area of the Mediterranean and became
the French equivalent of the Pillars of Hercules, Gibraltar.

---

[1]*expugner*. L. *expugnare*, to storm, subdue, violate.
[2]*Haemathion*. As Aemathion, Macedonian, or from Thessaly.

Century IX

IX.XCIIII

Foibles galleres feront vnies enfemble,
Ennemis faux le plus fort en rampart:
Faible affaillies l'ratiflaue tremble,
Lubecq & Myfne tiendront barbare
    part.

Weak galleys will be joined together, the false enemy is strongest on the ramparts. Bratislava trembles, the weak attacked. Lübeck and Meissen will take the Barbarian's side.

An incomprehensible quatrain, probably a failed one.

Century IX

IX.XCV

Le nouueau faict[1] conduyra l'exercite,[2]
Proche apamé[3] iufques au pres du
    riuage,
Tendant fecour de Milannoile[4] eflite,
Duc yeux priué à Milan fer de cage.

The new fact will lead the army almost cut off as far as the river bank, holding out for help from the Milanese elite. The duc loses his eyes in an iron cage in Milan.

Milan belonged to the Hapsburgs until 1859. A lot of commentators take the last line as referring to Mussolini, but his public hanging was somewhat different from losing his eyes in an iron cage. Probably a failed quatrain.

Century IX

IX.XCVI

Dans cité entrer exercit[5] defniee,
Duc entrera par perfuafion,
Aux foibles portes clam[6] armee amenee,
Mettront feu, mort de fang effufion.

The army denied entry to the city, the duke will enter through persuasion. Secretly the army led to the weak gates. They put it to fire, death and the flowing of blood.

I cannot interpret this quatrain.

---

[1]*faict.* a fact, or the newly elected one.
[2]*exercite.* L. *exercitus,* army.
[3]*apamé.* Gk. *apamao,* to cut off.
[4]*Milannoile.* probably Milanese.
[5]*exercit.* L. *exercitus,* army.
[6]*clam.* L. secretly.

Century IX

IX.XCVII

De mer copies en trois parts diuifees,
A la feconde les viures failleront,
Defefperez cherchant champs Helifees,
Premiers en breche entrez victoire
auront.

The forces at sea divided into three parts, the second one will run out of supplies. In despair, looking for the Elysian Fields, the first entering the breach will have victory.

In this quatrain we have two battles, one naval and one on land. The Elysian Fields were the Greek version of heaven, probably standing for the goal the army was attempting to reach. But I cannot grasp any solid facts from this quatrain.

Century IX

IX.XCVIII

Les affligez par faute d'vn feul taint,
Contremenant[1] à partie oppofite,
Aux Lygonnois mandera que contraint
Seront de rendre le grand chef de
Molite.[2]

Those afflicted through the fault of a single infected one, the transgressor will be in the opposite party. He will send to the Lyonnais and compel them to give themselves up to the great leader of Molite.

I cannot interpret this quatrain.

Century IX

IX.XCIX

Vent Aquilon fera partir le fiege,
Par murs gerer cendres, chaulz, &
poufiere,
Par pluye apres qui leur fera bein
piege,[3]
Dernier fecours encontre leur frontiere.

The North wind will cause the siege to be raised, to throw the cinders over the walls, lime and dust. Afterwards, through rain which does them much harm, the last help is met at their frontier.

Most commentators take this quatrain as describing Napoleon's retreat from Moscow, the north *(Aquilon)*. He finds help only at the frontiers of his empire, having lost so many men due to the appalling weather they encountered on the expedition.

[1]*Contremenant.* error for *contrevenant.*
[2]*Molite* ? either *Melita*, Malta, or Gk. *molos*, war.
[3]*piege.* A. Pr. *piegi*, worse, harmful.

Century IX

IX.C

Naualle pugne[1] nuit fera fuperee,[2]
Le feu aux naues[3] à l'Occident ruine:
Rubriche neufue la grand nef coloree,
Ire à vaincu, & victoire en bruine.

A naval battle will be overcome at night. Fire in the ruined strips of the West. A new coding, the great ship colored with anger to the vanquished. Victory in a mist.

This quatrain may well describe Pearl Harbor, which was attacked very early one morning in 1941 by Japanese planes which bombed the American fleet. The great tankers were set on fire to the ruin of America, the West, line 2. Does the new coding, *rubriche neufue,* mean the formula for this new type of warmongering attack, which finally brings anger to a defeated Japan and hazy glimpses of victory to a stunned America? The *coloree* of the ships is probably camouflage. A good quatrain.

Century X

X.I

L'ennemy l'ennemy foy promife
Ne fe tiendra, les captifs retenus:
Prins preme[4] mort & le reste en chemife,
Damné le refte pour eftre fouftenus.

To the enemy the enemy faith promised will not be kept, the captives retained. One is taken near to death the remainder in their shirts, the rest damned for being supporters.

This quatrain is usually read nowadays as a general quatrain about the Vichy régime, when the Germans failed to make collaboration a two-way proposition to the French people.

Century X

X.II

Voille gallere voil de nef cachera,
La grande claffe[5] viendra fortir la moindre
Dix naues[6] proches le torneront poulfer,
Grande vaincue vnies à foy ioindre.

The ship's sail will hide the sailing galley, the great fleet will drive out the lesser one. Nearby ten ships will turn to drive it back, the great one conquered, to join united in faith.

[1]*pugne.* L. *pugna,* battle.
[2]*fuperee.* L. *superatus,* overcome.
[3]*naues.* L., ships.
[4]*preme.* O.F. close, near.
[5]*claffe.* L. *classus,* fleet.
[6]*naues.* L. *navus,* ship.

There may possibly be a connection between this quatrain and IX.C. It describes a naval battle in which ships are either camouflaged or hidden by a smoke screen. The great one who is conquered may be the USA, which joins the Allies after the attack on Pearl Harbor 1941. Alternatively, it could apply to one of the many actions which took place in the Mediterranean from 1940 to 1943.

Century X

X.III

En apres cinq troupeau ne mettra hors
vn
Fuytif pour Penelon l'afchera,
Faulx murmurer fecours venir par lors,
Le chef le fiege lors habandonnera.

After the fifth will not put out a flock, a fugitive will be turned loose for Penelon. To murmur falsely, then to come in aid, then the chief will abandon the siege.

The key word to this quatrain is *Penelon,* which has not been deciphered. It may possibly be an anagram for *Polone,* Poland.

Century X

X.IIII

Sus la minuict conducteur de l'armee
Se fauluera, fubit efuanouy,
Sept ans apres la fame non blafmee,
A fon retour ne dira oncq ouy.

At midnight the leader of the army will run away, suddenly disappeared. Seven years later, his reputation unblemished to his return "yes" will not once be said.

After his defeat at the Battle of Worcester 1651, Charles II fled to France through Scotland, in disguise. His usurper, Cromwell, actually ruled for seven years, and Charles was restored in 1660. Nostradamus' last line is ambiguous. Not all the English welcomed the return of the Stuart monarchy. It is a general quatrain but fits these events quite simply.

Century X

X.V

Albi & Caftres feront nouuelle ligue,
Neuf Arriens Lisbons & Portugues,
Carcas, Tholoffe confumeront leur
brigue
Quand chief neuf monftre de
Lauragues.

Albi and Castres will make a new alliance, new Arians, Lisbon and the Portuguese. Carcassonne, Toulouse will join their intrigue when a new chief is the monster from the Lauragues.

The new Arians are the interesting subject here. Certainly Hitler used Portugal and the Portuguese as a Fifth Column during the Second World War. But it is more likely that Nostradamus was referring to the Albigensian Crusade, 1208–13.

Century X
X.VI

Sardon[1] Nemans fi hault desborderont,
Qu'on cuidera[2] Deucalion renaiftre,
Dans le coloffe la plus part fuyront,
Vefta fepulchre feu eftaint apparoiftre.

The Gardon will flood Nîmes so high that they will think Ducalion has been reborn. In the colossus the greater part will flee, Vesta's fire appears extinguished in the tomb.

According to Jaubert a storm broke out at Nîmes in 1557, which lasted from 5 A.M. to 9 P.M. and caused the local river Gardon to flood. Apparently many antiquities were revealed when the waters withdrew. Exactly the same thing happened October 3, 1988, when a cloudburst flooded Nîmes in several hours, 8 A.M. to 2 P.M., to a height of 2 meters of water. Shall we find further Roman remains when the floods and mud withdraw?

Century X
X.VII

Le grand conflit qu'on apprefte à Nancy,
L'aemathien dira tout le foubmetz,
L'ifle Britanne par vin, fel enfolcy,
Hem mi deux Phi long temps ne tiêdra Metz.

The great fight that they prepare at Nancy; Amathien will say, I subjugate all. The British Isles in trouble through wine and salt. Hem.mir, Philip two. Metz will not hold out for long.

The reference to wine and salt, taxes, the gabelle, are linked by this quatrain in some way with England (see IX.XLIX). But I am not happy with the various suggestions made by commentators to date. It seems more probable that *deux Phi* refers to Philip II, an everpresent personality in Nostradamus' *Prophéties,* who will attack French-occupied Lorraine. Metz was finally ceded to France in 1648 but had been under its control from 1552, so Nostradamus is simply stating a known, contemporary fact. Nancy was handed back to its duke in 1661 having been occupied for twenty-seven years.

[1] *Sardon.* probable error for Gardon.
[2] *cuidera.* O.F. to think, believe.

Century X

X.VIII

Index & poulfe parfondera[1] le front
De Senegalia le Conte à fon filz propre
La Myrnarmee[2] par plufieurs de
* prinfront*
Trois dans fept iours bleffes mors.

With index finger and thumb he will wet
the forehead, the count of Senegalia to his
own son. Through several, Venus in short
order, three are wounded to death in seven
days.

On June 15, 1856, the prince imperial, son of Napoleon III, was baptized *(index & poulfe parfondera)*. His godfather was Pope Pius IX, who was the son of Count Mastia Ferretti of Senegallia. Venus may be interpreted as the Empress Eugénie, but line 4 remains unexplained.

Century X

X.IX

De Caftillon figuires iour de brune,
De feme infame naiftra fouuerain prince
Surnon de chausses perhume luy
* pofthume,*
Onc Roy ne feut fi pire en fa prouince.

In the Castle of Figueras on a misty day
a sovereign prince will be born of an un-
worthy woman. The surname of Chausses
on the ground will make him posthumous.
Never was so bad a king in his province.

See X.XI also for another reference to posthumous child. Loomis suggests that this verse describes one of Nostradamus' Antichrists.

Century X

X.X

Tafche de murdre enormes adulteres,
Grand ennemy de tout le genre humain
Que fera pire qu'ayeulx, oncles, ne peres
En fer, feu, eau, fanguin & inhumain.

Stained with murder and enormous adul-
teries, great enemy of all mankind he will
be worse than his ancestor, uncles and
fathers. In steel, fire and water, bloody
and inhuman.

The epithet *grand ennemy de tout le genre humain* was applied to Napoleon by the Venetian ambassador, Morenigo. So perhaps the rest of the generalities also apply to him.

---

[1]*parfondera*. L. *parfundere*, to sprinkle, moisten.
[2]*Myrnarmee*. L. *Mimnermia*, a surname of Venus.

Century X

X.XI

Dessoubz Ionchere du dangereux paffage
Fera paffer le pofthume fa bande,
Les monts Pyrens paffer hors fon
　bagaige
De Parpignam courira duc à tende.

In the dangerous passage underneath Jun-
quera, the posthumous man will make his
men cross. To cross the Pyrenean moun-
tains without his baggage the duke will
hasten to Perpignan from Tende.

This quatrain may be related to X.IX through the connection of the posthumous child. Otherwise I cannot place it.

Century X

X.XII

Efleu en Pape d'efleu fera mocqué,
Subit foudain efmeu prompt & timide,
Par trop bon doulx à mourir prouocqué,
Crainte eftainte la nuit de fa mort
　guide.

Elected as pope he will be mocked when
elected, suddenly and unexpectedly moved,
prompt and timid. Caused to die through
too much goodness and kindness he will
fear for the guide killed on the night of his
death.

This quatrain is applied by most commentators to Cardinal Santa Severina, who was elected as Pope Gregory XIV in 1591, but who died two months later, his election having been declared illegal. But his successor, Innocent IX, also died within two months of taking office.

Century X

X.XIII

Soulz la pafture d'animaux ruminant
Par eux conduicts au ventre
　herbipolique[1]
Soldatz caichez les armes bruit menant,
Non loing temptez de cite Antipolique.

Beneath the food of ruminating animals;
led by them into the center of their feeding
place. Soldiers hidden, their weapons
being noisy, tried not far from the city of
Antibes.

[1]*herbipolique.* ? the marketplace?

Century X

X.XIIII

Vrnel Vaucile[1] fans confeil de foy
  mefmes
Hardit timide par crainte prins vaincu,
Accompaigné de plufieurs putains
  blefmes
A Barcellonne aux chartreux conuaincu.

*Vrnel Vaucile without a plan of his own,
bold, timid for fear of being taken and
captured. Accompanied by several pale
whores converted in the Carthusian convent at Barcelona.*

The interpretation here depends upon *Vrnel Vaucile* in line 1. It does not seem to have any connection with the monastery at St. Urgel. The Carthusian convent at Barcelona is that of Mont Allegro.

Century X

X.XV

Pere duc vieux d'ans & de foif chargé,
Au iour extreme filz defniant les guiere[2]
Dedans le puis vif mort viendra plongé,
Senat au fil[3] la mort longue & legiere.

*The duke, father, old in years and trou-
bled with thirst, on the last day his son
denying him the jug. Into the well,
plunged alive, he will die. The Senate to
the son, a death long and light.*

A son is hanged for denying his thirsty father water to drink and then puts him down the well! The worst type of Nostradamus' writing because it is open to ridicule.

Century X

X.XVI

Heureux au regne de France, heureux
  de vie
Ignorant fang mort fureur & rapine,
Par non flateurs feras mys en enuie,
Roy defrobé trop de foy ea cuifine.

*Happy in the kingdom of France, happy
in life, ignorant of blood, death anger and
rage. By a flattering name he will be en-
vied, a king robbed, too much faith in the
kitchen.*

When he is happily established on the French throne, Louis XVIII will not die a violent death but lives happily. Because of this he was given the nickname *"le Désiré,"* "the flattering name" (line 3). His guilt lies in the fact that he does not sufficiently occupy himself with the public good. He was also a renowned glutton, line 4.

[1]*Vrnel Vaucile. Llanos de Urgel,* Plain of Urgel?
[2]*les guiere.* F. *d'aiguiere,* jug.
[3]*fil.* probably *filz,* son.

Century X

X.XVII

La royne Ergafte¹ voiant fa fille blefme,
Par vn regret dans l'eftomach encloz,
Crys lamentables feront lors
* d'Angolefme,*
Et au germain mariage fort clos.

The barren queen, seeing her daughter pale because of the unhappiness locked up in her stomach. Lamentable cries will come from Angoulême and the marriage to the cousin greatly impeded.

The *royne Ergafte* is a queen confined to manual labor in a penitentiary. Marie Antoinette was compelled to sew her own clothes when imprisoned in the Temple. Perhaps this is not the general impression of manual labor, but it certainly was painful to the queen. *Ergafte* also means captive, which Marie Antoinette certainly was. She saw her daughter, Madame Royale, pale with suffering. Madame Royale was betrothed to the duc d'Angoulême in 1787, and married him in 1799. But she remained childless *(l'estomach encloz)*, probably due to the troubles experienced with her family when enclosed in the Temple.

Century X

X.XVIII

Le ranc Lorrain fera place à Vendofme,
Le hault mys bas & le bas mys en
* hault,*
Le filz d'Hamon² fera efleu dans Rome,
Et les deux grands feront mys en
* deffault.*

The house of Lorraine will make way for Vendôme, the high put low and the low exalted. The son of Hamon will be elected in Rome, and the two great ones will be put at a loss.

This is a very successful prediction for Nostradamus. Henri IV, duc de Vendôme, will eclipse the house of Lorraine, and Henri IV, earlier known as *"le petit Béarnais,"* will be elevated to the high rank of king of France. This son of Hamon, the heretic, will be accepted as king by Rome. The two great ones who lose are the two Pretenders, the duc de Guise and the duc de Mayenne.

---

¹*Ergafte. Ergastulus,* penitentiary.
²*Hamon.* ? *Mamon,* wealth, in some editions.

Century X

X.XIX

Iour que fera par royne faluee,
Le iour apres le falut, la priere,
Le compte fait raifon & valbuee,
Par auant humble oncques ne feut fi
    fiere.

The day she will be saluted as queen, the
prayer the day after the blessing. The account is right and valid, once humble
there was never so proud a woman.

It is suggested that this quatrain applies to Elizabeth I of England
when she succeeded her sister, the childless Mary Tudor.

Century X

X.XX

Tous les amys qu'auront tenu party.
Pour rude en lettres mys mort &
    faccagé,
Biens publiez par fixe grand neanty,[1]
Onc Romain peuple ne feut tant
    outragé.

All of the friends who have belonged to the
party, put to death and looked for the
uncouth letters. The public possessions,
the great one annihilated by six. Never
were the Roman people so wronged.

This quatrain made little sense in Nostradamus' day, but applies
quite accurately to post-Fascist Italy. The drastic remedy makes it
appear more modern.

Century X

X.XXI

Par le defpit du Roy fouftenant
    moindre,
Sera meurdry luy prefentant les bagues,
Le pere au filz voulant nobleffe poindre
Fait comme à Perfe iadis feirent les
    Mague.

Through the king's spite in supporting the
lesser one, he will be murdered presenting
the jewels to him. The father wishing to
impress his son with nobility did what the
Magi used to do in Persia.

I can offer no explanation of this complicated quatrain.

---

[1]*neanty.* O.F. *néantir,* to annihilate.

Century X

X.XXII

Pour ne vouloir confentir au diuorce,
Qui puis apres fera cogneu indigne,
Le roy des Ifles fera chaffé par force
Mis à fon lieu que de roy n`aura figne.

For not wanting to consent to the divorce which then afterwards will be recognized as unworthy, the king of the islands will be forced to flee, and no one put in his place who has no sign of kingship.

This, and quatrain X.LX, describe the abdication of Edward VIII in 1936. The king's act was not popular among the British people, who had little love for the already twice-divorced Mrs. Simpson. Edward was therefore forced to leave the court and England because of Mrs. Simpson's unsuitable social position *(cogneu indigne)*. Finally, George VI, who was not in line for the kingship, is forced to accede to the British throne.

Century X

X.XXIII

Au peuple ingrat faictes les
*   remonftrances,*
Par lors l'armee fe faifira d'Antibe,
Dans l'arc Monech feront les doleances,
Et à Freius l'vn l'autre prendra ribe.

Remonstrances are made to the ungrateful people, then the army will seize Antibes. In the arch of Monaco the complaints will occur, and at Fréjus the shore will be taken by one from the other.

When Louis XVIII issued a proclamation urging fidelity to his new régime, the only place that remained loyal to Napoleon was Antibes. Both Louis and Napoleon used Fréjus, the former to embark for England, the latter when leaving for Elba.

Century X

X.XXIIII

Le captif prince aux Italles vaincu
Paffera Gennes par mer iufqu'à
*   Marfeille,*
Par grand effort des forens[1] furuaincu
Sauf coup de feu barril liqueur
*   d'abeille.*

The captive prince conquered in Italy will cross from Genoa to Marseilles by sea. By a great effort the foreigners will be overcome except for a gunshot, a barrel of bee's honey.

This quatrain appears to be linked with IV.XXVI, in which Napoleon's emblem of the bee also appears. Napoleon, a closely guarded

[1]*forens.* O.F. foreigner, stranger.

prisoner on Elba, escapes by sea in March and lands at Cannes, on the south coast of France, as is Marseilles. He is overcome again at Waterloo, where he seeks death in vain. The bees of his emblem will spill all their sweetness.

Century X

X.XXV

Par Nebro ouurir de Brifanne[1] paffage,
Bien eflongnez el tago fara muestra,
Dans Pelligouxe[2] fera commis l'outrage
De la grand dame affife sur l'orchestra.

Through the Ebro will be opened a passage to Brisanne, far away the Tago will make a demonstration. The outrage committed in Pelligouxe, of the great lady sitting in the orchestra.

I find it difficult to interpret this quatrain.

Century X

X.XXVI

Le fucceffeur vengera fon beau frere,
Occuper regne fouz vmbre de vengeance,
Occis oftacle fon fang mort vitupere,
Long temps Bretaigne tiendra auec la
France.

The successor will avenge his handsome brother and occupy the realm under the shadow of vengeance. He is killed, the obstacle of the blameworthy dead, his blood. For a long time Britain will hold with France.

This quatrain appears to predict the assassination of Robert Kennedy, following upon that of his brother the president, John F. Kennedy. It is interesting to see that Nostradamus foresees two brothers killed within a short period of time. Robert Kennedy's stand in the name of his brother leads to his death. One wonders what may happen to the third brother, Edward Kennedy. The last line seems to imply that once de Gaulle is dead Britain's relationship with France and the Common Market is a successful one. (See I.XXVI, VIII.XLVI, VIII.LXXVII.)

---

[1] *Brifanne.* Unsolved place name.
[2] *Pelligouxe.* Unsolved place name.

Century X

X.XXVII

Par le cinquieme & vn grand Hercules
Viendront le temple ouurir de main
  bellique,
Vn Clement, Iule & Afcans recules,
Lefpe, clef, aigle n'euronc fi grand
  picque.

Through the fifth and a great Hercules,
they will come to open the temple with the
hand of war. One, Clement, Julius and
Ascans put back, the sword, the key. The
eagle never once felt so great a dislike.

Century X

X.XXVIII

Second & tiers qui font prime muficque
Sera par Roy en honneur fublimee,
Par graffe & maigre prefque demy
  eticque
Raport de Venus faulx rendra deprimee.

The second and third make first-class
music. They will be sublimely honored by
the king. Through fat and thin, even half
emaciated, to be made debased by the false
report of Venus.

Century X

X.XXIX

De POL MANSOL dans cauerne
  caprine
Caché & prins extrait hors par la
  barbe,
Captif mené comme befte maftine
Par Begourdans amenee pres de Tarbe.

In the great cave of St. Pol-de-Mausole,
hidden and seized, pulled out by the beard,
the captive led like an animal, a mastiff,
brought near to Tarbes by the people of
Bigorre.

As mentioned elsewhere St. Pol-de-Mausole is situated just outside
Nostradamus' birthplace in St. Rémy-de-Provence. The quatrain describes a captive who is taken to Bigorre in Navarre.

Century X

X.XXX

Nepueu & fang du fainct nouueau
  venu,
Par le furnom fouftient arcs & couuert
Seront chaffez mis à mort chaffez nu,
En rouge & noir convertiront leur vert.

Nephew and of the blood of the newly
created saint, through his surname he will
sustain the arches and the roof. They will
be driven out naked and chased to their
deaths, their queen will be converted to red
from black.

I cannot decipher this quatrain.

Century X
X.XXXI

Le faint empire viendra en Germanie,
Ifmaelites¹ trouueront lieux ouuerts.
Anes vouldront auffi la Carmanie,
Les fouftenens de terre tous couuerts.

The Holy Empire will come to Germany,
the Arabs will find open places. The asses
will also want Carmania, the supporters
completely covered with earth.

Hogue interprets the first line of this quatrain as "The Russians will enter Afghanistan." I cannot follow his train of thought. To me, this quatrain appears to relate to the Holy Roman Empire and its trouble with the Turks and the Arabs. Carmania is a province in Persia, now Iran, situated at the entrance to the Persian Gulf.

Century X
X.XXXII

Le grand empire chacun an deuoir eftre
Vn fur les autres le viendra obtenir,
Mais peu de temps fera fon regne &
*   eftre,*
Deux ans aux naues fe pourra fouftenir.

The empire each year should become great.
One will come to hold (power) over all the
others. But his kingdom and life will last
a short time. In two years he will be able
to maintain himself in his ships.

Yet another quatrain I cannot decipher.

Century X
X.XXXIII

La faction cruelle à robbe longue,
Viendra cacher fouz les pointus
*   poignars*
Saifir Florence le duc & lieu
*   diphlongue²*
Sa defcouuerte par immeurs &
*   flangnards.³*

The cruel party, wearing long robes will
hide sharp daggers beneath. The duke to
seize Florence and the place of two words.
Its discovery through young ones and
flatterers.

The first two lines are reminiscent of the assassination of Julius Caesar in Rome at the Ides of March. But the capture of Florence obviously places the quatrain in the sixteenth or seventeenth century.

¹*Ifmaelites.* Not Jews, but Arabs who claim descent from Ishmael, the son of Abraham.
²*diphlongue.* Error for *diphtongue,* double word.
³*flangnards.* Pr. flatterer, wheedler.

Century X
X.XXXIIII

Gauloys qu'empire par guerre occupera
Par son beau frere mineur sera trahy,
Par cheval rude voltigeant trayera,
Du fait le frere long temps sera hay.

The Gaul who gains his empire through war will be betrayed by his younger brother in law. He will be dragged by an untrained nervous horse. For the act the brother will be hated for a long time.

This quatrain describes very aptly the situation of the king of Naples, Joachim Murat, who married Napoleon's younger sister, Caroline. Murat first betrayed Napoleon in 1814, but joined up with him again in 1815. He was also a renowned cavalry leader and had a severe accident falling from his horse. Apparently, according to Robb, 1942, this quatrain converted the eminent professors Jacques Barzun and Professor Siceloff of Columbia University because of its accuracy. They were reputed to say that the chances of the quatrain being fulfilled were "about zero." This comment could probably refer to many of Nostradamus' quatrains.

Century X
X.XXXV

Puyfnay royal flagrand d'ardant libide,
Pour fe iouyr de coufine germaine,
Habit de femme au temple d'Arthemide:
Allant murdry par incognu du Marne.

The younger son of a king, flagrant with burning lust to enjoy his first cousin. Women's attire in the temple of Diana, who will be murdered by the unknown man from Marne.

The last line of this quatrain suggests that a duc, the younger son of a king, probably the duc de Maine or Mayenne, will be involved in a royal scandal. But, unfortunately, although a probable situation, it does not tie in with anything specific. Probably a failed quatrain.

Century X
X.XXXVI

Apres le Roy du foucq guerres parlant,
L'ifle Harmotique[1] le tiendra à mefpris,
Quelques ans bons rongeant vn &
    pillant
Par tyrannie à l'ifle changeant pris.

After the king (of the stump?) speaks of wars, the United Island will despise him. For several years the good one gnaws and pillages. Through tyranny on the island its values change.

[1] *Harmotique*. Dubious. Possibly from Gk. *armoskitos*, joined together, united.

The United Islands are probably the British Isles, bringing the date of the quatrain to 1604 or later. Line 3 may describe privateers of the late sixteenth and seventeenth centuries such as Drake, Hawkins and Raleigh. But *du foucq* in line 1 defies interpretation and I do not see its relevance to James, so that this may be a failed quatrain.

Century X

X.XXXVII

Laffemblee grande pres du lac de Borget,
Se ralieront pres de Montmelian,
Marchans plus oultre penfifz feront proget
Chambry, Moriane combat fainct Iulian.

The great crowd near the lake of Le Bourget will rally near to Montmelian. Going further ahead, the thoughtful ones draw up a plan. Chambery, St. Julien de Maurienne, fight.

Yet another incomprehensible quatrain.

Century X

X.XXXVIII

Amour alegre non loing pofe le fiege,
Au fainct barbar feront les garnifons,
Vrfins Hadrie pour Gaulois feront plaige,
Pour peur rendus de l'armee aux Grifons. [1]

"Light of love" will not hold the siege for long, all the garrisons will be for the converted barbarian. The Ursins and Adria give security for the French, for fear of the army being handed over to the Grisons.

The normal nickname for Henri IV of France among his contemporaries was *"vert galant,"* perpetually gallant, which is very close to Nostradamus' *Amour alegre,* light of love. During the siege of Paris in 1590, Henri was not able to hold the garrisons for more than four months because of the advance of the duc de Parma from Flanders. Nostradamus described the occupants of the garrisons as devoted to barbarous things, by which he means they are clerical revolutionaries. Henri himself also changed his religion to obtain the French throne: "Paris is worth a mass." The connection with Switzerland, other than Protestantism, is unclear.

---

[1]*Grifons.* people of southeast Switzerland.

Century X
X.XXXIX

Premier fils vefue malheureux mariage,
Sans nuls enfans deux Ifles en difcord,
Auant dixhuict incompetant eage,
De l'autre pres plus bas fera l'accord.

The first son, a widow, an unfortunate marriage without any children. Two islands thrown into discord. Before eighteen years of age, a minor. Of the other even younger will be the betrothal.

This is an excellent quatrain and appears to have been understood by Nostradamus' contemporaries at the French court. It describes the fate of François II and his child bride, Mary, Queen of Scots. François II, the eldest son of the widowed Catherine de' Medicis, married Mary Stuart. Their short marriage was childless. Mary's return to Scotland caused discord between Scotland and England. François was still not quite eighteen years old when he died (seventeen years, ten months, fifteen days). His younger brother, who became Charles IX, was betrothed to Elizabeth of Austria when he was only eleven years old. An accurate quatrain.

Century X
X.XL

Le ieune nay au regne Britannique,
Qu'aura le pere mourant recommandé,
Iceluy mort LONOLE¹ donra topique,
Et à fon fils le regne demandé.

The young one born to the kingdom of Britain, which his dying father has commended to him. Once he is dead, London will disagree with him and the kingdom will be demanded back from his son.

This quatrain continues upon X.XXII, the abdication of Edward VIII in 1936. He is the true heir to the throne of Britain, left to him by his dying father. But he causes scandal *(topique)* in London by his behavior with Mrs. Simpson. Public hostility towards her earlier divorces caused the king to abdicate, the kingdom taken back from him by popular opinion, and given to his brother.

¹*LONOLE.* probably error for *Londres,* London.

Century X

X.XLI

En la frontiere de Cauffade & Charlus,
Non guieres loing du fonds de la vallee,
De ville Franche muficque à fon de
luths,
Enuironnez combouls[1] & grand
myttee.[2]

On the boundary of Caussade and Caylus,
not very far from the depths of the valley.
Music from Villefranche to the sound of
lutes, surrounded by cymbals and many
stringed instruments.

Since all the places mentioned here are small villages within fifty miles of Agen, where Nostradamus once lived, could he be describing a local festival?

Century X

X.XLII

Le regne humain d'Anglique geniture,
Fera fon regne paix vnion tenir,
Captiue guerre demy de fa clofture,
Long temps la paix leur fera maintenir.

The human reign of English offspring will
cause the kingdom to be united in peace.
Half captured in his enclosure in the war.
For a long time peace will be maintained
by then.

This is a general but very apt quatrain which describes Britain and the Pax Britannica of the nineteenth century, or less probably, the long peace England enjoyed under Walpole and the early Georges.

Century X

X.XLIII

Le trop bon temps trop de bonté royalle:
Fais & deffais prompt fubit negligence,
Legier croira faux d'efpoufe loyalle,
Luy mis à mort par fa beneuolence.

Too much of the good times and too much
royal bounty, made and quickly undone by
sudden negligence. He will lightly believe
his loyal wife false, whom, benevolently is
put to death.

Both Louis XVI and his loyal wife Marie Antoinette were put to death by the Revolutionaries. Louis irritated his advisers because he did not apply himself properly to affairs of state. He displayed great weakness and irresolution of character, as seen in the case of the diamond necklace when he was quite prepared to believe the queen

[1]*combouls.* Gk. *kumbalou,* cymbal.
[2]*myttee.* dubious. Possibly Gk. *mitos,* stringed instrument?

was involved. All of these characteristics, plus a basic benevolence, left him defenseless before the Revolutionaries.

Century X

X.XLIIII

Par lors qu'vn Roy fera contre les fiens,
Natif de Bloys fubiuguera Ligures:
Mammel,[1] Cordube & les Dalmatiens,
Des fept puis l'ôbre à Roy eftrennes[2] &
* lemures.[3]*

When a king is against his people a native of Blois will subdue the league. Mammel, Cordoba and the Dalmatians. Of the seven then a shadow to the king, new money and dead ghosts.

Quatrain VIII.XXXVIII discusses a king who will come from Blois. They probably refer to Henri III of France, who subjugates the League, line 2. He was descended from the comte de Blois and is elsewhere called *le grand du Blois* by Nostradamus. The seven in line 4 are the children of Catherine de' Medicis and Henri II, who are but shades of their parents.

Century X

X.XLV

Lombre du regne de Nauarre non vray,
Fera la vie de fort illegitime:
La veu promis incertain de Cambray,[4]
Roy Orleans donra mur legitime.

The shadow of the kingdom of Navarre is not true, it will make the life of a strong man illegal. The uncertain promise of Cambrai, the king at Orléans will make a lawful boundary.

Henri de Navarre, Henri IV, initially had only the shadow of a kingdom because he had to storm Paris by force. He led an irregular life and kept many mistresses including the wife of a governor of Cambrai to whom in return Henri granted hereditary possession of the town, line 3. Cambrai may also have a retrospective meaning of the Peace of Cambrai of 1529. Orléans may stand for either the town or the family.

[1]*Mammel.* if place name perhaps Mamel in the Baltic. O.F. *mamelle,* breast.
[2]*eftrennes.* Handsel, New Year money.
[3]*Lemures.* L. *lemures,* ghosts.
[4]*Cambray.* The peace of Cambrai, 1529, at which the French gave up their claims to Flanders.

Century X

X.XLVI

Vie fort mort de L'OR vilaine indigne,
Sera de Saxe non nouueau electeur:
De Brunfuic mandra d'amour figne,
Faux le rendant au peuple feducteur.

Because of the gold, the life, fate and death of an unworthy, sordid man. He will not become the new Elector of Saxony. From Brunswick he will send for a sign of love, the false seducer giving it to the people.

In this quatrain, set in Germany, Nostradamus states that Saxony will not have a new Elector. Maurice of Saxony did not enter the war against Charles V until 1552 and the Duchy of Brunswick played no significant role during the sixteenth century. Quite an accurate quatrain but partially, at least, retrospective.

Century X

X.XLVII

De Bourze ville à la dame Guyrlande
L'on mettra[1] fus par la trahifon faicte,
Le grand prelat de Leon par
*   Formande,[2]*
Faux pellerins & rauiffeurs defaicte.

In the town of Burgos, at the lady of the Garland, they will deliver the verdict on the treason committed. The great prelate of Leon through Formade, undone by false pilgrims and thieves.

The secret of this quatrain lies with the "Lady of the Garland."

Century X

X.XLVIII

Du plus profond de l'Efpaigne enfeigne,
Sortant du bout & des fins de l'Europe,
Troubles paffant aupres du pont de
*   Laigne,*
Sera deffaicte par bandes fa grand
*   troppe.*

Banners from the furthest corners of Spain, coming out from the ends and borders of Europe. Trouble passing near the bridge at Laigne, its great army will be routed by bands (of men).

The first line of this quatrain contains a good description of the Spanish Civil War, with the increasing involvement of the Germans and Italians. Nostradamus sees this trouble growing, as indeed it did, to become the Second World War, raging throughout Europe.

[1]*mettra.* literally, impose a verdict.
[2]*Formande.*? Formentera in the Balearics?

Laignes is a town forty miles northwest of Dijon, which was occupied by the Germans. Nostradamus also foresees this occupying force being routed, which it was, by the Allied Forces in 1944–45. A good general quatrain.

Century X

X.XLIX

Iardin du monde au pres de cité neufue,
Dans le chemin des montaignes cauees,
Sera faifi & plongé dans la Cuue,
Beuuant par force eaux foulfre
* enuenimees.*

The garden of the World near the New City, in the road of the hollow mountains. It will be seized and plunged in the tank, forced to drink water poisoned with sulphur.

This extraordinary quatrain talks of a city, New York, being poisoned through its water supply, an idea more suited to James Bond than to Nostradamus. The *cité neufue* is New York. The *Iardin du monde* is possibly a way of describing it as a world center. The second line is interesting. Could the "road of hollow mountains" be the nearest Nostradamus could get towards describing a street lined with skyscrapers? The tank is unclear. It could well mean a reservoir which becomes poisoned by sulphuric acid. This is not as unlikely as one might think. A similar thing happened in Britain in summer 1988 when a load of chemicals was wrongly dumped into a reservoir. (See IX.XCII, I.LXXXVII.)

Century X

X.L

La Meufe au iour terre de Luxembourg,
Defcouurira Saturne & trois en lurne,
Montaigne & pleine, ville, cité &
* bourg,*
Lorrain deluge trahifon par grand
* hurne.*

By day the Meuse in the land of Luxembourg will find Saturn and three in Aquarius. Mountain and plain, town city and borough. A flood in Lorraine betrayed by the great urn.

Insufficient material for dating, this quatrain describes an enormous flood.

Century X

X.LI

Des lieux plus bas du pays de Lorraine,
Seront des baffes Allemaignes vnis,
Par ceux du fiege Picards, Normans, du
* Maifne,*
Et aux cantons ce feront reunis.

Some of the lowest places in the country of Lorraine will be united with the Lower Germany. Through the people of the seats of Picardy, Normandy and Maine, they will be reunited with the cantons.

In 1871, Lorraine and the regions to the south, *plus bas,* such as Alsace, were united with Lower Germany, with the consent of those defeated in the Siege of Paris in 1871. All the areas mentioned suffered German occupation. Lorraine was not returned to France until 1919. Quite a comprehensive quatrain.

Century X

X.LII

Au lieu où LAYE & Scelde fe marient,
Seront les nopces de long temps maniees,
Au lieu d'Anuers où la crappe[1]
* charient,[2]*
Ieune vieilleffe conforte intaminee.

At the place where the Laye and the Scheldt join, a long time earlier, the marriage will be arranged. At the place in Antwerp where the chaff is carried, a young, undefiled wife and old age.

An obscure marriage which takes place between a very young girl and her old suitor. The rest makes no sense. Probably a failed quatrain. The Laye and the Scheldt rivers join up at Ghent.

Century X

X.LIII

Les trois pellices de loing s'entrebatron,
La plus grand moindre demeurera à
* l'efcoute:*
Le grand Selin n'en fera plus patron,
Le nommera feu pelte blanche routte.

Three prostitutes will quarrel for a long time. The greatest will remain to hear the least. The great Selin will no longer be her patron. She will call him fire, shield, a white rout.

If Selin refers as usual to Henri II, this quatrain would describe his many royal mistresses, Diane de Poitiers' rivals, such as Gabrielle d'Estrées. White may refer to Diana, as she normally wore only this color and her château on the Loire, Annecet, was decorated entirely in black and white.

[1]*crappe.* O.F. chaff (of wheat)
[2]*charient.* O.F. to carry, cast about.

Century X

X.LIIII

Nee en ce monde par concubine fertiue,
A deux hault mife par les triftes
nouuelles,
Entre ennemis fera prinfe captiue,
Et amené à Malings & Bruxelles.

Born into this world of a furtive concu-
bine, to two raised high by the bad news.
She will be taken captive among enemies
and brought to Malines and Brussels.

I cannot decipher this quatrain.

Century X

X.LV

Les malheureufes nopces celebreront,
En grande ioye, mais la fin
malheureufe:
Mary & mere nore defdaigneront,
Le Phybe mort, & nore plus piteufe.

The unfortunate marriage will be cele-
brated with great joy, but the end is un-
happy. The mother will despise the daugh-
ter-in-law, Mary. The Apollo dead and
the daughter-in-law more pitiable.

The word *"Mary"* is, as can be seen, spelled with a *y* in the original text, which makes Mary, Queen of Scots an obvious target for this quatrain. Mary's wedding to François II was not the happiest. Her mother-in-law, Catherine de' Medicis, caused great trouble with England by insisting that the English standard be linked with Mary's Scottish one, a symbol which Elizabeth I did not take lightly. The feeling of dislike between the two women was reciprocal. Mary used to refer to Catherine as "the merchant's daughter." *Phybe* may stand for François II, Mary's husband in that the first syllable, *Phye*, phi stands for *F.* and the *be* for *beta,* the second letter of the Greek alphabet, thus F.II, François II. The young couple married in 1558 but by 1560 the young Apollo, François, the great hunter, was dead and Mary left in the perilous coils of the Scottish situation. A very good, convoluted quatrain.

Century X

X.LVI

Prelat royal fon baiffant trop tiré,
Grand fleux de fang fortira par sa
bouche,
Le regne Anglicque par regne refpiré,
Long temps mort vif en Tunys comme
fouche.

The royal priest bowing too low, a great
flow of blood will come out of his mouth.
The Anglican reign, the breathing realm,
for a long time dead as a stump of wood,
living in Tunis.

I cannot decipher this quatrain.

Century X
X.LVII

Le fubleué ne cognoiftra fon fceptre,
Les enfans ieunes des plus grands
*   honnira:*
Oncques ne fut vn plus ord[1] cruel eftre,
Pour leurs efpoufes à mort noir[2]
*   bannira.*

The uplifted one will not know his scepter,
he will disgrace the young children of the
great ones. There was never so filthy or
cruel a person. As for their wives, the king
will banish them to death.

Century X
X.LVIII

Au temps du dueil que le felin
*   monarque,*
Guerroyera le ieune Aemathien:
Gaule branfler perecliter la barque,
Tenter Phoffens[3] au Ponant[4] entretien.

At a time of mourning the feline monarch
will make war with the young Aemathien.
France will shake, the barque will be in
danger. Marseilles to be tried, a talk in the
West.

Aemathien, the child of dawn and therefore the sun, refers here to Louis XIV, who adopted the sun as his device and was also called the Sun King. While there is a time of mourning for Louis XIII, the wily Philip of Spain will go to war against the new king. France is deeply shaken by the War of the Fronde, and the Barque of the Papacy is threatened by the new development of Jansenism.

Phoffens is Marseilles, which Louis XIV entered by breaching its walls in 1660. A year earlier he had been to Ponant, in the west of France, and it was on the island of Bidussoa that he concluded the Peace of the Pyrenees and his marriage to the Infanta Maria Theresa. The island is still called *"Isle de la Conférence."*

---

[1]*ord.* O.F. filth.
[2]*noir.* usual anagram for *roi*, king.
[3]*Phoffens.* people of Phocea, Marseilles.
[4]*Ponant.* read Occident.

Century X

X.LIX

Dedans Lyons vingt cinq d'vne alaine,
Cinq citoyens Germains, Breffans,
   Latins,
Par deffous noble conduiront longue
   traine,
Et defcouuers par abbois de maftins.

In Lyons, twenty-five of the same breath.
Five citizens, Germans, Bressans, Latins;
under a noble they will lead a long trail
and are discovered by the barking of the
mastiffs.

Century X

X.LX

Ie pleure Niffe, Mannego, Pize, Gennes,
Sauone, Sienne, Capue, Modene,
   Malte:
Le deffus fang & glaiue par eftrennes,
Feu, trembler terre eau, malheureufe
   nolte.[1]

I weep for Nice, Monaco, Pisa, Genoa,
Savona, Siena, Capua, Modena and
Malta. The blood and sword above for a
gift fire, the earth will tremble. Water an
unhappy reluctance.

This quatrain appears to describe an earthquake which involves not only southern France, Nice, but Monaco and a great deal of Italy, including Malta. If this were to happen it would be an earthquake of calamitous effect. There are the usual additions of fire and fighting, but in this case it is followed by a flood. Possibly a future quatrain, or maybe a Millennium one for the end of this century.

Century X

X.LXI

Betta,[2] *Vienne, Emorre,*[3] *Sacarbance,*[4]
Voudront liurer aux Barbares Pannone:
Par picque & feu, enorme violance,
Les coniurez defcouuers par matrone.

Betta, Vienna, Emort, Sopron. They will
want to deliver Hungary to the barbari-
ans. Great violence through pikes and fire,
the conspirators discovered by a matron.

This quatrain appears to be linked with the two following ones, X.LXII and LXIII, but they all remain obscure.

---

[1]*nolte.* probably from L. *noluntas,* unwillingness?
[2]*Betta,* possibly *Baetis,* the Guadalquivir River?
[3]*Emorre.* uncertain place name.
[4]*Sacarbance.* L. *Scarbantia,* modern Sopron.

Century X

X.LXII

Pres de Sorbin pour affaillir Ongrie,
L'herault de Bude les viendra aduertir:
Chef Bizantin, Sallon de Sclauonie,
A loy d'Arabes les viendra conuertir.

Near Sorbia, in order to assail the hungry,
the herald of Brudes will come to warn
them. The Byzantine chief, Salona of Sla-
vonia, will come to convert them to Ara-
bian law.

Century X

X.LXIII

Cydron,[1] Ragufe,[2] la cité au sainct
    Hieron,[3]
Reuerdira le medicant fecours,
Mort fils de Roy par mort de deux
    heron,[4]
L'Arabe Ongrie feront vn mefme cours.

Cydonia, Ragussa, the city holy to
Hieron, the healing help will make it
green again. The king's son dead because
of the death of two heros, Arabia and
Hungary will take the same step.

Century X

X.LXIIII

Pleure Milan, pleure Luques, Florance,
Que ton grand Duc fur le char
    montera,
Changer le fiege pres de Venife
    s'aduance,
Lors que Colomne[5] à Rome changera.

Weep Milan, weep Lucca and Florence,
when your great duke climbs into the char-
iot. To change the seat it advances close to
Venice, when at Rome the Colonnas will
change.

This is a general quatrain about the situation in Italy during the nineteenth century. When the Grand Duke left Italy, Austria abandoned the province of Venetia to Napoleon III, who, in turn, gave it to Victor Emmanuel. Florence became Italy's new capital city until the seat of all Italian government was moved to Rome. It was from then onwards that the temporal powers to the Papacy declined. A good quatrain.

[1] *Cydron.* Cydonia, now modern Canea.
[2] *Ragufe.* now Denmark
[3] *Hieron.* a dubious personal name?
[4] *heron.* a false rhyme for heroes.
[5] *Colomne.* Colonna, a great Roman family.

Century X

X.LXV

O vafte Romme ta ruyne s'approche,
Non de tes murs de ton fang &
*   fuftance:*
L'aspre par lettres fera fi horrible coche,
Fer poinctu mis à tous iufques au
*   manche.*

O great Rome, your ruin approaches, not of your walls but of your blood and substance. The harsh one in letters will make so horrid a notch, pointed steel wounding all up the sleeve.

This quatrain probably refers to the attempt made to assassinate Pope John Paul II. Not the well-publicized attempt in Rome by Ali Agça, supposedly of the Bulgarian Secret Service, but another, less public event which occurred when he was touring the world. One of the priests in his entourage attempted to stab the Pope with a cut-down sword or knife which he had hidden up his sleeve. Nostradamus issues several warnings to John Paul II, whose papal reign he sees as being troubled not only by violence, but by *la peste,* the plague of AIDS.

Century X

X.LXVI

Le chef de Londres par regne l'Americh,
L'ifle Efcoffe tempiera par gellee:
Roy Reb auront vn fi faux antechrift,
Que les mettra treftous dans la meflee.

The London premier through American power will burden the island of Scotland with a cold thing. Reb the King will have so dreadful an Antichrist who will bring them all into trouble.

An interesting quatrain, definitely belonging to the twentieth century. During the Prime Ministership of Harold Macmillan, Scotland was certainly burdened by a "cold thing," the Polaris submarine. In this new age of the INF Treaty things will be drastically changed. It would be helpful if one could decipher *Roy Reb,* as it is during his time of power that the Third Antichrist will appear and there will be trouble in Britain and America. (See II.V.)

Century X

X.LXVII

Le tremblement fi fort au mois de May,
Saturne, Caper, Iupiter, Mercure au
*   beuf:*
Venus auffi Cancer, Mars, en Nonnay,[1]
Tombera greffe lors plus groffe qu'vn
*   euf.*

A very great troubling in the month of
May, Saturn in Capricorn, Jupiter and
Mercury in Taurus. Venus also in Can-
cer, Mars in Virgo, then hail will fall
greater than an egg.

This conjunction of planets is very rare, but Nostradamus predicts it in the month of May, together with extraordinary weather, in this case a fall of hail. Nostradamus seems to foresee an increase in earthquakes world-wide, starting in the 1980s. There are numerous quatrains referring to these quakes, and to one in particular on the west coast of America which will be so severe it will be recorded by seismographs as far away as New York. (See I.LXXXVII.) In other quatrains, such as this one, he places the quake in May at the end of the eighth decade. It is extraordinary that Nostradamus should be so aware of an event which will occur in a country which had scarcely been discovered in his time. The earthquake ties up with other major world disasters such as flood and famine. The three planets, Neptune, Mars and Uranus, all bad news, move into their malign aspects on May 8, 1989 our calendar. Neptune is the God of earthquakes.

Century X

X.LXVIII

L'armee de mer deuant cité tiendra
Puis partira fans faire longue alee,
Citoyens grande proye en terre prendra,
Retourner claffe reprendre grand
*   emblee.[2]*

The army of the sea will stand before the
city, then depart, without making a long
passage. A great prey of citizens will be
taken on land. The fleet returns to seize,
great robbery.

I cannot decipher this quatrain.

---

[1]*Nonnay.* Virgo. *Nonnay, nonne,* stands for a nun, a virgin.
[2]*emblee.* O.F. robbery, thieving.

Century X

X.LXIX

Le fait luyfant de neuf vieux efleué
Seront fi grand par midi aquilon,
De fa feur propre grande alles[1] leué.
Fuyant murdry au buyffon d'ambellon.[2]

The shining deed of the new old one exalted will be so great in the south and
north. Raised by his own sister, great
crowds arise. When fleeing, is murdered in
the bushes at Ambellon.

The clue to this unsolved quatrain lies in the word *Ambellon.*

Century X

X.LXX

L'oeil par obiect fera telle excroiffance,
Tant & ardante que tumbera la neige,
Champ arroufé viendra en defcroiffance,
Que le primat fuccumbera à Rege.

Because of an object the eye will swell so
much, burning so greatly that the snows
will fall. The watered fields will start to
shrink when the Primate dies at Reggio.

A failed quatrain in that no pope has died at Reggio and it seems
unlikely that this will happen before the end of the century. However,
I suppose it must always be borne in mind.

Century X

X.LXXI

La terre & l'air gelleront fi grand eau,
Lors qu'on viendra pour ieudi venerer,
Ce qui fera iamais ne feut fi beau,
Des quatre pars le viendront honnorer.

The earth and air will freeze so much
water when they come to venerate on
Thursdays. He who will come will never
be as fair as the few partners who come to
honor him.

An interesting quatrain. To date we have the Christians who worship on a Sunday, the Jews on Saturday and the Moslems, Friday. So
perhaps this relates to the quatrain which talks of *jeudi pour sa feste* and
may be the day of the Third Antichrist. (See quatrain X.XCV.)

[1]*alles.* O.F. trip, speed, crowd
[2]*ambellon.* Dubious, village of Ambal?

Century X

X.LXXII

L'an mil neuf cens nonante neuf fept
    mois
Du ciel viendra vn grand Roy
    deffraieur
Refufciter le grand Roy d'Angolmois.[1]
Auant apres Mars regner par bon heur.

*In the year 1999, and seven months from
the sky will come the great King of Terror.
He will bring to life the great king of the
Mongols. Before and after war reigns
happily.*

In this gloomy prediction of the coming of the Third Antichrist in July, 1999, Nostradamus seems to foresee the coming of the Millennium. He was greatly influenced towards this opinion by contemporary thought. This quatrain indicates that it will be preceded by the coming of the Third Antichrist from the East, "the king of the Mongols," before the Final Coming of the Great King of Terror. It is interesting to note that Nostradamus foresees war both before and after his coming. He therefore does not envisage an instant End of the World. (See IV.L, X.LXXIV, X.LXXV.)

Century X

X.LXXIII

Le temps prefent auecques le paffé
Sera iugé par grand Iouialifte,
Le monde tard luy fera laffé,
Et defloial par le clergé iuriste.

*The present time together with the past
will be judged by the great man of Jupiter.
Too late will the world be tired of him,
disloyal through the oath taking clergy.*

Century X

X.LXXIIII

Au reuolu du grand nombre feptiefme
Apparoiftra au temps Ieux
    d'Hacatombe,
Non efloigné du grand eage milliefme,
Que les entres fortiront de leur tombe.

*The year of the great Seventh number ac-
complished; it will appear at the time of
the games of slaughter. Not far from the
age of the great Millennium when the
dead will come out of their graves.*

Seven is always an important number for numerologists, it signifies many things. Nostradamus predicts that at the time of the seventh number (does this mean at the end of the seventies?) war will break out on an immense scale. In a sense this has been true, with localized wars breaking out all over the world. The date of the final war

[1]*Angolmois.* Anagram of the O.F. *Mongolois.*

will be not far from the Millennium (see X.LXXII). The last line is purely horrific. Does Nostradamus have a vision of the second judgment?

Century X

X.LXXV

Tant attendu ne reuiendra iamais
Dedans l'Europe, en Afie apparoiftra
I'n de la ligne yflu du grand Hermes,
Et fur tous roys des orientz croiftra.

Long awaited it will never return in Europe, he will appear in Asia. One of the league issued from the great Hermes, he will grow above all the other powers in the Orient.

This seems to be a continuation of quatrain X.LXXII where Nostradamus talks about the King of the Mongols bringing war to the world. It may also refer to the last quatrain, X.LXXIV, and the war of the seventh number. But Nostradamus sees this Third Antichrist as rising "above all powers in the Orient." At the present time it seems that he will probably surface in China.

Century X

X.LXXVI

Le grand fenat difcernera la pompe,
A l'vn qu'apres fera vaincu chaffé,
Ses adherans feront à fon de trompe,
Biens publiez ennemys defchaffez.

The great Senate will see the parade for one who afterwards will be driven out, vanquished. His adherents will be there at the sound of a trumpet, their possessions for sale, the enemies driven out.

Unfortunately no definite setting is given for these events.

Century X

X.LXXVII

Trente adherans de l'ordre des
*   quyretres[1]*
Bannys leurs biens donnez fes
*   aduerfaires,*
Tous leurs bienfais feront pour
*   defmerites*
Claffe efpargie deliurez aux corfaires.

Thirty members of the order of Quirites banished, their belongings given to their bold adversaries. All their good actions will be taken as wrong; the fleet scattered, delivered up to the Corsairs.

[1]*quyretres.* a) L. Roman citizens, b) Low L. renowned warriors.

This quatrain is usually applied to post-Fascist Italy in 1945. The Corsairs are then understood to be the Russians, who received a large part of the Italian navy. General, but satisfactory.

Century X
X.LXXVIII

Subite ioye en fubite trifteffe
Sera à Romme aux graces embraffees
Dueil, cris, pleurs, larm. Sang excellent
   lieffe
Contraires bandes furprifes & trouffees.

Sudden joy into sudden sadness will be at Rome for the graces embraced. Mourning, cries, tears, weeping, blood, great rejoicing. Contrary bands surprised and trussed up.

Century X
X.LXXIX

Les vieux chemins feront tous embelys,
Lon paffera à Memphis fomentrée,[1]
Le grand Mercure d'Hercules fleur de
   lys
Faifant trembler terre, mer & contree.

The old roads will all be improved, they will go (somewhere) similar to Memphis. The great Mercury of Hercules' fleur-de-lys will cause land, sea and country to tremble.

The key words of Memphis and the great Mercury of Hercules are the basis of this quatrain but I cannot decipher it.

Century X
X.LXXX

Au regne grand du grand regne
   regnant,
Par force d'armes les grands portes
   d'arain
Fera ouurir le roy & duc ioignant,
Port demoly nef à fons iour ferain.

In the kingdom of the great one, reigning with a powerful rule by force of arms, he will cause to be opened the great gates of brass. The king and the duke allied, the port demolished, the ship at the bottom. A severe day.

A difficult quatrain because it has no proper names on which to base an interpretation. Kings and dukes are frequent in the *Prophéties* and something more specific is needed. A failed quatrain?

[1]*fomentrée.* Gk. *symmetros,* like, dissembling.

Century X
X.LXXXI

Mys trefort temple citadins Hefperiques
Dans iceluy retiré en fecret lieu,
Le temple ouurir les liens fameliques.
Reprens rauys proye horrible au milieu.

Treasure is placed in a temple by Western citizens, withdrawn therein to a secret place. The temple to open by hungry bonds, recaptured, ravished, a terrible prey in the midst.

During the sixteenth century gold poured into Spain from her possessions in the New World. Can one take Nostradamus literally in this case, that a great amount of treasure is hidden in some Spanish cathedral? It must be remembered that most Spanish cathedrals were adorned with riches from the New World. But problems arise with line 3, *liens fameliques.* It has been suggested that this is an imaginative description of economic crisis in the United States—the other meaning of *Hesperique.* Is this to be followed by a raid on Fort Knox, the greatest gold hoard in the world? Perhaps it just means a great run on gold, as is happening at the moment.

Century X
X.LXXXII

Cris, pleurs, larmes viendront auec
      coteaux
Semblant fouyr donront dernier affault
Lentour parques planter profons
      plateaux,
Vifs repoulfez & meurdrys de
      prinfault. [1]

With the knives will come cries, tears and weeping. Seeming to flee they will make a final assault around the parks. They will set up high platforms, the living pushed back and murdered instantly.

A régime that throws people to their deaths from high platforms?

Century X
X.LXXXIII

De batailler ne fera donné figne,
Du parc feront contraint de fortir hors,
De Gand lentour fera cogneu l'enfigne,
Qui fera mettre de tous les fiens à mors.

The signal will not be given to fight, they will be obliged to go out of the park. The banner around Ghent will be recognized, he who will put all his followers to death.

[1]*prinfault.* O.F. first, at once, immediately.

Century X
X.LXXXIIII

La naturelle à fi hault non bas
Le tard retour fera martis contens,
Le Recloing[1] ne fera fans debarz
En empliant & perdant tout fon temps.

The illegitimate girl so high, not low, the late return will content the grieved ones. The Reconciled one will not be without disputes, by employing and wasting all his time.

Many commentators regard line 1 as describing Elizabeth Tudor, Elizabeth I, whom Pope Paul IV declared to be a bastard through the illegality of Anne Boleyn's marriage to Henri VIII.

Century X
X.LXXXV

Le vieil tribung au point de la
  trehemide
Sera preffee captif ne defliurer,
Le veuil non veuil le mal parlant
  timide
Par legitime à fes amys liurer.

The old tribune on the point of trembling will be pressed not to give up the captive. The old, not old, speaking timidly of the evil; to free his friends in a lawful manner.

This quatrain has been suggested as applying to France between 1940 and 1943, when Maréchal Pétain negotiated with the Germans about prisoners of war who were being used as slave labor.

Century X
X.LXXXVI

Comme vn gryphon viendra le roy
  d'Europe
Accompaigné de ceux d'Aquilon,
De rouges & blancz conduira grand
  troppe
Et yront contre le roy de Babilon.[2]

The king of Europe will come like a griffon, accompanied by those of the North. He will lead a great troop of red and white. They will march against the king of Babylon.

The king of Europe may be understood as standing for the Allied Forces who marched against Napoleon, king of Egypt, in 1815, before he was made First Consul. The red and white uniforms of the

---

[1] *Recloing.* Dubious? Possibly derived from L. *recolligo,* to regain, be reconciled.
[2] *Babilon.* In medieval texts the king of Babylon is usually interpreted as the king of Egypt.

great army are the tunics of the English and Austrian forces. The English may well be described as from the North in this context, as also Russia.

Century X

X.LXXXVII

Grand roy viendra prendre port pres de
   Niffe
Le grand empire de la mort fi enfera
Aux Antipolles pofera fon geniffe,
Par mer la Pille tout efuanoira.

A great king will come to anchor near Nice, the death of the great Empire is thus accomplished. He will place his heifer in Antibes, plunder at sea, all will vanish.

It would be interesting to be able to decipher exactly what Nostradamus meant by *geniffe,* the heifer of line 3.

Century X

X.LXXXVIII

Piedz & Cheual à la feconde veille
Feront entree vaftient tout par la mer,
Dedans le poil entrera de Marfeille,
Pleurs, crys, & fang onc nul temps fi
   amer.

Foot and horse at the second watch they will make an entry laying waste all at sea. He will enter the port of Marseilles. Tears, cries, blood, never a time so bitter.

Yet another quatrain of grief and lamentation.

Century X

X.LXXXIX

De brique en marbre feront les murs
   reduits
Sept & cinquante annees pacifiques,
Ioie aux humains renoué Laqueduict,
Santé, grandz fruict ioye & temps
   melifique.

The walls will change from brick to marble, seventy-five peaceful years. Joy to human kind, the aqueduct reopened. Health, abundant fruit, joy and mellifluous times.

Perhaps this quatrain is one that describes the peaceful world that Nostradamus envisages after the Millennium?

Century X

X.XC

Cent foys mourra le tyran inhumain.
Mys à fon lieu fcauant & debonnaire,
Tout le fenat fera deffoubz fa main,
Faché sera par malin themeraire.

A hundred times the inhuman tyrant will die and a wise and carefree man put in his place. He will have the whole senate in his hands, he will be troubled by a wretched scoundrel.

Napoleon died "a hundred deaths" through his enforced captivity on St. Helena. In his place Louis XVIII is elected, known popularly as *"le debonnaire,"* as in the text. Both Parliament and the Senate profess allegiance to their new king down to the last man *(le fenat fera deffoubz fa main).* The trouble in line 4 was the assassination of the duc de Berry, who had been in line for the throne through his father, Charles X.

Century X

X.XCI

Clergé Romain l'an mil fix cens &
* neuf,*
Au chef de l'an feras election
D'vn gris & noir de la Compagne yffu,
Qui onc ne feut fi maling.

In the year 1609, the Roman clergy at the night of the year will have an election. One of the gray and black come forth from Campania. Never was there one so wicked as he.

An almost successful quatrain, foiled by circumstances. Pope Paul V reigned from 1605 to 1621. He fell seriously ill in 1609, whether induced or not is not certain. However, according to contemporary reports there was a lot of intriguing going on in both the French and Roman courts, in the hope of his opportune death. Paul V recovered and whomever the French had hoped to put in the Vatican did not succeed.

Century X

X.XCII

Deuant le pere l'enfant fera tué:
Le pere apres entre cordes de ionc,
Geneuois peuple fera efuertué,
Gifant le chief au milieu comme vn
* tronc.*

In front of the father the child will be killed, the father afterwards, between rapes of rushes. The people of Geneva will be exercised, the chief lying in their midst like a trunk.

I cannot interpret this quatrain.

Century X

X.XCIII

La barque neufue receura les voyages,
Là & aupres transfereront l'empire,
Beaucaire, Arles retiendront les
  hoftages,
Pres deux colomnes trouuees de
  porphire.

The new Barque will go on voyages, far
and near they will transfer the Empire.
Beaucaire and Arles will retain the hostages, near where two columns of porphyry
are found.

The Papacy *(la barque neufue)* will move from the Vatican according to this quatrain. Both Beaucaire and Arles are near the Rhône river which borders on Valence where Pope Pius VI was held in captivity. There has long been a legend that the Papacy will leave Rome at the time of the Millennium.

Century X

X.XCIIII

De Nifmes, d'Arles, & Vienne
  contemner,
N'obey tout à l'edict Hefpericque:[1]
Aux labouriez[2] pour le grand
  condamner,
Six efchappez en habit feraphicque.[3]

Scorn from Nîmes, Arles and Vienne, not
to obey all the Western edict. In order that
the great may condemn the tormented, six
escape in Franciscan garb.

Possibly a failed quatrain.

Century X

X.XCV

Dans les Efpaignes viendra Roy tref
  puiffant,
Par mer & terre fubiugant or midy,
Ce mal fera rabaiffant le croiffant,
Baiffer les aefles à ceux de vendredy.[4]

Into Spain will come a very powerful
king, he will subjugate the south by land
and sea. This evil will cause a lowering of
the crescent again, a lowering of the wings
by the people of Friday.

The nearest this quatrain appears to be fulfilled is when Philip II of Spain, who persecuted the Moors, *ceux de vendredy*, made several futile expeditions to North Africa and became involved in the Battle of Lepanto 1571. (See also X.LXXI.)

[1]*Hefpericque.* Western, American?
[2]*labouriez.* O.F. *labourier*, to torment.
[3]*feraphicque.* The true name of the Franciscans is the Order of Seraphim.
[4]*vendredy.* The Moslems celebrate their Sabbath on a Friday.

Century X

X.XCVI

Religion du nom des mers vaincra,
Contre la fecte fils Adaluncatif,[1]
Secte obftinee deploree craindra,
Des deux bleffez par Aleph & Aleph.[2]

The religion called by the seas will over-
come, against the seat of the son Adalun-
catif. The stubborn lamentable sect the
two men wounded by Alpha and Alpha.

This quatrain should be easy to decipher but is not. The anagram *Adaluncatif* is unsolved, as are the two *Alephs* or *Alphas* in the last line.

Century X

X.XCVII

Triremes pleines tout aage captif,
Temps bon à mal, le doux pour
   amertume:
Proye à Barbares trop toft feront
   haftifs,
Cupid de veoir plaindre au vent la
   plume.

Triremes full of captives of all ages, good
times for bad, sweet ones for the bitter.
Hasty, they will be too quickly prey for the
Barbarians, anxious to see the plume (of
smoke) wail in the wind.

Again, probably a retroactive quatrain because of the use of the word *"triremes."*

Century X

X.XCVIII

La fplendeur claire à pucelle ioyeufe,
Ne luyra plus long temps fera fans fel:
Auec marchans,[3] ruffiens loups odieufe,
Tous pefte mefle monftre vniuerfel.

For the joyful maiden the bright splendor
will shine no more, for a long time she will
lack salt. With merchants, bullies, odious
wolves. All confusion, the universal mon-
ster.

Line 2 indicates a time of anarchy when the empire of the "joyful maiden" will no longer have enough control even to collect taxes (from *la gabelle,* the French tax on salt contemporary in France in Nostradamus' time). The Third Republic in France was typified as Marianne. If she is the *pucelle ioyeuse,* this quatrain may well refer to France between 1940 and 1944. Salt has a secondary meaning of

---

[1]*Adaluncatif.* Unsolved name, possibly containing the word Caliph in the anagram?
[2]Aleph & Aleph. *Aleph,* A in Hebrew, *Alif* in Arabic, *Alpha* in Greek.
[3]*marchans.* May mean mercenaries rather than merchants in this context.

wisdom. Perhaps France lacked this in some of her actions during the Occupation? The confusion and beasts would then refer to the Nazis.

Century X

X.XCIX

La fin de loup, le lyon, beuf, & l'afne,
Timide dama[1] feront auec maftins,
Plus ne cherra à eux la douce manne,
Plus vigilance & cuftode aux maftins.

The end of the wolf, the lion, ox and ass, the timid deer will be among the mastiffs. No longer will the sweet manna fall upon them. More vigilance and guarding of the mastiffs.

Does this quatrain indicate the end of the good time Nostradamus predicts after the Millennium, "when the ox shall lie down with the wolf," and bad times return, demanding guards and vigilance?

Century X

X.C

Le grand empire fera par Angleterre,
Le pempotam[2] des ans plus de trois
cens:
Grandes copies[3] paffer par mer & terre,
Les Lufitains[4] n'en feront pas contens.

A great Empire will be for England the all-powerful for more than three hundred years. Great forces cross by land and sea. The Portuguese will not be pleased.

In this powerful quatrain with which Nostradamus ends his *Prophéties,* he foresees a great future for Britain which will last for over three hundred years. Most commentators take this as starting with that of Elizabeth I and ending with that of Victoria. The forces of line 3 may mean both the First and Second World Wars, as by the end of those Britain had been stripped of most of her colonies and the rest were soon to claim independence of one kind or another. But what do the Portuguese, line 4, have to do with these matters? A good, ambiguous quatrain with which to end the Nostradamus legend.

[1]*dama.* L. a deer.
[2]*pempotam.* from Gk. *pan,* all, and L. *potens,* powerful, all-powerful.
[3]*copies.* L. *copia,* troops.
[4]*Lufitains.* Classical name for the Portuguese.

INDEX